GunDigest® Book of

RIMFIRE RIFLES

ASSEMBLY/DISASSEMBLY

Step-By-Step Photos and Instructions for Hundreds of Variants

Kevin Muramatsu

4th EDITION

Related titles from Gun Digest Books

Gun Digest Guide to Maintaining & Accessorizing Firearms
Gun Digest Guide to Customizing Your AR-15
Gun Digest Book of .22 Rimfire 2nd Edition
Customize the Ruger 10/22 2nd Edition

gundigeststore.com

Published by

Gun Digest® Books, an imprint of F+W Media, Inc.
Krause Publications • 700 East State Street • Iola, WI 54990-0001
715-445-2214 • 888-457-2873
www.krausebooks.com

To order books or other products call toll-free 1-800-258-0929
or visit us online at www.gundigeststore.com

ISBN-13: 978-1-4402-4584-8
ISBN-10: 1-4402-4584-3

Cover Design by Tom Nelsen
Designed by Rebecca Vogel
Edited by Corrina Peterson

Printed in the United States of America

10 9 8 7 6 5 4 3 2 1

Contents

Introduction

Term: Brown-bag special

Definition: *The completely and totally disassembled gun in a bag that a customer or buddy brings to you to put back together because said customer or buddy just "couldn't stop there." Usually the brown-bag special is missing one or more key components, and often has unrelated parts in it that were found on the floor adjacent to parts originating from the disassembled firearm.*

The brown bag special is one of the reasons for this book's existence. Gunsmiths around the country buy these books for a reason, sometimes just to add to the library (you can never have too many resources in your gun library). Of course, you don't have to be a gunsmith to make use of this book and it is quite handy for the average dude who simply wants to detail clean or just to learn more about how his firearm works.

Okay, straight to business, now. As useful as a book like this is, it is simply impossible to present perfect images of every step, from the best angle, through invisible fingers, palms, and receiver walls. There may come times where it is necessary for the user to read between the lines, or create simple mental images of the description. For example, we may instruct you to remove the four action screws from a rifle, but the picture shows and indicates only one or two, since the other two or three happen to be in similarly obvious locations on the gun. Or a decent image is simply impossible to capture so we point out what needs to be done and the effect that it will have. For example: "This receiver is narrow enough to preclude a good internal image. Drive out this pin and this will happen. Drive out that pin and that will happen. Catch the twelve and a half springs that drop free when you do." You will find that parts schematics will be of immense help in these instances.

The truth is that most gunsmithing or takedown tasks can be accomplished with a handful of useful tools. Many guns require special tools to do this and that, and such will be noted in the text, when applicable. Otherwise, the items detailed in the Tools section in the beginning of this book should suffice for any of the rifles detailed in this guide. There are four tools that are the most useful and I would like to touch on those here.

The first and most useful is a functioning brain. "Guns are always loaded" is the maxim and I can confirm that removing any distractions, particularly when unloading or checking the load status, can be critical. Otherwise the operation can result in holes in things that shouldn't have them. A gun's primary safety is your well-functioning head, because if that isn't working, you shouldn't be anywhere near a firearm. Or me. Triple-check that the firearm is unloaded, especially for firearms with detachable magazines. Too often, people remove a loaded magazine and forget that there is still a live cartridge in the chamber. Stick your finger in the chamber, in addition to a visual check. If the bolt slams shut on your digit, you've a pretty good indication that the check was successful. It's really a treat when it happens with a bolt or other manual action. Please don't ask me how I know this.

The second tool is the digital camera. Its value cannot be overstated. Taking what are essentially free pictures whenever you feel the need will make disassembly and reassembly much more practical. This is not to mention the proof you will have when you tell the customer that you found a bunch of grass, or a key (yes, that really has happened) in his receiver and he meets that statement with profound skepticism. It isn't unusual when compiling these books to discard half again as many pictures that were, in the end, used.

The third tool is the internet. In the 21st century we have access to a tremendous amount of information, because it seems that everybody wants everybody else to know what they are doing and how they are doing it. You will find everything from idiocy to priceless wisdom, so you will have to filter it out. But when you find that schematic you couldn't find elsewhere you will be thankful indeed for the information superhighway.

The fourth tool is the third hand. Every gunsmith needs one, but alas, not a single one possesses it. So we make do with a heavy, sturdy bench vise with padded jaws.

A few more suggestions. Don't work on guns in thick carpet or outside, since you will drop parts. Always wear safety glasses, since your eyes are way, way more important than your comfort. Read the firearms' user manuals. I know this is a tall order for the American male (any American honestly), but please do it. Finally, brute force is the enemy. If it doesn't come out with a light tap, there is probably a good reason. Like a set screw. Or you are trying to tap it out the wrong way. "Hit it harder" and "get a bigger hammer" generally aren't mantras to live by when working on a firearm.

Check out the index in the back if you don't see the gun you are looking for. Some models are similar or identical to others, and generally the steps to take down the basic model of rifle are going to be the same for the more enhanced target/tactical/deluxe versions of the same gun. It's also interesting to note that, of late, many replicas of popular centerfire rifles such as the M4 or Uzi have emerged, and several such examples are included in this revision. Furthermore, as traditional rifle sales have given way to "black" rifle and concealed carry pistol sales, manufacturers have had to reimagine how to make a quality and effective rifle at a cheaper cost, i.e. below $400. The result is the use of some interesting technologies and design trends that result in such guns as the Ruger American and Savage B.Mag.

Limited space requires new additions to displace older models, so please don't be offended if the takedown you are looking for is not found here. There are a number of older editions available online and you can also contact the publisher for pdf copies of older chapters. Lastly, space also precludes the inclusion of the oh-so-useful schematics. Many or all of these can be found in the huge *Gun Digest Book of Exploded Gun Drawings*.

Kevin Muramatsu
Sleep deprived, yet caffeine supplied
White Bear Township, Minnesota
October 2015

Dedication

As I finished up this revised edition on October 25th (yes, the manuscript deadline date), I took a break and looked up events that happened on this day in history. One remarkable occasion stood out.

On the morning of October 25th, 1944, occurred what is known as the Battle at Samar. This was an adjunct engagement of the rather larger Battle of Leyte Gulf when (the insufferable buffoon) General MacArthur "returned" to the Philippines. Without going into too much detail, because I'd like the readers to look it up, this engagement was one of the most lopsided in naval history yet had a surprisingly lopsided result in turn. For those with short attention spans, Wikipedia has a surprisingly concise account. There are better resources written by many that were present, and these accounts tell the whole story. Anyway, in a nutshell, a powerful fleet of IJN surface warfare ships, four battleships, eight cruisers, and eleven destroyers got into shooting range of a much smaller USN task force composed of six escort carriers, three destroyers and four destroyer escorts.

Needless to say, the USN was in as poor a set up as can be imagined, yet the destroyers and escorts plunged head first into a surface engagement that was tactically hopeless, in order to buy time for the six small carriers to escape. In theory, the IJN had all the advantages, yet they lost the battle, being turned away in frustration (their target was the invasion force at Leyte), largely due to the boldness of the attacking escorts and aircraft from the carriers and the mass confusion that erupted in what amounted to a massive melee at short ranges. In the end, we lost "only" two escort carriers, two destroyers, and one destroyer escort.

Of particular interest to me was the account of the destroyer USS Johnston and its CO, and of the destroyer escort Samuel B. Roberts. The Johnston was eventually lost after suffering tremendous damage and casualties, with Commander Evans receiving the Medal of Honor, posthumously. The Roberts was also lost after inflicting far disproportionate amounts of damage to the Japanese.

Here's the point. A lot more Americans would have died had not the escorts of Taffy 3 boldly charged into the far larger and more numerous guns of the Japanese battleships. These actions and others similarly performed yet uncounted ensure the freedom we all take for granted. The actions continue to be performed today.

I'll give you one guess to whom this revised edition is dedicated.

Acknowledgements

As with the last of these books that I revised, I pretty much did and obtained everything myself. So I guess I'm left with thanking Gun Digest for the job of making these revisions and putting my name and mug on the covers. I suppose I should thank the several gun distributors for making sure they had what I needed in stock. Now if only they could produce a PMR-30.

Oh, and thanks, Corrina, for not firing me.

A Note on Reassembly

Most of the rifles covered in this book can be reassembled by simply reversing the order of disassembly, carefully replacing the parts in the same manner they were removed. In a few instances, special instruction are required, and these are listed with each gun under "Reassembly Tips." In certain cases, reassembly photos are also provided.

If there are no special instructions or photos with a particular gun, you may assume that it can just be reassembled in reverse order. During disassembly, note the relationship of all parts and springs, take digital photos of the installed arrangements, and lay them out on the workbench in the order they were removed. By following this procedure, and referring to your own digital images, you should have no difficulty.

TOOLS

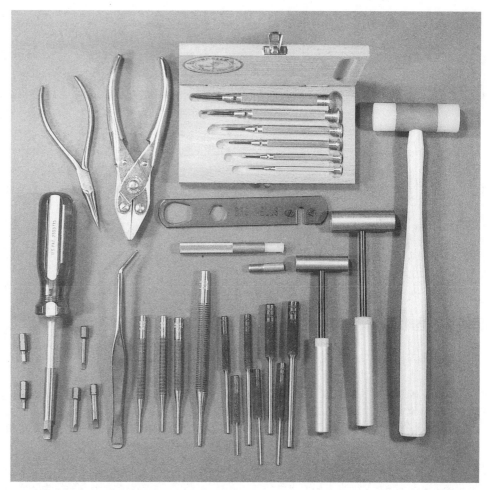

Countless firearms, old and new, bear the marks, burrs and gouges that are the result of using the wrong tools for taking them apart. In the interest of preventing this sort of thing, I am including here a group of tools that are the best types for the disassembly of rifles. Except for the few shop-made tools for special purposes, all of those shown here are available from one of these three sources.

Brownells, Inc.
200 South Front Street
Montezuma, IA 50171

B-Square Company
P.O. Box 11281
Fort Worth, TX 76109

Williams Gun Sight Company
7389 Lapeer Road
Davison, MI 48423

General Instructions:

Screwdrivers: Always be sure the blade of the screwdriver **exactly** fits the slot in the screw head, both in thickness and in width. If you don't have one that fits, grind or file the top until it does. You may ruin a few screwdrivers but better them than the screws on a fine rifle.

Slave pins: There are several references in this book to slave pins, and some non-gunsmith readers may not be familiar with the term. A slave pin is simply a short length of rod stock (in some cases, a section of a nail will do) which is used to keep two parts, or a part and a spring, together during reassembly. The slave pin must be very slightly smaller in diameter than the hole in the part, so it will push out easily as the original pin is driven in to retain the part. When making the slave pin, its length should be slightly less than the width of the part in which it is being used, and the ends of the pin should be rounded or beveled.

Sights: Nearly all dovetail-mounted sights are drifted out toward the right, using a nylon, aluminum, or brass drift punch.

1. The tiniest of these fine German instrument screwdrivers from Brownells is too small for most gun work, but you'll see the rest of them used frequently throughout the book. There are many tight places where these will come in handy.

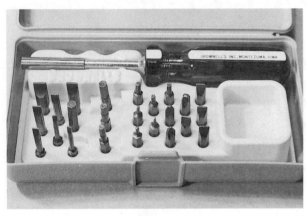

2. When a larger screwdriver is needed, this set from Brownells covers a wide range of blade sizes and also has Phillips- and Allen-type inserts. The tips are held in place by a strong magnet, yet are easily changed. These tips are very hard. With enough force you might manage to break one, but they'll never bend.

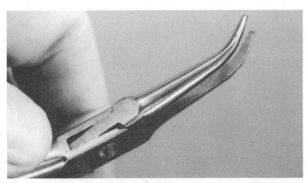

3. You should have at least one good pair of bent sharp-nosed pliers. These, from Brownells, have a box joint and smooth inner faces to help prevent marring.

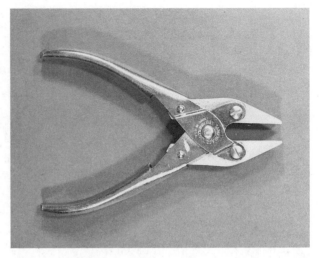

4. For heavier gripping, these Bernard parallel-jaw pliers from Brownells have smooth-faced jaw-pieces of unhardened steel to prevent marring of parts.

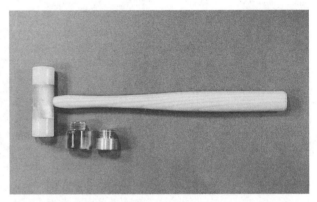

5. For situations where a non-marring rap is needed, this hammer from Brownells is ideal. It is shown with nylon faces on the head, but other faces of plastic and brass are also available. All are easily replaceable.

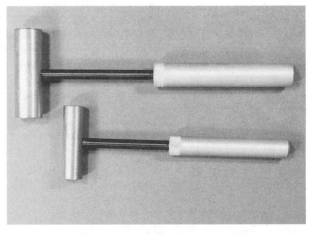

6. For drifting out pins, these small all-metal hammers from B-Square are the best I've seen. Two sizes (weights) are available and they're well worth the modest cost.

7. For situations where reach and accessibility are beyond the capabilities of sharp-nosed pliers, a pair of large sharp-nosed forceps (tweezers) will be invaluable.

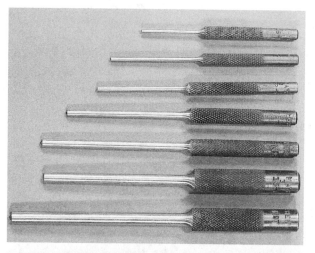

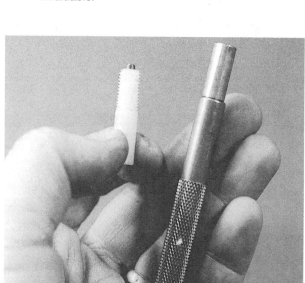

8. One of the most-used tools in my shop is this nylon tipped drift punch, shown with an optional brass tip in place on the handle. It has a steel pin inside the nylon tip for strength. From Brownells, and absolutely essential.

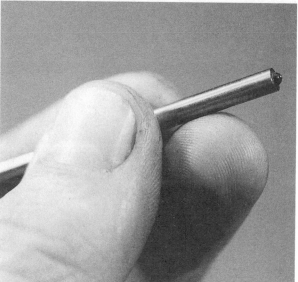

10. These punches by Mayhew are designed specifically for roll pins and have a projection at the center of the tip to fit the hollow center of a roll pin, driving it out without deformation of the ends. From Brownells.

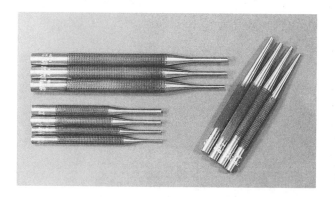

9. A good set of drift punches will prevent a lot of marred pins. These, from Brownells, are made by Mayhew. The tapered punches at the right are for starting pins, the others for pushing them through. Two sizes are available-4 inches or 6 inches.

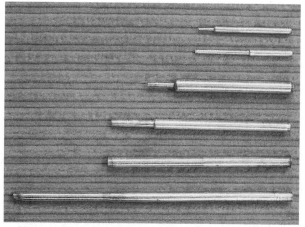

11. Some of the necessary tools are easily made in the shop. These non-marring drift punches were made from three sizes of welder's brazing rod.

12. From Brownells, this wrench is specifically designed for use on the barrel nut on the Winchester 150/250 and 190/290 series.

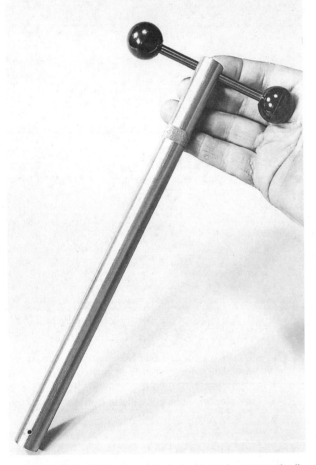

15. This excellent new hammer from B-Square is the same size and weight as the larger of the two hammers shown elsewhere in the tool section, and has an additional feature-knurled replaceable striking faces, in your choice of brass or steel.

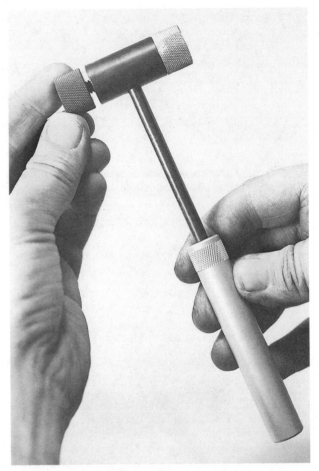

13. The B-Square stock bolt tool automatically centers in the access hole at the rear of the stock, and its wide cross-piece easily "finds" the screw slot. The T-handle gives good leverage.

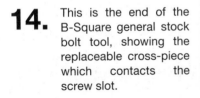

14. This is the end of the B-Square general stock bolt tool, showing the replaceable cross-piece which contacts the screw slot.

16. When dovetail-mounted sights are not super-tight, this "Sight-Pusher" will move them out or into place gently, without the marring which can occur with the hammer-and-drift method. From Williams.

17. A digital camera, even a cheap, low-resolution model can be invaluable. The ability to take a quick, free photo of anything that you are doing for reference is a modern convenience that one would be foolish to neglect.

Inner Magazine Tube Disassembly:

With very few exceptions, the disassembly of the inner magazine tube is the same for most rifles having this type of magazine system. The knurled knob at the end of the tube is retained by a cross pin, with one or both ends of the cross pin protruding to lock the tube in the gun. Most of the pins are driven out toward the non-protruding (or smooth) side. The tube should be supported in a V-block or a slightly opened bench vise during this operation, to avoid deformation of the thin walls of the tube. When the pin is out, the knob can be removed from the end of the tube, and this will release the magazine spring and follower. In some cases, the spring will be slightly compressed, so take care that it doesn't get away, and ease it out. In those cases where the cross pin protrudes on both sides, the pin will be slightly tapered. These should be driven out toward the larger end of the pin. Some box-type magazines can be disassembled, but most of them are of staked construction, and in normal disassembly should not be taken apart.

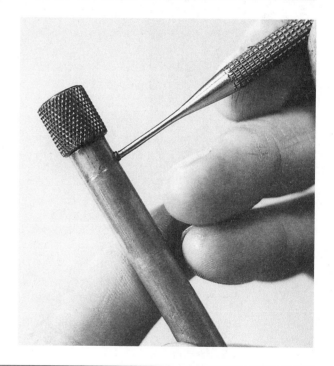

A Note On Coin-Slotted Screws

Many action takedown screws and main stock retaining screws have slots designed for use with a coin, the theory being that a shooter in the field might not have a large screwdriver at hand, but would be likely to have pocket change. The slots in these screws are wider than normal, and the floor of the slots will be curved, to match the curve of a coin edge. It is possible, and advisable, for the gunsmith or advanced amateur to alter a large shop screwdriver to exactly fit these screws. In general, though, the following advice applies: *Do not use an ordinary, unaltered large screwdriver on coin-slotted screws.*

Anschutz MSR RX22

Similar/Identical Pattern Guns

The same basic assembly/disassembly steps for the MSR RX22 also apply to the following gun:

ISSC MK22

Data	Anschutz MSR RX22
Origin:	Germany
Manufacturer:	J.G. Anschutz GmbH, Ulm, Germany
Cartridge:	.22 Long Rifle
Magazine capacity:	16 rounds
Overall length:	35.8 inches
Barrel length:	16.5 inches
Weight: 6.9	pounds

The Anschutz RX22 is a match grade bulky-looking thing that resembles the FN SCAR rifle. Unlike the SCAR, the RX22 is a rimfire rather than centerfire and is somewhat lighter in weight. Available in several configurations and colors, this rifle is quite accurate with a match grade barrel and adjustable match grade trigger. The ISSC MK22 is virtually identical, with some minor cosmetic changes and with a different trigger group. The takedown steps should apply greatly for that rifle as well, and they should, since both companies collaborated in order to make the rifles.

Disassembly:

1. Remove the two screws at the forward and rear ends of the fire control housing. The push the remaining pins out to the left.

2. Lift the upper assembly from the fire control assembly.

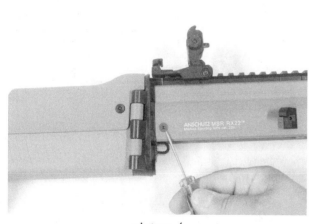

picture A

picture B

3. Remove this screw and its opposite on the left side (picture A). Fold the stock and then remove this screw (picture B). Removal of this screw frees the buttstock, the stock unit being pushed from the receiver by the thick recoil reduction spring.

4. Pull the bolt assembly out of the receiver.

5. Remove the folding sights, if not already done.

6. Remove the Picatinny rails from the sides and bottom of the forend. Each is held by two hex screws (picture A). Beneath each side rail are two Torx screws, front and rear (picture B). Remove them.

picture A

picture B

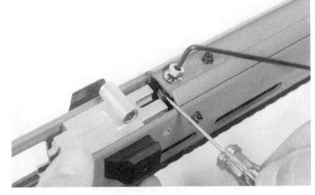

7. Unscrew this bolt from the front plate of the forend, and then the two screws immediately behind the plate on either side of the forend. Then pull the plate forward and off the barrel. Do not lose the small nut resting in the back of the plate.

8. Loosen this nut, and then the set screw within it. This will allow the forend bottom to slide forward out of the forend.

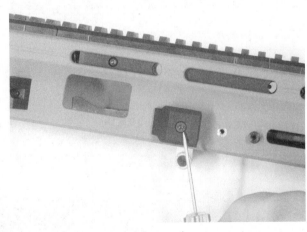

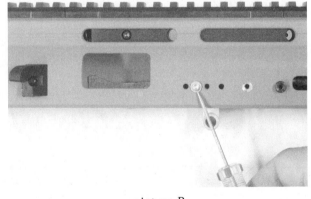

picture A

picture B

9. Removing this screw will release the rear end of the side rail (picture A). Beneath this end cap is another Torx screw. Remove it (picture B). Repeat on the other side.

10. Remove the barrel from the receiver. The bolt stop, pivot pin, and spring will be free to fall off as soon as it clears the receiver wall. Do not attempt to remove the barrel from the barrel block.

11. Remove this screw at the rear inside top of the receiver. This will free the charging handle stop and spring.

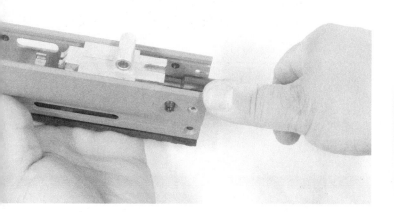

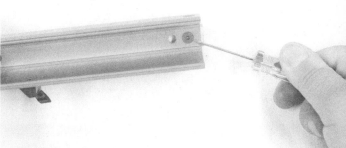

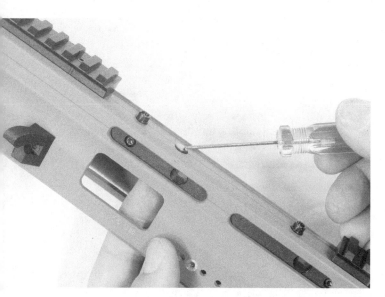

12. Remove the top middle section of the optics Picatinny rail. Inside the receiver is a pin that limits travel of the charging handle bar. Align this pin with the hole underneath the middle portion of the optics rail and push it up and out of the receiver. The charging handle bar will then slide forward or rearward out of the receiver. The bar is composed of two halves with detents and springs for the charging handle sandwiched in between. Do not disassemble this bar without good reason.

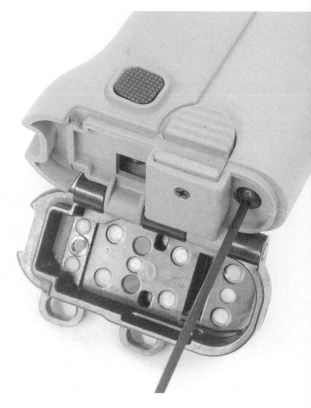

13. Remove this screw in the front wall of the stock. This will free the collapsible buttpad section from the hinge section of the stock.

14. The following steps to the buttstock should only be followed if necessary. To disassemble the comb adjustment, remove this screw. The beneath the screw is the retaining bushing. Inside the stock are the spring, bearing washer, and the button itself.

15. The hinge piece can be removed by driving the hinge pin out.

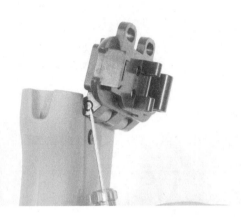

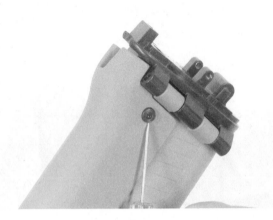

16. The folding latch can be removed by taking this screw out of the stock.

17. Remove this set screw to free the stock adjustment rail, and then the rail can be removed from the front.

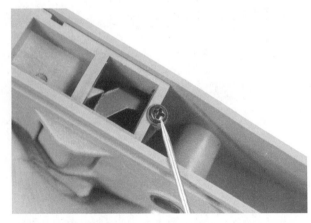

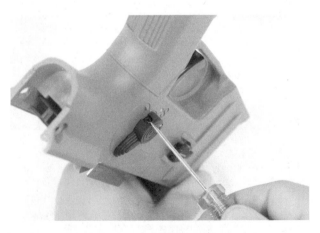

18. Remove this phillips head screw. Fully depress the stock adjustment and remove the button assembly out of the rear of the stock. The buttpad simply snaps on the rear of the stock and can be easily pried off.

19. Under the left side safety lever is a screw. Remove it to remove the lever from the safety. Then press the safety body out to the right of the grip housing.

20. The fire control housing is retained in the pistol grip by a screw up inside the grip. Remove this screw.

21. Lift the fire control assembly out of the grip housing. Be careful not to lose the two brass bushings on the left of the assembly.

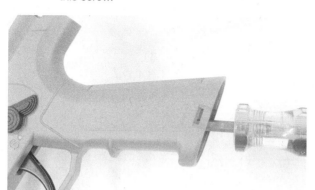

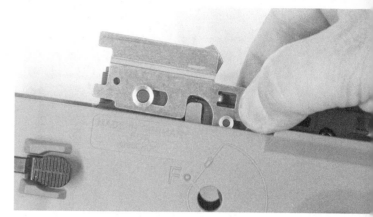

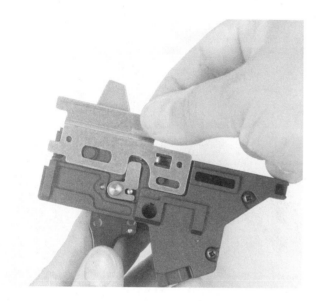

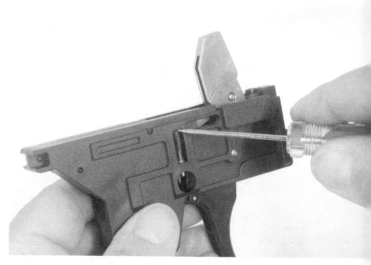

22. Remove the firing pin bar and its spring, which lies beneath.

23. The safety detent can be removed by merely displacing the top of the spring, then removing it, followed by the plunger.

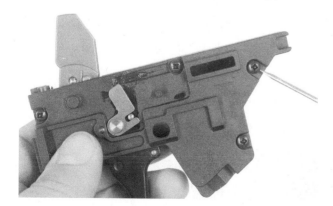

24. Remove the four phillips screws that hold the fire control housing halves together. Separate the halves, ensuring that as many of the internals stay in the left side of the housing as possible.

25. The fire control housing with the right side removed. The hammer strut bushing and the retainer nut will likely remain in the left side.

26. Remove the hammer with its strut, spring, and bushing. Between the hammer and left wall is the retractor spring.

27. Lift the trigger assembly out. The sear also pivots on the trigger pivot pin and will, with its spring, separate from the trigger. Do not disassemble it further without need.

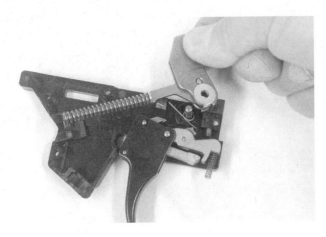

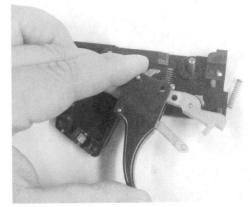

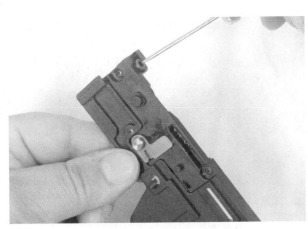

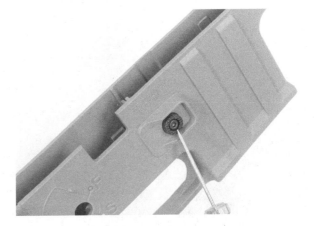

28. The firing pin safety bar lever is staked into the left housing wall (by the thumb); the indicated trigger adjustment screw can be removed if necessary.

29. To remove the magazine catch, remove this screw, and the catch, spring, barrel, and button will be freed.

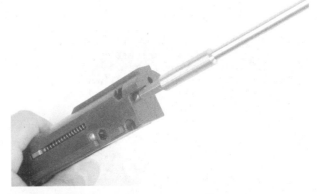

30. Remove the bolt rebound spring at the rear of the bolt assembly and then remove the small screw at the back to separate the spring seat from the bolt assembly.

31. The two guide rods have flat screw heads on them at the back end. Unscrew these guide rods from the bolt. The springs will be freed as you remove these rods, so control them.

32. There are five small dome headed Torx screws holding the two pieces of the bolt assembly together. Remove them to separate the left and right halves of the assembly module. Remove the bolt.

33. A small set screw is in this hole. Remove it and push the pin that the screw retains out from the other side through this screw hole. This frees the firing pin to be removed out the rear of the bolt, and the firing pin safety plunger out to the left.

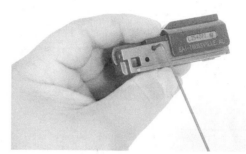

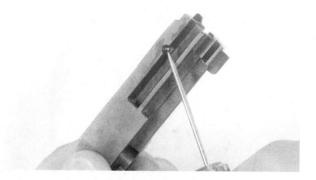

34. The bolt cover on the top of the bolt is held by three Torx screws. Remove this cover. Inside the top of the cover lies the firing pin return spring.

35. Tap out this pin from the bottom up to remove the extractor and spring.

Reassembly Tips:

1. When rebuilding the fire control assembly, place the parts in the right side housing wall. Be sure to control the hammer spring. Then reattach the left side wall (which should have the hammer rebound spring mounted in it) to the right side. As the hammer is about to seat, pull the long upward pointing leg of the rebound spring in front of the hammer spud that it sits against.

2. The bolt guide rods are easily reassembled into the bolt assembly by partially inserting the rods from the rear as the springs are inserted from the side and forward. The springs will be compressed, but not by much.

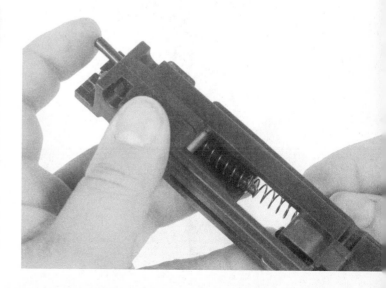

Beretta ARX-160

Data:	Beretta ARX-160
Origin:	Germany
Manufacturer:	Walther Arms, Germany
Cartridge:	.22 Long Rifle
Magazine capacity:	15 rounds
Overall length:	36.2 inches
Barrel length:	18.1 inches
Weight:	6.6 pounds

Beretta has a new full sized "assault rifle" called the ARX-100 in service with their military. As with many such rifles, there is a rimfire replica imported into the U.S. that otherwise looks and feels like the original. The ARX-160, made by Walther, does not have the ambi switching features of the centerfire rifle, but just about everything else is there.

Disassembly:

1. With the stock folded, rotate the safety up past the safe position. You will feel the tension. At this time, depress the bolt backstop plate inside the rear of the receiver. When the plate is fully depressed, pull the pistol grip down and off the receiver.

2. Pull the bolt assembly all the way to the rear of its motion and pull the operating handle out to the side. Then the bolt assembly can be fully removed out the back of the receiver.

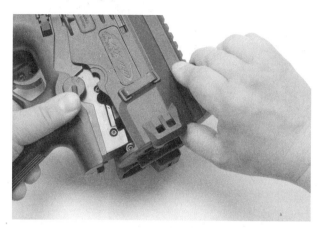

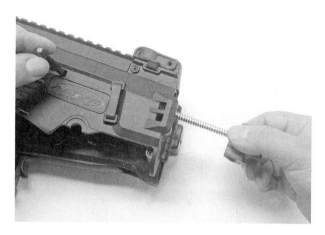

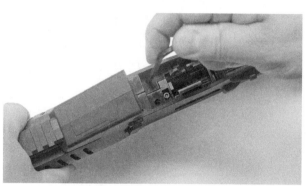

3. Loosen these two screws in the slots to release the barrel.

4. The pseudo gas block can be removed by punching out his roll pin. A similar but smaller pin holds on the flash hider. Remove the pin and unscrew the flash hider.

picture A

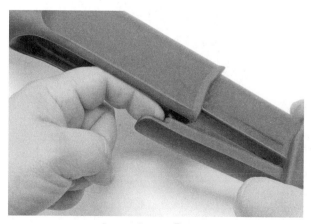

picture B

5. The stock, if necessary, can be removed by punching out the hinge pin(s). This catch should be depressed to remove the stock latch and spring (picture A). The buttplate can be removed by manually pulling down on the long adjustment latch and pulling the plate out to the rear (picture B). The latch and spring can be removed by driving out the pin in the middle of the sides of the buttplate.

6. The rails are retained by spring pins. The receiver halves are held together by several screws which are concealed by the top and bottom rails (picture A), and the "Beretta" and "ARX-160" panels on the left side. The panels are snapped in place; the snap tabs can be displaced with a small screwdriver by reaching up inside the receiver from the bottom (picture B). Further disassembly should not be required unless the bolt catch (just below the left ejection port) is broken.

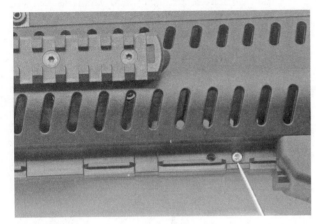

picture A

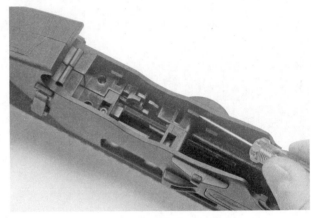

picture B

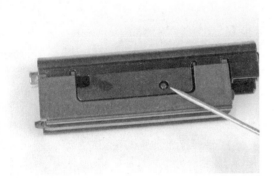

7. Tap out this pin to separate the bolt pieces.

8. The extractor spring and plunger can be removed by inserting a small tool in order to lift the spring out of its slot. The extractor can be removed once the spring and plunger are gone.

9. Lift the rear of the firing pin up slowly to remove it and its underlying return spring.

10. Should it be necessary to disassemble the recoil spring assembly, it can be done by unscrewing the guide rod from its nut. The nut is positioned on the backside of the buffer/takedown section at the rear of the assembly.

11. This small spring in the underside of the bolt carrier is a detent for the pin that was punched out in step 7. Leave it there and try not to break it.

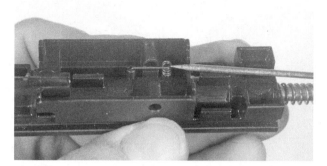

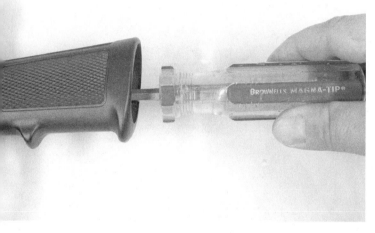

13. Remove the bolt inside the pistol grip. Then lift the trigger housing assembly out of the pistol grip.

14. Pull the safety levers out to either side.

12. Fully depress the right side magazine catch button to expose the left button. Pull the left button to the rear and off the assembly (picture A). The remaining assembly can be broken down by removing this screw (picture B).

picture A

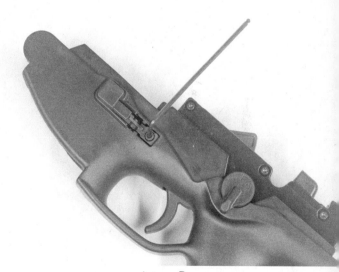

picture B

15. Remove the six screws on the left side of the trigger housing (picture A). Note that the bottom three are shorter than the top three. Remove the left side of the housing (picture B). This is the orientation of the internals.

picture A

picture B

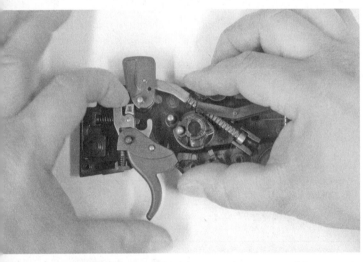

16. Remove the trigger and sear assembly.

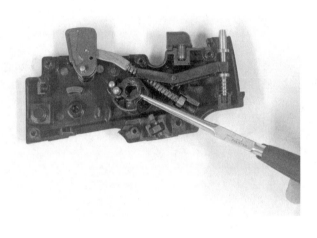

17. Remove the safety. Do not lose its spring and plunger, inserted in the left side of the safety.

18. This large plunger is the device that holds the bolt assembly and pistol grip in place in the receiver. Remove it next, taking care to control the assembly, as well as the hammer assembly springs, as both continue to be under tension.

19. This is the hammer spring seat. Tease it out and control the spring, then remove the hammer. The hammer and strut are connected with a pivot pin that should ordinarily stay in place.

20. The trigger/sear assembly can be broken down by removing the two large pins. The disconnector is a small "Y" shaped piece on the right side that is held in place by a coil spring wrapped around the rearmost pin. Don't lose this spring, should the need arise to break this assembly down.

21. This screw holds a spring that tensions the takedown extension movement of the safety. Remove if necessary.

22. The front and rear sight assemblies are both retained by large roll pins. Punching out these pins will allow the sights to slide off the receiver to the front and rear respectively. Further disassembly of the sight assemblies is not recommended.

Reassembly Tips:

1. When replacing the left trigger housing wall, make sure the spring that is screwed into the left wall, shown at the right in this picture, enters the safety at this location, shown on the left.

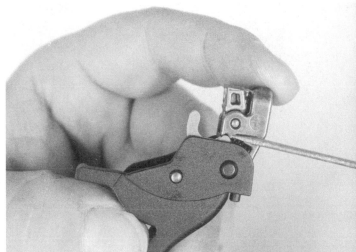

2. The disconnector and sear arm must be arranged in this fashion when reinstalling. Failure to do so will immobilize the trigger.

BRNO Model ZKM 452

Similar/Identical Pattern Guns

The same basic assembly/disassembly steps for the BRNO Model ZKM 452 also apply to the following gun:

BRNO Model ZKM 452D

Data:	BRNO Model ZKM 452
Origin:	Czechoslovakia
Manufacturer:	Zavody Presneho Strajirenstvi, Uhersky Brod
Cartridge:	22 Long Rifle
Magazine capacity:	5 rounds
Overall length:	43½ inches
Barrel length:	23.6 inches
Weight:	6.9 pounds

The ZKM-452 was introduced in 1992, and this high-quality rifle was imported from Czechoslovakia by Action Arms. There was also a Deluxe version, which differs only in stock quality and added checkering. A synthetic stock is also offered as a lower-priced option. The present importer of the rifle is CZ-USA.

Disassembly:

1. Remove the magazine. Hold the trigger to the rear, open the bolt, and remove the bolt toward the rear.

2. Remove the front stock mounting bolt.

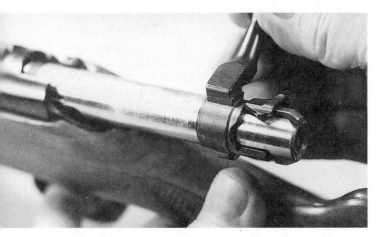

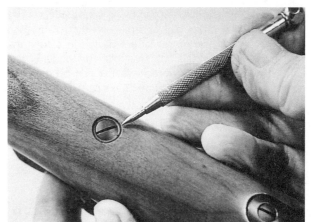

3. Remove the rear stock mounting bolt, located between the trigger guard and magazine well.

4. Remove the action from the stock.

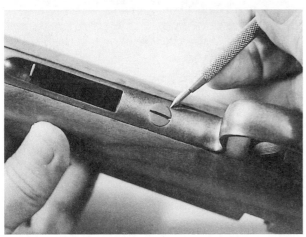

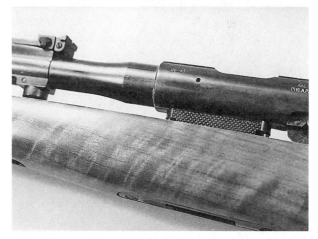

5. The stock buttplate and the trigger guard unit are retained on the stock by two wood screws.

6. Push out the trigger pin toward either side. Restrain the trigger, as the spring is under tension.

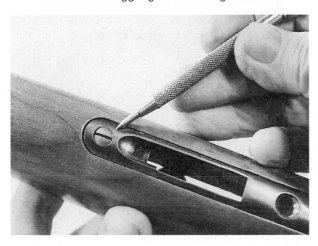

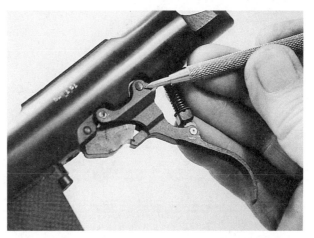

7. Ease the trigger downward. It is not taken off at this time, as it is still retained by its sear-contact cross pin. That cross pin, and the one that pivots and retains the spring guide, are riveted in place, and routine removal is not advisable. The trigger spring and the adjustment lock-washer can be removed from the guide at this point. Take care that the small washer isn't lost.

8. Restrain the sear, and push out the sear cross pin. **Caution:** *The sear spring is powerful, and there is a small ball bearing between the spring and the receiver. Control it and ease it out.* Considering the reassembly difficulty, this system is probably best left in place unless removal is necessary for repair or refinishing.

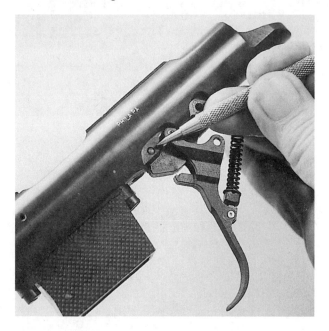

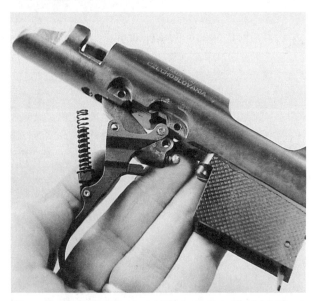

9. Remove the sear and trigger assembly downward. After removal, the parts are easily separated.

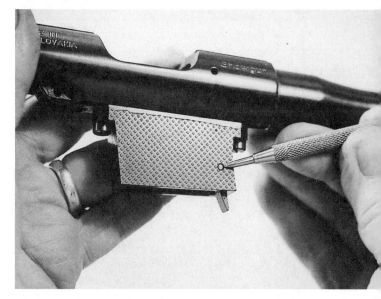

10. The magazine catch and its spring are pivoted and retained by a cross pin. **Caution:** *Control the catch and its spring as the pin is drifted out.* The magazine housing is retained on the receiver by two screws, at front and rear.

11. The front sight hood can be sprung outward slightly and slid forward out of its tracks. Backing out the front sight elevation adjustment screw will allow the sight blade to be slid down and forward for removal.

12. The rear sight is retained Mauser-style. Push down at the front and slide it toward the rear for removal. There is no cross pin.

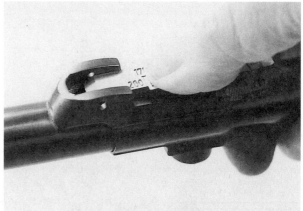

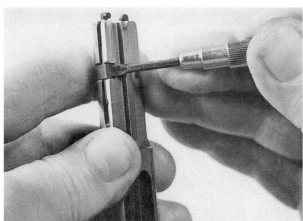

13. To remove the twin extractors, insert a tool and pry the end of the saddle-spring outward, just enough to clear its retaining shelf. As the spring is removed, control it. The extractors are then lifted out of their recesses.

14. With the bolt held securely, use a tool to push the combined striker and firing pin toward the rear, and turn the bolt handle, allowing the striker to move forward to fired position.

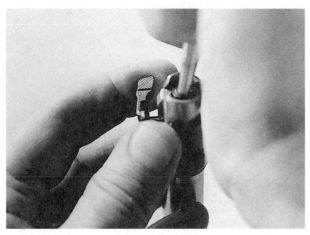

15. Grip the front part of the bolt in a padded vise, and use a tool to depress the safety retainer until the safety can be lifted out. **Caution:** *Control the retainer.*

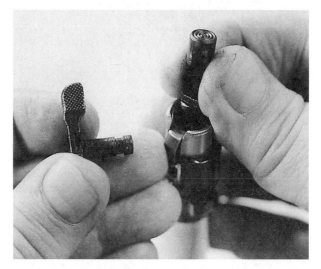

16. Easing the spring tension, remove the safety and the retaining plunger.

17. Remove the striker assembly toward the rear. The spring is easily removed from inside the striker.

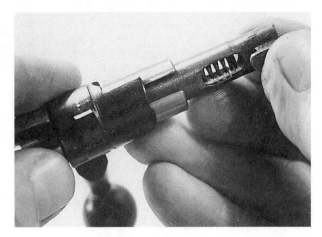

18. Remove the bolt handle toward the rear.

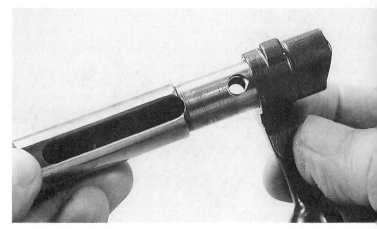

Reassembly Tips:

1. When replacing the sear and trigger assembly, temporarily install the rear stock-mounting bolt in order to supply a compression surface for the sear ball bearing and spring, as shown. Remember to hook the forward trigger cross pin over the sear. Temporarily insert the bolt body to stop the sear inside the receiver. When the ball and spring are compressed, insert a small drift to hold the sear for insertion of the sear cross pin. This is a difficult operation. Keep a shop cloth or apron around the receiver to arrest the ball if it slips.

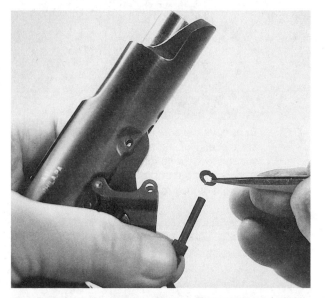

2. Be sure the trigger spring adjustment washer is installed in the proper orientation, with the locking dimples downward toward the adjustment nut, as shown. Remember that the upper end of the guide must enter its hole in the receiver before the trigger cross pin is reinserted.

3. When replacing the striker assembly in the bolt, remember that the angled lug goes at the bottom to contact the like surface on the bolt handle, as shown.

4. When the safety and its retaining plunger are installed, it will be necessary to again use a padded vise to hold the front of the bolt. Be sure the plunger is oriented as shown, and that the safety is straight across as it is inserted.

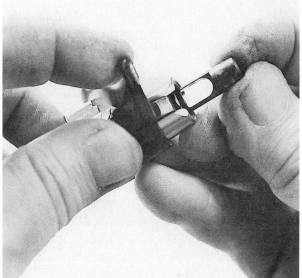

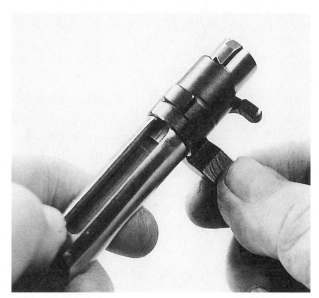

5. Before the bolt can be reinserted in the receiver, the striker must be re-cocked. Hold the front part of the bolt firmly, and turn the handle until the locking lug is at the bottom, as shown.

Browning A-Bolt 22

Similar/Identical Pattern Guns

The same basic assembly/disassembly steps for the Browning A-Bolt 22 also apply to the following gun:

Browning A-Bolt 22 Gold Medallion

Data:	Browning A-Bolt 22
Origin:	Japan
Manufacturer:	Miroku
Cartridge:	22 Long Rifle
Magazine capacity:	5 rounds
Overall length:	40¼ inches
Barrel length:	22 inches
Weight:	5 pounds 9 ounces

The Browning A-Bolt in 22 LR and 22 WMR was also offered in a Gold Medallion version that differs only in fancy stock wood and other embellishments. The standard rifle was introduced in 1986, but fewer than 150 were made in that year. The deluxe model was first made in 1988, and the 22 WMR version in 1989. Among the high-class 22 bolt actions, the A-Bolt ranks as one of the best. The A-Bolt 22 was discontinued in 1996.

Disassembly:

1. Remove the magazine, open the bolt, and depress the bolt latch. Remove the bolt toward the rear.

2. Remove the stock mounting bolt, located just forward of the magazine well.

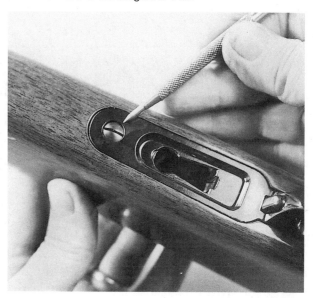

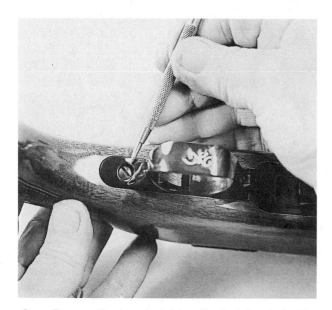

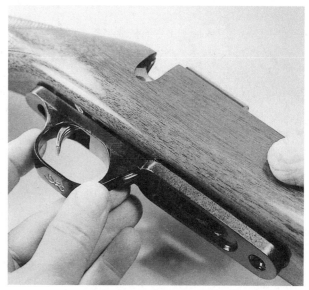

3. Remove the rear stock mounting bolt, located at the rear of the trigger guard unit.

4. Remove the trigger guard assembly downward. The magazine catch and its spring, located in the guard forward of the trigger, are best left in place in normal takedown. If removal is necessary for repair, insert a drift or rod through the loop at the rear of the catch, and draw it back until its side wings align with the exit cuts; then lift it out. Control the spring.

5. Remove the action from the stock, upward.

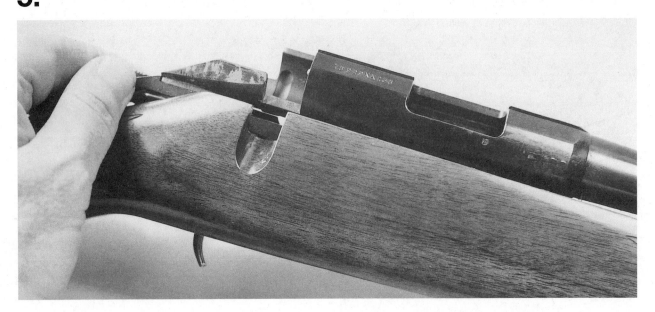

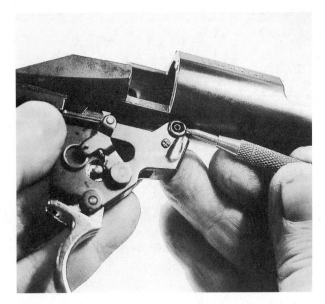

6. Drift out the roll pin at the front of the trigger housing.

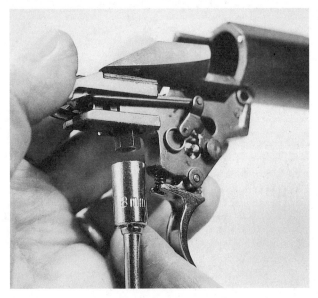

7. Use an 8mm socket to remove the mounting bolt at the rear of the trigger housing. Take care that the lock washer is not lost.

8. Remove the trigger housing downward.

9. The bolt latch can be removed from the left side of the receiver by backing out its retaining and pivot screw. Restrain the latch as the screw is taken out, and ease it off. Remove the spring. In the front of the latch, a vertical roll pin retains the bolt stop/guide pin.

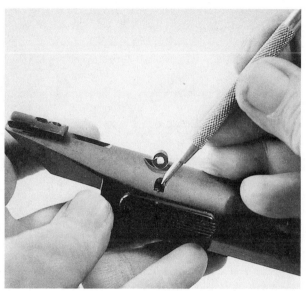

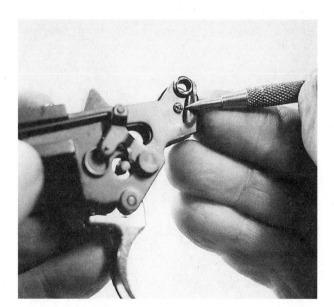

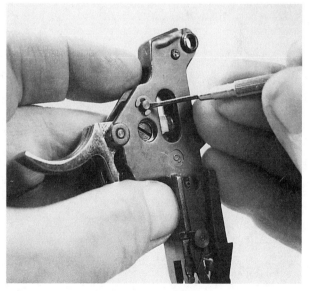

10. Because several of the parts in the trigger group are set or staked at the factory, disassembly of this system should be reserved for repair purposes. The sear pivot, for example, is riveted on both sides, and it is not routinely removable.

11. If necessary, the safety system can be removed. First, pry off the C-clip on the left side of the housing. Control it during removal, as it will snap off when freed.

12. Control the torsion spring, and remove the safety toward the right.

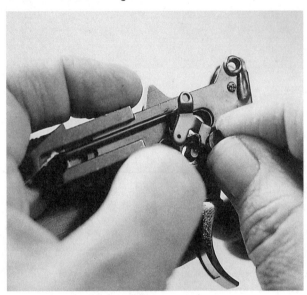

13. Remove the safety spring.

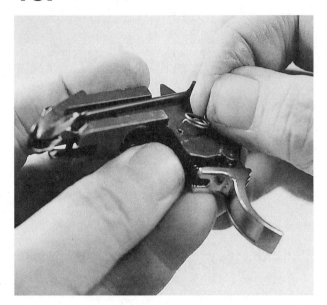

14. Move the connecting rod and the safety button out toward the rear.

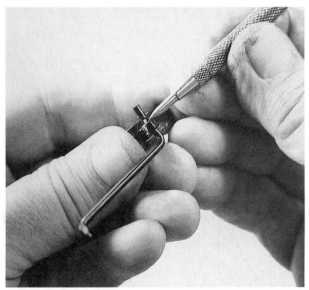

15. The connecting rod is staked on the left side of the button, and these parts are not routinely separated.

16. Unhook the safety-lever spring at the rear to release its tension.

17. Insert a drift in the access hole on the right side, and drift out the safety-lever post toward the left. Remove the lever and spring.

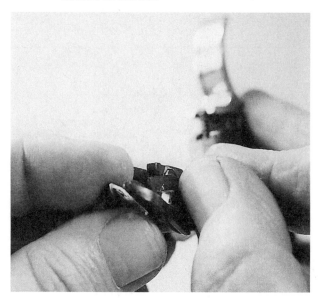

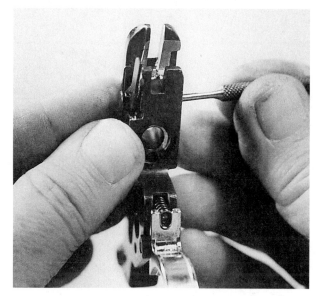

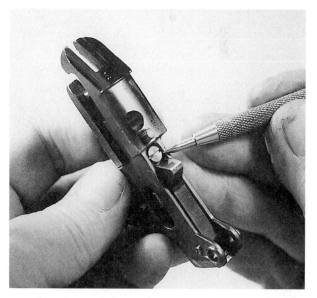

18. In order to remove the safety bolt lock pin, it is necessary to grip its side roll pin with pliers and pull it out. The lock pin is then taken out upward. Damage to the roll pin is likely, so this should not be done in normal takedown.

19. While the sear is not routinely removed, its spring is accessible by removal of the sear limit screw. However, this screw is factory set for proper engagement of the sear contact stud in the top of the trigger. If the screw is disturbed, it must be reset.

20. If the trigger has to be removed for repair, the first step is to unscrew and take out the safety post, shown here.

21. After the safety post is removed, drift out the trigger pin and take out the trigger and its spring downward. The sear contact stud in the top of the trigger is a separate part. In normal takedown, this system is best left undisturbed.

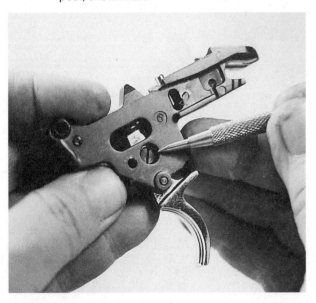

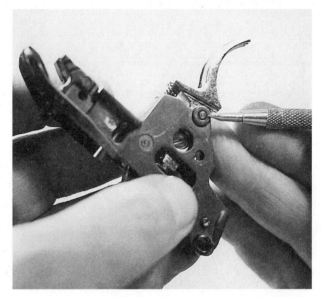

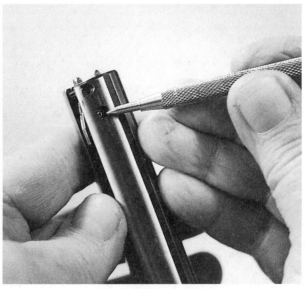

22. To remove the extractor, insert a small tool to depress the plunger and spring toward the rear, and lift out the extractor. **Caution:** *Keep the plunger and spring under control and ease them out.*

23. The combination ejector and firing pin can be removed by drifting out this roll pin, but the plunger and spring may be difficult to remove without further disassembly of the bolt. It can be done, though, if only this part needs to be replaced in repair. The forward roll pin is a guide only, and it does not have to be removed.

24. Hold the bolt firmly at the front, and turn the handle to lower the striker to fired position, as shown.

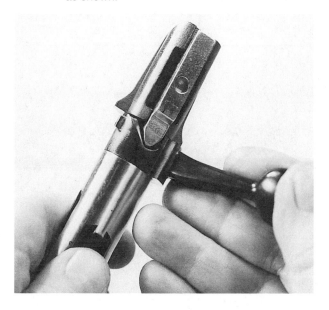

25. Restrain the bolt end piece and use an Allen wrench to remove the bolt sleeve retaining screw. **Caution:** *Even in fired mode, the striker spring has some compression, so control the end piece.*

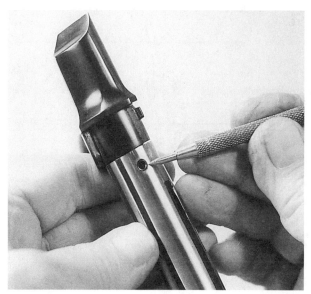

26. Remove the end piece and striker assembly toward the rear.

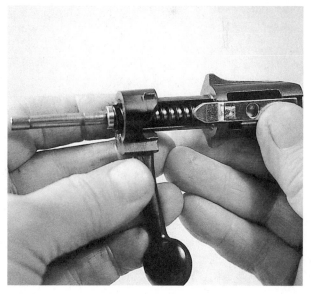

27. Remove the bolt handle toward the front.

28. With the front of the striker against a firm surface, such as a workbench edge, tip the striker and spring assembly downward, out of the bolt end piece.

29. The striker, its spring, and the collar at the rear can be separated from the cocking piece by drifting out the roll cross pin. **Caution:** *The captive spring is still under tension. Except for repair, this system should be left intact.*

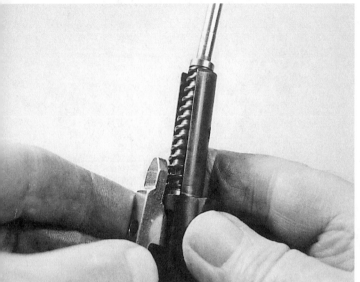

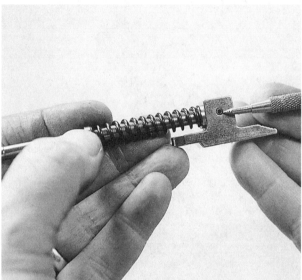

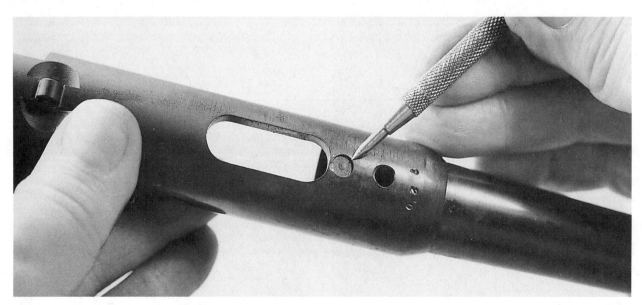

30. The cartridge guide is a separate part, driven into a well in the underside of the receiver. If it is damaged and must be replaced, it can be driven out downward. Replacement requires precise positioning. In normal takedown, even for refinishing, it is best left in place.

Reassembly Tips:

1. When installing the striker assembly in the bolt end piece, place the spring collar against the shoulders in the end piece, and push the assembly back and inward to snap it into place.

2. When replacing the Allen screw, be sure the screw hole is precisely aligned before turning the screw into place.

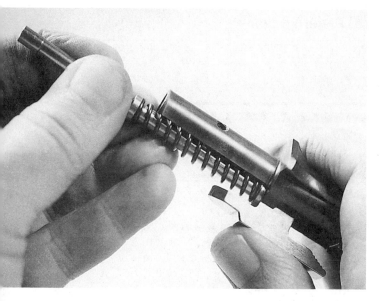

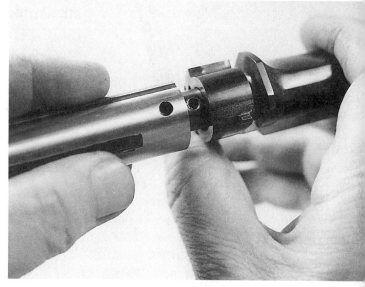

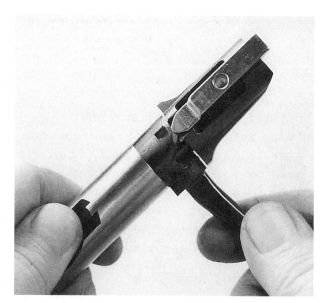

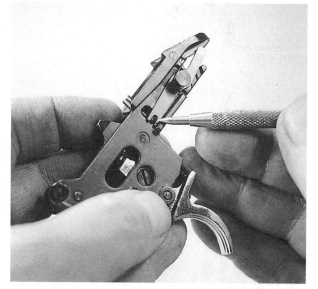

3. Before the bolt can be put back into the receiver, the striker must be in cocked position. Grip the front of the bolt firmly in a shop cloth or a padded vise, and turn the handle until the lug is in the position shown.

4. When installing the safety-lever, be sure its front fork engages the bolt lock side pin, as shown. After the post is drifted into place, remember to rehook the spring under the lever at the rear.

Browning Model BL-22

Similar/Identical Pattern Guns

The same basic assembly/disassembly steps for the Browning BL-22 also apply to the following gun:
Browning BL-22 Grade II

Data:	Browning BL-22
Origin:	Japan
Manufacturer:	Made in Japan by Miroku for Browning Arms, Morgan, Utah
Cartridge:	22 Short, Long, or Long Rifle
Magazine capacity:	22 Short, 17 Long, 15 Long Rifle
Overall length:	36¾ inches
Barrel length:	20 inches
Weight:	5 pounds

Browning's neat little lever-action 22 has been made by Miroku of Tokyo for many years, and it will probably be around for many years to come. It is unique among currently-made 22-caliber lever actions in having the trigger mounted in the lever, rather than in the receiver. It also has a very short lever arc that allows operation of the action without removing the hand from the wrist of the stock. For the nonprofessional, some elements of the takedown and reassembly can be rather difficult. Note that in 2005 the same rifle was offered in 17 Mach 2 chambering as the BL-17.

Disassembly:

1. Remove the inner magazine tube, and set the hammer on its safety step. Partially open the action. Take out the large cross-screw at the rear of the receiver.

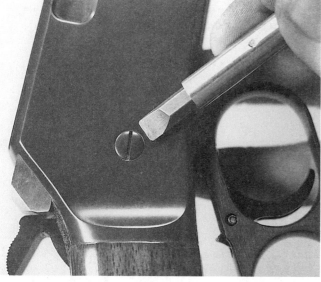

2. Move the sub-frame and buttstock assembly straight out toward the rear. Move it slowly, and insert a fingertip through the ejection port to restrain the ejector, as it will be released as the front of the bolt clears it.

3. Remove the ejector spring from its recess in the left inner wall of the receiver. Move the ejector downward off its fixed pivot post, and take it out.

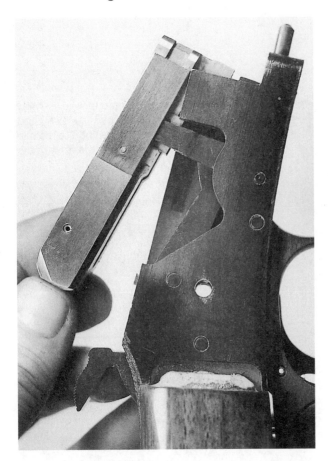

4. Tip the bolt upward at the rear, and move it a short distance toward the front.

5. Bring the rear of the bolt back down parallel with the top of the sub-frame, then lift the bolt off upward.

6. The firing pin and its return spring are retained in the bolt by a roll cross pin. Drift out the pin, and remove the firing pin and spring toward the rear.

7. The bolt cover plate on the right side is taken off by prying it gently outward at the rear, equally at the top and bottom, until it snaps off its fixed mounting pin.

8. Insert a screwdriver blade between the extractor and its plunger, depress the plunger, and remove the extractor from its recess in the bolt. **Caution:** *Take care that the screwdriver doesn't slip, and ease out the plunger and spring.*

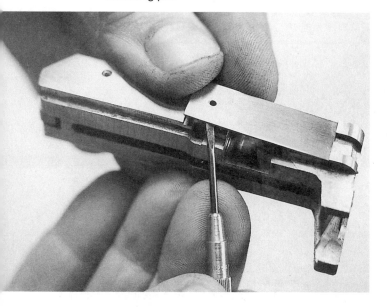

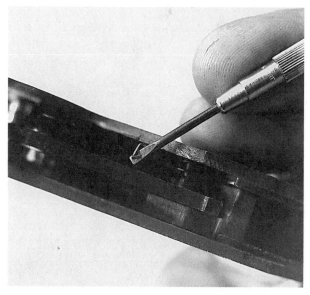

9. Depress the carrier, and remove the locking block from the lever link toward the left.

10. Unhook the carrier spring and allow its front arm to swing upward, relieving its tension.

11. Drift out the carrier pivot pin toward the right, and remove the carrier and its spring upward.

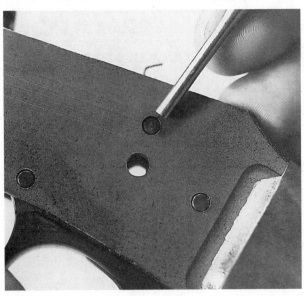

12. Removal of the carrier pin will also release the hammer stop block, and it can now be removed upward.

13. Restrain the hammer, pull the trigger, and ease the hammer down beyond its normal forward position, relieving the tension of its spring. Drift out the hammer pivot pin toward the right, and remove the hammer and its attached spring guide upward. The guide pin is staked in place, and should not be removed in normal takedown.

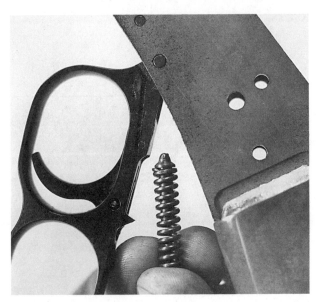

14. Open the lever, and remove the mainspring and its lower guide downward.

15. Drift out the lever link pivot pin.

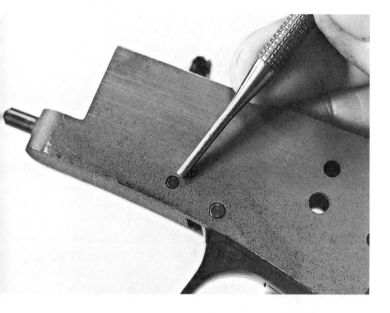

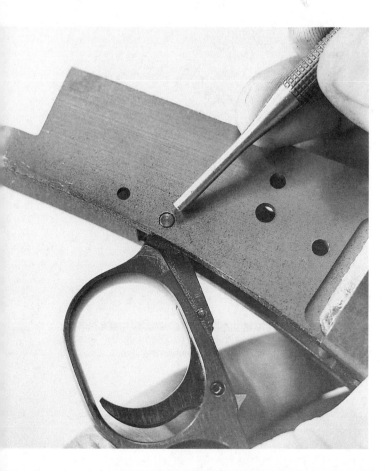

16. Removal of the pin will allow the lever to be pivoted downward beyond its normal position, and the link can then be removed toward the right.

17. Drift out the lever pivot pin, and remove the lever downward.

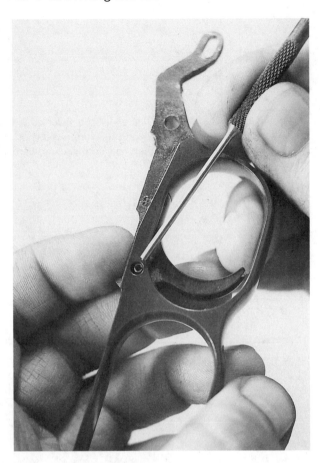

18. Drift out the roll cross pin at the rear of the trigger, restrain the sear link, and remove the link and its spring upward.

19. Drift out the trigger cross pin and remove the trigger and its spring upward.

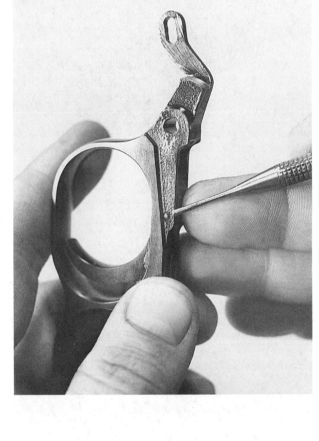

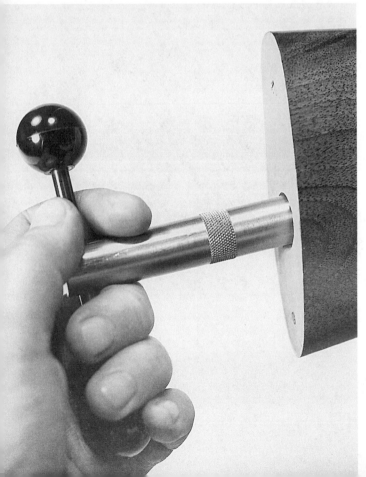

20. Remove the buttplate, and use a B-Square stock tool or a long screwdriver to remove the stock bolt. Take off the stock toward the rear.

21. Push out the cross pin that retains the sear, and remove the sear and its spring downward.

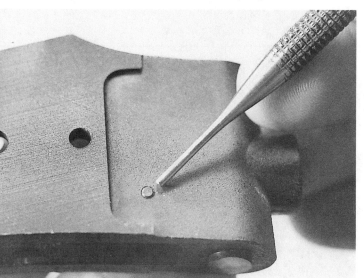

22. Remove the cross-screw in the front barrel band.

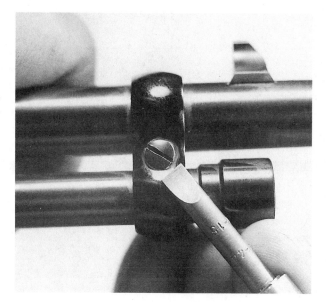

23. Drift out the cross pin in the rear barrel band, and slide the band off the forend toward the front. Remove the outer magazine tube toward the front, and take off the forend downward. The front barrel band can be removed only after the front sight is drifted out of its dovetail.

Reassembly Tips:

1. After the sear is installed, flip it over and insert the spring, then rotate it back into position, and insert a tool from the top to nudge the spring onto its plate inside the frame.

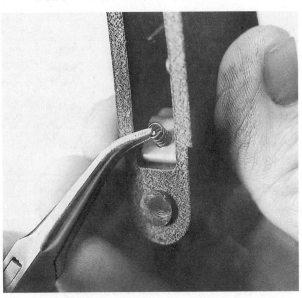

2. After the hammer is installed, tip its spring guide upward, and fit the spring and lower guide onto it.

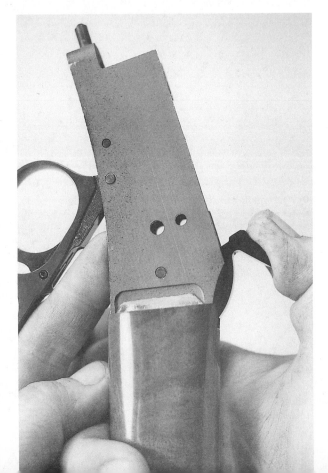

3. Swing the mainspring assembly downward, with the lever in closed position. Pull the trigger to release the hammer, and tip it forward beyond its normal lowered position. Snap the nose of the lower spring guide into its recess on the lever. Open the lever, and insert a fingertip to support the underside of the spring while slowly cocking the hammer. **Caution:** *If solid resistance is felt, stop and be sure that the spring is being kept straight (it will tend to bow downward).*

5. Grip the ejector spring with forceps or sharp-nosed pliers for insertion. The same procedure can be used for the ejector. When the spring and ejector are in place, insert a fingertip through the ejection port to hold them while sliding the bolt and sub-frame back in.

4. When replacing the locking block on the lever link, note that its side projection must be at the right rear, as shown.

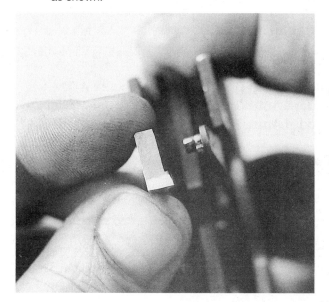

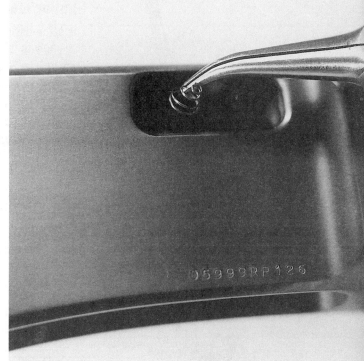

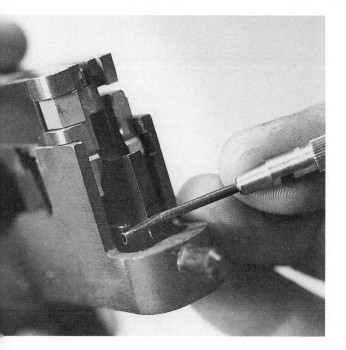

6. When replacing the carrier and lever link, be sure the pointed front arm of the lever link lies on top of the carrier guide pin.

Browning Semi-Auto 22

Similar/Identical Pattern Guns

The same basic assembly/disassembly steps for the Browning Semi-Auto 22 also apply to the following guns:

Browning Standard Auto Grade II   **Norinco 22 ATD**
Browning Standard Auto Grade III   **Remington Model 24**
Browning Standard Auto Grade VI   **Remington Model 241**

Data:	Browning Semi-Auto 22
Origin:	Belgium
Manufacturer:	Browning Arms Company, Morgan, Utah (Made for Browning by FN in Belgium)
Cartridge:	22 Long Rifle
Magazine capacity:	11 rounds
Overall length:	37 inches
Barrel length:	19¼ inches
Weight:	4¾ pounds

This neat little semi-auto rifle was first produced in 1914 by FN in Belgium. In 1922, production rights for the U.S. were leased to the Remington company, and it was made by them as the Model 24 and Model 241 until 1951. In 1956, a slightly altered version was introduced by Browning, and it was made for them at FN until 1974. From that time to the present, the gun has been made for Browning by Miroku of Japan. Through all of this time, the internal mechanism has been essentially unchanged. There are some minor differences in the extractor and cartridge guide systems, but the instructions will still apply.

Disassembly:

1. The takedown latch is located on the underside of the forend, at its rear edge. Push the latch forward into its recess in the forend.

2. Retract the bolt slightly, and turn the barrel assembly clockwise (rear view) until it stops. Then, remove the barrel assembly toward the front.

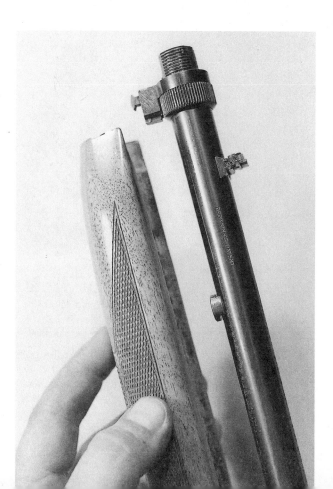

3. Remove the screw on the underside of the forend, and take off the forend downward.

4. Slide the takedown latch forward out of its base at the rear of the barrel. **Caution:** *Two plunger-and-spring assemblies will be released, and must be restrained to prevent loss.* The first will be the positioning plunger and spring at the rear of the latch, and the second will be the wedge-shaped plunger under the latch which bears on the barrel adjustment nut serrations. Ease both of these out, and take care that these small parts aren't lost.

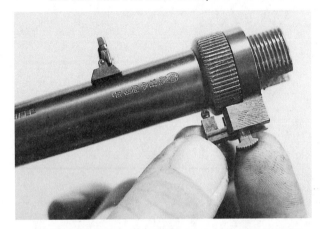

5. Remove the takedown latch base ring toward the rear. Unscrew the knurled barrel adjustment nut and remove it toward the rear.

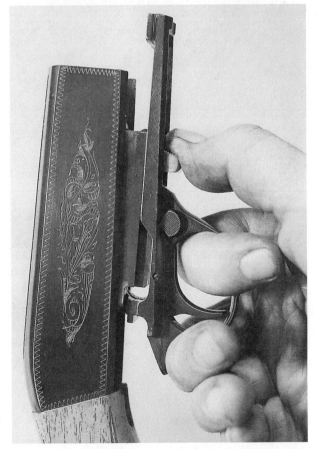

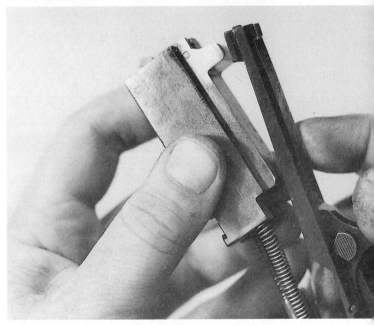

6. Insert a finger through the trigger guard, place the thumb on the bolt handle, and retract the bolt to the rear while exerting forward pressure on the guard. The trigger group and bolt assembly can now be moved forward together and removed downward.

7. Pull the trigger to release the striker into the bolt, then move the front of the bolt upward out of the guard unit and ease it off forward. **Caution:** *Both the bolt spring and the striker spring are under some tension, so take care that they don't get away.* Remove the springs and their guides from the rear of the bolt.

8. Remove the striker from the rear of the bolt.

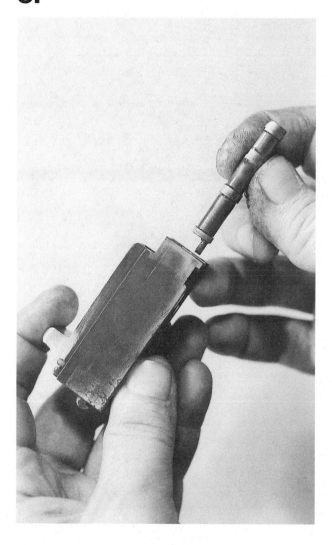

9. Drifting out the cross pin at the lower front of the bolt will release the extractor retainer and allow removal of the extractor and its spring downward.

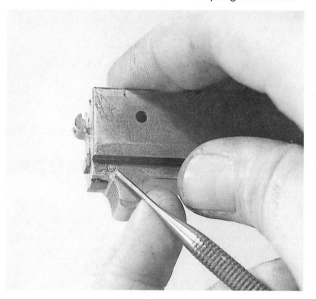

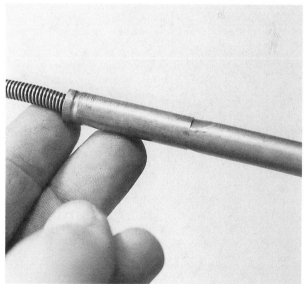

10. To remove the inner magazine tube, pull it out until it stops, then turn it 180 degrees to clear its side steps from the detents in the outer tube and take it out toward the rear.

11. Drifting out the locking cross pin at the head of the inner magazine tube will allow removal of the handle piece, spring, feed cable, and follower.

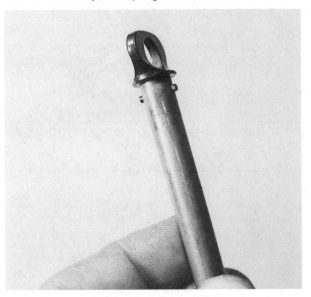

12. Use a very wide screwdriver or a special shop made tool to remove the nut at the rear of the buttstock, and its lock washer, and take off the stock toward the rear. The outer magazine tube can now be unscrewed from the rear of the receiver. **Caution:** *Avoid gripping the tube too tightly and deforming it.*

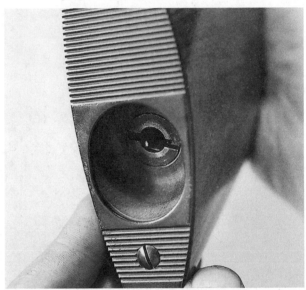

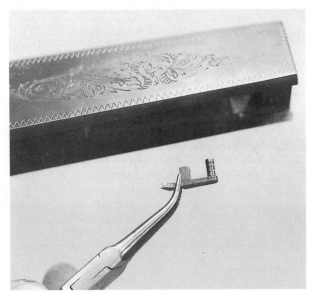

13. Swing the cartridge stop toward the inside wall of the receiver to clear its inner arm and lift it out of its pivot-hole in the roof of the receiver. It should be noted that on older guns that have seen a lot of use, the cartridge stop may fall out when the bolt and trigger assembly are removed, so be sure it isn't missed and lost.

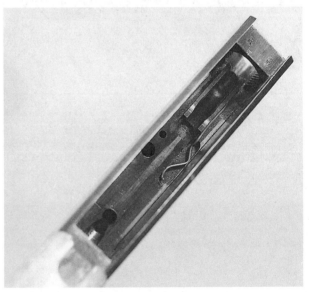

14. Removal of the cartridge guide spring in the top front of the receiver will release the cartridge guide to be taken out toward the front. To remove the spring, use a small tool to pry its rear loop from beneath its flange in the receiver.

15. Drifting out the small cross pin (upper arrow) at the top of the vertical trigger group extension will release the sear spring and plunger for removal upward. Drifting out the sear pivot pin (lower arrow) will allow the sear to be taken out toward the front. The trigger and disconnector pivot on the same pin, are removed as a unit, along with the disconnector spring. The disconnector can be separated from the trigger by drifting out the short pin that mounts it in the trigger. To remove the safety, use a small screwdriver to depress the plunger and spring inside, at the center, under the safety, and move the safety out toward the right. **Caution:** *Control the compressed spring and plunger and ease them out.*

Reassembly Tips:

1. When replacing the striker in the bolt, note that the striker has a guide lug on its left side that mates with a track inside the bolt.

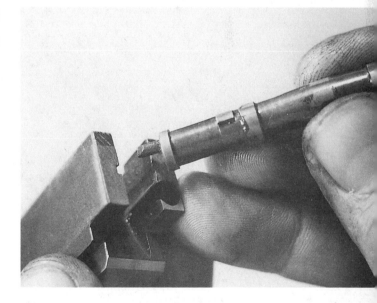

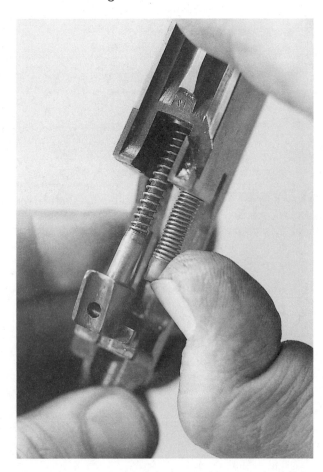

2. When replacing the bolt in the trigger group, carefully compress the recoil spring on its guide, then use a fingertip to hold the spring and guide in place on the bolt while fitting the bolt into place, inserting the tip of the striker spring guide into its hole in the vertical extension. Then, fit the rear bracket of the bolt spring guide onto its lug on the extension. **Caution:** *While the bolt spring is compressed, keep it aimed away from your eyes, in case the finger should slip.*

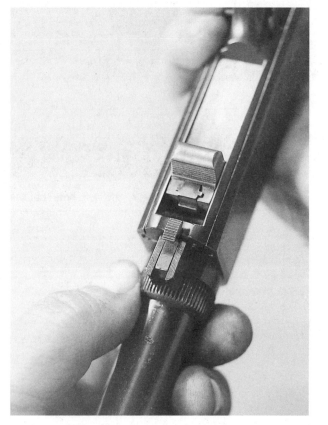

3. When reassembling the takedown latch system, be sure the small wedge-tipped plunger on the underside of the latch is oriented so the wedge tip aligns with the serrations on the adjustment nut. Use a small screwdriver to depress the two plungers alternately as the latch is moved into place.

4. To readjust the barrel nut, install the barrel on the gun before replacing the forend, lock the takedown latch in place, and turn the knurled adjustment nut until the ring is snug against the receiver. Then, reinstall the forend.

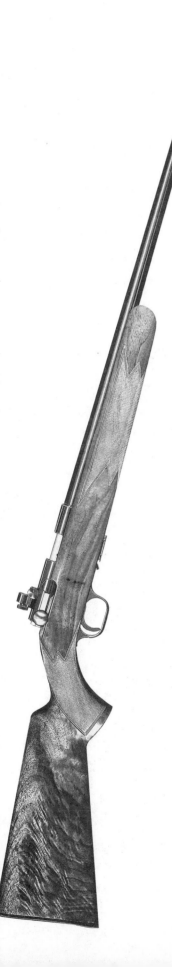

Browning T-Bolt

Similar/Identical Pattern Guns

The same basic assembly/disassembly steps for the Browning T-Bolt also apply to the following gun:

(Classic)
Browning T-2 T-Bolt

(Reintroduced)
Browning T-Bolt Sporter
Browning T-Bolt Target/Varmint

Data:	Browning T-Bolt
Origin:	Belgium
Manufacturer:	Fabrique Nationale, Herstal (for Browning Arms Company, Morgan, Utah)
Cartridge:	22 Long Rifle
Magazine capacity:	5 rounds
Overall length:	39¼ inches
Barrel length:	22 inches
Weight:	5½ pounds

The unusual "straight pull" bolt of this fine little gun is a masterpiece of good engineering, and works beautifully. Unfortunately, the average American shooter has never been fond of unusual actions, and the T-Bolt was imported for less than ten years, from 1965 to 1973. In addition to the plain T-1 model, a T-2 was offered, with 24-inch barrel and fancy stock. The gun was also available in a left-hand version. An accessory single-shot adapter would allow the use of 22 Short or Long, as well as Long Rifle. Except for the reversal of some directions in the left-hand model, the instructions will apply to all of them. In 2006, Browning reintroduced the T-Bolt rifle, manufactured using more modern technology, and has since expanded the line to rifles with heavy, target-style barrels, composite or wood stocks, and stainless steel actions. There is little difference in methods of disassembly or reassembly.

Disassembly:

1. Remove the magazine, and remove the main stock mounting screw, on the underside just forward of the magazine well. Separate the action from the stock.

2. Removal of the wood screw at the rear of the trigger guard unit will allow the guard to be taken off downward.

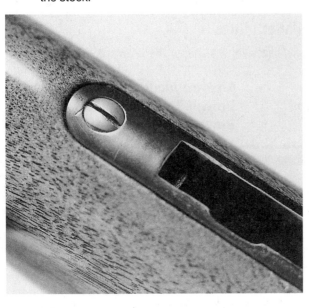

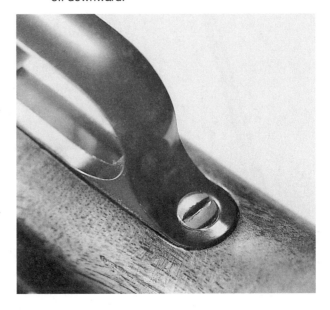

3. To remove the bolt, hold the trigger to the rear, and move the bolt out the rear of the receiver.

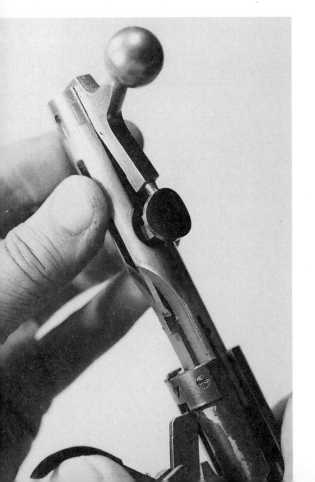

4. With the bolt handle in the closed (locked) position, push the vertical pin at the rear of the bolt upward, and remove it.

5. Remove the bolt handle toward the rear.

6. Remove the striker spring and its plunger toward the rear.

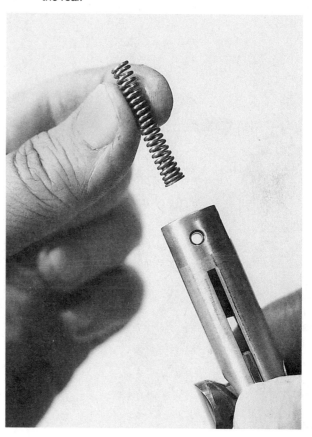

7. Turn the locking block ("cross-bolt") slightly to raise the firing pin out of its inside shoulder, and remove the locking block toward the right.

8. Remove the firing pin from its channel in the top of the bolt.

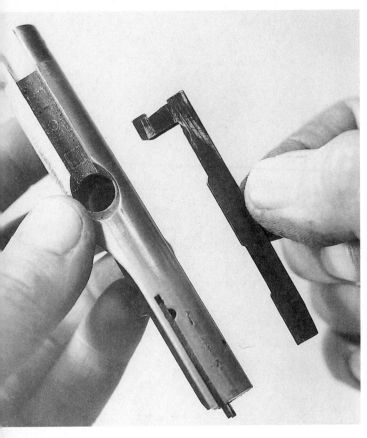

9. The twin extractors are retained by two vertical roll pins at the front of the bolt. Use a roll pin punch to drift out the pins, and remove the extractors from each side, along with the single transverse coil spring that powers both.

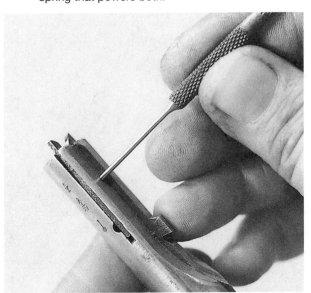

10. Push out the magazine catch cross pin, and remove the magazine catch and its coil spring downward.

11. Removal of the magazine catch will give access to the magazine housing screw, which is taken out downward.

12. Remove the magazine housing downward.

13. Push out the cross pin at the top of the magazine housing, and remove the sear upward and toward the front.

14. Note the relationship of the trigger and its spring before removal, to aid in reassembly. Push out the cross pin at the lower rear of the magazine housing, and remove the trigger and its spring toward the rear and downward. Take care that the trigger spring isn't lost. Restrain it, and ease it out.

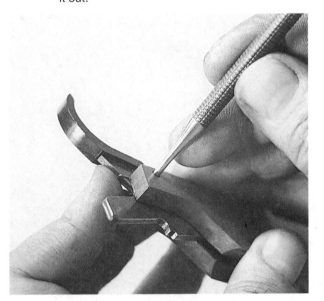

15. The trigger stop pin can also be drifted out, but can be left in place, as it retains no part.

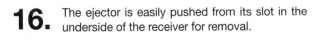

16. The ejector is easily pushed from its slot in the underside of the receiver for removal.

17. Removal of the two screws in the outer band of the safety catch at the rear of the receiver will allow the catch to be taken off. **Caution:** *Removal of the safety will release the safety positioning plunger and spring, so restrain them and ease them out.*

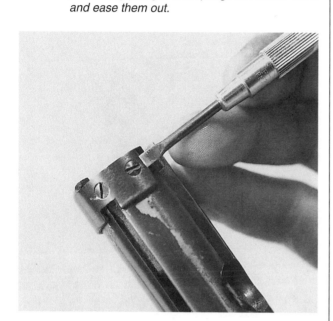

Reassembly Tips:

1. When replacing the ejector in its slot in the underside of the receiver, be sure its vertical face is toward the front, and its angled end toward the rear, as shown.

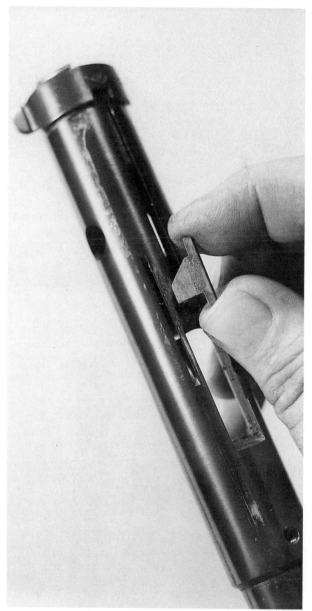

2. When replacing the trigger and its spring, taking out the trigger stop pin will make this operation easier. Insert the cross pin from the right, just far enough to hold the spring in position, then put in the trigger, and move the cross pin the rest of the way across. Be sure the front arm of the spring is against its shoulder or shelf inside the housing.

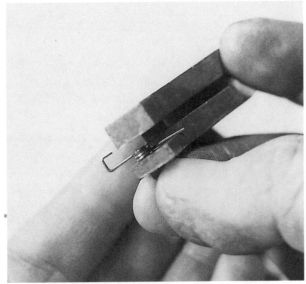

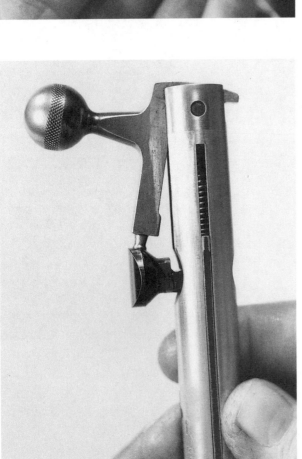

3. When replacing the locking cross bolt in the body of the bolt, note that the face with the deep cut and hole must be oriented toward the rear, and install the locking bolt before the firing pin is returned to its channel.

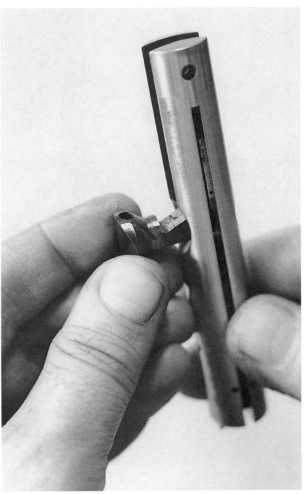

4. When replacing the bolt handle, be sure its front projection enters the hole in the rear face of the locking bolt, and note that the handle must be in the unlocked position, as shown, when the bolt is inserted into the receiver.

Calico M-100

Similar/Identical Pattern Guns

The same basic assembly/disassembly steps for the Calico Model 100 also apply to the following gun:

Calico M-105 Sporter

Data:	Calico M-100
Origin:	United States
Manufacturer:	California Instrument Co.
	Bakersfield, California
Cartridge:	22 Long Rifle
Magazine capacity:	100 rounds
Overall length:	35.8 inches (stock extended)
	29.8 inches (stock folded)
Barrel length:	16.1 inches
Weight:	4.2 pounds

In 1986, the California Instrument Company startled the world of 22 rimfire rifles by bringing out a semi-auto with a unique helical-feed magazine that had a capacity of 100 rounds. This was not the only innovation-the design has many nice little touches of engineering. The M-105 Sporter, with a wood stock and forend, was introduced in 1989. It is the same mechanically, and the instructions will apply.

Disassembly:

1. Remove the magazine and open the stock. Cycle the action to cock the hammer, and set the safety in on-safe position. It is not necessary to take off the folding stock for further disassembly, but if removal is required, drift the stock. retaining pin out upward. The stock can then be slid off toward the rear.

2. The stock latch can be removed by drifting out the roll cross pin. If this is done, the coil spring and the magazine ejector plunger can then be taken out.

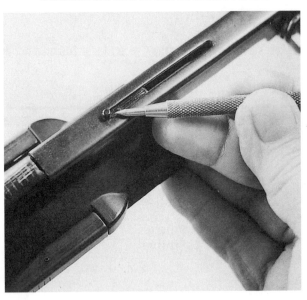

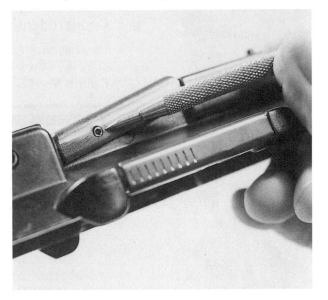

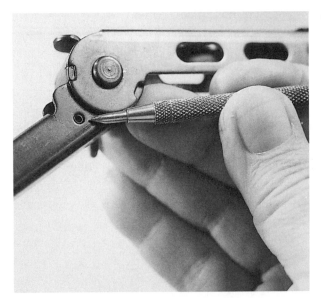

3. The stock release lever and its coil spring can be removed by drifting out this roll cross pin. The other stock components are riveted in place, and routine removal is not advisable.

4. The lower receiver is retained by two hollow cross pins at the rear, and a hinge post at the front. The cross pins are flared on one side and must be pushed out in that direction-in this case, toward the left.

5. Drift or push out the rear cross pin.

6. Drift out the other cross pin.

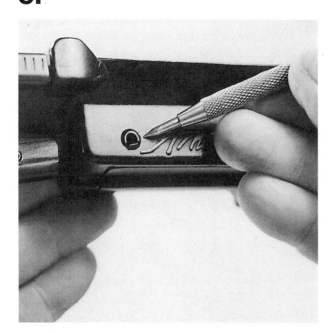

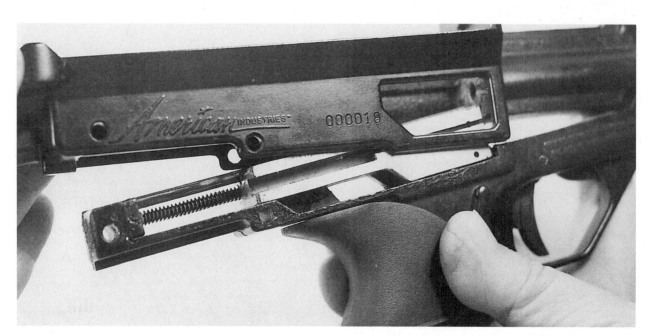

7. Draw the bolt back slightly to clear the extractor from its recess in the barrel, and keeping the bolt snugged against the lower receiver, pivot the upper receiver upward.

8. Remove the bolt assembly from the top of the lower receiver. Take care that the plastic buffer at the rear is not lost.

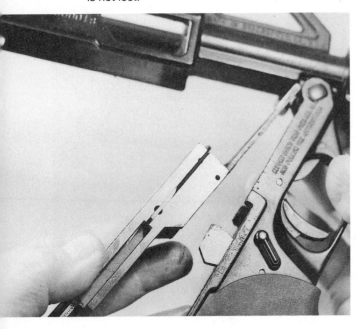

9. Remove the ejector from its recess in the top of the bolt.

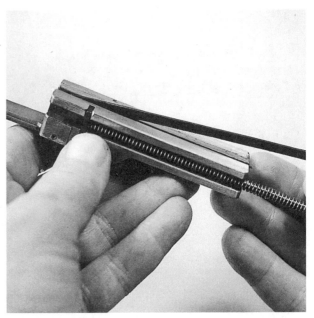

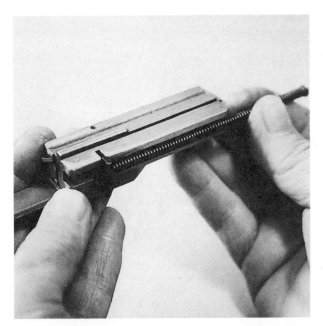

10. Remove the recoil spring assembly from the side of the bolt. This unit is staked at the ends, and routine disassembly is not advisable.

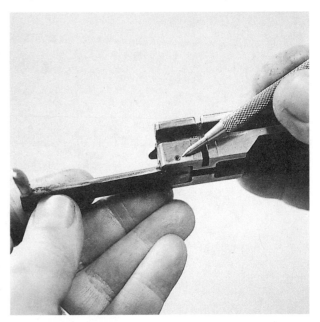

11. Drift out the cross pin at the lower front of the bolt.

12. Remove the cocking handle plate toward the front. Take care that the firing pin return spring is not lost.

13. Remove the firing pin return spring.

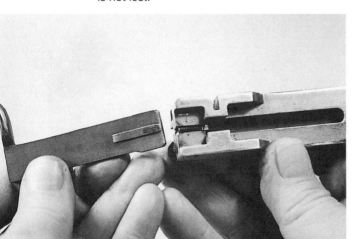

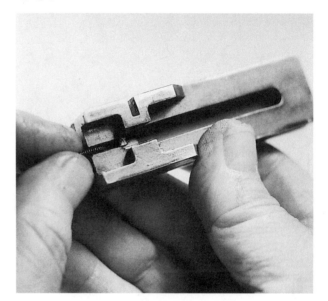

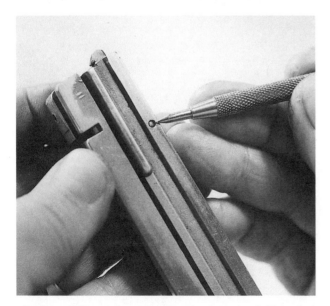

14. Drift out the extractor pin downward. Note that this pin is angled toward the center of the bolt, not straight downward. Control the extractor and its spring.

15. Remove the extractor from its recess.

16. Remove the extractor spring from its well in the bolt.

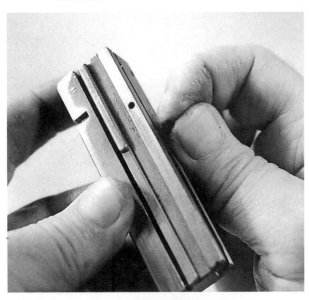

17. Tip the firing pin out of its recess. The cross pin is staked in place, and it is not removed in normal takedown.

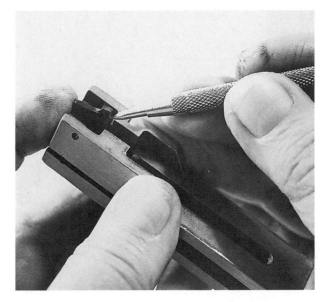

18. For easier access to the parts in the lower receiver, you may wish to separate it from the upper receiver. To remove the pivot shaft, use a properly-fitted screwdriver to take off the cap screw. It will be necessary to hold the head of the shaft on the other side. Grip it with non-marring pliers, or, as I did, just press it against the wooden edge of a workbench. The finish is easily marred, so work with care.

19. Push out the pivot shaft and separate the upper and lower receivers.

20. Drifting out the cross pin at the front of the sight unit will allow this assembly to be pushed off toward the front. If this is done, take care that the positioning key, in a recess on top of the barrel, isn't lost. If necessary, the flanged nut at the rear of the forend can be unscrewed for removal of the barrel. There is also a positioning key at the barrel flange, at the rear. In normal takedown, this entire system is best left in place. The factory suggests that it not be dismounted.

21. The twin magazine catches and their coil springs are pivoted and retained by vertical roll pins.

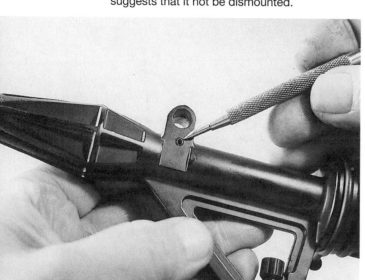

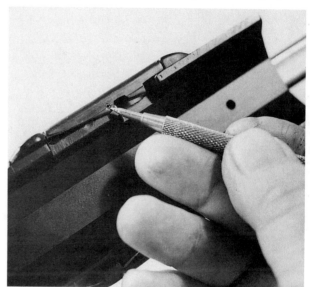

22. Slide open the pistol grip cap and use a screwdriver to remove the mounting screw.

23. Remove the pistol grip from the lower receiver.

24. Move the safety to off-safe position, restrain the hammer, pull the trigger, and ease the hammer down to fired position. Restrain the hammer and drift out the hammer pivot pin.

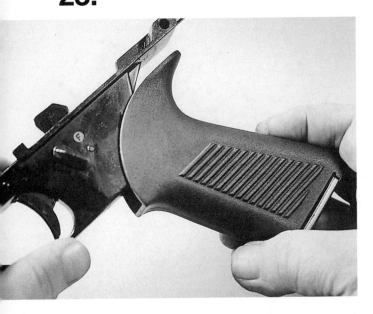

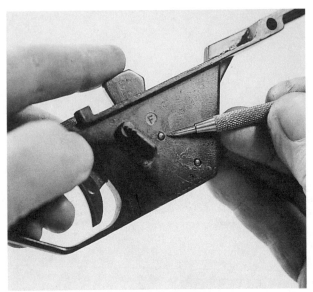

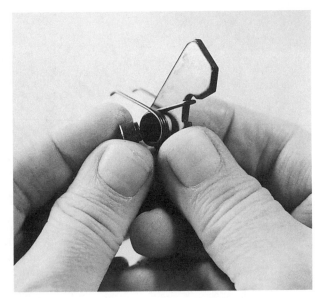

25. Remove the hammer and its spring assembly.

26. The bushings are easily removed from the hammer.

27. Further disassembly of the trigger group is not advisable because of possible damage and the difficulty of reassembly. However, in repair situations, it may be necessary to take out certain parts, so we will show the sequence without removal. The safety-levers are retained on each side by internal C-clips. When these are turned to position and pried off upward, the levers can be removed, along with the center shaft and the safety block.

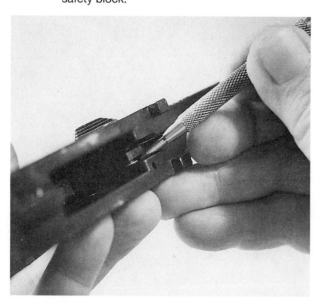

28. Drifting out this cross pin will release the bolt hold open and its coil spring for removal.

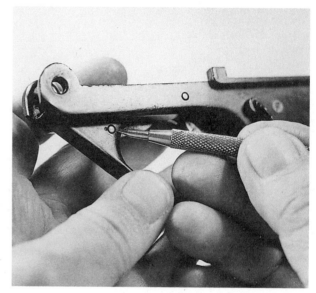

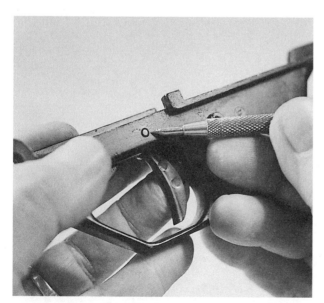

29. Drifting out the trigger cross pin will allow the trigger to be moved forward and turned down into the guard opening for removal.

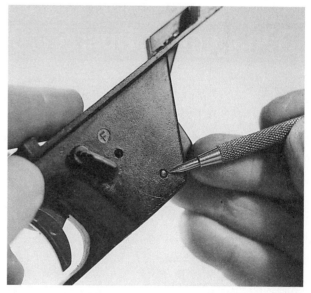

30. Drifting out this cross pin will release the sear assembly for removal. **Caution:** *The primary and secondary sears and their coil and torsion springs will be released, so control them.* A slave pin and much patience will be necessary for reinstallation. In normal takedown, this system is definitely best left in place.

31. By sliding off the upper and lower ribbon clamps, it is possible to disassemble the magazine. The winder assembly, however, should not be taken apart. If a magazine malfunctions, it is best to return it to Calico for service.

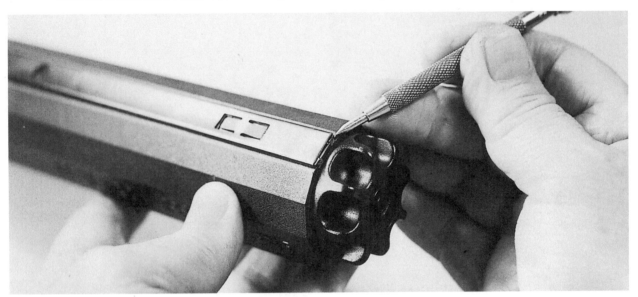

Reassembly Tips:

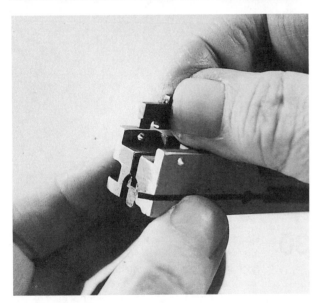

1. When installing the firing pin in the bolt, be sure it is oriented properly, as shown.

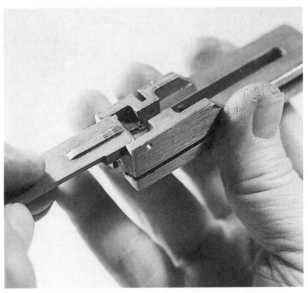

2. When attaching the bolt handle plate, be sure its rear lug engages the firing pin return spring.

3. When the bolt assembly is put back into the lower receiver, be sure the buffer is oriented properly to engage the tail of the ejector and the rear tip of the recoil spring unit.

4. As the bolt is installed, be sure the ejector is hooked into its recess at the rear, and push it forward as the upper receiver is tipped back into place. Also, draw the bolt back slightly to clear the extractor.

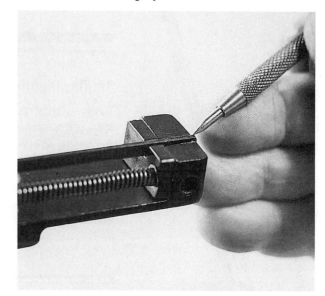

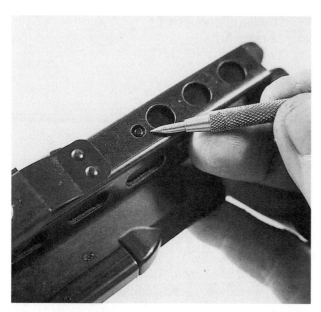

5. If the stock has been removed, drift the retaining pin down until its tip is level with the exterior of the stock piece, as shown.

Charter AR-7 Explorer

(now from Henry Repeating Arms)

Similar/Identical Pattern Guns

The same basic assembly/disassembly steps for the Charter AR-7 Explorer also apply to the following guns:

Armalite AR-7   **Armalite AR-7C**

Armalite AR-7 Custom   **Survival Arms AR-7**

Armalite AR-7S

Data:	Charter AR-7 Explorer
Origin:	United States
Manufacturer:	Charter Arms Corp.
	Stratford, Connecticut
Cartridge:	22 Long Rifle
Magazine capacity:	8 rounds
Overall length:	35 inches
Barrel length:	16 inches
Weight:	2½ pounds

In 1959, Armalite, Incorporated of Costa Mesa, California, introduced the AR-7 Explorer, and this little semi-auto carbine instantly became popular with backpackers, fishermen, pilots, and everyone who might eventually be faced with a survival situation. The barrel, receiver, and magazine can be stowed inside the hollow plastic stock, and with the rubber buttplate/cover in place, the whole thing will even float. From 1973 to 1990, the AR-7 was made by Charter Arms. Between 1990 and 1995, the AR-7 was produced by Survival Arms. An improved version has been made by Henry Repeating Arms since 1997.

Disassembly:

1. The stock retaining bolt is accessible in a recess at the bottom of the pistol grip portion of the stock, and its head has a raised center piece that is easily grasped with finger and thumb. Turn the bolt counterclockwise until the stock is released from the receiver, and remove the stock down and toward the rear.

2. The barrel is retained by a knurled collar which is threaded onto the front of the receiver. Turn the collar counterclockwise (front view) until it is free of the receiver, and remove the barrel toward the front. Note the guide or key on top of the barrel, which mates with a slot in the top of the receiver extension.

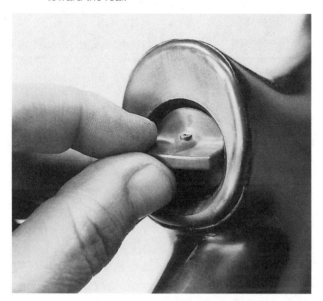

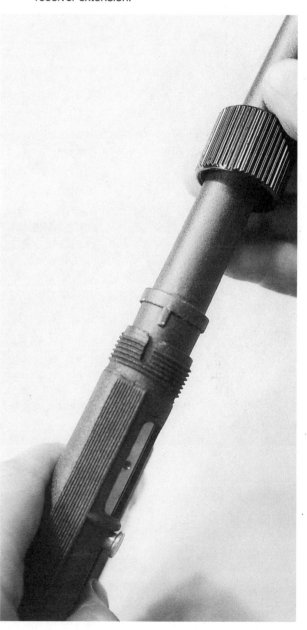

3. The barrel collar can be removed from the barrel only after the front sight is drifted out of its dovetail.

4. Be sure hammer is at rest (in the fired position) and remove the large screw on the left side which retains the sideplate.

Remove the sideplate toward the left. Proceed cautiously, as the left end of the hammer pivot rests in a small hole in the sideplate. If the plate is tight, it may have to be nudged from inside the magazine well and pried gently at the lower rear.

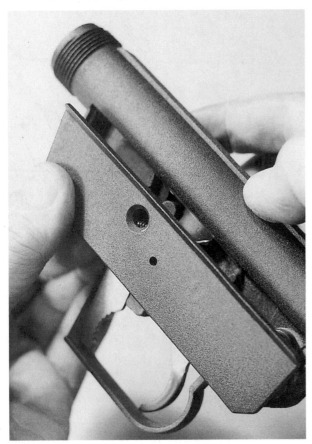

5. After the plate is removed, take note of the relationship of the internal parts before taking them out.

6. Restrain the magazine catch spring to prevent its loss, and remove the catch and spring toward the left.

7. Disengage the outside (left) rear arm of the mainspring from its groove in the bearing pin at the rear of the trigger, and swing the spring arm down and forward to relieve its tension.

8. With a small screwdriver, lift the inside (right) rear arm of the mainspring from its groove in the pin at the rear of the trigger, and remove the pin toward the left.

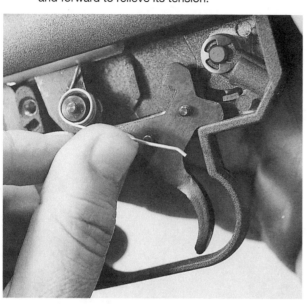

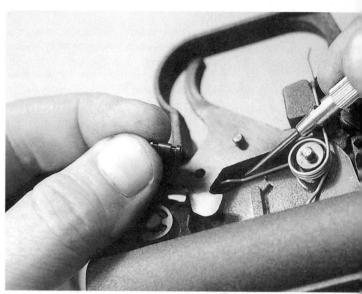

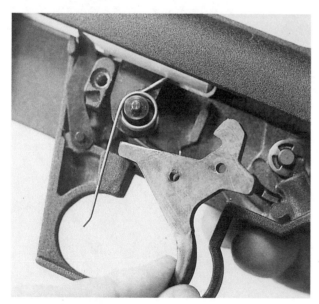

9. Remove the trigger and its pivot pin toward the left.

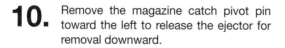

10. Remove the magazine catch pivot pin toward the left to release the ejector for removal downward.

11. Tip the hammer toward the rear and remove the hammer, spring and pivot assembly toward the left. The spring is easily detached from the hammer. In normal disassembly, the pivot should not be removed from the hammer.

12. Depress the bolt very slightly to align the bolt handle with the enlarged portion of its track in the receiver, and remove the handle toward the right.

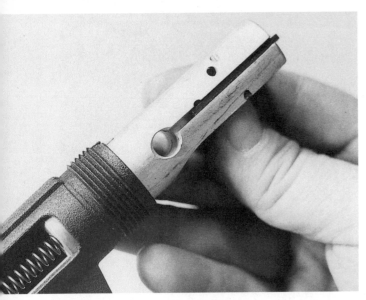

13. Remove the bolt, along with its twin springs and spring guide unit, toward the front.

14. Remove the springs and spring guide unit from the rear of the bolt.

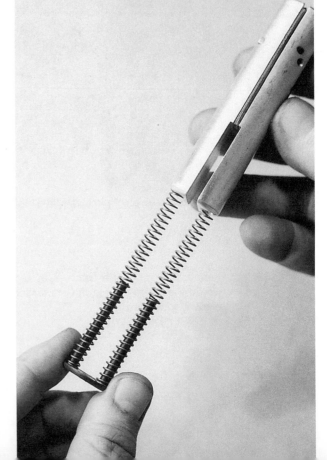

15. Drifting out a horizontal roll pin will release the firing pin for removal from the top of the bolt.

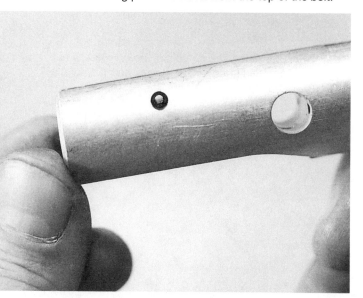

16. Drifting out a vertical roll pin (arrow) on the right side of the bolt will release the extractor and its spring for removal toward the right.

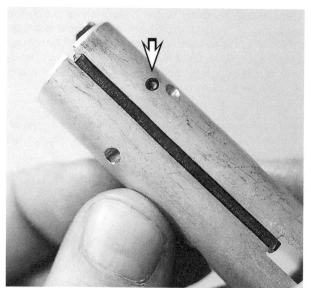

17. The safety is retained by a spring C-clip inside the receiver. After removal of the clip, the safety is removed toward the right.

18. Backing out the screw at the rear of the receiver will release the rear sight for removal.

Reassembly Tips:

When replacing the bolt and bolt spring assembly in the receiver, be sure the two springs are completely seated on the guide, and that the guide is horizontally oriented so the springs will not kink.

Before replacing the trigger in the receiver, swing the inside arm of the mainspring up to the rear and rest it on the inside of the receiver. When the trigger is in place, use a small screwdriver to lift the inner arm of the spring while inserting the spring base pin. Be sure the tip of the spring engages the groove in the pin.

1. When replacing the rear sight, note that the position of the sight plate is adjustable, and any change will affect the point of impact.

2. When replacing the sideplate, be sure the small tip of the hammer pivot is aligned with its hole in the sideplate.

3. When replacing the barrel, be sure the guide key on the top of the barrel enters its slot in the front of the receiver. Tighten the barrel collar firmly, by hand, but do not over-tighten, as both collar and receiver are made of alloy.

Chiappa Little Badger

Data:	Chiappa Little Badger
Origin:	Italy
Manufacturer:	Armi Sport de Chiappa, Italy
Cartridge:	.22 Long Rifle, .22 Magnum
Overall length:	32 inches
Barrel length:	16.5 inches
Weight:	2.9 pounds

The Little Badger, made and imported by Chiappa Firearms, is a new entry into the "survival" rifle market. The rifle has an attractive price tag and has surprisingly few plastic parts, the most notable being the sights and the buttplate, as well as a threaded barrel for use with a sound suppressor. The rifle also folds nearly in half and as such can be stored in its included carry bag inside most backpacks, while holding cartridges in a small rack inside the wire stock. Several accessory rails allow the mounting of pistol grips, lights, and optics, etc. The Chiappa Double Badger, M6, and X-Caliber models are similarly derived but rather differ in design due to the presence of two barrels.

Disassembly:

1. Open the action. Remove the pivot pin screw from the right side of the receiver. Then push the pivot pin out to the left and separate the barrel from the receiver.

2. Remove this screw and pull the extractor out of the barrel to the rear.

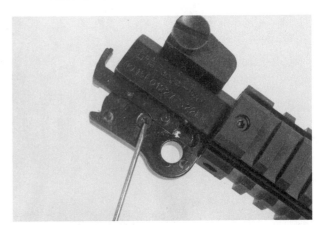

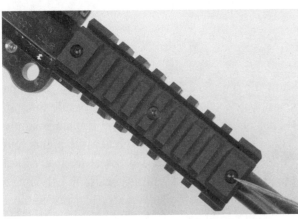

3. The barrel is held inside a sleeve that contains the extractor. If necessary the sleeve can be removed by first removing the two side Picatinny rails from the barrel, each held by three screws. There is no need to remove the top and bottom rails.

4. Drive out these two cross pins and pull the barrel sleeve off to the rear of the barrel.

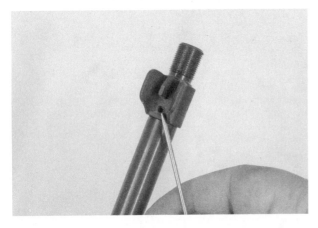

5. The rear sight is attached to the barrel sleeve. The front sight is retained by means of this set screw.

6. Remove the two large Torx head screws in the receiver, one on each side.

7. Remove the left side plate of the receiver to reveal the inner workings.

8. The buttstock can be removed by simply lifting it from the receiver.

9. Remove the locking lever and its spring.

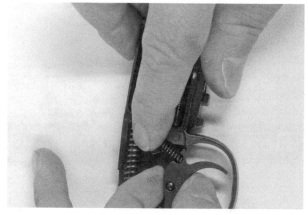

10. Lift out the trigger and spring. Guard the spring.

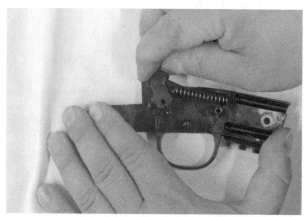

11. Lift out the hammer, spring, and guide. The spring is still slightly compressed and should be contained.

12. The buttstock should be left intact as further disassembly will likely cause breakage.

13. The firing pin can be removed by driving out this pin.

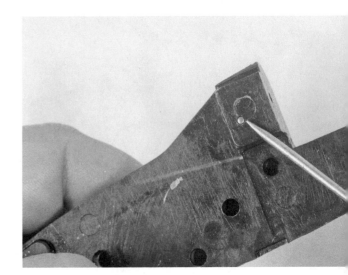

Reassembly Tips:

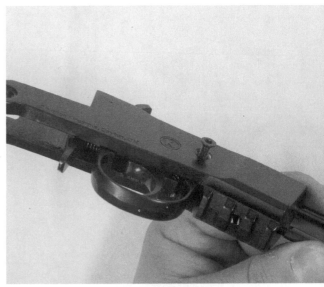

1. The hammer and spring are easily installed as the pin projects out from the right side receiver inner wall. Place the hammer on the pin, the spring in its seat and lever the hammer slightly to the rear; then push the hammer fully on to the hammer pin.

2. Note that the two large receiver Torx head screws have different heads: one is a flat head and the other is a square head. The flat head screw goes into the left side hole.

Chiappa M1-22

Data:	Chiappa M1-22
Origin:	Italy
Manufacturer:	Kimar (Chiappa Group), Azzano Mella
Cartridge:	.22 Long Rifle
Magazine capacity:	5 rounds
Overall length:	35 inches
Barrel length:	18 inches
Weight:	5.5 pounds

Made by Chiappa, the M1-22 is a low cost rimfire replica of the well-loved M1 Carbine. It is roughly the same weight, with the same dimensions and operating controls and sights as the later models of the M1 carbine. It simply fires .22 LR instead of .30 Carbine ammo. This model wears a black synthetic stock, but the rifle can be purchased with a wood stock as well. There is also a similar model chambered in 9mm and some of the steps will work for that model as well.

Disassembly:

1. Remove the screw holding the barrel band closed (picture A). Then depress this spring and push the barrel band forward on the barrel and off the stock (picture B). Remove the upper handguard by pulling if forward slightly and off the barrel.

picture B

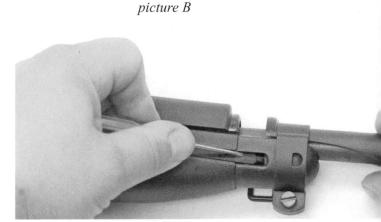

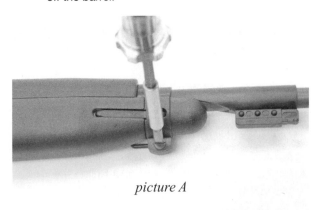

picture A

2. Lift the barrel up and pull the action out of the stock.

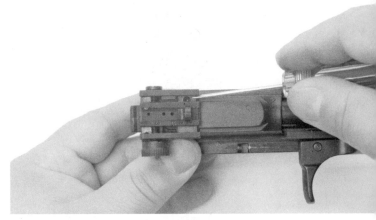

3. The front and rear sight assemblies are retained by set screws. Do no remove the sights unnecessarily.

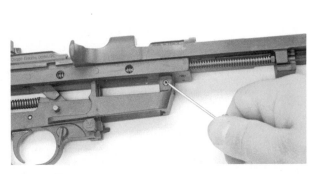

4. Drive out this roll pin. Then pull the trigger assembly slightly forward or rearward to clear the rear dovetail and remove it from the action.

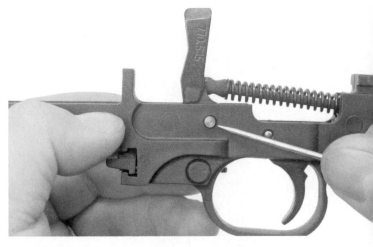

5. Push out the hammer pin to remove the hammer, strut, and spring.

6. Push out this pin to remove the trigger and its spring, and the sear, sear spring, and plunger.

7. There is a small gap underneath the front of the magazine catch. Insert a small tool and push the plunger toward the trigger guard. At the same time push the magazine catch in the direction of the button, to the right, to remove it and its spring from the assembly. The plunger, spring, and another plunger that works against the safety will fall out of this hole to the front once the magazine catch has been removed.

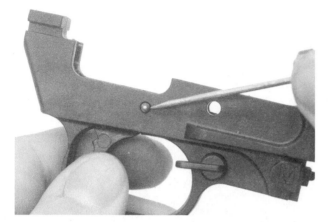

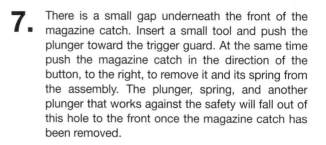

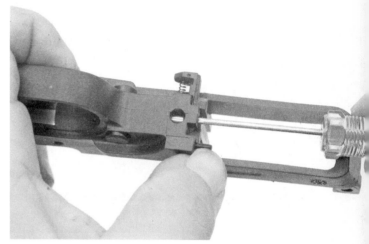

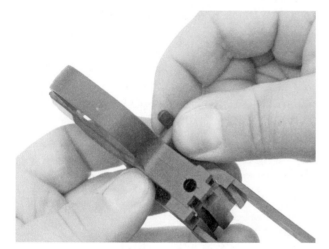

8. Remove the safety lever to the right.

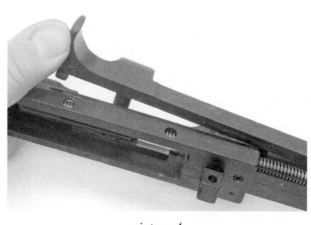

picture A

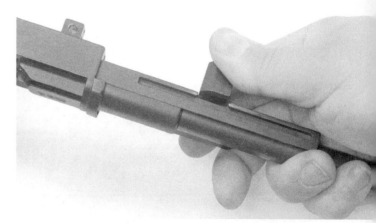

picture B

9. Push the charging handle back until the rear section can be rotated up and out of its track (picture A). The allow it to come forward until the front section reaches the point where it can rotate up and out of the track (picture B). Allow the operating handle to come fully forward to separate from the recoil spring and the receiver. Remove the bolt up and forward through the ejection port.

10. Drive out this pin from left to right to free the firing pin and spring.

11. Drive out this pin to free the extractor and spring.

Reassembly Tips:

1. When reassembling the trigger group, replace the trigger assembly and then insert the trigger return spring as shown here. Then simply use a punch to push it into place behind the trigger. Note that the loop of the spring rests on the top of the rear of the trigger.

Chipmunk

Similar/Identical Pattern Guns

The same basic assembly/disassembly steps for the Chipmunk also apply to the following gun:

Chipmunk Deluxe

Data:	Chipmunk
Origin:	United States
Manufacturer:	Oregon Arms, Inc. Medford, Oregon
Cartridge:	22 Long Rifle
Overall length:	30 inches
Barrel length:	16⅛ inches
Weight:	2½ pounds

This elegant little rifle was designed for young shooters, but it has also seen some use by campers, backpackers and others who value its small size and reliable mechanism. It was first made by the Chipmunk Manufacturing Company from 1982 to 1988, then by Oregon Arms between 1988 and 1996. At the present time, it is being produced by Rogue Rifle Company. The instructions can be applied to all Chipmunk rifles.

Disassembly:

1. Hold the trigger to the rear, open the bolt, and remove the bolt toward the rear.

2. Remove the stock mounting bolt, located on the underside, just forward of the trigger guard. Remove the action from the stock, straight upward. The fitting is often tight, so use care, and apply equal pressure at each end.

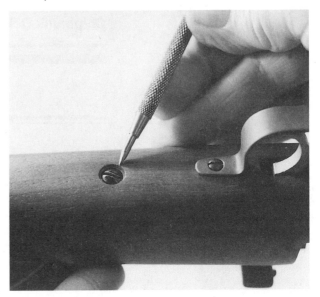

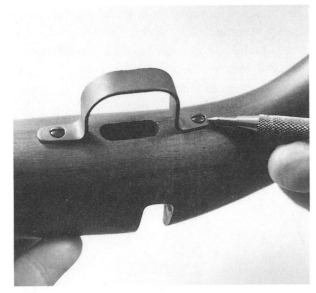

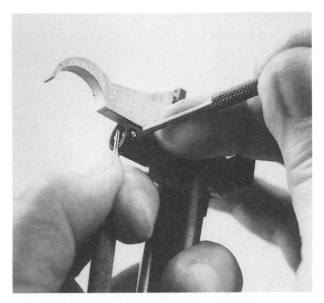

3. The trigger guard and the stock buttplate are each retained by two wood screws.

4. The cross pin that retains the combination sear and trigger spring is rebated at each end. To remove it, depress it upward with a tool or fingertip until its larger central portion is aligned with the exit hole on either side. Then, push it out. **Caution:** *The spring is under tension, so control it.*

5. Remove the spring from its recess.

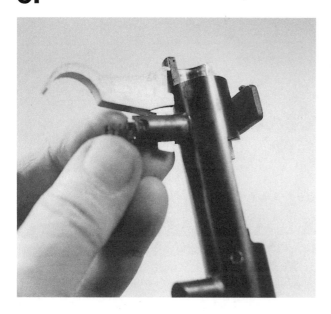

6. Remove the trigger downward.

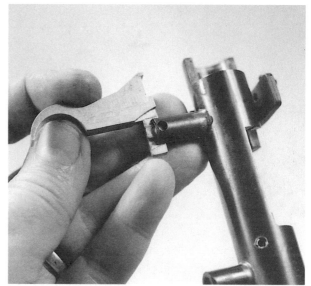

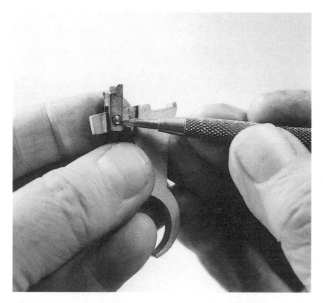

7. Pushing out the cross pin will allow the sear to be separated from the trigger.

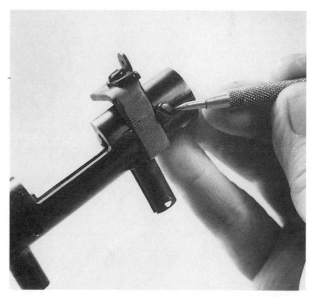

8. The elevation adjustment screw also retains the rear sight on the receiver. The windage adjustment screw retains the aperture on the sight base.

9. A cross pin retains the barrel in the receiver. In normal takedown, this is not disturbed. If removal is necessary, drift out the pin and use a hardwood block to drive the receiver off the barrel. Note that the cross pin is a roll pin, so use a roll pin punch to avoid deformation.

10. With a tool or a strong thumbnail, depress the extractor plunger and remove the extractor toward the side. **Caution:** *Control the strong spring and plunger.*

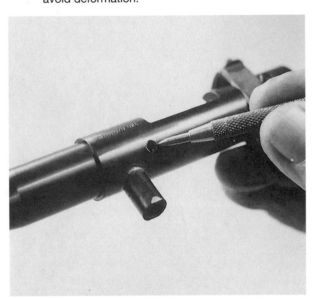

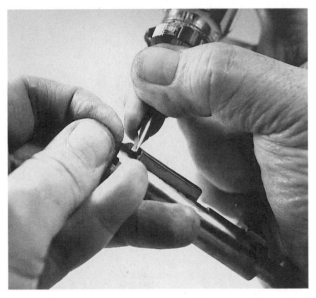

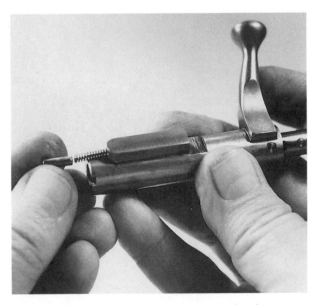

11. Remove the extractor plunger and spring.

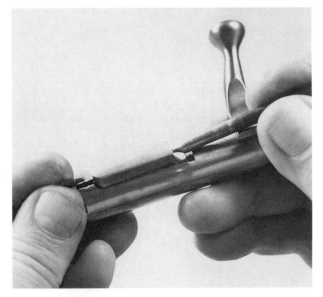

12. Use a small tool to nudge the bolt detent plunger forward, into the extractor spring tunnel, and take the plunger out toward the front.

13. Drift out the cross pin that retains the cocking knob. When the drift is withdrawn, control the knob, as it is under tension of the rebound spring.

14. Remove the cocking knob and rebound spring toward the rear. The spring is easily removed from inside the knob shaft.

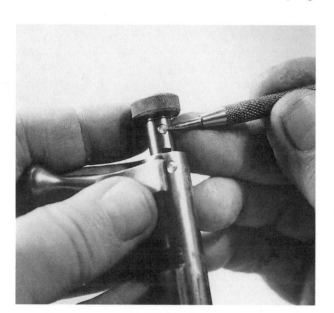

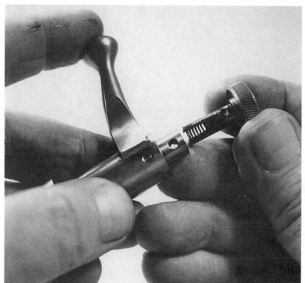

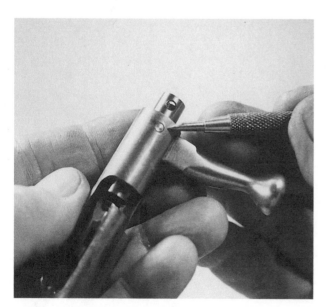

15. Drift out the striker retaining pin upward. Avoid canting the pin after it clears one wall of the bolt. **Caution:** *Control the striker spring as the drift is withdrawn.*

16. Remove the striker and spring toward the rear. The spring is easily removed from inside the striker.

Reassembly Tips:

1. When installing the striker retaining pin, insert a tool at the rear to slightly compress the striker spring, keeping it forward of the pin.

2. When installing the bolt detent plunger, note that its smaller tip goes toward the rear.

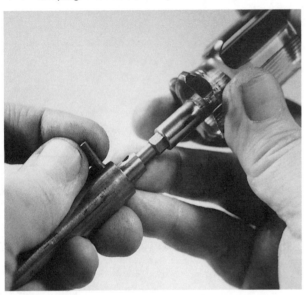

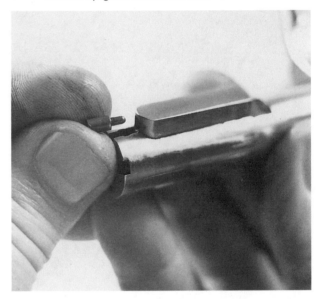

3. If the sear has been removed from the trigger, be sure it is reinstalled as shown, with its step toward the front.

Colt M4 Carbine .22

Data:	Colt M4
Origin:	Germany
Manufacturer:	Walther Arms, Ulm
Cartridge:	.22 Long Rifle
Magazine capacity:	30 rounds
Overall length:	34.5 inches
Barrel length:	16.1 inches
Weight:	6 pounds

Just as the AR-15 and M4 rifles are heavily copied in centerfire versions, they are also heavily copied in rimfire. This is Colt's own .22 version of their M4 carbine, even though it, like those made for HK and one or two other companies, is actually license built by Walther Arms of Germany. In fact some of the basic designs are quite comparable, and the magazines are usually interchangeable. For those who desire a full sized, full weight replica of the normal rifle, these rifles fit the bill.

Disassembly:

1. Push out the two takedown pins and separate the upper assembly from the lower assembly.

2. Pull back on the handguard ring in order to remove the handguard pieces.

3. Remove this large set screw from the back of the bolt assembly to free the recoil spring and its two plungers.

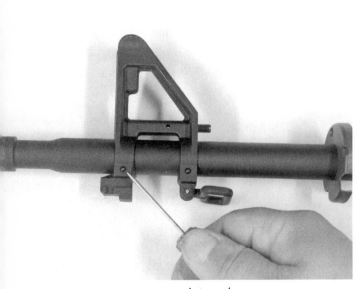

picture A

picture B

4. Unscrew and remove the flash hider from the muzzle. Then drive out these two pins from left to right (picture A). Drive out the small spring pin that retains the swivel in place. Beneath the swivel is a small set screw that must also be removed (picture B). Then pull the front sight tower off the barrel.

5. Use a standard AR action wrench to remove the barrel retaining nut assembly. (Vice omitted for clarity).

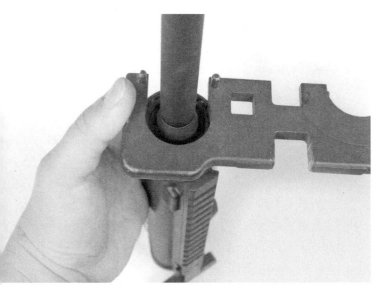

6. With the nut removed, pull the barrel cover forward off the inner barrel.

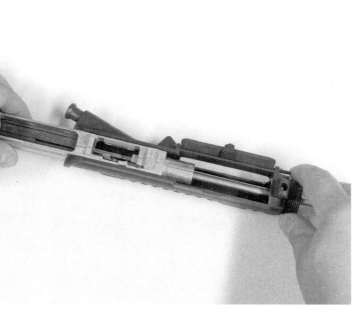

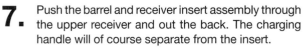

7. Push the barrel and receiver insert assembly through the upper receiver and out the back. The charging handle will of course separate from the insert.

picture A

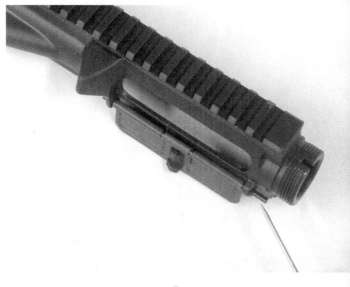

picture B

8. Drive out this pin to remove the non-functional forward assist button and spring (picture A). To remove the ejection port cover, pull the pivot pin out to the front. Do not remove the small spring clip from the pivot pin (picture B).

9. There are five socket screws that hold the two halves of the receiver insert together. Remove them and lift the right side half off the left side half.

10. Remove the barrel (picture A) and the bolt (picture B).

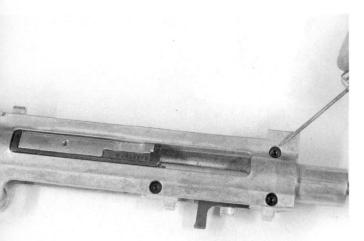

picture A

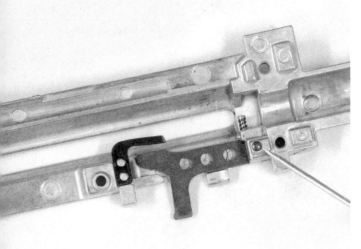

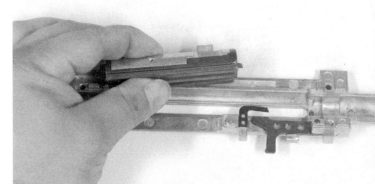

11. Remove the ejector. Then push out this pin to remove the bolt catch with spring.

picture B

12. To separate the bolt pieces, this pin must be removed. It is staked in from the right. A punch must be applied at an angle in order to get a purchase. Do this only if something is broken.

13. With the top of the bolt removed, the firing pin and underlying spring can be removed, as can the extractor spring and plunger (above, in this picture). The extractor can be removed to the front as soon as the plunger has been cleared.

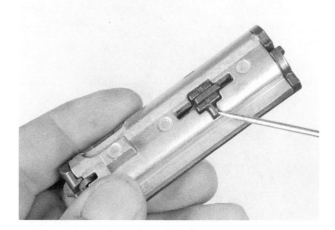

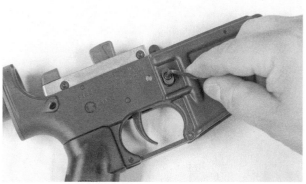

14. Remove this screw to disassemble and remove the magazine catch, button, and spring.

15. Push out the safety from the right.

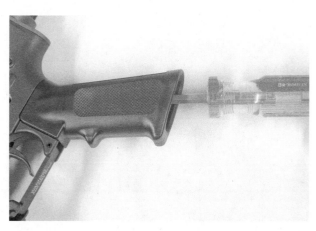

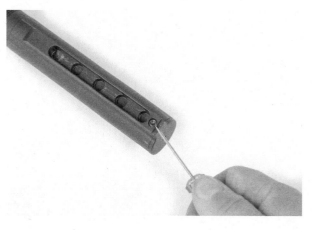

16. Remove the pistol grip. This frees the trigger housing to be removed upwards out of the lower receiver. The fake bolt catch will fall out after the housing is removed.

17. If necessary, the receiver extension tube can be removed. It is held onto the receiver by a single screw through the center of the tube's front wall. It can be accessed by removing this small socket screw and removing the rear face plate from the tube.

18. Remove the four socket head screws from the right side of the housing and their corresponding nuts from the left (picture A). Gently remove the right half wall of the housing to reveal the contents. Take care to control springs as you can.

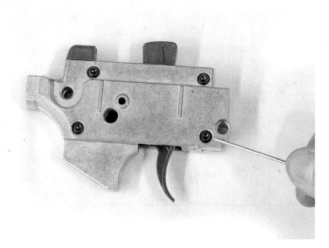

picture A

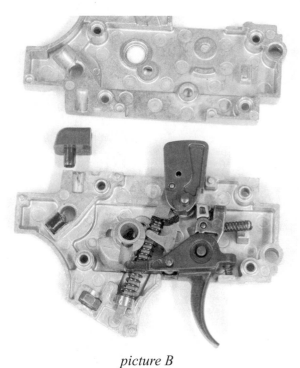

picture B

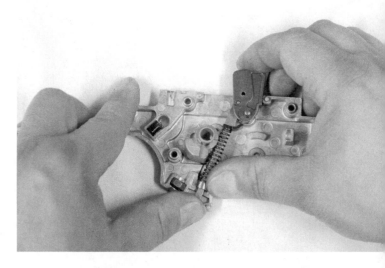

19. The trigger and sear mechanism can be disassembled by pushing out the three pins that hold them together, as can the hammer and hammer strut by pushing out the pivot pin.

20. Carefully displace the hammer spring seat, and then the hammer from the left housing wall. The safety behind it can also be removed at this time. The safety's plunger and spring bear against the left wall "beneath" the safety. Do not lose them.

21. The trigger parts assembled. If there is no need to disassemble further, do not do so. Note that the disconnector (the "Y" shaped piece) is rotated far to the rear of its functional location, in contact with the sear.

Reassembly Tips:

1. Note when reassembling the upper receiver insert, that the screws are two different lengths. As shown in this picture, the two short screws go in the two top holes. Also, though it need not be said, do not lose the nuts.

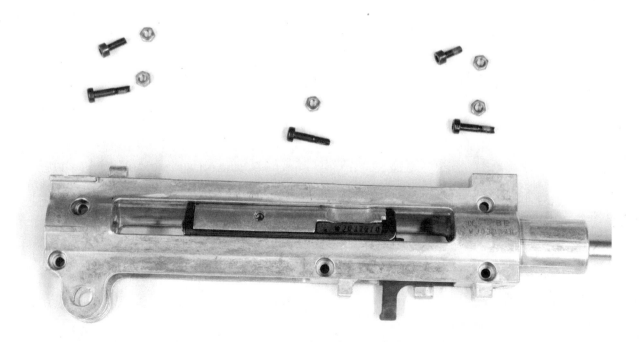

Cooper 57M Jackson Squirrel Rifle

Similar/Identical Pattern Guns
The same basic assembly/disassembly steps for the Cooper 57M also apply to the following guns:

57M LVT　　　　　　**57M Classic**
57M Western Classic　**57M TRP-3**
57M Jackson Hunter

Data:	Cooper Model 57M Jackson Squirrel Rifle
Origin:	United States
Manufacturer:	Cooper Firearms of Montana, Stevensville, Montana
Cartridge:	17 HMR
Magazine capacity:	5 rounds
Overall length:	40½ inches
Barrel length:	22 inches
Weight:	7¾ pounds

Cooper Firearms of Montana delivers several lines of very high-quality bolt-action rifles. Even the synthetic stocked models show fine craftsmanship, and all are sold with an impressive accuracy guarantee. The 57M is the rimfire model and is chambered in both 22 and 17 caliber varieties. For those willing to pay the premium charge for such a firearm, a pinpoint-accurate rifle with high-quality finishing, stock wood and a fully adjustable trigger are at hand for their shooting enjoyment.

Disassembly:

1. Remove the magazine and depress the bolt stop button to pull the bolt from the receiver.

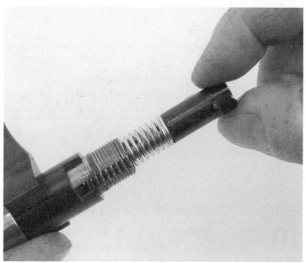

3. Pull the firing pin assembly from out of the rear of the bolt.

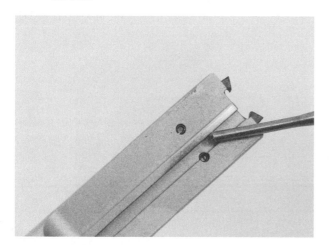

5. The extractors and extractor springs can be removed by punching out these two roll pins. The extractors are not identical, so make note of which extractor is the left and which is on the right.

2. Unscrew the bolt shroud from the back of the bolt. Caution: the rear of the bolt is threaded and split to allow passage of the firing pin assembly. This split can make it susceptible to pinching, expanding or other bend damage.

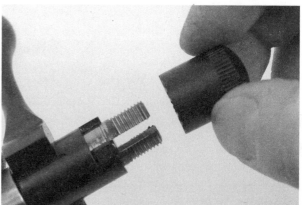

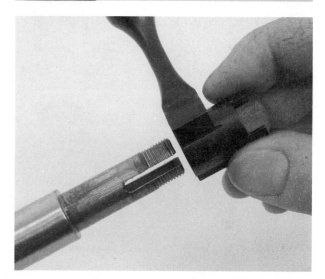

4. Remove the bolt handle from the bolt body by pulling it from the rear of the bolt.

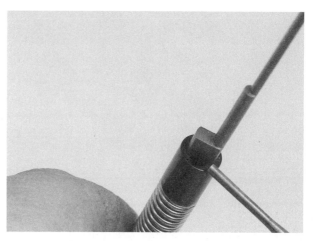

6. The firing pin spring cap should be pushed slightly to the rear and rotated 90 degrees to remove it from the firing pin. CAUTION: the firing pin spring is under a great deal of compression.

7. With the firing pin spring cap removed, the firing pin spring and cocking piece can be removed from the firing pin.

8. Remove the front action screw just in front of the magazine well.

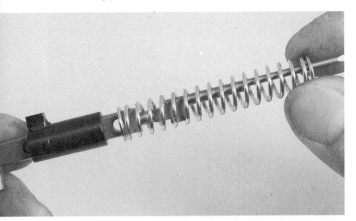

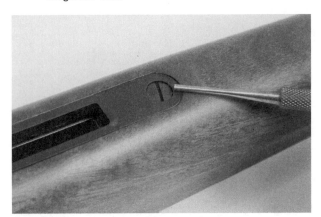

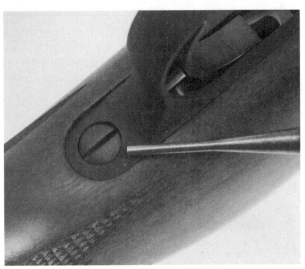

9. Remove the rear action screw located just behind the trigger guard.

10. Press the magazine catch forward slightly and lift the action from the stock. The trigger guard can then be easily pulled from the stock. If you do not depress the magazine catch, it will nick the trigger guard piece as the action is removed.

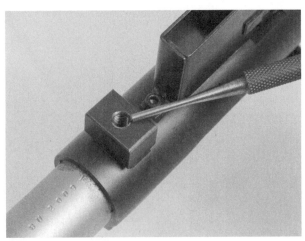

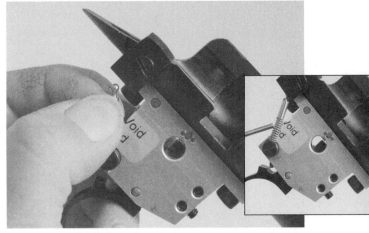

11. The recoil lug attaches to the receiver by a dovetail and is locked in place by a set screw, which passes through the lug. Do not remove it unless necessary.

12. Remove the safety arm and spring by pulling slightly down and rotating to the rear. The spring is no longer retained and should be captured to prevent loss.

13. Unscrew the safety lever screw and remove the safety lever.

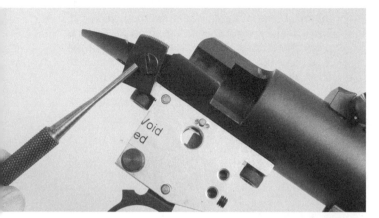

14. The front and rear trigger housing screws retain the trigger housing to the receiver. Save for trigger pull adjustments, work on the trigger should only be conducted by the factory.

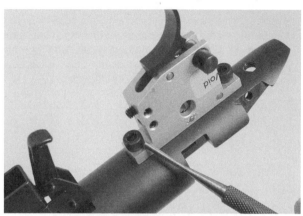

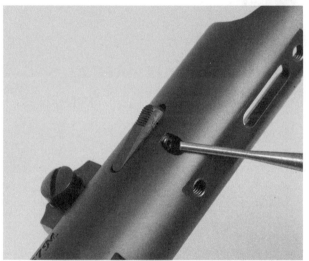

15. Removal of this screw will release the bolt stop and spring.

16. To remove the magazine housing and catch, first push out the magazine catch spring stop pin. This will release tension from the magazine catch spring.

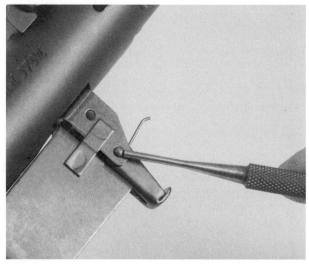

17. Press out the magazine catch pivot pin.

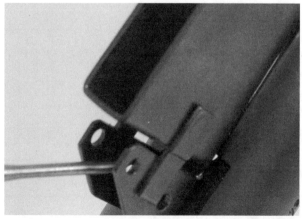

18. To remove the magazine box, remove the retaining screws, one of which is in front of the box. The other is here between the magazine catch wings. This will also release the feed ramp/bolt guide from inside the receiver.

Reassembly Tips:

1. Replace the front magazine box retaining screw until it is just snug. Then insert the feed ramp back into the receiver. Align it and then reinstall the rear magazine box retaining screw. This screw passes through the receiver and screws into the rear portion of the feed ramp/bolt guide. Now tighten both screws. Test to see that the bolt will slide in and align with the feed ramp/bolt guide.

2. When reinstalling the magazine catch spring into the catch, the short leg of the magazine spring passes through the hole in the front of the catch and rests in a small indentation. When reinstalling the catch assembly, fully seat the mag catch pin. Then partially insert the spring stop pin. Using a small pliers or screwdriver, lift the long leg of the mag catch spring over the pin and then continue to finish inserting the mag catch spring stop pin.

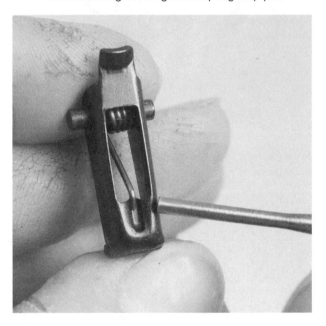

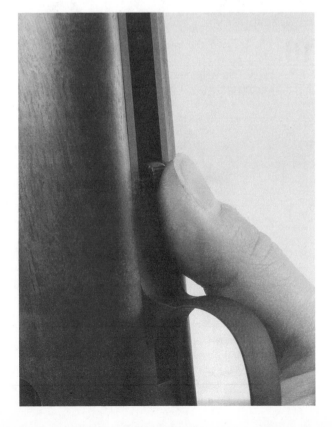

3. As the action is being reinserted into the stock, press the magazine catch forward as it approaches the bottom of the magazine well to allow it to clear the trigger guard piece. It hangs over the trigger guard slightly and can cause damage.

CZ Model 511

Data:	CZ Model 511
Origin:	Czech Republic
Manufacturer:	CZ-USA Kansas City, Kansas
Cartridge:	22 Long Rifle
Magazine capacity:	8 rounds
Overall length:	38⅜ inches
Barrel length:	22.2 inches
Weight:	5.39 pounds

The elegant CZ 511 has been around for quite a while, and was briefly discontinued about 20 years ago. Fortunately, at the time this is written, it is once again available in Standard and Lux versions. Aside from the usual Czech good design and high quality, it is notable for having very easy takedown for routine cleaning. Complete disassembly is discouraged by numerous staked and riveted parts.

Disassembly:

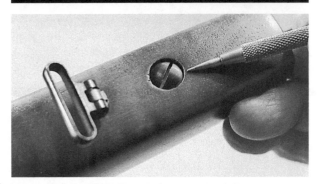

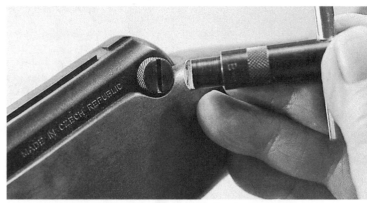

1. Remove the magazine. Cycle the action to cock the hammer and set the safety in on-safe position. With a screwdriver of the proper dimensions, loosen the large screw on the underside near the front end of the stock. About four turns is right.

2. You can use a coin for this, but a suitably-shaped tool is better. Shown here is a B-Square scope-base tool. Back out the takedown screw (the CZ parts list calls it the "connection screw") until it is free of its threads, and pull it out. It will not move far.

3. Push the rear of the action slightly upward, with pressure on the trigger guard. Retract the bolt a half-inch, move the action forward, and take it out of the stock.

4. Depress the trigger group latch, and hold it in as the trigger group is moved rearward.

5 Remove the trigger group from the receiver.

6. Move the base of the recoil spring guide forward about ⅜-inch and tip it out of its recess for removal of the guide and spring. **CAUTION:** *The spring is under tension, control it. If necessary for repair, the base can be removed from the guide rod by drifting out the cross pin.*

7. Move the bolt assembly rearward far enough to clear the ejector, and take it off downward.

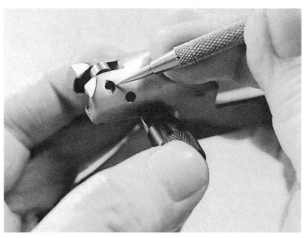

8. The roller at the upper rear of the bolt should be removed only for repair purposes. If necessary, drifting out the cross pin will free it.

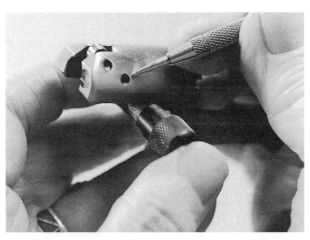

9. A single cross pin retains the firing pin and its return spring, and the extractor, which is its own spring. The bolt handle is heavily staked in place, and is not routinely removable.

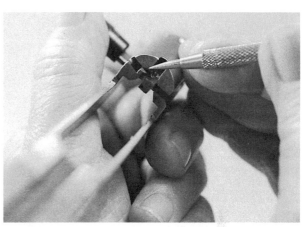

10. If removal of the extractor is necessary, after the cross pin has been taken out, the front beak of the extractor must be flexed to clear the face of the bolt as the extractor is moved out rearward.

11. The factory discourages disassembly of the trigger group by riveting or staking all of the cross pins. If disassembly is absolutely necessary, the hammer and its spring assembly can be removed by drifting out this pin. The hammer should first be eased down to fired position, and grinding away the rivet flange on one side will make it easier to remove. **CAUTION:** *Control the powerful spring.*

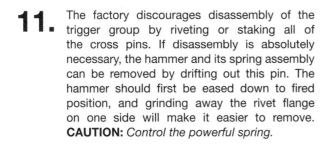

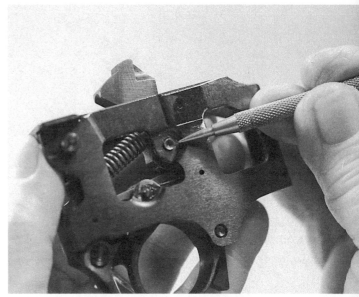

12. The trigger/sear cross pin is staked, but can be drifted out toward the left. However, the hammer must first be taken out for their removal. The sear spring is located inside the trigger, and the trigger spring is vertical under the front extension of the trigger. The safety and its detent plunger and spring are accessible for removal only after the trigger is taken out. If the trigger/sear system is removed, a slave pin will be necessary for re-installation. Really, in the unlikely event that something goes wrong, it would be best to simply send this unit to CZ-USA.

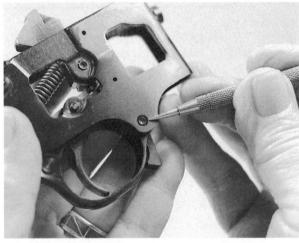

13. The magazine catch and its spring are retained by this heavily-riveted cross pin. The advice in the previous step applies.

14. The trigger group latch and its spring are retained by a nut on the right side which requires a two-point wrench for removal. Here, again, the nut is staked.

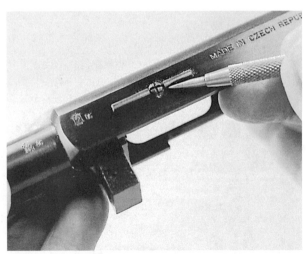

15. The ejector is mounted in the left side of the receiver by a single screw, which is heavily staked.

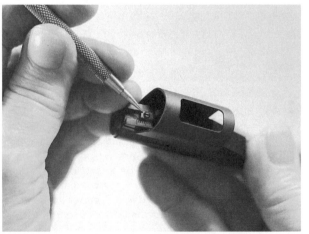

16. The front sight base is a sleeve that is permanently heat-mounted at the muzzle. The adjustable sight blade can be removed toward the front by backing out the adjustment screw.

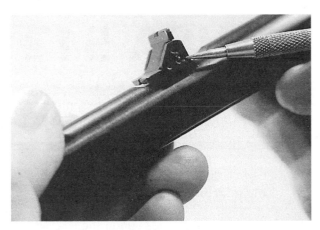

17. The rear sight is dovetail-mounted, and may be drifted out toward the right. While it is possible to drift out the cross pin and take the flip-over sight out of its base, this will release a spring and two tiny steel balls, which you will probably never see again.

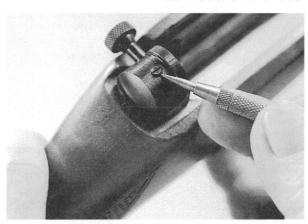

18. If necessary for repair or refinishing, backing out this small vertical screw will allow removal of the takedown screw. If the receiver base (CZ calls it the "catch") needs to be taken out of the stock, it is retained by a long screw that enters at the bottom of the stock pistol grip.

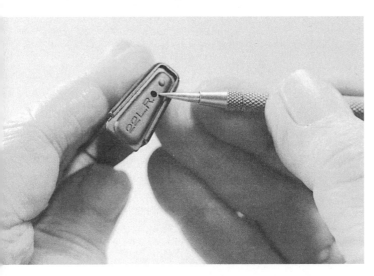

19. The magazine can be disassembled for cleaning by inserting a small tool through the hole in the floorplate to depress the lockplate, then sliding the floorplate off toward the rear. **CAUTION:** *Control the lockplate and spring, ease them out, and then take out the follower.*

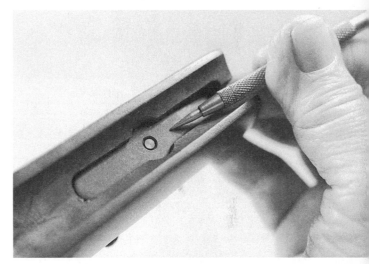

20. The front hook-plate (CZ: "suspension") can be taken out of the stock by removing its screw. Note its orientation before removal.

Reassembly Tips:

1. When the action is put back into the stock, keep firm downward and rearward pressure on the action while reengaging the takedown screw. Remember to retighten the hook-plate screw at the front. Also, as the action is being put into the stock, remember to slightly retract the bolt, to clear its front extension inside.

CZ-USA 512

Data:	CZ 512
Origin:	Czech Republic
Manufacturer:	Czeska Zbrojovka Uhersky Brod
Cartridge:	.22 Long Rifle, .22 WMR
Magazine capacity:	5 rounds
Overall length:	39.3 inches
Barrel length:	20.5 inches
Weight:	5.9 pounds

CZ makes a very nice little semi-auto rimfire called the CZ 512. It has hardwood stocks with an aluminum upper receiver and well-made plastic lower receiver. It's sort of a meld of European and American aesthetics and it fits well into the medium price range rimfire rifles currently on the market.

Disassembly:

1. Remove the bolt in the bottom of the pistol grip to remove the buttstock.

2. Remove the large slotted screw at the forward end of the forend and pull the forend off the barrel.

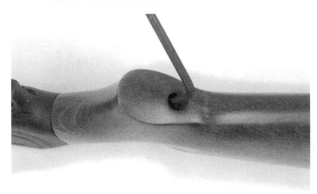

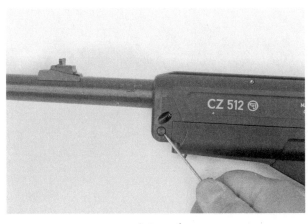

picture A

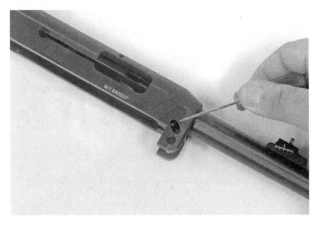

picture B

3. Tap out this pin (picture A). Then pull the lower receiver to the rear until the charging handle aligns with its hole and can be removed (picture B). Then finish pulling the lower receiver half out of the upper half.

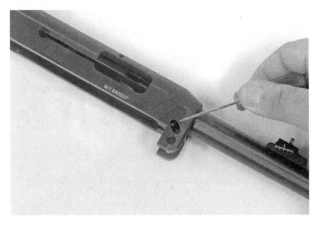

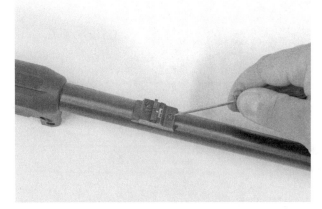

4. There are two large angled set screws in the receiver that retain the barrel into the receiver. Unless the barrel is to be replaced, there is no need to remove them.

5. The rear sight is retained by two screws, one here and one beneath the ramped sight itself. The front sight has a single retention screw.

6. Lift the rear end of the recoil spring assembly out of the lower receiver. Take care as the springs are quite compressed. Lift the bolt out of the receiver and the springs out of the bolt.

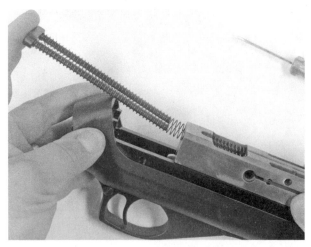

7. Drive out this short roll pin from right to left to remove the firing pin and spring. It will be damaged if you drive it out the other way.

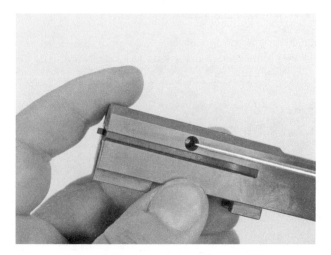

8. Drive this pin out from bottom to top to free the extractor.

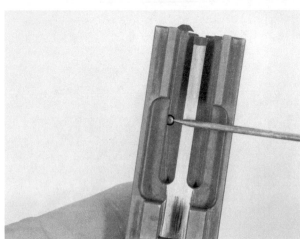

9. Push the trigger guard to the rear slightly and remove the magazine well.

10. The magazine catch and spring can be removed by driving out this pin. The larger pin to the rear (left) simply retains the magazine well spacer used on the .22 LR.

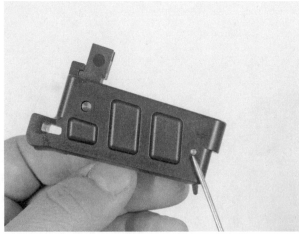

11. Use the stock bolt to remove the nut up and forward out of the receiver.

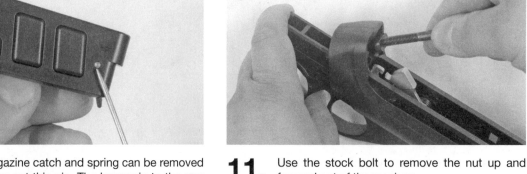

12. Pull the trigger guard fully out of the receiver to the rear. The hammer must be forward, in the magazine well area for clearance.

13. Push out this pin to remove the hammer and spring. There are two bushings in the spring that should not be misplaced.

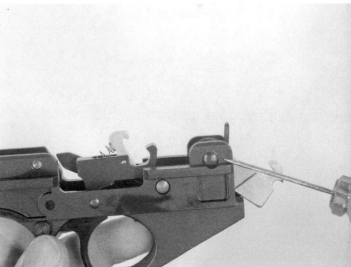

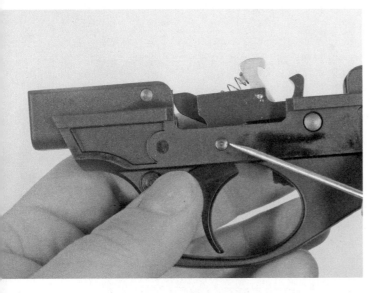

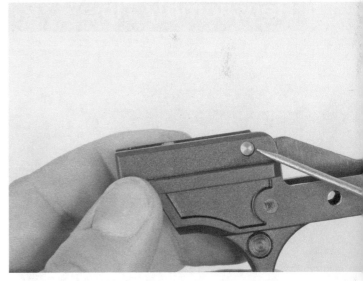

14. Push out this pin to remove the trigger assembly and trigger return spring.

15. Push out this pin to remove the safety spring and plunger. The safety can then be removed from the trigger guard to the side.

16. Push out this pin to remove the bolt catch and spring.

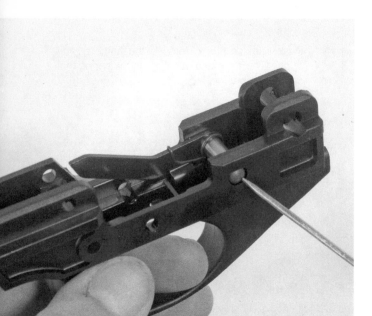

17. Remove the disconnector spring by either pulling the coil out of the trigger or off of the back of the disconnector. Don't lose it. The disconnector pin is staked in place, so leave it.

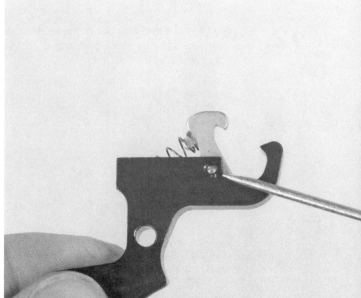

Reassembly Tips:

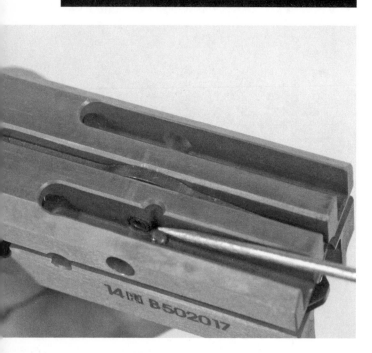

1. When reinstalling the firing pin retaining roll pin, it should be seated so that it makes contact with the extractor pin. The firing pin retaining pin blocks the upward movement of the extractor pin. Do not damage the pins as you abut them.

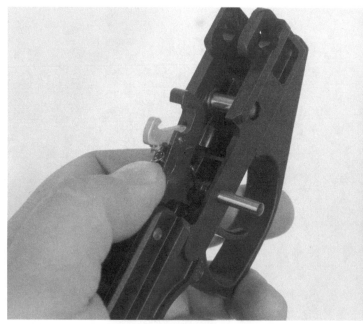

2. When reinstalling the trigger return spring, insert the pin through the spring from the right, with the trigger in the position shown. Then push down on the trigger assembly until the pin can pass through the trigger and the other side of the trigger guard.

Excel Arms MR-22 Accelerator

Similar/Identical Pattern Guns

The same basic assembly/disassembly steps for the Excel Arms Accelerator also apply to the following gun:
Mitchell's Mausers Black Lightning

Data:	Excel Arms MR-22 Accelerator
Origin:	United States
Manufacturer:	Excel Arms, Ontario, CA
Cartridge:	.22 WMR, 5.7x28mm
Magazine capacity:	9 rounds
Overall length:	32.5 inches
Barrel length:	18 inches
Weight:	8 pounds

The Accelerator rifle is one of the few semi-auto rifles chambered in .22 Magnum. The overall length is kept relatively short, despite the 18" barrel, by the magazine being inserted into the pistol grip. A heavy fluted barrel is typical as is a full length Weaver optics rail along the top of the receiver. Affordable, it had an MSRP of just over $500.

Disassembly:

1. Remove the operating handle by removing this screw.

2. Remove the two bolts on the top of the optics rail and then lift the optic rail/shroud off the gun.

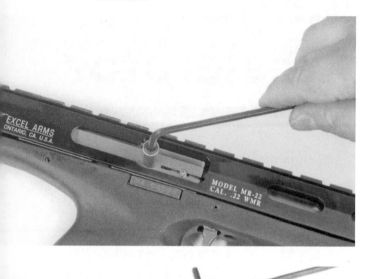

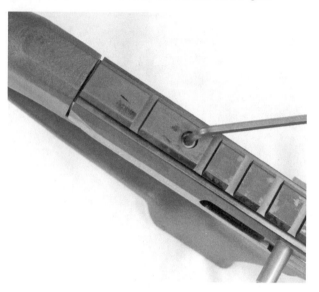

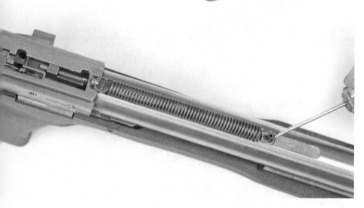

3. Unhook the recoil spring from the bolt and barrel and lift the bolt off the receiver.

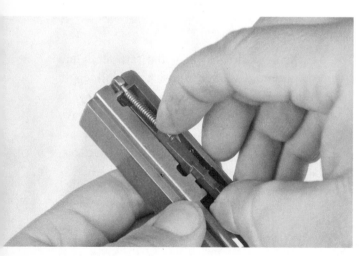

4. Drive out this pin to free the firing pin safety spring. The safety will come out to the top after the spring has been removed.

5. Remove the firing pin and return spring.

6. To remove the extractor, first take out this set screw (picture A). Then depress the plunger and roll the extractor forward to slide it out of its slot.

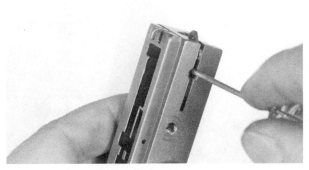

picture A   *picture B*

7. Remove the two bolts from the underside of the stock. One is inside the trigger guard and the other is at the forward end of the handguard area (picture A). Lift the barrel off the action. A slight wiggle may be necessary (picture B).

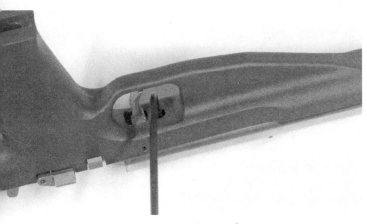

picture A   *picture B*

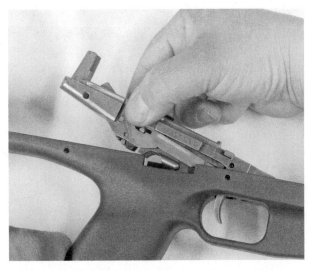

8. Drive out the two spring pins in the stock, one just above and behind the pistol grip and one above and just ahead of the pistol grip.

9. Pull the trigger housing up and out of the stock.

10. Remove the bolt catch and spring.

11. Remove the trigger, trigger bar, and spring. The pivot pin was the forward roll pin removed in step 8.

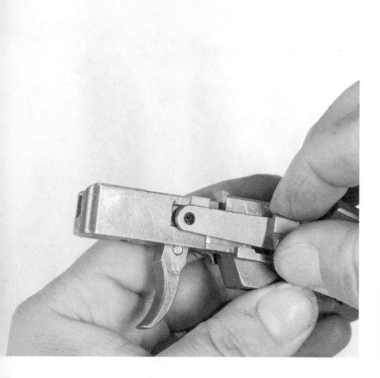

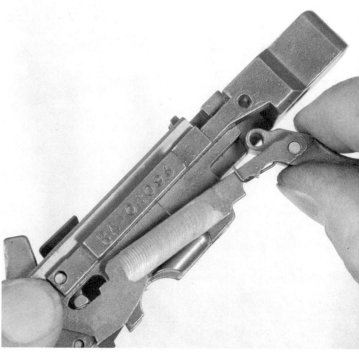

12. Tap out the hammer pin. Withdraw your punch with care to avoid loss of the springs, mounted to either side of the hammer.

13. Pull the safety off to the left (picture A). The ejector and firing pin safety lifter can be removed at this time as well. Pull out the ejector first and then the safety lifter and the spring contained within (picture B).

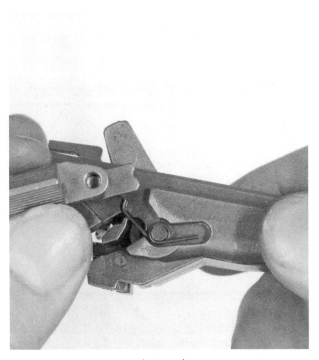

picture A

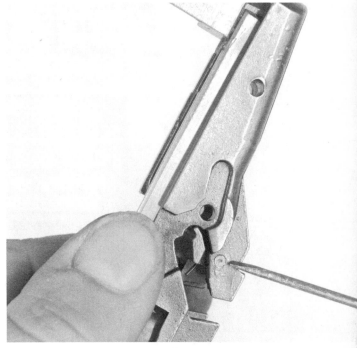

picture B

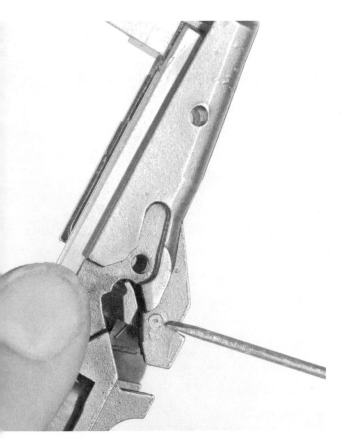

14. Push out this pin to remove the sear and spring.

Reassembly Tips:

1. Use a slave pin to hold the trigger in place for reinstallation into the stock.

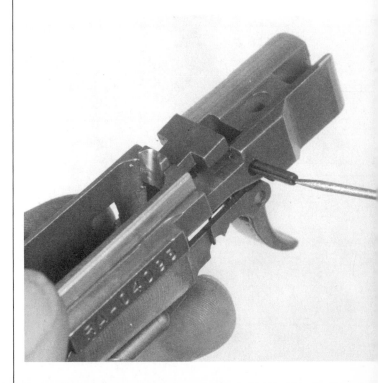

Feather
AT-22

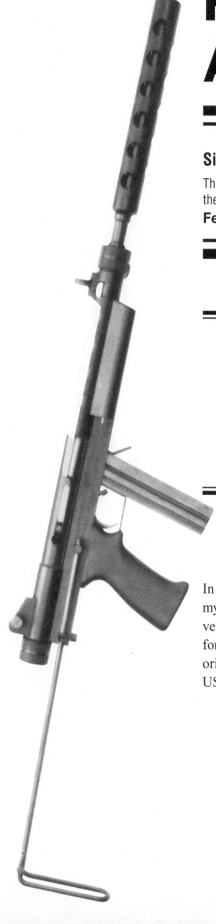

Similar/Identical Pattern Guns

The same basic assembly/disassembly steps for the Feather AT-22 also apply to the following gun:

Feather AT-22 F2

Data:	Feather AT-22
Origin:	United States
Manufacturer:	Feather Industries
	Boulder, Colorado
Cartridge:	22 Long Rifle
Magazine capacity:	20 rounds
Overall length:	35 inches (stock extended)
	26 inches (stock stored)
Barrel length:	17 inches
Weight:	3¼ pounds

In 1986, Feather Industries introduced a neat little gun that was to become my favorite 22 semi-auto carbine. The gun shown here has an optional vented barrel sleeve. There was also a fixed-stock version, the F2. Except for the difference in stock attachment, it was mechanically the same. The original Feather company closed in 1995, but recently a new firm, Feather USA, resumed production.

Disassembly:

1. Remove the magazine, and pull the trigger to drop the striker to fired position. Unscrew the barrel collar at the front of the receiver, and remove the barrel toward the front.

2. The cartridge guide above the chamber and its coil spring are retained by a roll-type cross pin.

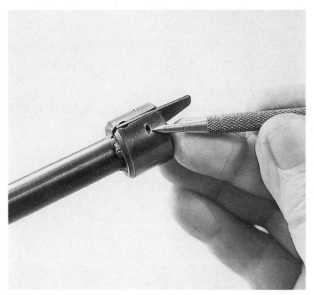

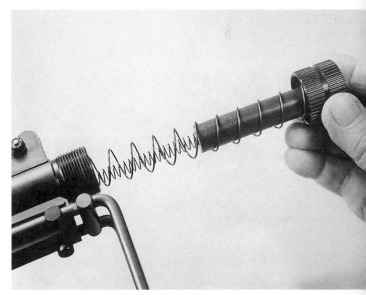

3. Unscrew the knob at the rear of the receiver. **Caution:** *Control the knob, as the recoil and striker springs will be released.*

4. Ease the spring tension slowly. Remove the knob, the guide, and the striker spring toward the rear.

5. Remove the recoil spring and its guide toward the rear.

6. Move the bolt toward the rear until the handle aligns with the exit cut in its track, and take out the bolt handle toward the right.

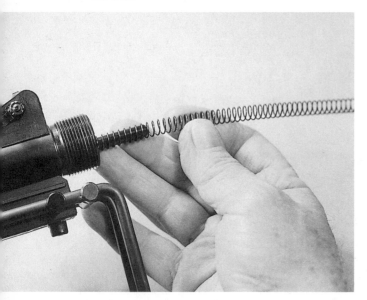

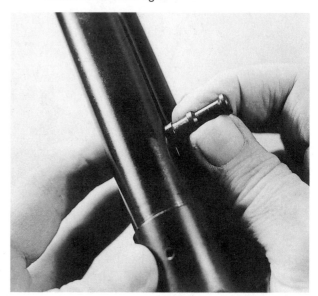

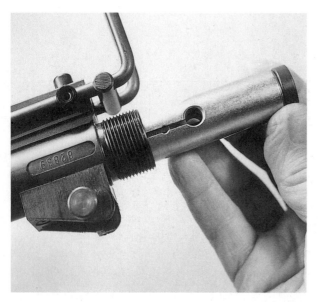

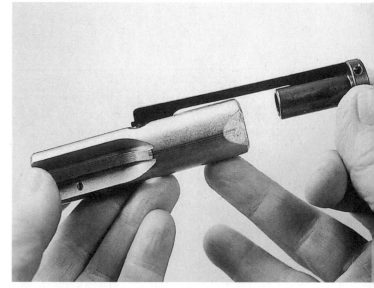

7. Use a tool to push the bolt assembly toward the rear, and remove the bolt assembly.

8. Move the striker assembly rearward out of the bolt. When its central guide clears, it can be lifted off.

9. The firing pin is attached to the striker unit by a roll-type cross pin. The cross pin is factory-staked on both sides, and it should be removed only for repair purposes.

10. The extractor and its coil spring are retained in the bolt by a vertical roll pin that is best drifted out upward. The pin is lightly staked in place and should be removed only for repair.

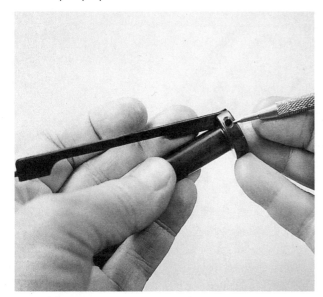

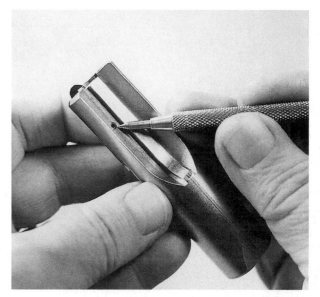

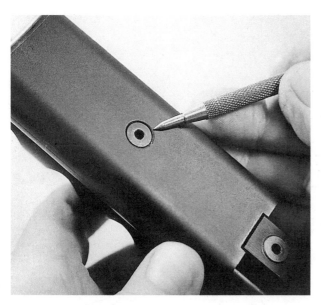

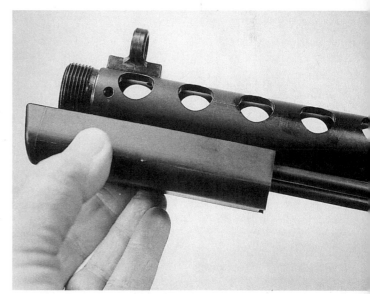

11. The forend is retained by a single Allen screw.

12. If the stock is in stored position, take off the forend toward the front.

13. If the stock is to be removed, drift the roll pin in its right shaft out toward the right. The stock can then be removed toward the rear.

14. Remove the large Allen screw at the front of the lower receiver.

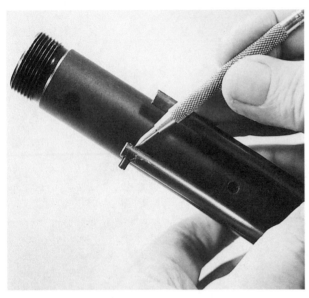

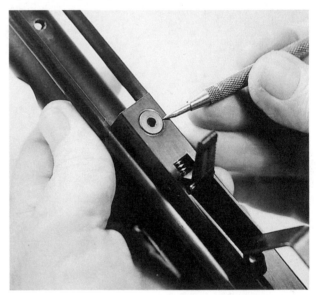

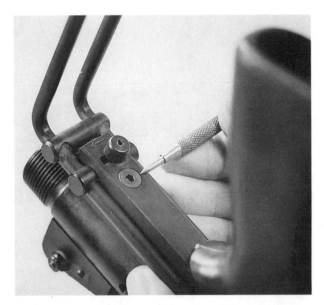

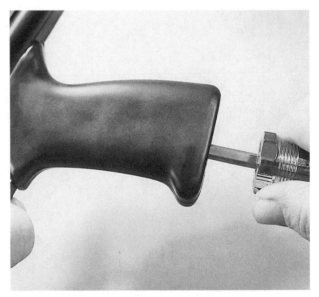

15. Remove the large Allen screw at the rear of the lower receiver.

16. With a larger Allen bit, remove the screw inside the pistol grip. Note that there are two washers on this screw. Take care that they are kept in order and not lost.

17. Remove the pistol grip downward.

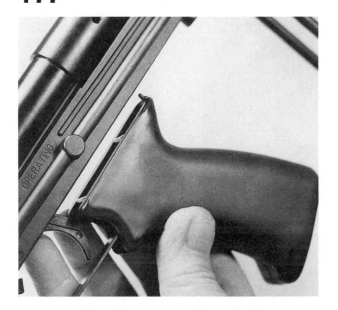

18. Remove the middle Allen screw in the lower receiver.

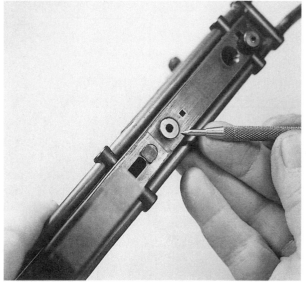

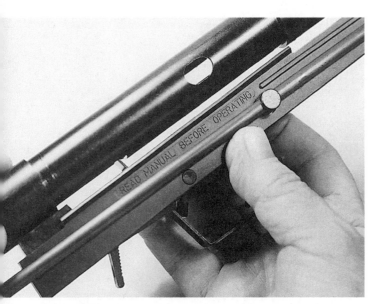

19. Remove the lower receiver downward.

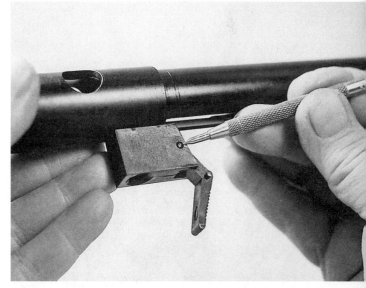

20. The magazine catch is pivoted and retained by a cross pin. Control the catch and its coil spring as the pin is removed.

21. The front and rear sights are retained on the receiver by two Allen screws in each location. For access to the rear screw in the rear sight, the aperture must be removed from the sight.

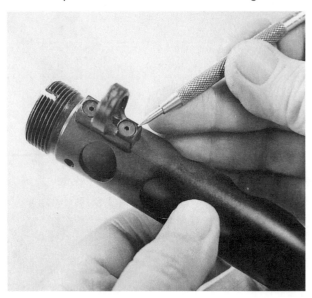

22. Inside the rear of the lower receiver are two polymer spacer blocks, through which the mounting screws pass. Remove these and keep them in the correct order and orientation, as they are not interchangeable.

23. The lower receiver parts should not be removed unless necessary for repair. If the trigger system is to be removed, first drift out the stock retaining pin (see step 13), and remove the stock toward the rear. Push out the front stock cross pin.

24. With the safety in off-safe position (forward), carefully move the trigger group sub-frame slightly upward and forward, taking the tip of the trigger through the recess in the safety cross-piece.

25. Put the safety back in on-safe position, tilt the sub-frame as shown, and remove it upward.

26. The safety detent spring, mounted on the left tip of the trigger cross pin, will be freed as the sub-frame is removed. Retrieve the spring from inside the sub-frame.

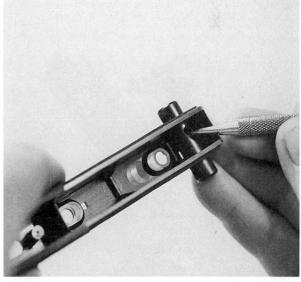

27. In most cases, the safety is best left in place. If it must be removed, its handle pin is drifted out of the cross-piece, downward. The cross-piece is then easily removed.

28. If the rear stock cross pin is to be removed, the pin in its release knob must be drifted out downward. **Caution:** *Control the plunger and spring.*

29. The forward pin in the trigger group is the trigger stop pin. It retains no part, and is easily removed.

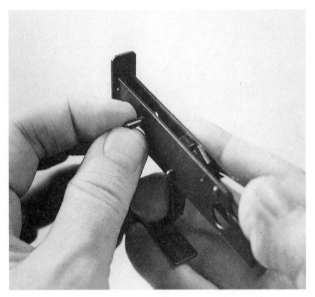

30. Push the trigger forward and push out the trigger cross pin toward either side.

31. Remove the trigger and disconnector assembly upward. This is more easily done by depressing the disconnector slightly at the rear, and moving the trigger forward. A cross pin retains the disconnector on the trigger.

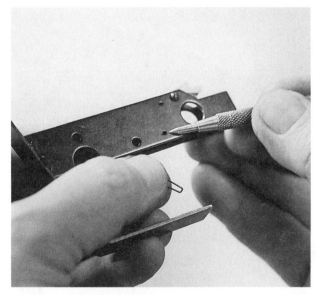

32. Unhook the combination trigger and disconnector spring from its lock hole in the left side of the sub-frame and remove it.

33. Tip the sear upward, and push out the sear cross pin.

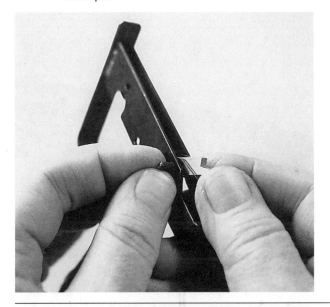

34. Remove the sear upward. The sear spring is easily detached from its lock holes on each side.

Reassembly Tips:

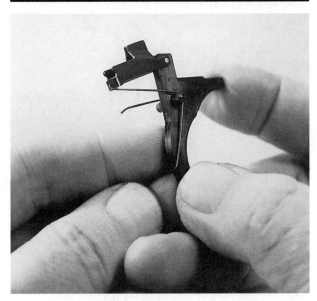

1. When installing the trigger and disconnector system, remember to re-hook the spring in its lock hole. The long rear arm of the spring must be hooked into a notch beneath the rear tip of the disconnector, as shown. The parts are assembled here for purposes of illustration, as they would be in the sub-frame.

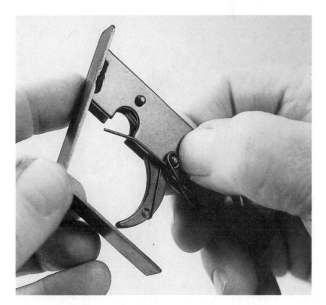

2. The safety detent spring is shown here in the proper orientation, as it should be when it is installed in the sub-frame.

3. As the trigger system is put back into the sub-frame, tip the disconnector upward and use it to position the trigger, as shown.

4. Be sure the two spacer blocks are installed in the proper order, as shown.

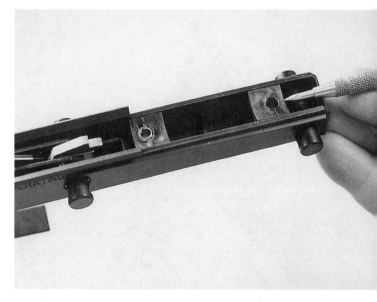

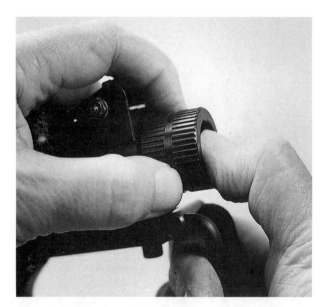

5. As the rear receiver end cap is turned into place, be sure the striker is in the fired position. In the last few turns, depress the button at the center of the knob to be sure the guide seats properly.

6. As the barrel assembly is put back into place, retract the bolt slightly. Note that the barrel has a positioning stud that must enter a slot at the front of the receiver.

German Sport Guns ATI GSG-5

Similar/Identical Pattern Guns

The same basic assembly/disassembly steps for the GSG-5 also apply to the following guns:

GSG-5 SD

GSG-522

Data:	GSG-5
Origin:	Germany
Manufacturer:	German Sport Guns GmbH
Cartridge:	22 Long Rifle
Magazine capacity:	22
Overall length:	33¾ inches
Barrel length:	16 inches
Weight:	7¼ pounds

Many heads were turned when American Tactical Imports began importing the German Sport Guns GSG-5 in 2009. It has since branched out into several different configurations and even pistol variants. The main selling point, of course, is its striking visual similarity to the HK MP-5 submachinegun. In fact, ATI was the object of litigation because of this, which forced a temporary halt in sales, and a significant redesign. It is a relatively heavy gun (for a 22) and, as a result, closely duplicates the feel and look of an MP-5. A brief note: the original SD model's barrel shroud was recalled due to legal issues in relation to the National Firearms Act and any of these rifles serviced should be checked to verify that it has the replacement barrel shroud.

Disassembly:

1. With the action closed and the gun decocked, remove the buttstock screw. Push the buttstock bolt out the opposite direction. The bolt head is slightly splined.

2. Remove the trigger housing screw from behind the magazine well. Push the trigger housing bolt out the opposite direction. Like the buttstock bolt, the head of the trigger housing bolt is splined.

3. Pull the buttstock off to the rear.

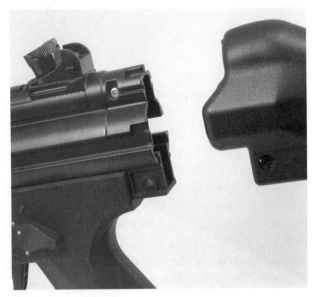

4. Remove this hex screw and its lock washer to take out the bolt stop.

5. With the action upside down, use a punch to lift the bolt stop out of its slot in the rear of the receiver.

6. Pull the pistol grip unit back about 1 inch.

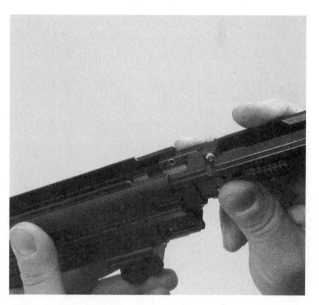

7. Lift the pistol grip off of the receiver.

8. Pull the breech housing out to the rear of the receiver.

9. Remove the screw from the forend front and push the front forend bolt out the opposite direction.

10. Remove the forend by pulling down on the front and then pulling it off.

11. Unscrew the barrel shroud and remove it from the barrel.

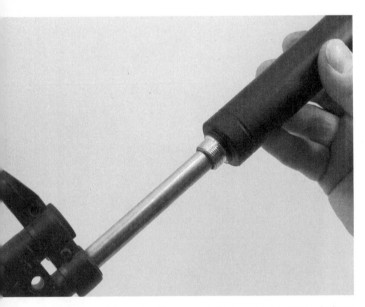

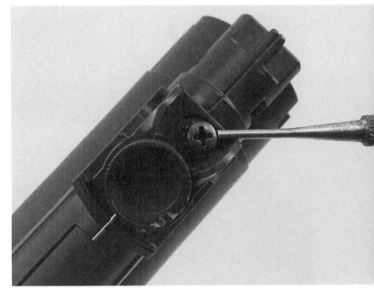

12. Remove the rear sight by taking out this screw. There is a star washer beneath it that tensions the sight. Be careful not to lose it. The windage adjustment screw lies just beneath the right side of the rear sight assembly. It can be unscrewed if necessary.

13. Lock the charging handle back to the rear and unscrew the handle retaining screw through the hole in the right side of the tube to release the charging handle from the cocking bar.

14. Remove the screw in the center of the magazine catch button on the right side of the receiver and push the magazine catch out to the left. Removing the bolt catch spring at this time would be wise. Gently pry it out with a small screwdriver through the ejection port.

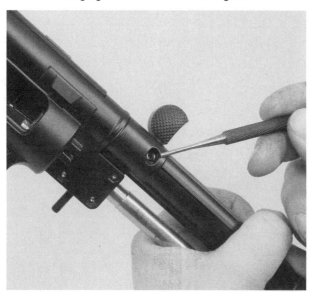

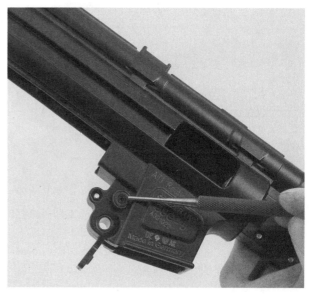

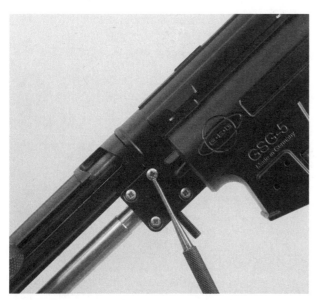

15. There are six screws that now need to be removed: these four, one behind the magazine catch and one behind the rear sight. This particular screw is shorter than the rest and acts as a tension pin for the charging handle tube, while the others hold the receiver halves together.

16. While firmly holding the two receiver pieces together, grasp the front sight and pull the front sight and charging handle tube forward about 3/8ths of an inch until it stops against the step on the barrel.

17. Holding the right side down, lift the left side of the receiver straight up. At this point, virtually everything remaining in the receiver is loose. The bolt catch spring will fall out if it has not already been removed.

18. Remove the bolt stop.

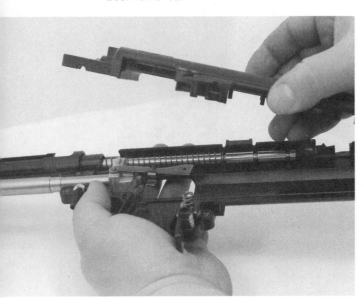

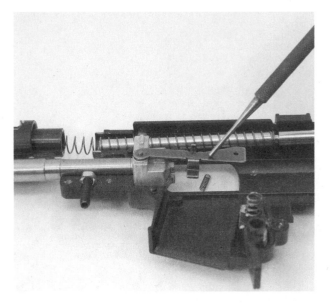

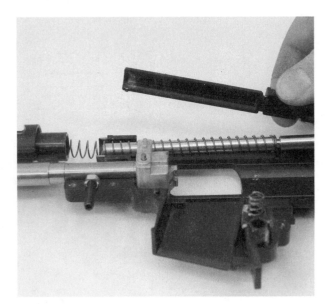

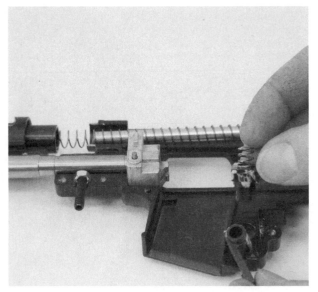

19. Remove the center plate at the top of the receiver.

20. Remove the magazine catch, first the top half (the button and spring) then the bottom half (latch).

21. The guide rod and charging handle spring can be lifted up and pulled straight back and out.

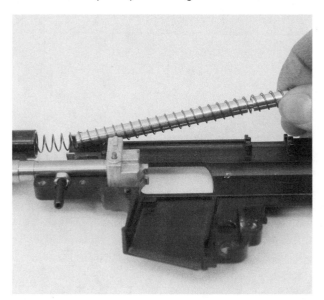

22. The barrel can now be lifted from the receiver and the barrel tension screw will fall out. Pull the front sight assembly off the barrel.

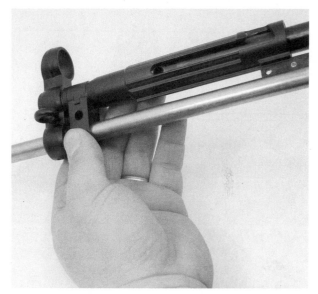

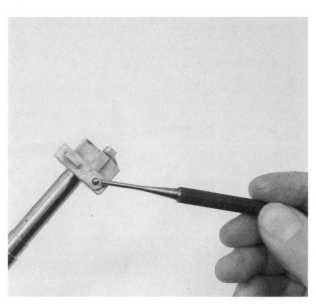

23. The barrel block has a loose alignment pin on the left side. Do not lose it.

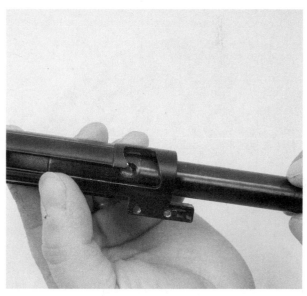

24. Pull the charging handle tube out of the front sight assembly.

25. The front sight can be replaced by removing the indicated set screw. The Phillips head screw below it secures the sling swivel on the left side. Further take down of the front sight assembly should only be done by the factory.

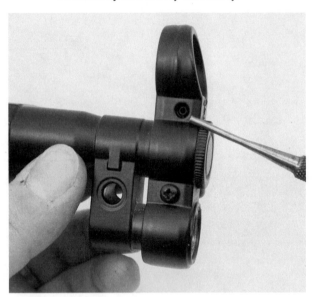

26. Remove this screw to remove the left side safety switch. Pull the switch straight off of the receiver. It is tight fitting and a bit of jiggle will likely be necessary. Do not pry it off. Then push the rest of the safety assembly through the receiver out to the right.

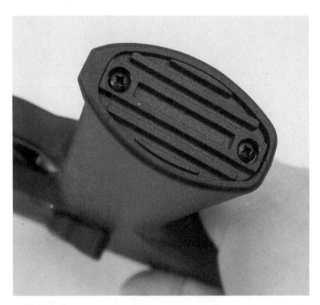

27. Remove these two screws to access the grip screw. Caution: the internal slots that these screws turn into are very easily stripped.

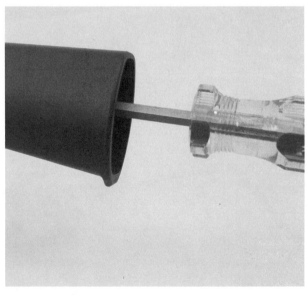

28. Remove the grip screw and the trigger housing can be pulled from the pistol grip.

29. There are two brass spacers sitting on top of a large plate, which is the firing pin safety arm. There is a spring pushing this plate to the rear. Remove the spacers and then gently remove this plate and the spring from the slot underneath it. The J shaped trigger bar below it is riveted to the trigger housing and should not be removed.

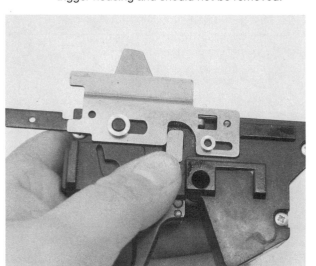

30. On the right side, the vertical safety detent plunger and spring and the horizontal magazine safety spring can be removed. Caution: control these springs.

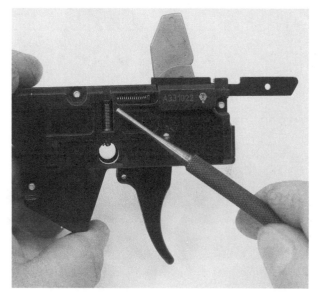

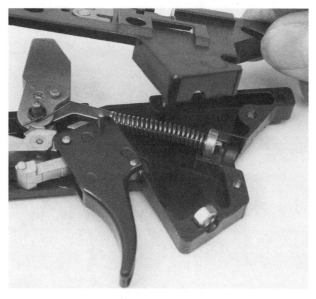

31. Remove the four Phillips screws from the left side to separate the halves of the trigger housing. Place the trigger housing on its right side and slowly lift the left half off.

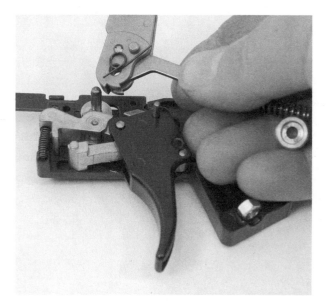

32. Release the tension from the hammer spring and pull the hammer, hammer spring and bushings, hammer strut and the small coiled hammer rebound spring on top of the hammer out. After these have been removed, the hammer pin and spacer can also be removed.

33. The sear spring can be removed and then the entire trigger and sear assembly can be pulled from the housing. Then the long bar-like magazine safety can be lifted from the housing.

34. The disconnector and spring can be removed from the trigger unit by pushing out the rear top corner pin in the photo. The lower trigger arm can be removed by pushing out the pin in the lower rear corner. The sear arm can be removed by pressing out the front top corner pin. The sear can be removed from the sear arm by pressing out the small pin indicated here.

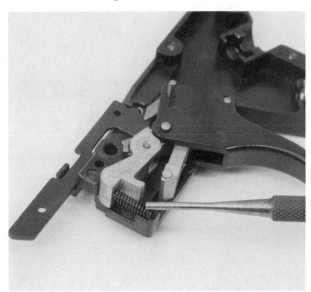

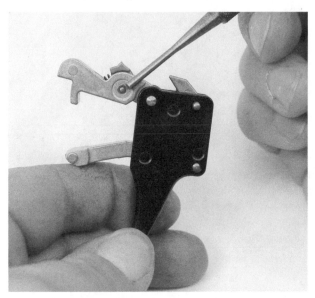

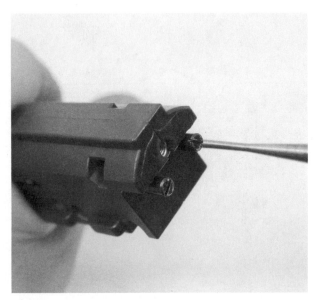

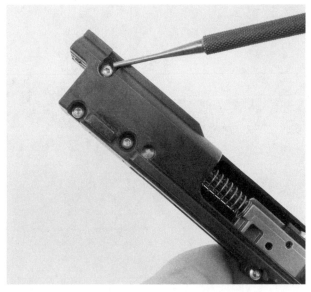

35. To disassemble the bolt, the right side guide rod should be unscrewed and pulled out the back of the breech assembly. Control the spring as it is under tension.

36. There are five Torx screws that retain the right half of the breech assembly housing to the left. Remove these screws and gently lift the right half of the breech from the left half.

37. Push the bolt slightly to the rear and lift it out of the breech assembly's left side. Remove the left guide rod spring and unscrew the left guide rod from the back of the bolt.

38. In this hole is a set screw that blocks the firing pin retaining pin. After the screw is removed, the pin can be pushed out from the left side.

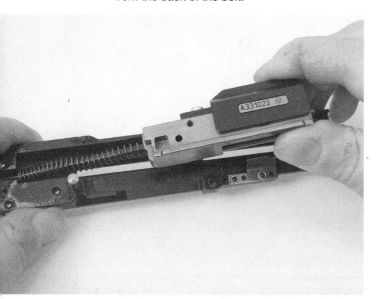

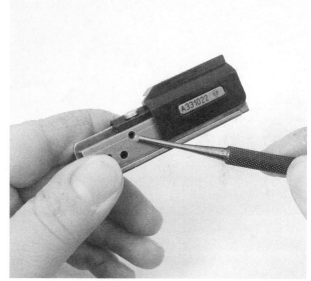

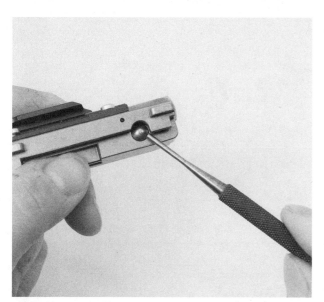

39. With the firing pin retaining pin removed, depress the firing pin safety button. This will allow the firing pin to be pulled from the back of the bolt. Control the firing pin as it is under spring pressure. With the firing pin removed, the firing pin return spring will fall out the rear of the bolt, and the firing pin safety button with its spring will fall out the left side.

40. Take off the bolt cover by removing the Torx screws that fasten it to the bolt.

41. Drive out the extractor pin from the bottom as the top is splined.

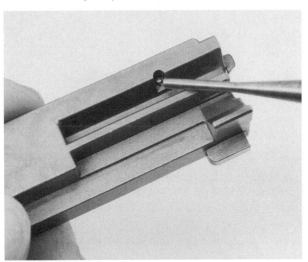

42. The ejector is riveted in. Do not remove it unless it needs to be replaced.

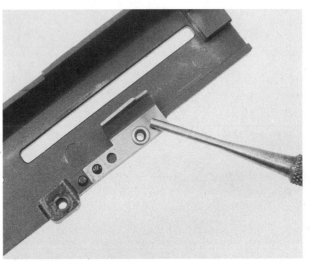

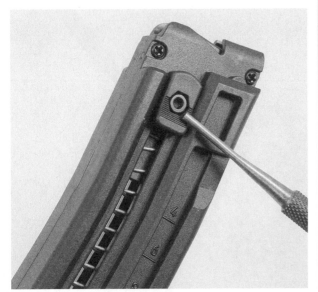

43. To disassemble the magazine, remove the two screws from the base plate and the bolt and cross bolt from the finger pieces. If it is necessary to separate the two halves of the magazine for cleaning, then the two screws beneath the feed lips at the top of the magazine can be removed as well.

Reassembly Tips:

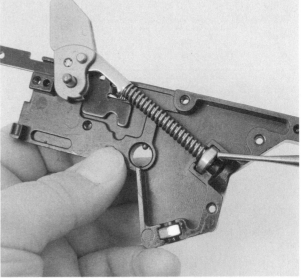

1. When reassembling the fire control, first insert the firing pin safety and then the hammer. With the hammer in this well forward position, little tension is placed on the hammer spring and the hammer spring retaining bushing can easily be placed into its slot.

2. Emplace the hammer rebound spring in its place in this orientation in the trigger housing's left side before placing the trigger housing halves together.

3. To ease assembly of the receiver sections, reassemble the charging handle assembly into the front sight assembly. Place the front sight assembly over the barrel and attach the muzzle shroud. This will allow the barrel and front sight unit to be installed as one unit into the receiver, thus easing assembly.

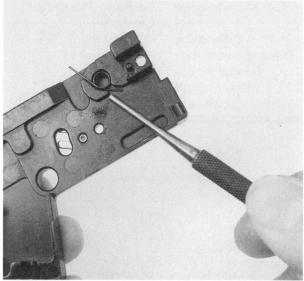

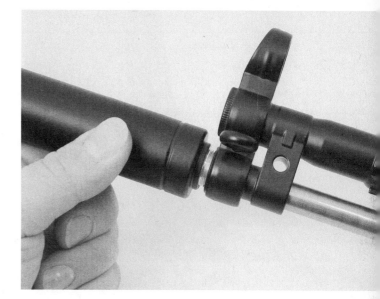

4. When the receiver assembly has been completely assembled around the barrel, tension the barrel by tightening this long set screw in. This will keep the barrel stabilized inside the receiver. The short upper right screw in this photo should also be tightened at this time. It prevents the charging handle tube from rattling.

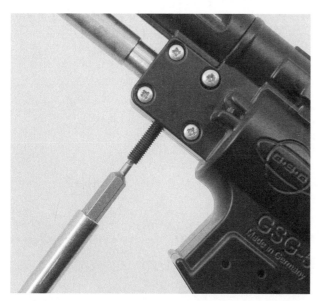

5 The bolt stop spring is easily inserted after the receiver has been reassembled with needle nose pliers.

GSG StG-44

Data:	GSG StG-44
Origin:	Germany
Manufacturer:	German Sport Guns, Germany
Cartridge:	.22 Long Rifle
Magazine capacity:	25 rounds
Overall length:	37.24 inches
Barrel length:	16.3 inches
Weight:	9.9 pounds

One of the most desired rifles of the 20th century was the StG-44, and those that exist are treasured collectables. German Sport Guns has made a replica chambered in .22 LR, but is the same dimensionally and of a close weight. Almost entirely made of metal and wood, it is a faithful copy in all but the cartridge, and many of the units sold were packed in a pine "collector's" box.

Disassembly:

1. Push out the stock retaining pin and pull the stock piece off the receiver.

2. Pull the bolt recoil block out (picture A). Then pull out the plastic sleeve and operating handle spring (picture B).

picture A

picture B

3. Remove the bolt assembly.

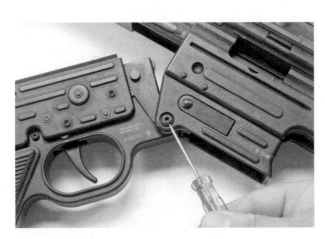

4. Unscrew this screw to separate the pistol grip from the receiver.

5. Remove this screw to take the grip panels off.

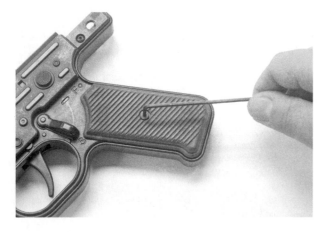

6. The safety lever is held on by a screw on the right side of the housing. Remove it and pull the lever off and out to the left. There is a small spring and detent ball within the underside of the lever.

picture A

picture B

7. There are five screws that retain the left grip housing wall to the right wall. Remove them and gently lift the left wall off the right wall (picture A). This is what you should see with the left wall removed (picture B).

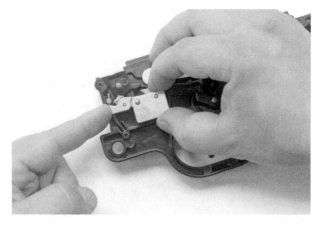

8. First, remove the hammer assembly. Do not lose the small hammer rebound spring on the hammer's left side. When free the assembly will further break down to brass spring bushing, small brass bearing washer, spring, strut, and hammer.

9. Remove the sear/disconnector assembly.

10. Pushing out this pin will separate the disconnector and spring from the sear block.

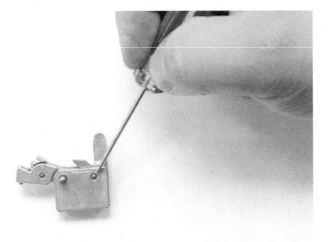

11. Pushing out this pin will separate the sear arm from the sear block.

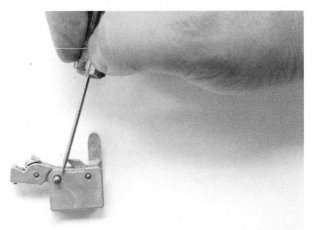

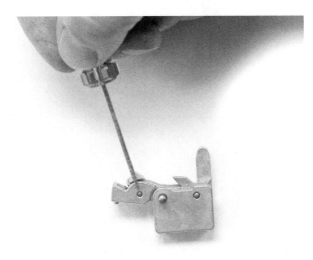

12. Pushing out this pin will separate the sear and sear spring from the sear arm.

13. Detach this trigger spring from the trigger or anchor pin and remove the trigger and trigger bar from the housing.

14. If necessary, the trigger pull adjustment set screw and bushing can be removed from the housing.

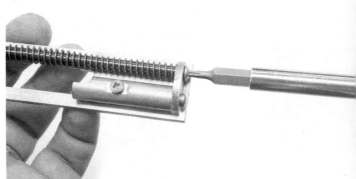

15. The screw holds the bolt rails onto the carrier via the recoil spring guide rod. Remove it. The bolt will then be freed from the rails, as will the spring.

16. The buffer piece can be removed if necessary by removing this screw and the screw on top of the buffer.

17. Tap out this roll pin to remove the extractor and spring.

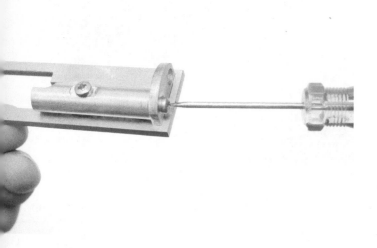

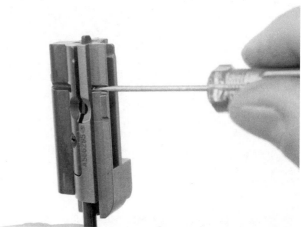

18. Tap out this pin. Then remove the screw at the top front left side of the bolt.

19. Lift the top of the bolt off the bottom to expose the firing pin and firing pin spring.

20. To remove the operating handle, remove the small set screw in the underside of the handle, up inside the receiver. With the handle removed, the op handle body can be removed out the rear.

21. The handguard is held on by spring tension and can simply be pulled down firmly and off.

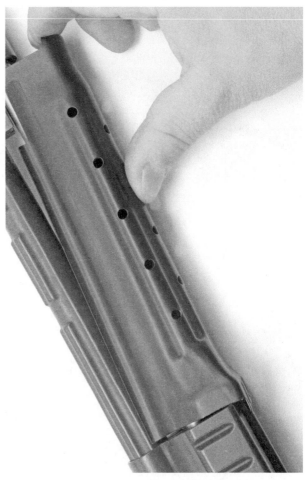

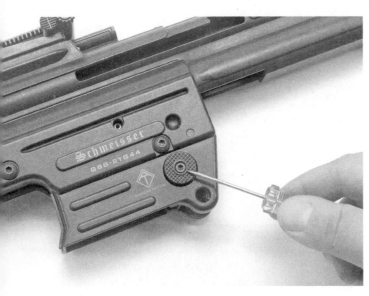

22. The magazine catch is disassembled by removing this screw. The button and spring beneath it will come off to the left and the latch itself will move out to the right.

23. Remove these two screws on the magazine well and lift the well off the receiver. The ejector is riveted inside of the mag well.

24. The barrel sleeve can be removed by taking this screw out and driving the two pins out to the left (picture A). Then remove the stainless Torx screw above the chamber.

25. The barrel can then be removed, with the bolt catch and spring underneath it.

Reassembly Tips:

1. Place the hammer rebound spring in its slot in the left trigger housing wall like this. Emplace the left wall onto the right wall. Just prior to fully closed, reach in with a thin tool or fingernail and hook the long leg in front of the round boss on the left side of the hammer.

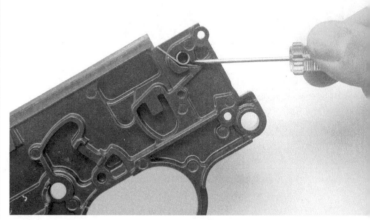

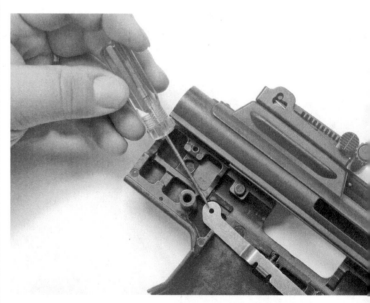

2. Place the bolt catch and spring in place and then place the barrel, ensuring the bolt catch pin inserts properly in the bolt catch.

Grendel R-31

Data:	Grendel R-31
Origin:	United States
Manufacturer:	Grendel, Incorporated
	Rockledge, Florida
Cartridge:	22 WMR
Magazine capacity:	30 rounds
Overall length:	31 inches (stock extended)
	24 inches (stock stored)
Barrel length:	16 inches
Weight:	4 pounds

Introduced in 1991, the carbine version of the Grendel P-31 pistol has a longer barrel and a storable buttstock. Available in 22 WMR only, it is perhaps the ultimate "survival"-type carbine. There are some elements of takedown and reassembly that could be very difficult for the non-professional.

Disassembly:

1. Cycle the action to cock the internal hammer. Set the safety in on-safe position and remove the magazine. Open the stock to its extended position. Unscrew the barrel retaining collar.

2. Move the left sidepiece forward and lift it off.

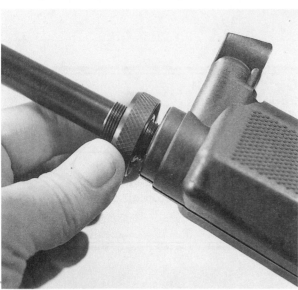

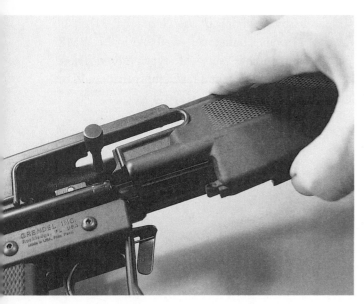

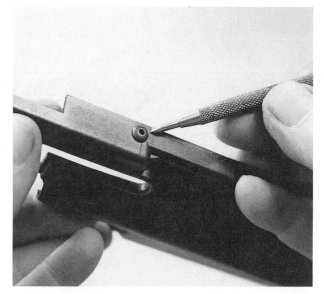

3. Move the right sidepiece forward and lift it off. Note that it must be moved far enough to clear the cocking handle.

4. The Phillips-type screws in the top of each sidepiece are bearing screws that lock into a recess in the receiver, and they are not to be removed.

5. Using the serrated wings provided, push the recoil spring assembly forward until it is clear of the rear vertical plate of the receiver. **Caution:** *Keep the unit under control.*

6. Tip the assembly out toward either side and remove it. Ease the spring tension slowly.

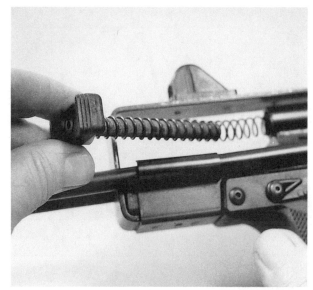

7. Move the bolt assembly all the way to the rear, and tip the bolt handle downward. Remove the bolt assembly toward the right.

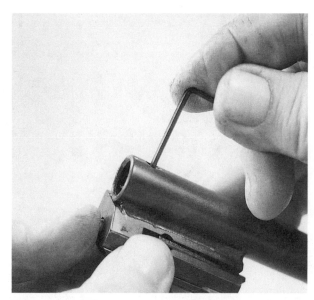

8. Use an Allen wrench to back out the screw which retains the firing pin and its spring. **Caution:** *The return spring is quite strong, so keep the firing pin under control.*

9. Ease the spring tension carefully and remove the firing pin and its spring toward the rear.

10. The extractor pin is drifted out toward the left and upward, at an angle. Restrain the extractor and spring and ease them out.

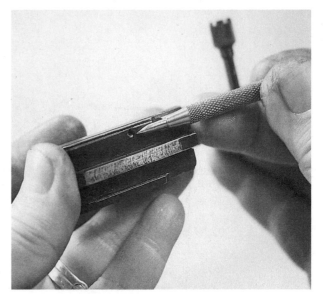

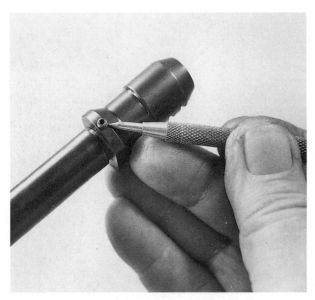

11. If removal of the muzzle brake is necessary, it is locked by an Allen screw on the underside. After the screw is backed out, the brake can be unscrewed from the muzzle. This will also allow the barrel collar to be taken off.

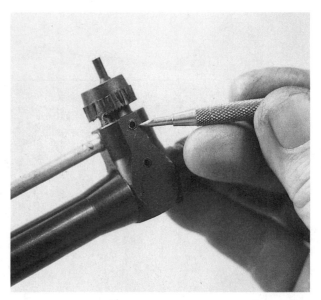

12. The adjustable front sight can be unscrewed from its base, and the detent plunger and its spring can be lifted out. If removal of the bolt guide rod is necessary, it is retained by this roll pin.

13. The lower roll pin retains the base for the sight and guide rod on the barrel.

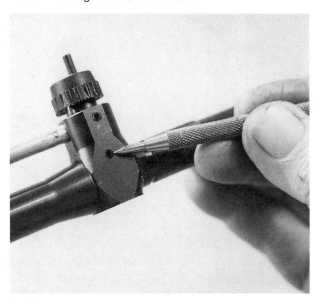

14. Use an Allen wrench to remove the screw in the inside floor of the receiver at the rear.

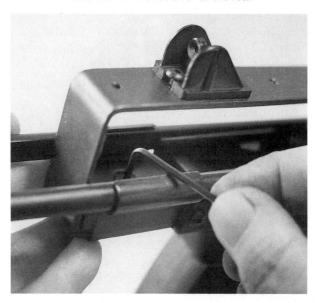

15. Move the stock mounting plate upward and forward, detach it from the stock, and remove the stock toward the rear.

16. Remove the nylon screw spacer from inside the receiver.

17. Remove the stock support piece from the rear of the receiver.

18. Move the safety to off-safe, and restrain the hammer with a fingertip. Pull the trigger, and ease the hammer over forward until it is resting against the ejector. Use an Allen wrench to remove the screw from the left safety-lever.

19. Remove the safety-lever toward the left. **Caution:** *Take care that the small detent plunger is not lost.*

20. The plunger and spring are easily removed from inside the lever.

21. Repeat this operation with the right safety-lever.

22. Restrain the hammer and push out the safety cross-piece, which is also the hammer pivot.

23. Remove the hammer and hammer spring assembly. The bushing and spring are easily removed from inside the hammer.

24. Remove the internal safety-lever from inside the receiver, on the right side.

25. Remove the hammer spacer from inside the receiver, on the left side.

26. Remove the Allen screw on the left side at the rear of the grip frame.

27. Remove the Allen screw on the right side at the rear of the grip frame.

28. Remove the center screws on both sides of the grip frame. Note that there is an internal nut on each of these screws, and these will have to be held with a small wrench.

29. Remove the front screws on both sides of the grip frame. Note that these, also, have internal nuts. Insert a screwdriver to hold them. Also note that the right screw is longer, and its nut holds the stock latch spring.

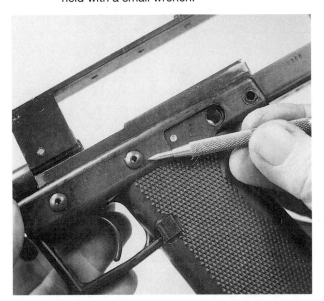

30. Remove the grip frame and the stock latch spring.

31. Unhook the right arm of the magazine catch spring from its recess inside the grip frame and take out the spring upward.

32. Move the magazine catch toward the left until its right end clears the opening in the grip frame. Turn it as shown, and move it inward for removal. The roll-type stop pin in the catch is not removed in normal takedown.

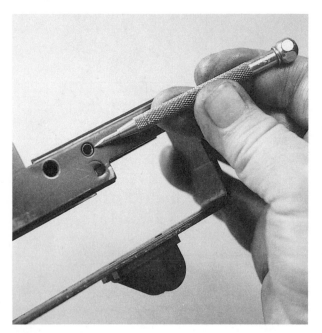

33. If removal of the sear and its torsion-coil spring is necessary, push out the sear pivot. **Caution:** *The spring will be released, so control it.*

34. The spring that powers the trigger bar can be seen here, protruding below the receiver. To remove it, insert a tool to unhook its upper arm from the bar, then move the loop of the spring inward, toward the center, for removal.

35. In normal takedown, the barrel is not removed. If this is necessary, drifting out this cross pin will release the barrel for removal toward the front. This will also release the barrel sleeve and the stock latch.

36. Drifting out this cross pin will allow the trigger to be taken out downward. **Caution:** *The trigger spring will be released.* The trigger bar is turned upward to follow the trigger out.

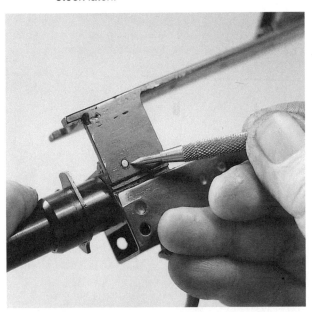

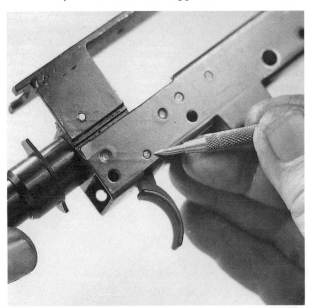

Reassembly Tips:

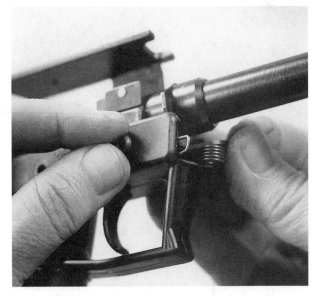

1. Use slim pliers to position the nut for the right front grip frame screw. Start it, but do not tighten it at this point.

2. Fit the long loop of the stock latch spring onto the right front screw. Use a tool to hold it in place, and tighten the screw, with the nut retaining the spring.

3. If the hammer spring has been removed, be sure the spring and bushing are replaced so the arm of the spring enters the recess on the hammer, as shown.

4. A slave pin will be necessary to stabilize the spring and bushing in the hammer for reassembly.

5. When the safety cross-piece/hammer pivot is in the receiver, the internal safety-lever and the spacer must be in the relative positions shown. For illustration, they are assembled here, outside.

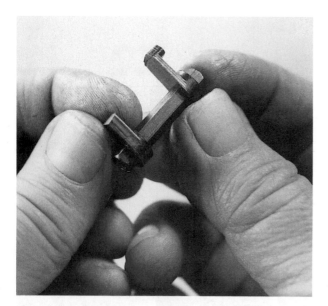

6. Because the rear arm of the hammer spring bears on the right side, the cross-piece is best inserted from the left, as shown. Start it through the spacer, then insert the hammer, tipped over forward, and align it for entry of the cross-piece.

7. After the internal safety-lever is installed, move it back into on-safe position. Then, install the external safety levers in on-safe position.

8. If the firing pin has been removed, check the free movement of the firing pin as the Allen screw is tightened. If it binds the firing pin, back it off until the pin moves freely.

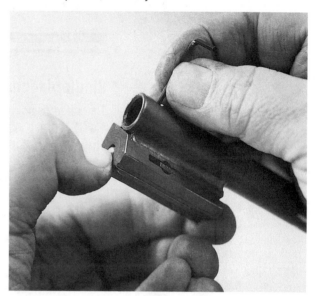

9. As the bolt assembly is reinstalled, it must be depressed downward to properly engage the rails, working against the tension of the hammer spring. This is easily done by using a large screwdriver at the top, as shown.

Harrington & Richardson Model 700

Similar/Identical Pattern Guns

The same basic assembly/disassembly steps for the Harrington & Richardson Model 700 also apply to the following gun:

Harrington & Richardson Model 700 Deluxe

Data:	Harrington & Richardson Model 700
Origin:	United States
Manufacturer:	Harrington & Richardson
	Gardner, Massachusetts
Cartridge:	22 WMR
Magazine capacity:	5 or 10 rounds
Overall length:	42½ inches
Barrel length:	22 inches
Weight:	6½ pounds

There had been earlier attempts to make a semiauto rifle in 22 WMR—Kodiak in the U.S., Landmann in Germany—but they were not successful. Then, in 1977, two fine rifles in this chambering were introduced. One was the Heckler & Koch Model 300; the other was the Harrington & Richardson Model 700. Beautifully engineered and elegantly styled, the Model 700 was made from 1977 until the original H&R company ceased operations at the end of 1985.

Disassembly:

1. Remove the magazine and pull the trigger to drop the striker to fired position. Back out the two screws in the magazine plate (they are captive in the plate).

2. Remove the plate and the attached screws.

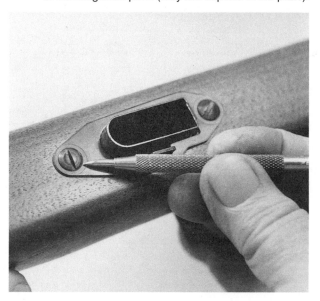

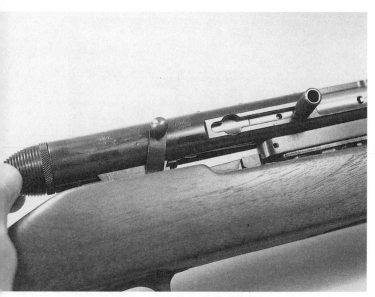

3. Remove the action from the stock.

4. The trigger guard and the stock buttplate are retained on the stock by two Phillips-type screws in each location.

5. Unscrew the receiver end piece. **Caution:** *Even in fired mode, the striker spring retains some tension.*

6. Remove the end piece toward the rear. In normal takedown, the nylon buffer is not removed from the end piece.

7. Remove the striker spring toward the rear.

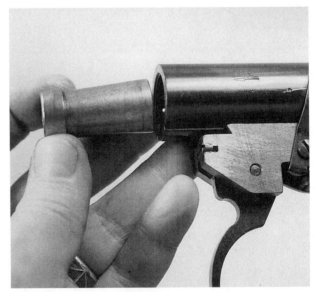

8. Cycle the bolt to nudge the striker toward the rear. Pull the trigger and remove the striker toward the rear.

9. Use a ⅝-inch wrench to remove the large nuts at the front and rear of the magazine housing.

10. Remove the magazine housing. Take care that the two lock washers are not lost.

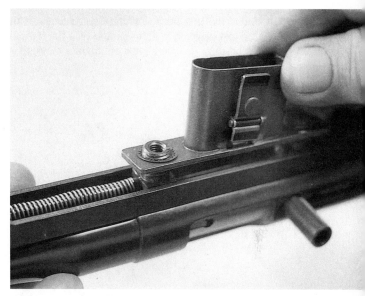

11. The magazine catch pivot is factory staked at one end. For removal, it would have to be cut off and a new pivot made. If this system is taken off, the coil catch spring will be released.

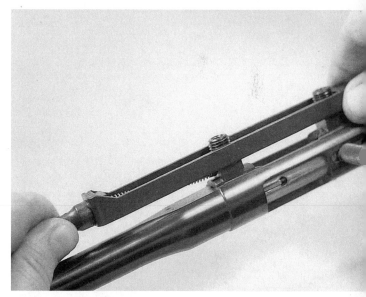

12. Lift the recoil spring assembly equally at front and rear and use a shop cloth (not shown) over the spring to arrest it as it is released. An alternative method is to draw the assembly back until the small holes in the spring housing and guide are aligned, and insert a sharp tool to trap the spring (see Reassembly Step 3). **Caution:** *Either way, keep control of the spring.* The spring housing at the front of the unit can be unscrewed from the harness and the bolt contact block can be removed by drifting out its roll-type cross pin. In normal takedown, this is not done.

13. Move the bolt back until the handle aligns with the exit opening in its track and give the handle a half-turn. Pull the handle out toward the right.

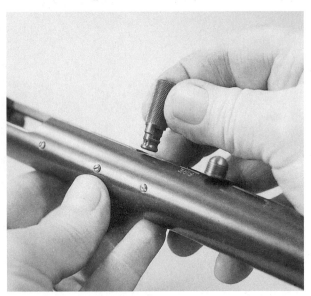

14. Pull the trigger and remove the bolt toward the rear.

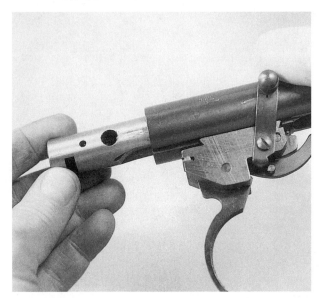

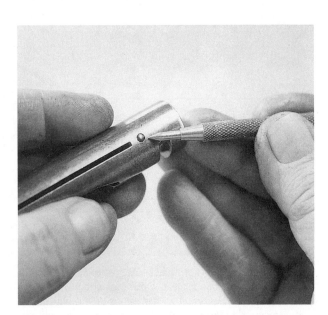

15. Restrain the firing pin, drift out this cross pin and remove the firing pin and its return spring toward the rear.

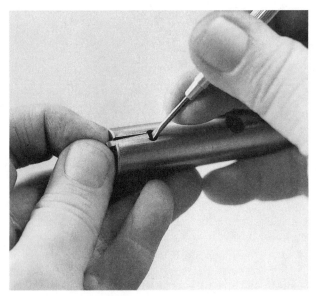

16. Insert a small tool between the extractor and its plunger and lever the plunger toward the rear. Lift out the extractor and remove the plunger, spring and bolt handle detent plunger toward the front. **Caution:** *Control the spring.*

17. While the recoil spring assembly is off the action, do not attempt to move the safety to on-safe position or it could be damaged. Remove the safety lever screw and take off the safety-lever toward the right.

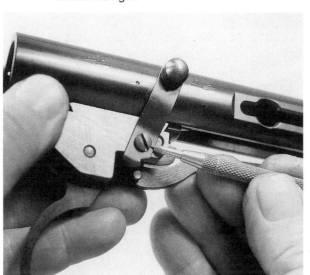

18. Restrain the trigger and push out the trigger pivot pin. **Caution:** *Two small plunger-and-spring systems are mounted in the trigger, so control them.*

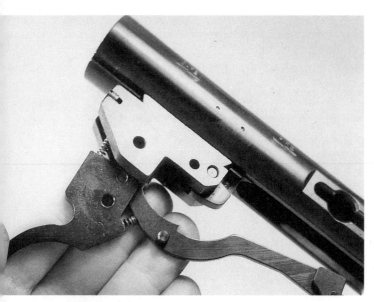

19. Remove the trigger and disconnector assembly downward.

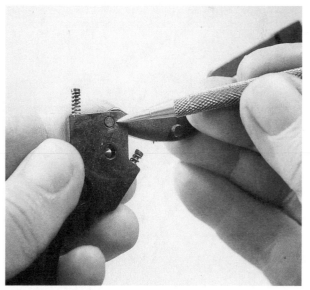

20. Push out the disconnector pivot and detach the disconnector from the trigger. The trigger and disconnector springs and plungers are easily removed from their wells in the trigger.

21. The trip block on the front of the disconnector has a riveted pivot, and this part and its coil spring should be removed only for repair.

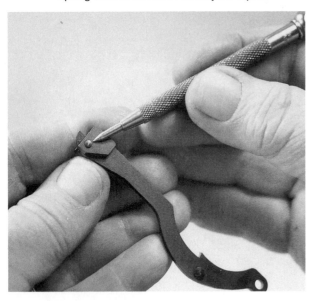

22. Restrain the sear and push out the sear cross pin. **Caution:** *The spring is under tension.*

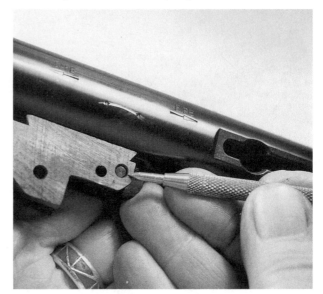

23. Remove the sear and its spring downward.

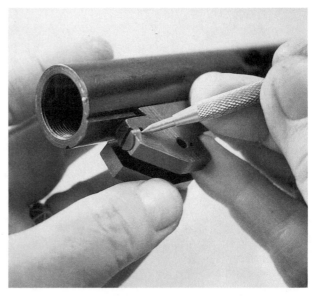

24. The screw at the rear of the trigger housing is the trigger adjustment screw. It is pre-set by the factory, and should not be disturbed.

Reassembly Tips:

1. When installing the bolt handle, note that there is a small lock-recess at one point in its circumference. After the handle is pushed into place, turn it until this recess engages the detent plunger.

2. The recoil spring housing and the spring guide have holes to allow trapping of the recoil spring.

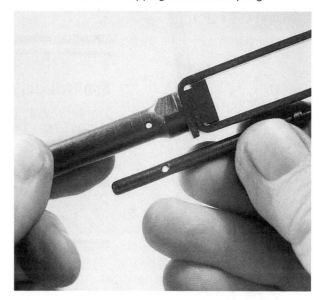

3. With the spring compressed and the holes aligned, a sharp tool is used to trap the recoil spring, as shown.

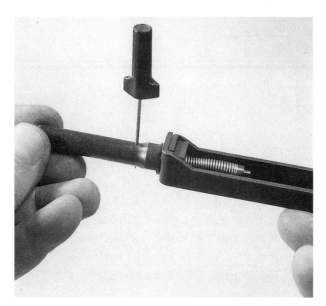

4. After the system is in place, with the rear lug engaging the bolt, draw the bolt back until the tip of the recoil spring guide enters its recess in the frame. The tool can then be taken out to release the spring.

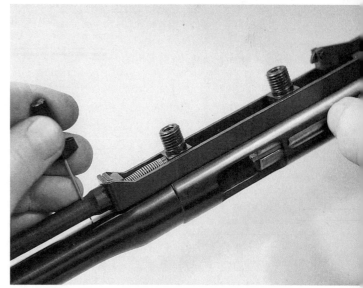

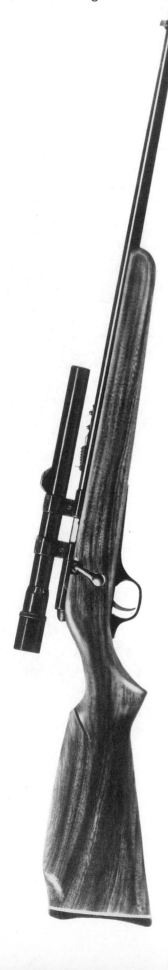

Harrington & Richardson Model 750

Similar/Identical Pattern Guns

The same basic assembly/disassembly steps for the Harrington & Richardson Model 750 also apply to the following gun:
Harrington & Richardson Model 751

Data:	Harrington & Richardson Model 750
Origin:	United States
Manufacturer:	Harrington & Richardson
	Gardner, Massachusetts
Cartridge:	22 Short, Long, or Long Rifle
Overall length:	39 inches
Barrel length:	22 inches
Weight:	5 pounds

Introduced in 1954, the Model 750 was named the "Pioneer" like the Model 765 which preceded it. The Model 750 is a good, solid single shot rifle. As a general rule, single shot bolt-action rifles are mechanically very simple, since there are no cartridge feed systems. Each one, though, has a firing mechanism that is unique to its particular manufacturer. There are certain general similarities, however, and the Model 750 H&R is a typical representative of the type. The instructions can also be used for the H&R Model 751.

Disassembly:

1. Back out the large screw on the underside of the stock, forward of the trigger guard, and separate the action from the stock.

2. To remove the bolt, open it and move it toward the rear. Pull the trigger, hold it back, and press the lower lobe of the sear to tip it downward, holding it down while removing the bolt toward the rear.

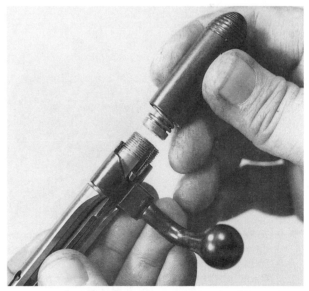

3. Grip the forward portion of the bolt in a padded vise and turn the bolt handle to allow the striker to move forward to the fired position. The photo shows the striker in the forward position, with the tension of its spring partially relieved.

4. With the front portion of the bolt still gripped in the padded vise, unscrew the domed rear end piece. **Caution:** *The striker spring is quite powerful and has considerable tension, even when at rest. Hold the end piece firmly, control it, and ease the spring tension off slowly.*

5. Remove the striker spring and its guide from the bolt end piece.

6. Move the bolt handle sleeve off toward the rear, taking with it the striker/firing pin unit.

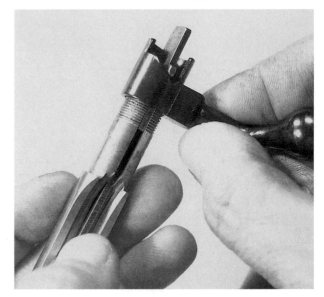

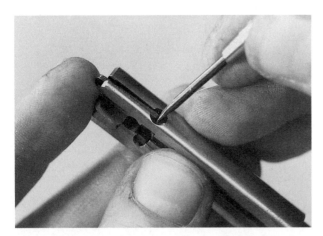

7. To remove the twin extractors, use a small screwdriver to depress the extractor spring plungers, and lift the extractors out of their recesses on each side. **Caution:** *Take care to keep the depressed plungers under control, as the springs can propel them quite a distance if they are released suddenly.* Keep the springs with their respective extractors, as they are not interchangeable.

8. Remove the spring clip on the left side of the trigger housing from the end of the trigger pivot and take out the pivot pin toward the right.

9. As the pivot pin is removed, restrain the trigger against the tension of its spring, and take it off downward. The safety-lever will also be released for removal toward the right. The trigger spring and its plunger are easily removed from their well in the upper rear of the trigger.

10. Remove the spring clip from the left end of the sear pivot and push the pivot pin out toward the right. This will allow removal of the sear and its spring downward, and the safety bar and its spring toward the right. The sear spring is easily removed from its well in the top rear of the sear.

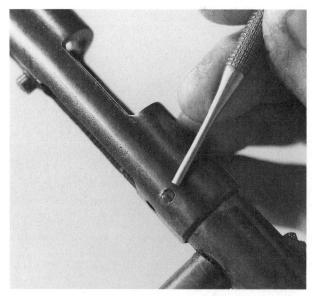

11. The cartridge guide platform with its integral ejector is retained inside the receiver by a screw on the underside, just forward of the trigger housing.

12. The barrel is retained in the receiver by a cross pin, but removal is not recommended in normal disassembly.

Reassembly Tips:

1. When replacing the safety positioning spring, note that the dimple at its center must have its convex side inward, to bear on the recesses in the safety bar.

2. When replacing the safety-lever, be sure the lower turned-in portion of the lever engages its opening in the safety bar.

3. When replacing the spring clips on the sear and trigger pins, be sure the pins are turned fully toward the left, so the clips will engage their grooves in the heads of the pins.

4. When replacing the striker/firing pin unit in the bolt, insert it only as far as shown, then install the bolt handle sleeve, and let it carry the striker into the bolt.

5. Replacement of the rear end piece of the bolt, working against the tension of the striker spring, will require that the front portion of the bolt be gripped in a padded vise. Be sure the bolt handle is turned so the striker is in fired position. Be very careful not to cross-thread the end piece. When the end piece is in place, the bolt must be in cocked condition for reinsertion in the receiver. With the bolt still in the padded vise, turn the bolt handle to recock the striker. The photo shows the striker in the cocked position.

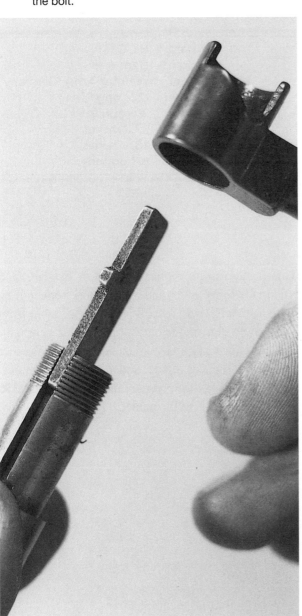

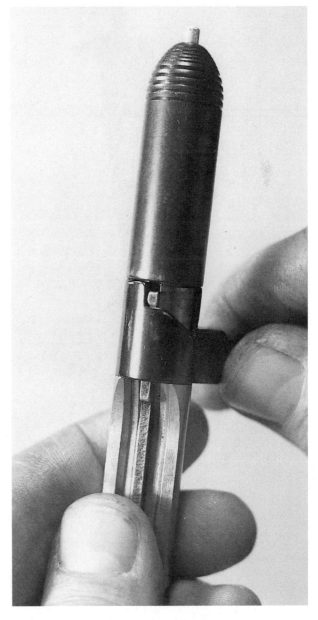

Heckler & Koch G36

Data:	HK G36
Origin:	Germany
Manufacturer:	Walther Arms, Germany
Cartridge:	.22 Long Rifle
Magazine capacity:	20 rounds
Overall length:	37.8 inches
Barrel length:	18.1 inches
Weight:	6.8 pounds

This is the rimfire replica version of the HK G36 rifle made by Walther, and a very close replica it is. Dimensionally, it's virtually indistinguishable from the parent gun, and is only a hair lighter in weight. It uses the common magazine made by Walther for the replicas made under other companies' brands, in multiple capacities, though this G36 was shipped with a 20-rounder.

Disassembly:

1. Push out the retaining pin in front of the trigger guard. Rotate the rear of the magazine well down, and then the entire unit off the receiver.

2. This pin can be tapped out to disassemble the magazine catch and spring.

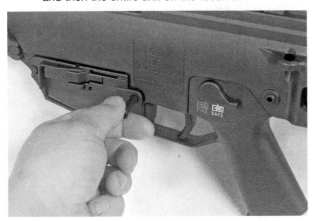

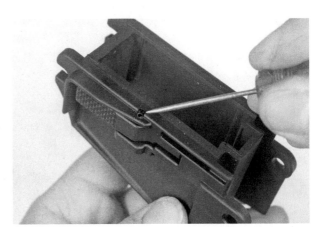

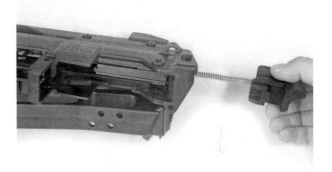

3. Push out the retaining pin behind the pistol grip and pull the pistol grip down and out of the receiver.

4. Pull the bolt assembly out of the rear of the receiver.

5. Push out the retaining pin at the rear top of the handguard and pull the handguard forward and off the barrel.

6. The optics rail is held on by six screws. There is no need to remove the rail unless something needs to be replaced.

7. Tap out the pivot hinge pins to take the stock off the receiver.

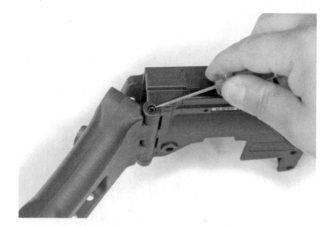

8. Should it be necessary to replace the bolt catch or spring, the receiver halves can be separated by removing the several screws from the right side of the receiver that hold the halves together.

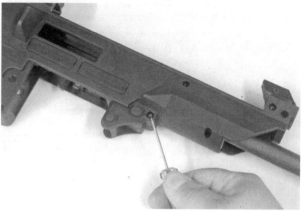

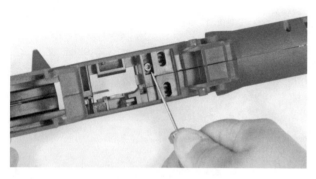
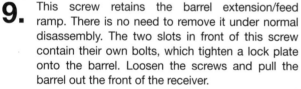

9. This screw retains the barrel extension/feed ramp. There is no need to remove it under normal disassembly. The two slots in front of this screw contain their own bolts, which tighten a lock plate onto the barrel. Loosen the screws and pull the barrel out the front of the receiver.

10. The flash hider can be removed by driving out this small spring pin and unscrewing the device from the barrel.

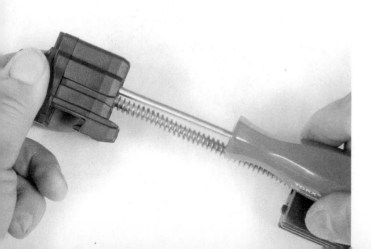

11. The recoil block must be disassembled in order to take down the bolt's recoil spring. There are two small Torx screws inside the front piece that must be removed to separate the front and rear pieces. Then the screw at the rear of the guide rod can be removed, the recoil spring removed from the rod, and the rod removed forward through the bolt.

12. Tap this pin out carefully to separate the bolt from the carrier (picture A). With the carrier removed, the firing pin and spring, and the extractor with spring and plunger can be removed from the bolt.

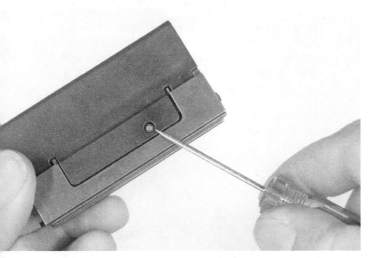

picture A

picture B

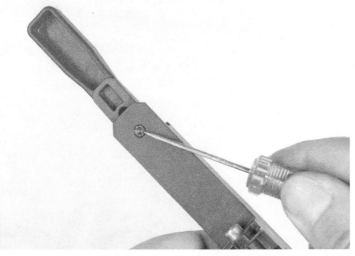

13. The charging handle is staked in place on the bolt carrier. Leave it alone.

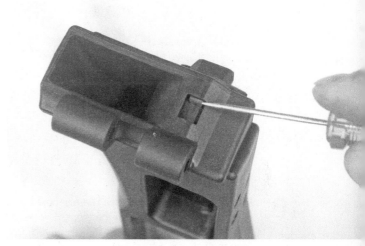

14. Depress this small latch to remove the stock button and spring.

15. Remove the bolt in the pistol grip.

16. Lift the trigger housing slightly until it stops, then pull the safety levers out to each side and finish lifting the housing out of the trigger grip.

17. Remove the screws holding the trigger housing halves together and lift the right half of the left half. All the internals should stay in the left half. There is a buffer pad at the top rear of the housing that will be freed when the halves are separated.

18. Remove the trigger assembly. There should be no need to further break down the trigger. However if further disassembly is somehow required, this trigger assembly is virtually identical to that of the Colt M4-22 on page 99.

19. Remove the hammer assembly. The hammer strut passes through the safety and this round piece will certainly come out with the hammer. Do not lose the plunger and spring from the safety.

Reassembly Tips:

1. This is the disconnector spring in place on the left trigger housing wall. Note the bent tip (picture A). This tip must rest in the notch shown (picture B) when the disconnector and hammer are replaced back into the housing.

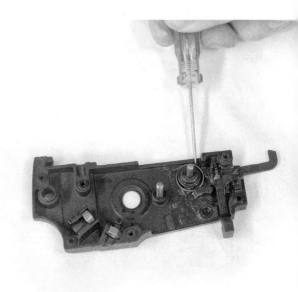

picture A

picture B

Henry Golden Boy

Data:	Henry Golden Boy
Origin:	United States
Manufacturer:	Henry Repeating Arms, Brooklyn, New York
Cartridge:	22 Long Rifle
Magazine capacity:	16 rounds
Overall length:	38 inches
Barrel length:	20 inches
Weight:	6¼ pounds

Introduced in 1998, the Golden Boy was designed to resemble the classic Winchester Model 1866. The Winchester was a redesign of an earlier gun by B. Tyler Henry, and the present firm was named in his honor. The Golden Boy is also offered in 22 Magnum and 17 HMR versions. Any complete takedown of this rifle should be done very carefully, to avoid marring its elegant exterior. Henry produces a number of rimfire rifles with different names and cosmetics that ultimately are based on the same Golden Boy design.

Disassembly:

1. Remove the wood screw near the end of the lower tang.

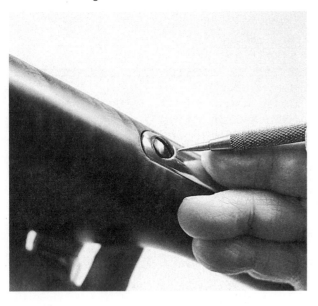

2. Remove the screw at the end of the upper tang.

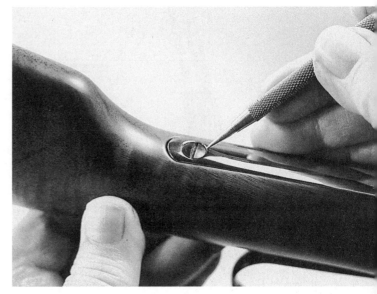

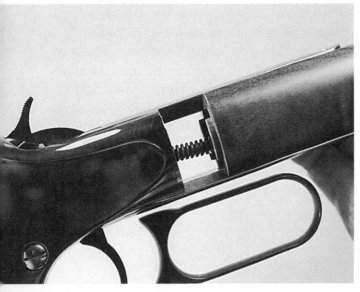

3. Remove the butt-stock toward the rear. The buttplate is retained by two wood screws.

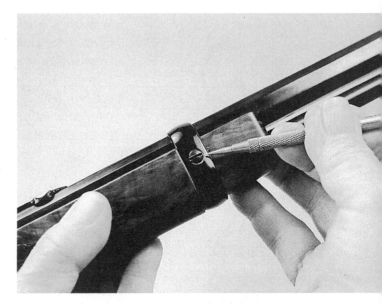

4. Remove the cross-screw in the barrel band.

5. Move the barrel band off toward the front. It may be necessary to nudge it with a non-marring tool.

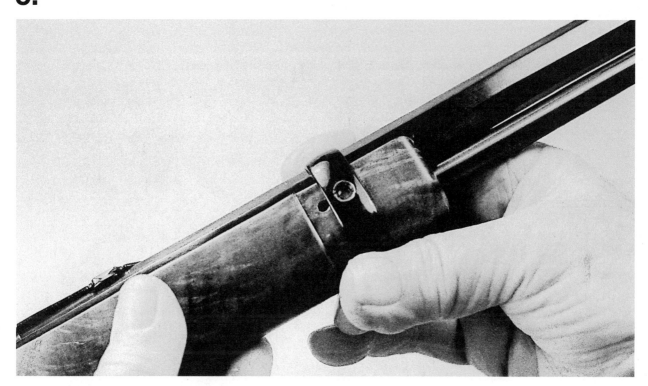

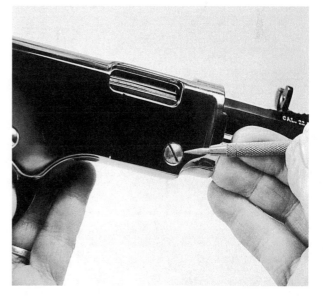

6. Remove the forend. Take out the inner magazine tube. If disassembly of the magazine tube is necessary, see the note at the end of the tool section.

7. Remove the four receiver cover screws, two on each side of the receiver. Note that each has a lock-washer, and take care that those are not lost.

8. Remove the receiver cover slightly upward and toward the rear for removal.

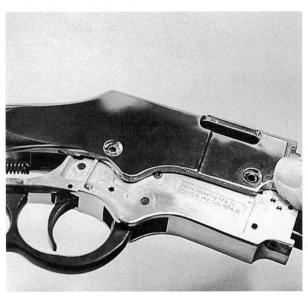

9. Remove the bolt.

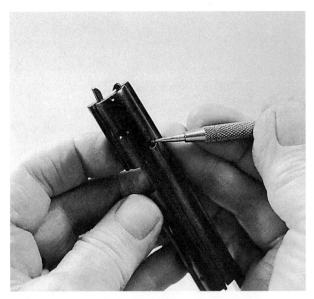

10. The primary extractor and the secondary (holding) extractor are retained on each side of the bolt by vertical pins that are drifted out upward. The coil extractor springs will also be released, so control them.

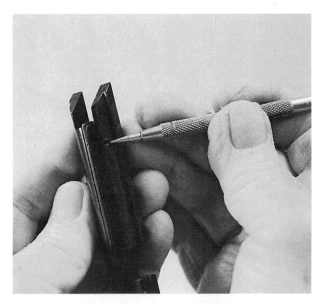

11. The firing pin and its return spring are retained by a cross pin at the rear of the bolt.

12. With the hammer fully "down," it is possible to grip the hammer spring guide with pliers, move it rearward, and tip it to the side for removal. **CAUTION:** *If you have sufficient hand and arm strength to do it this way, remember that you are compressing the powerful hammer spring.* The receiver should be in a padded vise.

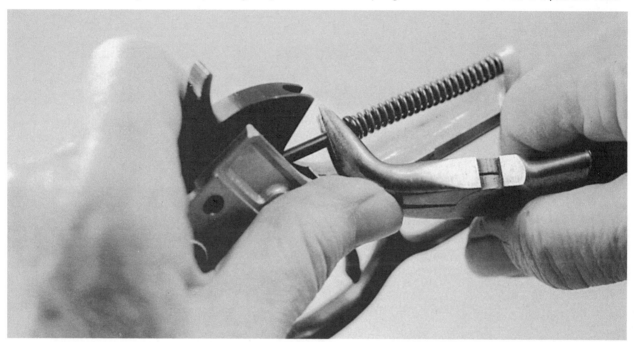

13. Here is an alternate way to remove the hammer spring and its guide: Cock the hammer, and use vise-grip pliers to grip the rear tip of the spring guide. Pull the trigger, and move the hammer to full down position. At this point, with the spring trapped, the hammer pin can be pushed out and the hammer removed, or, another vise-grip can be used to control the front of the spring guide for its removal. **CAUTION:** *Either way, take care the spring is not accidentally released. It is powerful. If removal of this system is not necessary for repair, it is best left in place.*

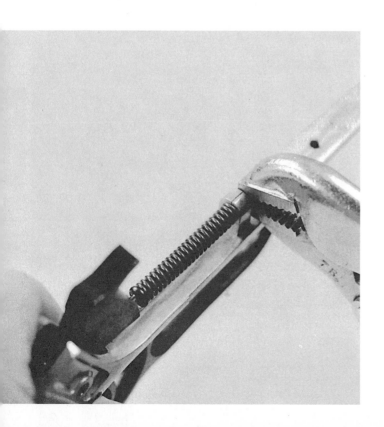

14. Assuming the hammer spring and guide are either restrained or removed, push out the hammer pivot pin, and take the hammer out upward.

15. Drift out the trigger cross pin.

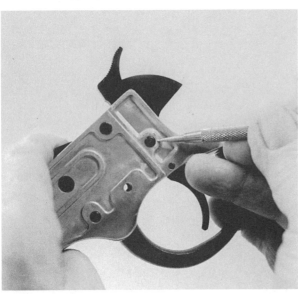

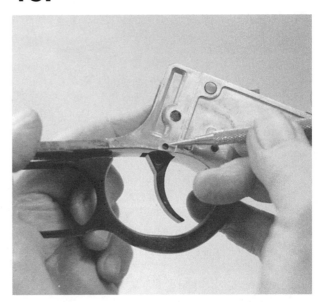

16. Remove the trigger and its spring.

17. Drift out the bolt locking bar pin.

18. With the lever in closed position, move the bolt locking bar slightly rearward, and take it out upward.

19. Remove the bolt locking bar spring.

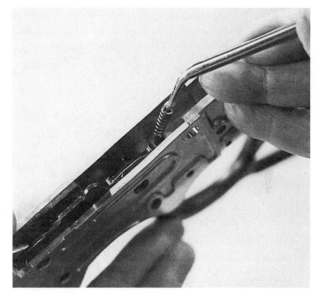

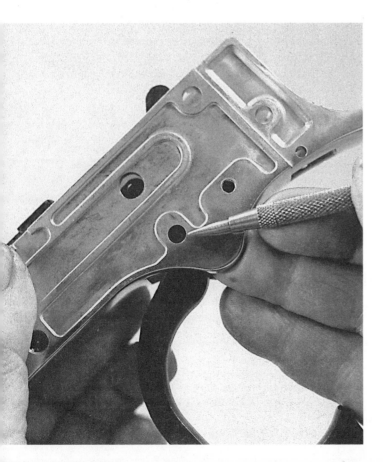

20. Push out the lever pivot pin, and remove the lever downward. It will be necessary to manipulate the lever slightly during removal, to clear its internal projections.

21. Do not disturb the carrier pivot post. It is riveted in place.

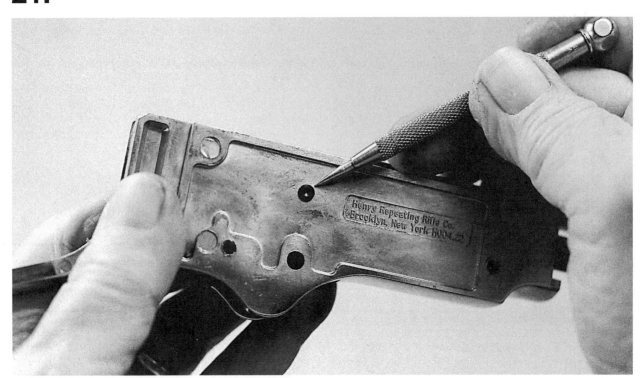

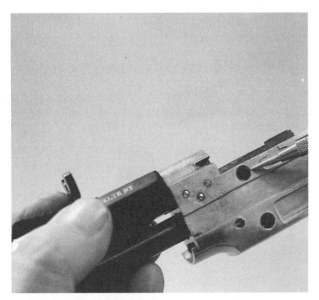

22. Remove the two screws on the left side of the receiver that retain the cartridge feed assembly.

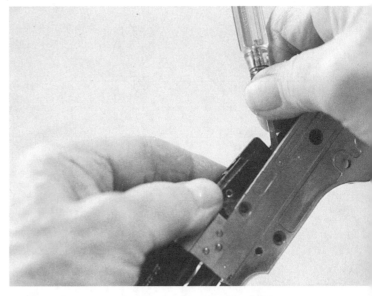

23. Depress the carrier lever and remove the feed assembly upward.

24. Allow the carrier lever to pivot over toward the rear, and slide the feed assembly off the lever.

25. Remove the carrier lever spring and plunger.

26. Move the carrier lever off its post toward the left side, and take it out upward.

27. The two upper pins retain the barrel and the lower pin retains the outer magazine tube. In normal takedown, these are left in place.

28. Both sights and the magazine tube hanger are dovetail-mounted and can be drifted out toward the right. Removal of the hanger would require prior removal of the magazine tube, of course.

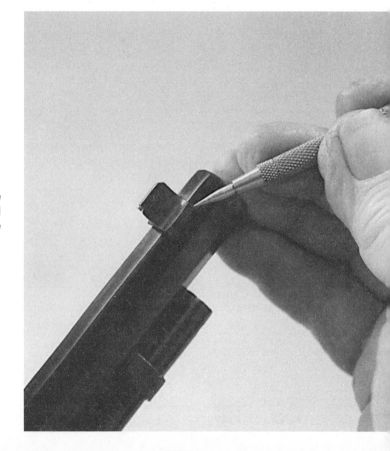

Reassembly Tips:

1. Before the hammer is reinstalled, it's best to install and restrain the hammer spring and guide. Use the same method as in takedown, as shown here.

2. Once the hammer is in place, fit the ball at the front of the spring guide into its recess in the hammer, cock the hammer, and release the pliers at the rear.

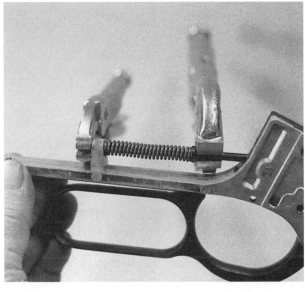

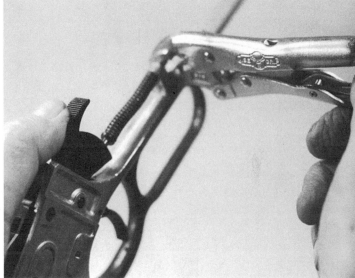

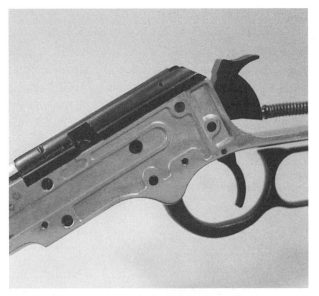

3. When re-installing the receiver cover, set the bolt in position on the receiver. The lever should be closed, and the hammer cocked.

4. As the receiver cover is moved back on, be sure the bolt rails mate with their recesses in the cover.

ISSC SPA

Data:	ISSC Austria SPA
Origin:	Austria
Manufacturer:	ISSC, Ried, Austria
Cartridge:	.22 Long Rifle, .17 HMR, .22 WMR
Magazine capacity:	10 rounds
Overall length:	38.6 inches
Barrel length:	20.1 inches
Weight:	5.6 pounds

The SPA is a recently imported rifle chambered in the ubiquitous .22 LR, but also in .22 WMR and .17 HMR. Black synthetic, camouflage, and a rather nice, if only barely finished wood stock contain the rifle and other little bits. The SPA uses a sort of side toggle lock bolt that amounts to a straight pull type of operation. An accurate gun, it has no provision for sights, nor is the stock comb low enough to even allow their use without modification. Be aware that the plastic magazine can be inserted and seated backwards, despite not being designed to do so.

Disassembly:

1. With the magazine removed, begin disassembly by removing the two Phillips head screws that retain the trigger guard and magazine well, at the front of the mag well, and behind the trigger guard. Then gently pull the trigger guard unit from the stock.

2. Remove the flat-headed action retaining screw just in front of the forward edge of the trigger guard/magazine well piece.

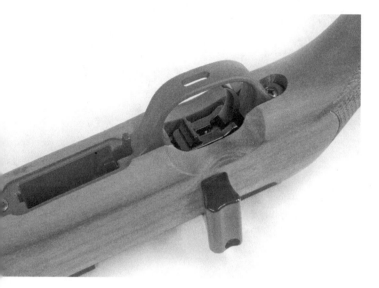

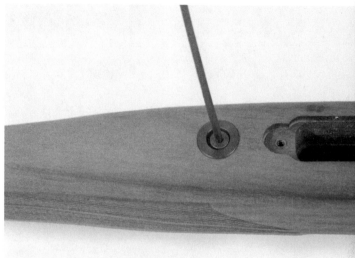

3. Lift the barreled action out of the stock.

4. Remove this screw at the lower rear corner of the receiver's right side wall. It retains two bushings, one entering each side of the receiver. Then push out both bushings. The screw, when partially removed, can be used to push out the left side bushing.

5. Unlock the bolt and pull the bolt assembly out of the rear of the receiver.

6. Two screws retain the trigger assembly. They are located at the lower edge of the receiver on either side, the left screw approximately 1/4 the distance from the rear of the receiver, and the right screw approximately 1/3 the distance. Remove them.

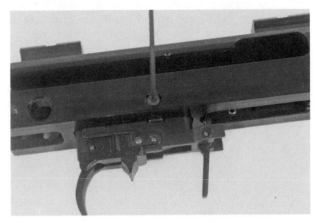

7. Remove the barrel only if necessary. This screw has a duplicate on the left side. To begin removing the barrel, remove these two screws.

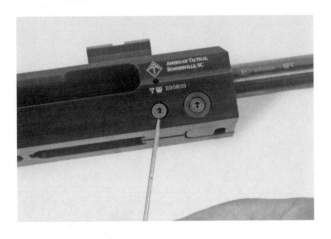

8. This screw is identical to the bolt block retaining screw at the rear of the receiver. Remove the screw and then push out both bushings.

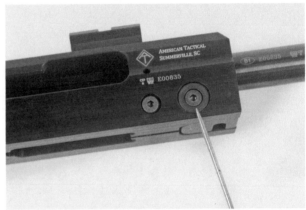

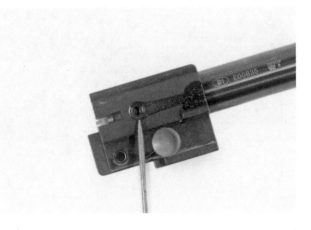

9. Now the barrel can be removed from the receiver. A small nut will fall from a slot in the bottom of the barrel block. This is the nut to which the action retaining screw engages.

10. The barrel is held in the barrel block by means of a highly thread-locked set screw. Unless you are replacing the barrel, leave this assembly intact.

11. The ejector is held inside the receiver by means of a pair of brass rivets. Do not remove this part.

12. Tap out this pivot in from bottom to top to separate the rear block from the toggle arm.

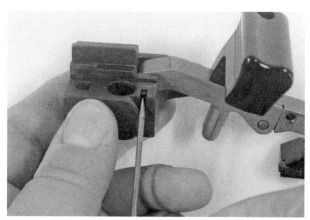

13. Take out these three screws to remove the plate that sits on top of the bolt.

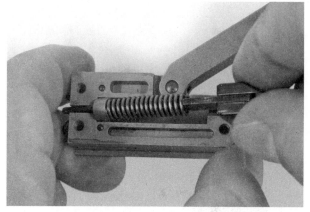

14. With the plate removed, the firing pin assembly can be removed. Beneath the assembly is a very small spring that sits in the bottom of the firing pin channel that serves as a return spring. Don't lose it.

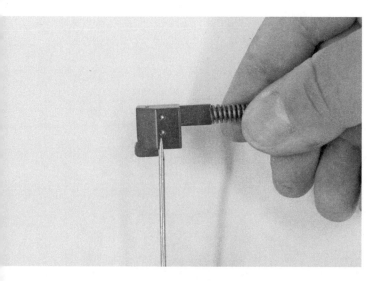

15. Do not remove these pins.

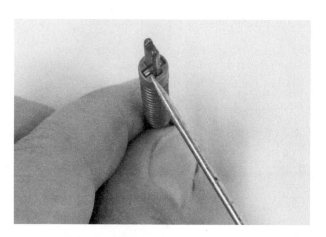

16. The firing pin spring retaining collar and firing pin spring are retained by this small pin. Compress the spring enough to push out the small pin and free the collar and spring.

17. To remove the toggle arm from the bolt, tap out this pin from bottom to top.

18. Tap out these two pins from bottom to top. They are splined. This will free both extractors and their springs.

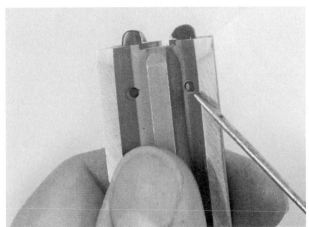

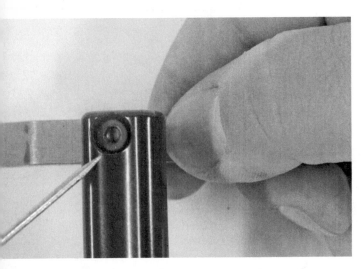

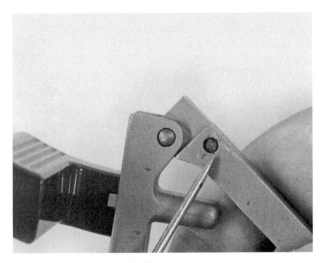

19. The screw can be removed to separate the operating handle from the bolt toggle arm.

20. This small set screw retains the ball bearing detent. Don't take it out or you will lose the ball bearing and spring.

21. Tap out this pin to remove the magazine catch and spring.

22. Tap out this pin to free the sear spring legs.

23. Tap out this pin (picture A) and remove the sear and spring (picture B).

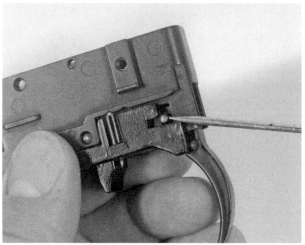

24. Tap out this trigger limiter pin.

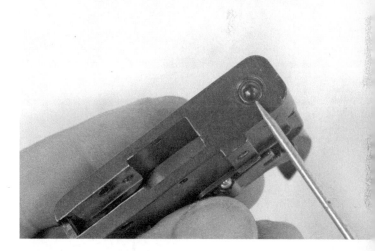

25. Remove this set screw and the spring and large plunger that sit beneath it.

26. Tap out the rear of these two pins to remove the trigger. It should not be necessary to remove the set screw in the trigger body.

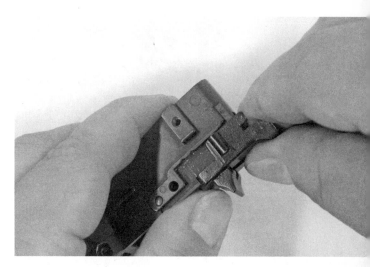

27. Push the safety bar to the rear and off the trigger housing. The two self -contained detent spring assemblies may fall out of the safety.

28. Tap out this pin to remove the trigger connector and spring.

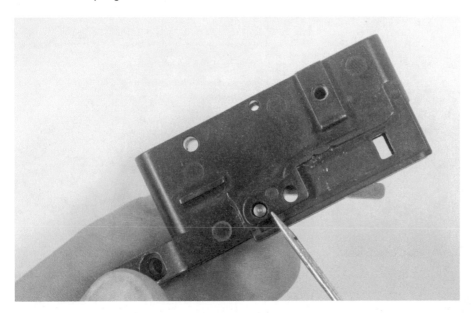

Reassembly Tips:

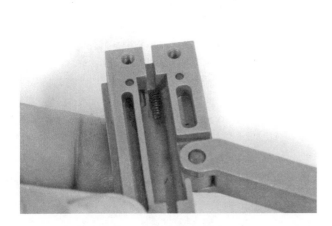

1. When reinstalling the firing pin assembly, drop the small return spring in first and so it touches the front wall, and is sitting on top of but not compressed and inside its slot. Then insert the firing pin in by sliding it forward across the bottom of the firing pin slot. The collar should catch the return spring and then, pushing the assembly down and seating it fully in the slot should cause the return spring to seat in its own slot properly.

2. The rear pin has a flat on it that needs to face forward. Don't try to hammer it in in any other orientation.

IWI Uzi

Data: Israel Weapon Industries Uzi
Origin: Germany
Manufacturer: Walther Arms, Germany
Cartridge: .22 Long Rifle
Magazine capacity: 20 rounds
Overall length: 26 inches
Barrel length: 17.9 inches
Weight: 7.7 pounds

This is an Uzi that is full size, full weight, but mini-caliber, being chambered for .22 LR. It retains the stamped, folding metal stock and ridiculously uncomfortable pistol grip with grip safety. The designers obviously decided to keep the body counts accumulated by the purchasers low by making the barrel 16" long and shrouding it with a heavy fake silencer. It was a fortunate decision too, because when I opened the box and pulled out my sample for this book, my innate gun-collector blood lust was instantly eliminated by its presence, forever it seems, even though it was shipped with a 20 round magazine, also known as a "score box." No longer in production, this Uzi is a fun little gun for backyard (legal) mayhem.

Disassembly:

1. Push the takedown button back into the rear sight housing and lift the top cover off the receiver.

2. Push out the takedown pin and pull the pistol grip down off the receiver.

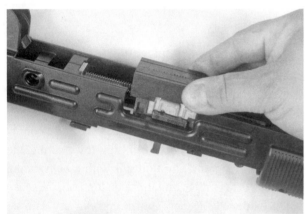

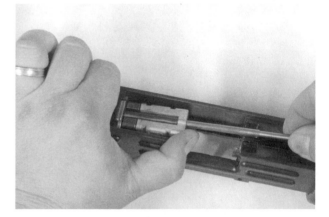

3. Lift off the bolt cover from the bolt.

4. Carefully push the bolt all the way to the rear and lift up on the front end of the guide rod to remove the bolt assembly from the receiver. The recoil spring will be very tightly compressed, caution is indicated.

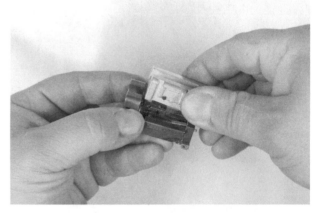

5. Tap out this pin from right to left.

6. Lift the top bolt piece from the bottom piece. Inside the bolt are the firing pin with return spring beneath it, and the extractor with plunger and spring. Lift the extractor spring to displace it, allowing the plunger and extractor to be removed. Don't lose the springs.

7. Drive out this roll pin (picture A). Tap out this pin from left to right (picture B). It is splined. Then lift out the trigger housing.

picture A

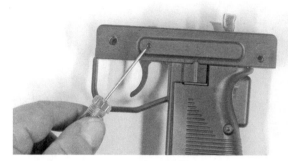

picture B

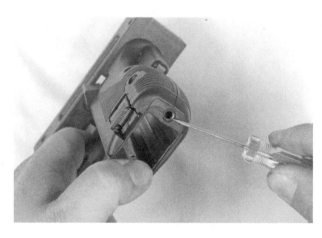

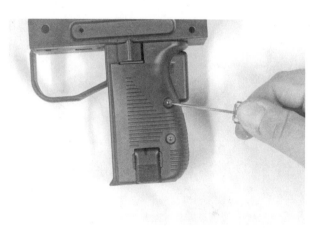

8. This set screw should be removed to remove tension from the hammer. Inside is the hammer spring and two plungers.

9. Remove the left grip panel. There is no need to remove the right panel unless it is cracked.

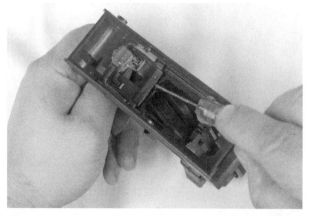

10. The grip safety button can be pulled slightly to the left and down to remove it. Don't lose the springs.

11. This retainer holds down the safety bars. Gently pry it up, taking care not to damage the plastic stud it projects into the receiver. Lift out the safety bars. Note the small flat spring used to tension the manual safety under the left bar. The manual safety button will be free now as well.

12. Push out this pin to free the magazine catch and spring.

13. Remove the three screws from the right side of the trigger housing. The top/middle screw is shorter than the other two. Remove the right half of the housing. Attempt to keep all the parts inside the left side of the housing.

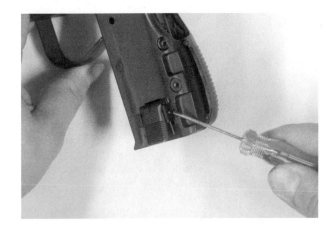

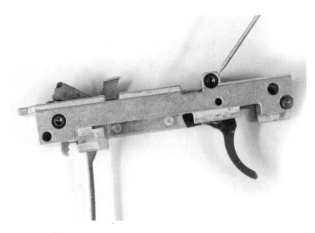

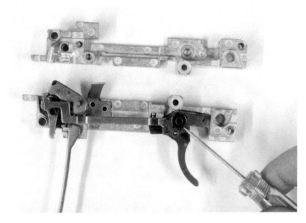

14. Remove the trigger by pulling the trigger bar at the rear out to the right slightly to disengage it from the hammer and sear. Then lift the trigger assembly off its pin. There is a return spring and plunger under the rear of the trigger.

15. Remove the hammer assembly. There should be no need to further disassemble the hammer.

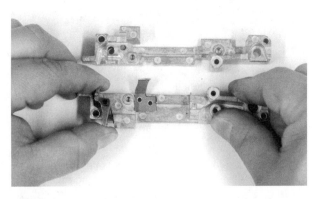

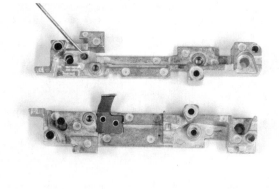

16. Remove the sear and the underlying sear spring.

17. This is the disconnector spring and plunger in the right wall. It may have fallen out in a previous step.

18. The charging handle is held to the top cover by means of a screw. Remove the screw (picture A). On the underside, another screw holds the two halves of the slide together. Remove the screw to separate the halves, and remove them and the spring (picture B).

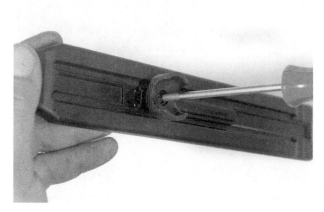

picture A

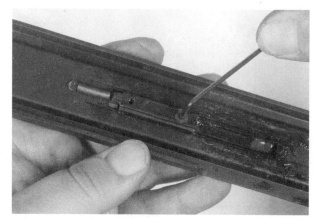

picture B

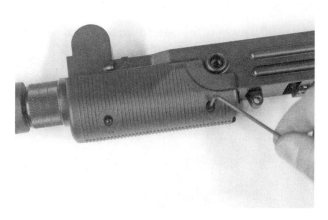

19. Remove the screws from the handguard and remove the handguard pieces.

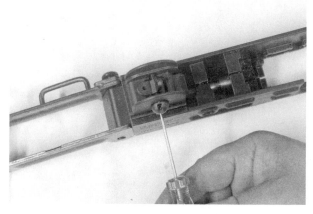

20. Drive out this small spring pin. Then unscrew the keeper it was retaining, and unscrew the adjustment screw out the left side, removing the sight when it has been freed.

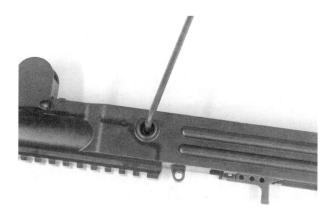

21. There are two large bolts, one on either side of the receiver, sunk into their holes. Remove these two bolts.

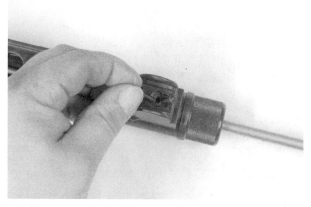

22. Remove the front sight by depressing the plunger and then unscrewing the sight post.

23. Unscrew the fake silencer from the barrel and then pull the sleeve off the front of the barrel as well.

24. Unscrew and remove the barrel nut and its attendant O-ring.

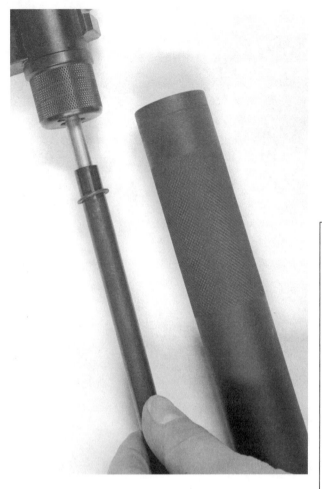

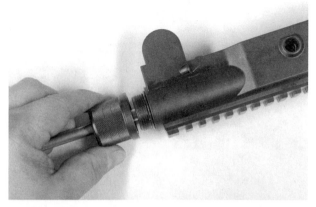

Reassembly Tips:

1. The sear spring bent tip wraps around the front of the bottom of the sear. There is a small cut-out to accept it. The straight leg rests against the housing left wall boss.

25. Further disassembly should not be done outside the factory. The stock is riveted and staked together, as is the assembly to the receiver. If necessary, the barrel can be removed by spreading the front receiver apart, like so.

2. Note the orientation of the trigger bar spring, with the long squared tip over the top of the bar and the shorter bent tip resting on the back bottom of the trigger.

Ithaca Model 49

Similar/Identical Pattern Guns

The same basic assembly/disassembly steps for the Ithaca Model 49 also apply to the following guns:

Ithaca Model 49 Youth   **Ithaca Model 49 Presentation**
Ithaca Model 49 Deluxe   **Ithaca Model 49R**
Ithaca Model 49 Magnum   **Ithaca Model 49 St. Louis**

Data:	Ithaca Model 49
Origin:	United States
Manufacturer:	Ithaca Gun Company
	Ithaca, New York
Cartridges:	22 Long Rifle, 22 Magnum (WMR)
Overall length:	35 inches
Barrel length:	18 inches
Weight:	5½ pounds

Designed to resemble a Western-style lever-action repeating rifle, the Ithaca Model 49 is actually a single shot with a Martini-type action. The "magazine tube" below the barrel is a dummy. The gun was introduced in 1961, and soon became popular as a "first gun" for young shooters. To accommodate the younger group, Ithaca produced a version with a shorter-than-standard stock. While the Model 49 is a simple gun, there are several points in the takedown where a wrong move can result in damaged parts. The instructions can be used for all of the variants listed above.

Disassembly:

1. Take out the screw at the bottom of the barrel band and remove the barrel band toward the front.

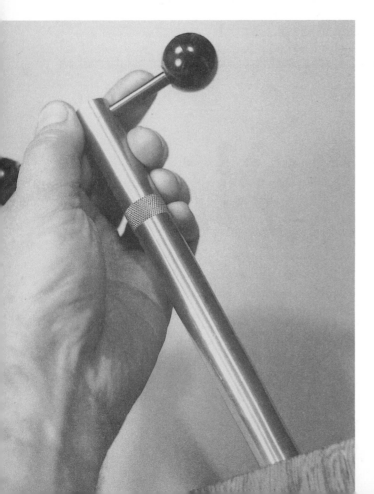

2. Drift out the small cross pin in the magazine tube loop (arrow), and slide the dummy magazine forward. Remove the forend downward and slide the tube out of the loop toward the rear. Take care not to lose the small plastic cap at the end of the tube. It is a friction fit, and may come out as the tube is removed.

3. Take off the buttplate and use a B-Square stock tool, a ⅜-inch socket wrench, or a long screwdriver to remove the stock mounting bolt. Take off the stock toward the rear. Grip the stock mounting stud firmly with leather-padded pliers and unscrew it from the rear of the receiver. Take out the hammer spring toward the rear, and take care not to lose the lock washer on the neck of the stud.

4. Drift out the lever pivot pin (arrow) toward the right. It should be noted that on all late production guns, the cross pins are knurled on the right side and must be taken out in that direction. On some very early guns, certain pins may have the knurled end on the left side. If you have an older gun, it would be best to check the heads of the pins before removal.

5. Remove the lever downward, and remove the trigger spring and plunger from the back of the lever base.

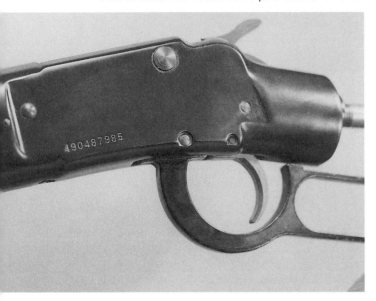

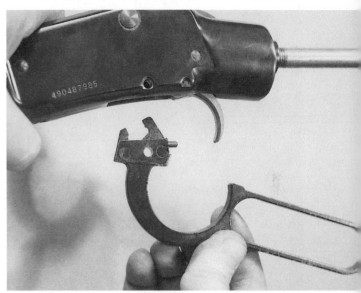

6. Remove the bolt spring plunger, bolt spring and bolt pivot lock plunger from the hole in the bottom of the lower lobe of the bolt. The lower plunger and the spring should come out easily. If the upper plunger is reluctant to come out, hold the gun right-side up, and move the large bolt pivot gently from side to side. If this fails, give the receiver a few light taps with a plastic mallet.

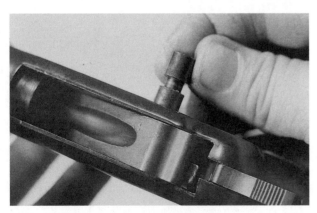

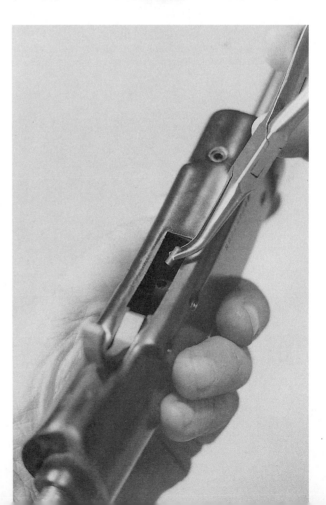

7. When the spring and both plungers are removed from the breechblock pivot, the pivot can easily be pushed out toward either side. It should be noted, though, that any attempt to remove the pivot with the upper plunger still in place can result in damage to the pivot, receiver and plunger.

8. Remove the breechblock (bolt) from the top of the receiver. Restrain the firing pin spring on the left side to prevent its escape, as it is held in place only by the inside wall of the receiver.

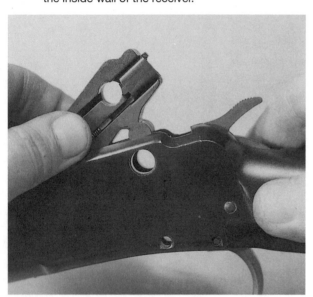

9. The firing pin, return spring and lock pin are shown in their proper positions, before disassembly.

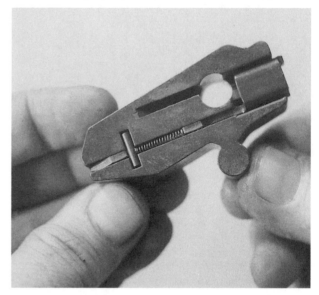

10. Remove the spring, lock pin and firing pin toward the left.

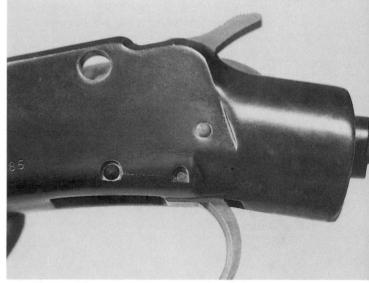

11. Drift out the hammer and trigger pivot pins toward the right. Remove the hammer and hammer spring strut toward the top, and the trigger from the bottom.

12. Use an Allen wrench of the proper size to remove the ejector trip spring screw from the bottom front of the receiver and take out the spring and plunger.

13. Drift out the large cross pin at the front of the receiver toward the right. Depress the ejector trip to ensure that it is disengaged from the ejector, and remove the ejector and its spring toward the rear. The large cross pin also retains the barrel. Drift out the smaller cross pin toward the right to release the ejector trip, and use a large hardwood dowel or some other non-marring tool to prevent damage while driving the barrel out forward. The ejector trip can then be removed from inside the receiver.

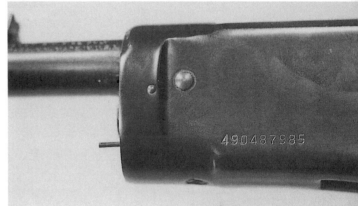

Reassembly Tips:

When replacing the breechblock pivot, remember that the retaining plunger groove must be on the right side of the receiver.

When replacing the retaining plunger in the bottom of the breechblock, remember that the shorter plunger with the flat ends goes in first. The longer plunger with one rounded end goes at the bottom, with the rounded end downward. As the plungers and spring are installed, move the breechblock pivot slightly from side to side, to ensure that the top plunger enters its groove.

Keep the gun inverted while installing the lever to avoid losing the spring and plungers from their hole in the breechblock.

Remember to reinsert all cross pins from right to left, because the knurled ends will have slightly expanded the holes on the right side.

When replacing the dummy magazine tube, be sure the groove for the cross pin is at the top and aligned with the hole in the hanger loop before driving in the pin.

Kel-Tec SU-22

Data:	Kel-Tec SU-22
Origin:	United States
Manufacturer:	Kel-Tec CNC Industries, Inc., Cocoa, Florida
Cartridge:	22 Long Rifle
Magazine capacity:	26 rounds
Overall length:	34 inches
Barrel length:	16 inches
Weight:	4 pounds

The SU-22 rifle is very lightweight, and with an accessory rail on the bottom of the forend, it makes for a very handy, robust utility and plinking rifle. Composed of a mostly hollow clamshell-like stock assembly and fire control, the rear half of the rifle could, with removal of a retaining cross pin, fold for compact storage, with the notch on the buttstock toe snapping onto the barrel. The buttstock could also store two 10-round magazines in its hollow cavity.

The forward half was composed of the polymer receiver with the barrel held on by a retaining nut system, with an internal steel framework upon which the bolt reciprocates. It is an excellent example of what can be done with modern CNC and polymer molding manufacturing technology.

This rifle is one of several introduced by multiple manufacturers that uses a common magazine type based on the Atchisson/Ciener system.

Disassembly:

1. Push out the Assembly Pin in either direction.

2. Unscrew the bottom screw from either side of the back of the magazine well and push the spacer out to the other side. The buttstock with fire control can then be removed from the receiver.

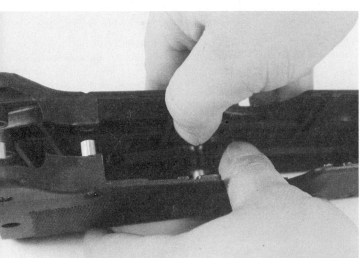

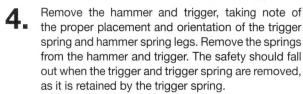

3. Remove the 10 Phillips screws from one side of the buttstock. This will allow you to separate the two halves. Do so slowly and gently as the trigger and hammer pins are retained only by the stock halves. The hammer spring is quite powerful and unless controlled, the hammer, spring and pin will energetically separate from the stock pieces if care is not observed. Separating the stock halves will also free the recoil pad.

4. Remove the hammer and trigger, taking note of the proper placement and orientation of the trigger spring and hammer spring legs. Remove the springs from the hammer and trigger. The safety should fall out when the trigger and trigger spring are removed, as it is retained by the trigger spring.

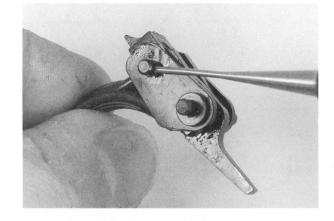

5. Pushing out the trigger axis pin indicated in the photo will free the trigger block. Pushing out the sear pin in front of it will release the sear. The sear spring and sear spring pin are held in by the sear.

6. Removing all the spacers from the stock is not necessary unless one needs replacement.

7. Remove the thread protector.

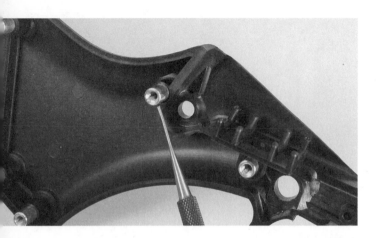

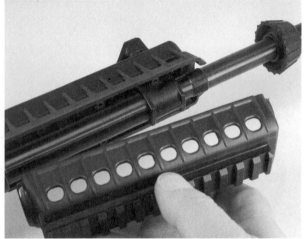

8. Remove the compact forecap by unscrewing it and sliding it forward and off the barrel. This will allow the compact bottom forend to be removed.

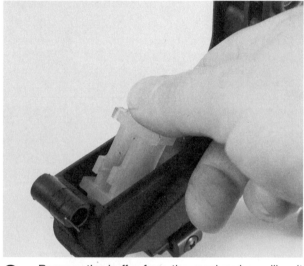

9. Remove the buffer from the receiver by pulling it down and out.

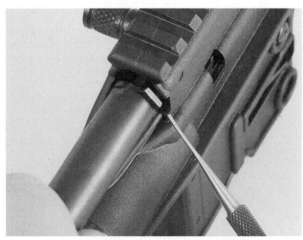

10. To remove the bolt, the recoil spring tube must be pushed forward slightly and then rotated 90 degrees so that the small tab points upward. This removes tension on the recoil spring.

11. The bolt assembly can then be pulled all the way to the rear and the bolt handle pulled straight out to the right once it reaches its clearance notch at the end of its rearward movement.

12. The bolt can then be pulled all the way back, tipped down and then pulled back out of the receiver.

13. Remove the compact forend top.

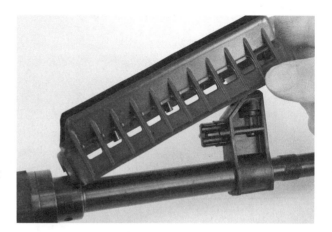

14. Push the recoil spring lock button slightly into the recoil spring tube and rotate 90 degrees. This will allow the recoil spring to push the lock button off. Caution: capture the spring as it is under compression, and remove from tube.

15. The recoil spring tube can then be removed from the recoil spring guide. Invert the tube to remove the recoil spring washer.

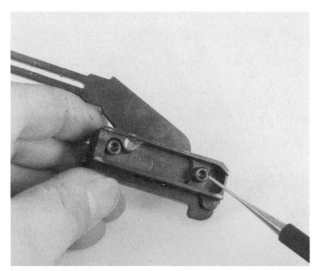

16. Remove the two bolt screws to free the bolt left half.

17. Pull the bolt left half away from the right half. Remove the firing pin. Note that the firing pin return spring might no longer be captured. Note also that the extractor spring helps to retain the firing pin in the bolt during disassembly.

18. The extractor spring can be pulled from its hole and the recoil spring guide can be removed from the bolt right half.

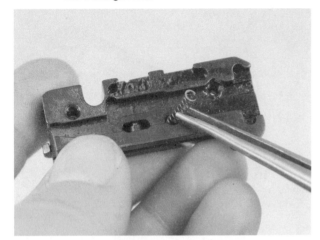

19. Drive out the extractor axis to remove the extractor.

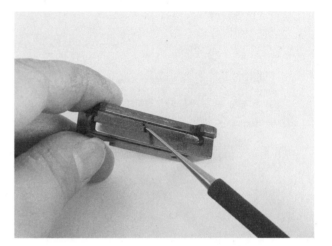

20. Unscrew the Phillips head screw at the top rear of the magazine well and then push the spacer out one side. This will free the bolt stop.

21. Pull the bolt stop down and press forward to angle it out of its position and pull it out of the receiver. Catch the short stubby bolt stop spring as it will fall out.

22. Pull the mag well piece down until it stops. Using a small screwdriver or similar tool, dislodge the magazine catch spring from the receiver by prying it back from the stud that it rests upon. Once dislodged, push it down into the body of the magazine catch and push the catch out to the left.

23. The magazine well can now be pulled out of the receiver.

24. The internal framework consisting of the two guide plates, two guide rails, mid support plate and feed ramp can now be removed by sliding the assembly to the rear of the receiver and pulling it down and out of the receiver. Note the arrangement of the parts as they will promptly fall apart.

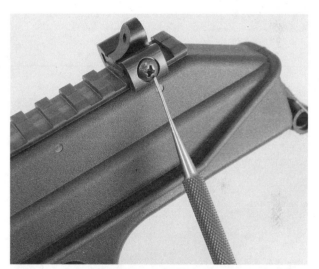

25. The rear sight can be removed by loosening or removing both adjustment screws.

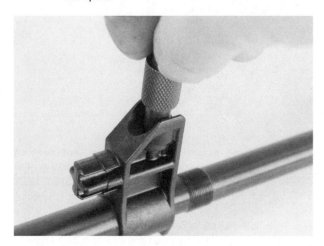

26. The front sight can be unscrewed off the front sight block using a punch to depress the detent, or by using an M-16/AR-15 front sight adjustment tool.

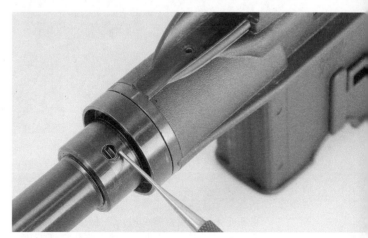

27. The barrel can be removed by using a spanner wrench to loosen the compact forend barrel nut. This is not necessary unless barrel replacement is warranted.

28. The magazine snap ring and pin assemblies in the buttstock should only be disassembled for replacement. This is done by pushing the pin out from the inside and removing the e-rings, allowing the pin and snap ring to come free.

29. Remove the stock pin spring with a small screwdriver by prying out the right leg.

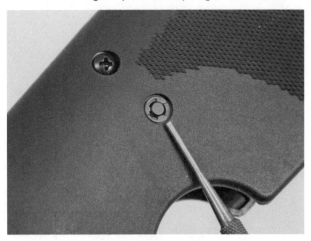

Reassembly Tips:

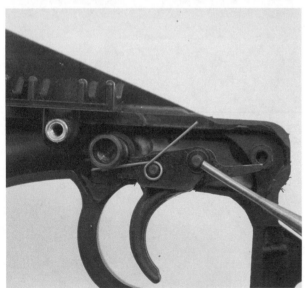

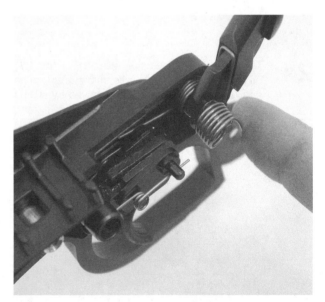

1. On the trigger assembly, the front pin is the sear pin. The trigger return spring tensions off of this pin. Install the trigger with the inside spring leg under this pin. Leave the other leg loose. This reduces tension enough to easily install the safety. The trigger spring will retain the safety. Then place the loose trigger return spring leg under the near side of the sear pin. This sequence will help to keep the trigger in place as the hammer is reinstalled. The sear pin is indicated in the photograph.

2. When reinstalling the hammer, ensure that the hammer spring is installed properly on the hammer with the loop wrapping around the back of the hammer and wrapping around the front of the hammer's bosses. Place one leg of the hammer spring on the sear pin to the far side of the trigger, then push the hammer and pin into position. Place the second hammer spring leg temporarily on top of the trigger as it is unlikely to remain on top of the sear spring without the other stock half in place.

3. Then align the opposite stock half, press the two stock sides together and reinstall the stock screws. Then, through the hole above the trigger, displace the hammer spring leg from off of the trigger and onto the sear pin.

4. Insert the magazine catch spring into the magazine catch as shown in the picture. Insert the mag well into the receiver as shown so that the full square magazine catch hole can be seen through the receiver.

5. Push the magazine catch in all the way until it stops. Then use a small screwdriver to displace the spring from the left side off the magazine catch down onto the inner wall of the magazine well. Then push the magazine well up until it stops. The spacer (cross bolt) holes at the back of the magazine well should be clear and fully open.

6. When putting the bolt assembly back together, ensure that the bolt face itself is flat and that both sides of the bolt face are on the same plane.

7. When reinstalling the buffer, the corner with the 90-degree angle is to the back and bottom of the receiver.

8. When pushing the assembly pin back in place to fully connect the two halves of the rifle, the pin drags the assembly pin spring legs slightly. Push the pin through and just slightly out the other side until you hear a small click. Then push the pin back into the stock until a second click is heard. The pin will now be fully seated with both spring legs resting in the pin's grooves.

Kimber Model 82

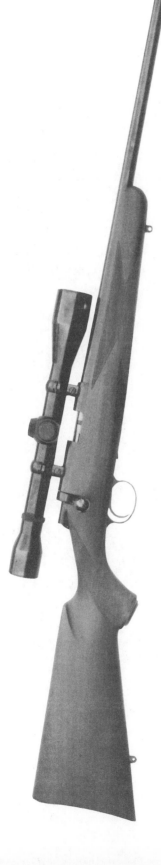

Similar/Identical Pattern Guns

The same basic assembly/disassembly steps for the Kimber Model 82 also apply to the following guns:

Kimber Model 82 Gov't. Target

Kimber Model 82 All Amer. Match

Kimber Model 82 Sporter

Kimber Model 82 Varminter

Kimber Model 82 Deluxe

Kimber Model 82 Custom Classic

Kimber Model 82 Hornet

Kimber Model 82 America

Kimber Model 82 Super

Kimber Model 82B

Kimber Model 82A Gov't.

Kimber Model 82 Mini-Classic

Kimber Model 82 Hunter Grade

Kimber Model 82 Classic

Data:	Kimber Model 82
Origin:	United States
Manufacturer:	Kimber of Oregon, Inc.
	Clackamas, Oregon
Cartridge:	22 Long Rifle
Magazine capacity:	5 rounds
Overall length:	41 inches
Barrel length:	24 inches
Weight:	6¼ pounds

Quality and price were both notably high, and the Kimber rifle lasted for about 11 years, from 1980 to 1991. Now, treasured by both shooters and collectors, the original Kimber guns have become difficult to find. The Model 82 was made in several grades and styles, but all were mechanically essentially the same.

Disassembly:

1. Remove the magazine. Hold the trigger to the rear, open the bolt and remove the bolt toward the rear.

2. Remove the large screw in front of the magazine opening.

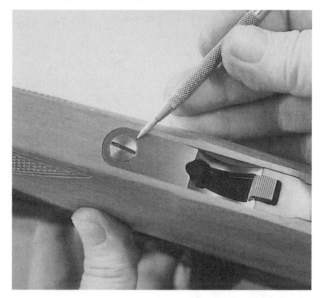

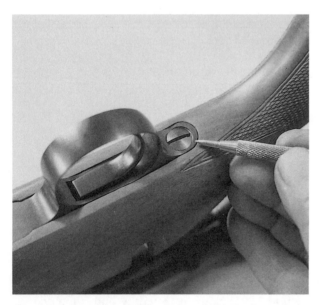

3. Remove the large screw behind the trigger guard. Keep the two screws in order, as they are not interchangeable.

4. Remove the action from the stock.

5. Remove the trigger guard unit from the stock.

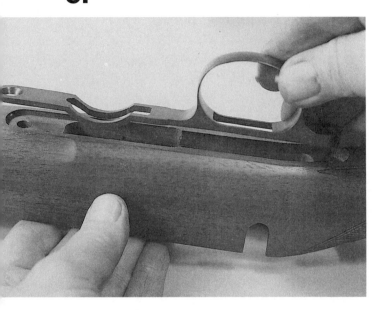

6. Hold the front of the bolt firmly with a shop cloth and turn the handle to lower the striker to fired position, as shown.

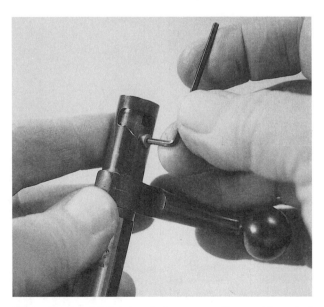

7. Use an Allen wrench to remove the cocking stud from the striker.

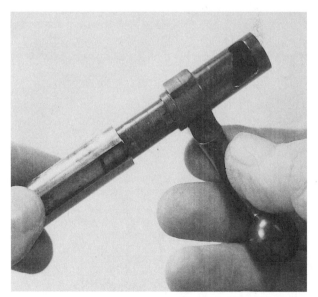

8. Remove the bolt handle unit toward the rear.

9. Insert a tool at the rear to arrest the striker spring and push out the retaining cross pin. **Caution:** *Control the spring.*

10. Remove the striker spring toward the rear.

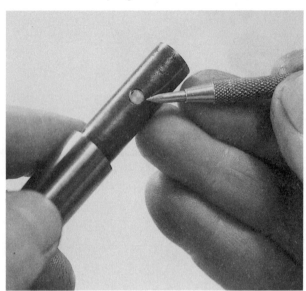

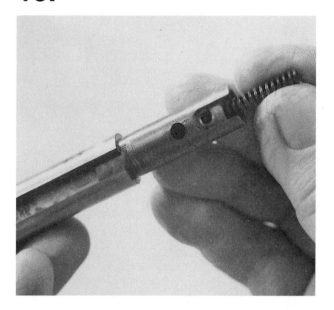

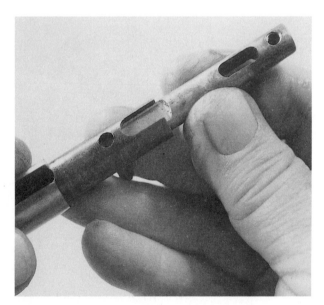

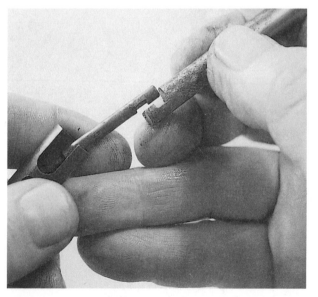

11. Remove the striker toward the rear.

12. As the striker emerges, the firing pin will be released from its hook at the front of the striker.

13. Carefully pry the narrow left arm of the saddle-type spring from its engagement with the left extractor. Control the spring as it is taken off.

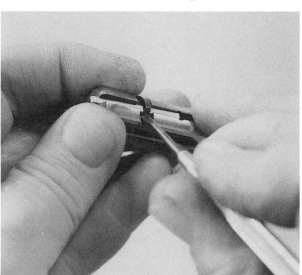

14. The extractors are now easily lifted out of their recesses in the bolt. Keep them in order, as they are not interchangeable.

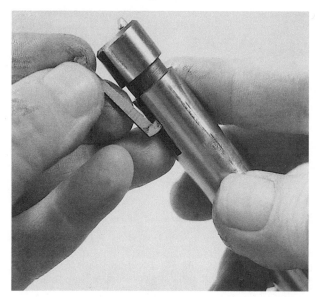

15. Grip the shaft of the safety positioning spring guide and move it downward to disengage its upper tip from the recess in the safety disc. Keep control of the guide and spring, and swing them out toward the rear for removal.

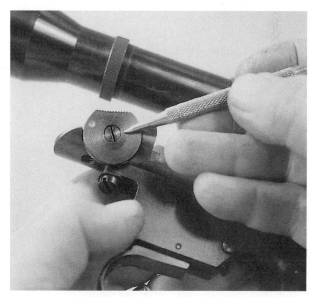

16. The safety disc need not be removed for further disassembly. However, if it is to be taken off, its pivot screw is the retainer.

17. Remove the vertical screw at the front of the trigger and magazine housing. Take care that the lock washer is not lost.

18. Remove the screw and lock washer at the rear of the housing.

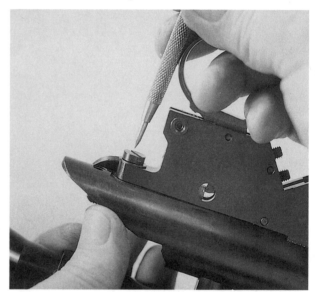

19. Restrain the magazine catch and push out the cross pin.

20. Remove the magazine catch and its spring downward.

21. Remove the center housing screw and its lock washer.

22. Remove the trigger and magazine housing downward.

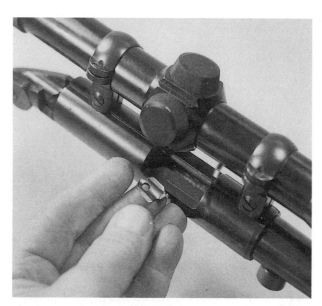

23. The ejector is released internally with removal of the center screw. Retrieve it from inside the action.

24. The sear spring is easily removed from its well in the front of the sear. Drifting out this cross pin will allow removal of the sear upward.

25. Except for repair, removal of the trigger is not advisable, as the original adjustments will be cancelled. However, if it is necessary, the first step is to back out the cinch screw that locks the adjustment screws.

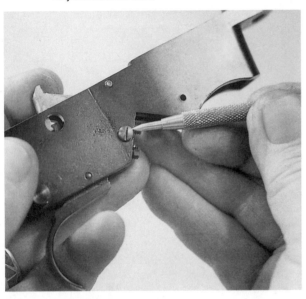

26. The next step is to remove the trigger spring adjustment screw and the spring. The upper screw is the over-travel stop and it can be left in place.

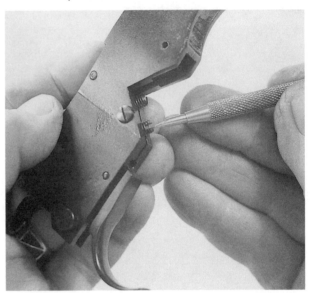

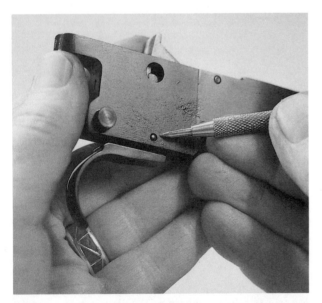

27. If the previous steps have been done, drift out the trigger cross pin and remove the trigger downward.

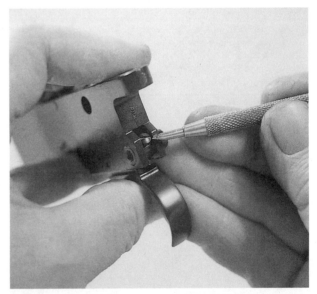

28. To remove the safety cross-piece, the adjustment screw must first be backed out. Here, again, it is best left in place in normal takedown. If the screw is removed, it will have to be carefully reset for proper bearing on the trigger. Also at the rear of the receiver (not shown) is the bolt handle detent plunger and spring, retained by a small pin in the right side of the receiver. The pin is drifted inward to release the plunger and spring. In normal takedown, leave it in place.

Reassembly Tips:

1. When the ejector is reinstalled, it must be oriented as shown, with the ejector projection at left front. Use a fingertip inside the receiver to hold it in place as the screw is inserted. Before this is done, it is best to put the trigger and magazine housing in place with the front and rear screws.

2. Use a screwdriver blade the same width as the diameter of the striker spring to compress the spring for insertion of the retaining cross pin. This is more easily done with the front part of the bolt in a well-padded vise.

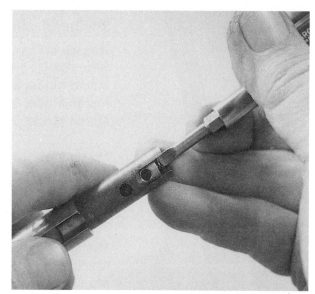

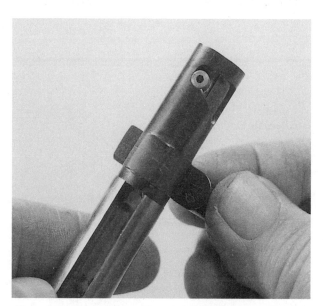

3. Before the bolt can be reinserted in the receiver, the striker must be in cocked position, as shown. Hold the front of the bolt in a shop cloth (or in a padded vise), and turn the handle to recock the striker.

Marlin Model 39A

Similar/Identical Pattern Guns

The same basic assembly/disassembly steps for the Marlin Model 39A also apply to the following guns:

Marlin Model 39	**Marlin Model 1892**
Marlin Model 39TDS	**Marlin Model 1897**
Marlin Model 39AS	**Marlin Model 39A 90th Anniv.**
Marlin Model 39A Mountie	**Marlin Model 39M Mountie**
Marlin Model 39 Carbine	**Marlin Model 39A Octagon**
Marlin Model 39D	**Marlin Model 39M Octagon**
Marlin Model 39M	**Marlin Golden 39M Carbine**
Marlin Model 39M Golden Carbine	**Marlin Model 39A-DL**
Marlin Model 39 Century LTD	**Marlin 39A Article II**
Marlin Model 39M Article II	

Data:	Marlin Model 39A
Origin:	United States
Manufacturer:	Marlin Firearms North Haven, Connecticut
Cartridge:	22 Short, Long or Long Rifle
Magazine capacity:	26 Short, 21 Long, 19 Long Rifle
Overall length:	40 inches
Barrel length:	24 inches
Weight:	6½ pounds

When the Marlin Company introduced the first lever-action, repeating 22 rimfire rifle in 1891, it had one particularly notable feature: It was the first repeating 22 rifle that would feed Short, Long and Long Rifle cartridges interchangeably. The basic gun was slightly redesigned in 1897, 1922 and 1938, finally arriving at the excellent Model 39A that is so popular today. Except for slight manufacturing change—such as the use of modern round-wire springs—the internal mechanism is basically unchanged from the original 1891 version. With the exception of a shorter barrel and carbine-style, straight-gripped stock, the Mountie model is mechanically identical. The instructions can be used for all of the variants listed above.

Disassembly:

1. Use a coin to start the large, knurled takedown screw on the right side of the receiver. Then use your fingers to back it out until its threads are free. An internal shoulder will keep the screw from coming completely out.

2. Set the hammer on the safety step and bump the left side of the stock with the heel of your hand to force the stock and receiver plate toward the right. Separate the stock and its attached parts from the front portion of the gun.

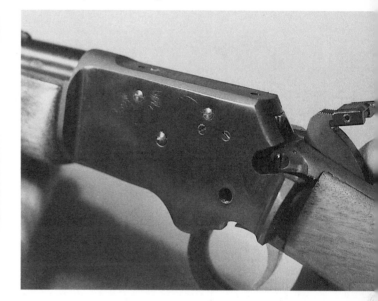

3. Slide the breechblock (bolt) toward the rear until its lower projection stops against the shoulder of the receiver, and then remove the bolt toward the right side of the frame.

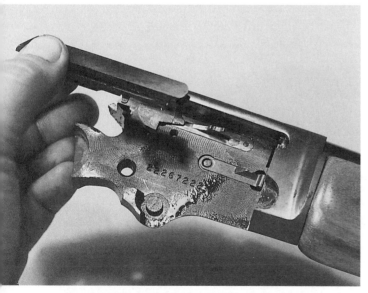

4. The firing pin is easily lifted from the top of the breech block.

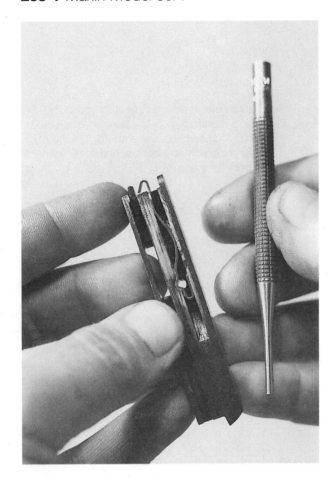

5. Insert a drift punch of the proper size through the small hole in the underside of the breechblock and push the extractor upward and out of its recess in the top of the bolt.

6. The ejector housing is retained on the inside of the receiver by two screws .which enter from the outside left of the receiver, near the top. Back out the two screws and remove the ejector assembly toward the right. The ejector spring will be released by removal of the housing, and drifting out a vertical pin will free the ejector for removal. In normal takedown, the ejector lock rivet is not removed. The cartridge stop (arrow), located below the ejector and toward the front, is retained by a single screw which also enters from the outside left of the receiver. Back out this screw and remove the stop and its spacer block toward the right.

7. The cartridge guide spring, located just above the chamber, is retained by a screw which enters from the top of the receiver. This is the larger screw near the front scope mount screw. The cartridge guide spring is removed downward.

8. Drifting out the small cross pin in the magazine tube hanger will allow removal of the outer magazine tube toward the front. If the inner magazine tube is to be taken apart, drifting out the cross pin which also locks the tube in place will allow removal of the knurled end piece, spring and follower. There is some risk of damage to the thin tube, and in normal take down the inner tube should be left assembled.

9. Removal of the two screws in the forend cap will allow it to be taken off forward, and the forend cap base can then be driven out of its dovetail toward the right side. When doing this, take care not to damage the screw holes. The forend can now be moved slightly forward and taken off downward.

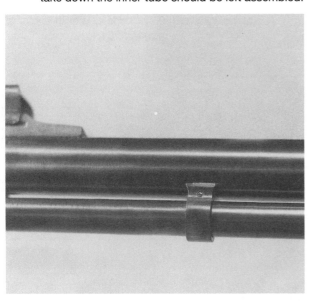

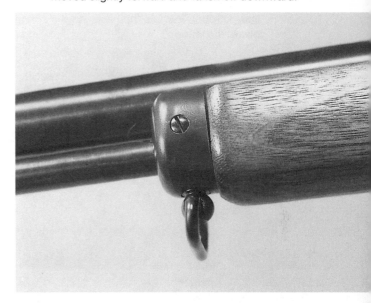

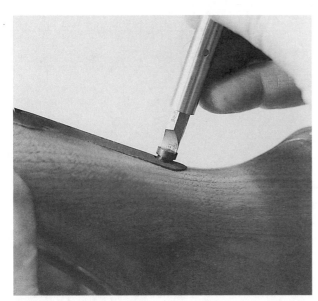

10. Take out the stock mounting bolt-the large screw at the rear tip of the upper tang. The stock can now be removed toward the rear. If the fitting is very tight, it may be necessary to bump the front of the comb with the heel of your hand or a soft rubber hammer.

11. The firing mechanism is shown in proper order, prior to disassembly. Note the relationship of all parts, to aid in reassembly.

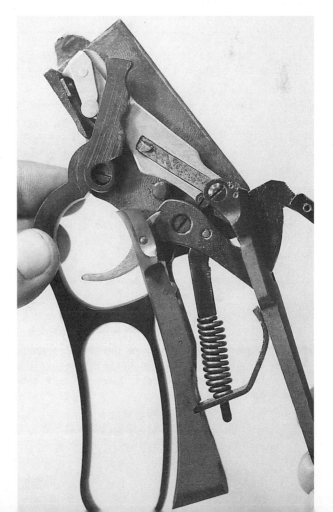

12. Grip the upper part of the hammer spring base with pliers and slide it out toward either side, moving its lower end out of its slot in the lower tang. The hammer, of course, must be at rest (in fired position). Remove the base and the spring toward the rear.

13. Take out the hammer pivot screw and remove the hammer from the top of the frame. During this operation, it will be necessary to tilt the attached hammer strut slightly to one side or the other to clear. Proceed carefully, and use no force.

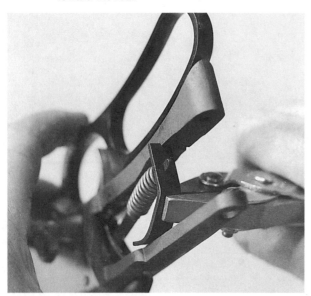

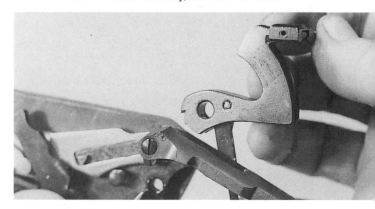

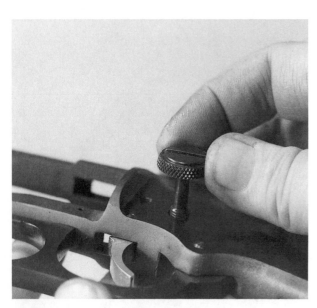

14. Move the takedown screw over until its threads engage the threads in the right side of the receiver, and unscrew it toward the right side for removal.

15. Remove the small screw on the underside of the frame, just forward of the lever, and take out the lever spring from inside the frame.

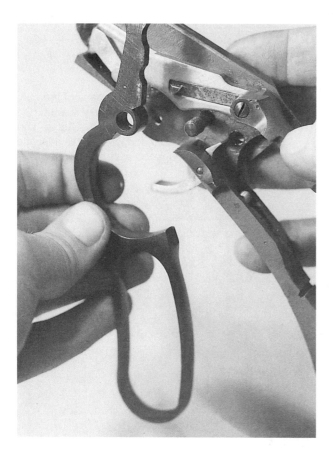

16. Take out the lever pivot screw and remove the lever toward the left.

17. Take out the carrier pivot screw and remove the carrier assembly toward the front. Taking out the carrier rocker screw will allow removal of the rocker and its spring from the carrier.

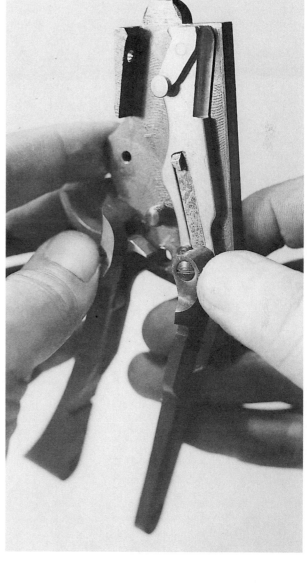

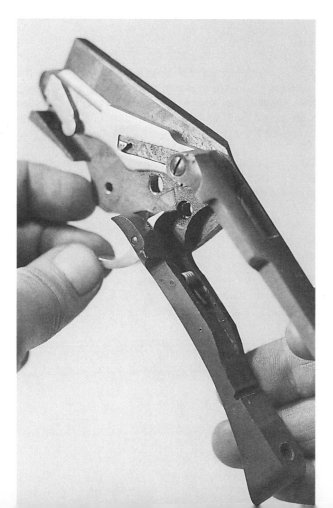

18. Drift out the trigger pin toward the right, and remove the trigger downward. Drift out the trigger spring pin and remove the trigger spring from inside the frame.

Reassembly Tips:

1. When replacing the hammer spring and its base, be sure the hammer is at rest and insert a lower corner of the base into its slot in the lower tang. Then tip the upper part downward and slip it under the upper tang, moving it inward into place.

2. When rejoining the front and rear parts of the gun, be sure the breechblock is all the way forward, the hammer is at full cock or on the safety step, and take care that the front tongue of the sideplate (arrow) is properly engaged with its mating recess in the main frame.

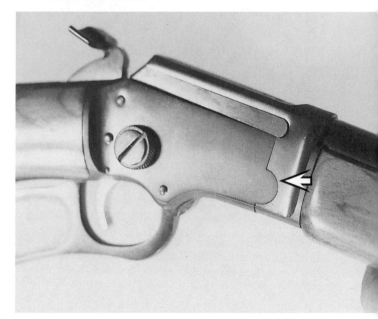

Avoid over-tightening the small screw which holds the cartridge guide spring above the chamber, or the spring may crack. This advice also applies to the cartridge stop screw. Both should be firm and snug, but use no excessive force.

When replacing the extractor in the top of the breechblock, start its rear portion into the recess; then flex the front portion slightly for proper alignment and push it into place.

Marlin Model 57

Similar/Identical Pattern Guns

The same basic assembly/disassembly steps for the Marlin Model 57 also apply to the following guns:

Marlin Model 57M   **Marlin Model 56**

Data:	Marlin Model 57
Origin:	United States
Manufacturer:	Marlin Firearms Company
	North Haven, Connecticut
Cartridge:	22 Short, Long or Long Rifle
Magazine capacity:	27 Short, 21 Long, 19 Long Rifle
Overall length:	42¾ inches
Barrel length:	24 inches
Weight:	6 pounds

In 1955, Marlin introduced a new internal hammer lever-action rifle with an accelerated short-lever movement, the box-magazine Model 56. Three years later, they added the gun covered here, the tube magazine Model 57, and a 22 WMR chambering, the Model 57M. Except for the different feed systems, these three guns are mechanically the same, and the instructions will apply to any of them. The Model 56 and Model 57 were discontinued in 1964 and 1965 respectively, and the Model 57M in 1969.

Disassembly:

1. Remove the inner magazine tube. Back out the large screw on the underside of the stock, forward of the lever plate.

2. Open the lever and remove the larger of the two screws at the rear of the lever plate. Move the action upward and then forward out of the stock.

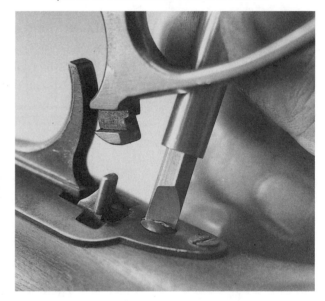

3. Remove the cap screw on the cross-post at the rear of the sub-frame. It may be necessary to use another screwdriver to stabilize the screw-slotted cross-post on the opposite side. After the cap screw is removed, push out the cross-post.

4. Remove the two small screws on each side, at the front of the sub-frame.

5. With the lever opened, remove the sub-frame downward.

6. Drift out the lever link pin, in the lower rear section of the bolt, and remove the bolt upward. If the pin is as originally installed, it should be drifted out toward the right. Take care not to lose the small bolt cam roller, which will be released as the pin is taken out.

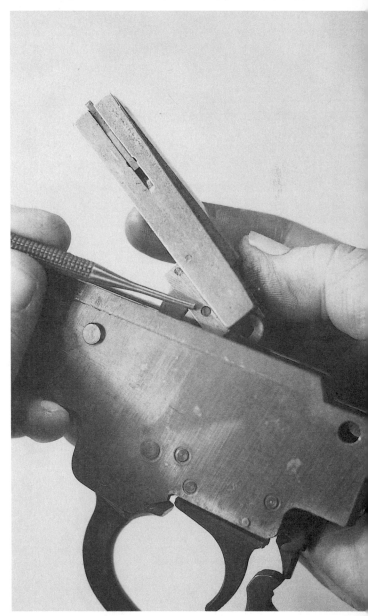

7. Restrain the hammer, pull the trigger and ease the hammer down to fired position. Remove the sideplate screw on the right side of the sub-frame.

8. The sideplate can now be removed toward the right. If the plate is very tight, pry it gently at several points until it is free and carefully lift it off.

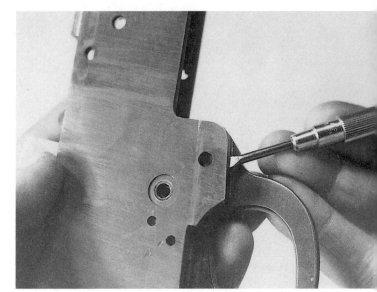

9. Taking care not to disturb the other parts, unhook the upper arm of the carrier spring from the carrier, slowly release its tension, and remove the spring from its post toward the right.

10. Detach the upper arm of the hammer spring from its groove at the back of the hammer and slowly release its tension, allowing it to swing over toward the front and downward. Remove the spring from its post toward the right. **Caution:** *This spring is quite strong, and if it slips can cause injury, so proceed carefully.*

11. Move the safety catch off its two posts and take it off toward the right.

12. Use a small screwdriver to detach the sear spring from the rear of the sear and allow it to swing downward, relieving its tension.

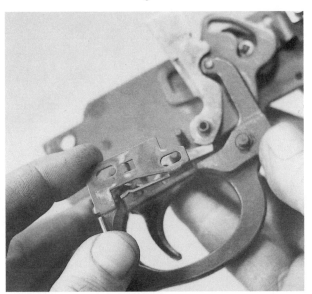

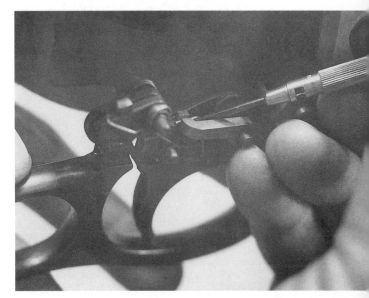

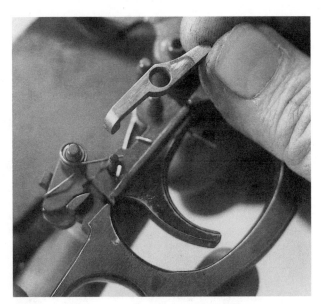

13. Remove the sear toward the right.

14. Remove the hammer toward the right.

15. With the lever opened, use sharp-nosed pliers to remove the front arm of the trigger block spring from the trigger limit pin and remove the spring toward the right.

16. Remove the spacer sleeve and the trigger block toward the right. It will be necessary to push the lever latch slightly upward to free the trigger block.

17. Disengage the lever latch spring from the back of the lever latch and allow the spring arm to swing forward, releasing its tension.

18. Remove the lever latch toward the right.

19. Disengage the trigger spring from the top of the trigger, swing it inward, and allow it to swing downward, releasing its tension. Keep fingertips out of the way!

20. Remove the trigger toward the right. The lever latch spring and the combination sear and trigger spring can now be removed from their posts toward the right.

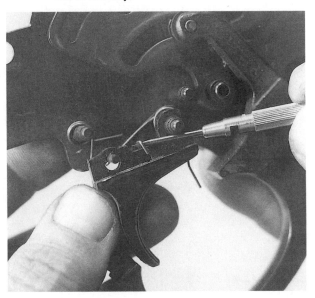

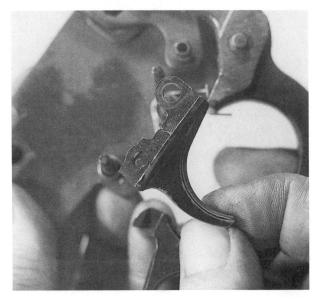

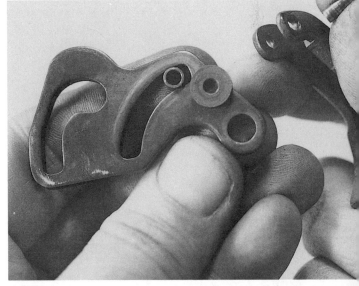

21. Move the lever and lever cam plate off their posts toward the right. The cam plate may be tight and will have to be worked and pried gently off.

22. The lever cam plate can be separated from the lever by drifting out the connecting pin. The cam roller and the washer-like hammer-cocking roller will also be released, so take care that they aren't lost.

23. Remove the C-clip on the inside tip of the carrier pivot and take out the carrier pivot toward the left.

24. Remove the carrier toward the rear.

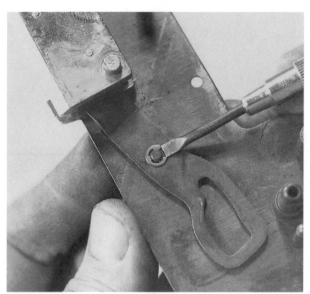

25. Remove the cartridge feed throat toward the right. If necessary, the two sides of the feed throat can be separated.

26. Drifting out the cross pin in the magazine tube hanger loop will allow removal of the magazine tube toward the front.

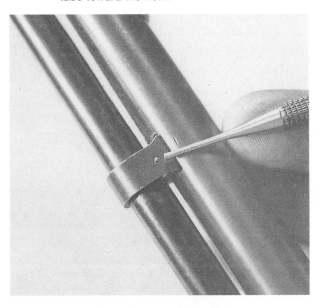

27. The barrel is retained in the receiver by a single cross pin. After removal of the pin, grip the barrel in a padded vise and use a non-marring tool to drive the receiver off toward the rear.

28. The firing pin is retained in the bolt by a small rectangular block, and the block is held in place by two cross pins. Drifting these out will release the block and allow removal of the firing pin toward the rear.

29. The twin extractors are retained by two vertical pins near the front of the bolt. After these are drifted out, the extractors and their coil springs are taken off toward each side.

Reassembly Tips:

1. This photo shows the internal parts of the sub-frame in proper order. The safety is not in place, to allow a view of the other parts.

2. This photo shows the safety catch in place and in the on-safe position. Note that the spring arm at its lower edge goes below the stop pin.

3. When replacing the bolt on the lever cam plate, remember that the bolt cam roller must be put back in its track on the plate, and the pin must pass through.

When replacing the sub-frame on the underside of the receiver, the action must be partially opened.

Marlin Model 80

Similar/Identical Pattern Guns

The same basic assembly/disassembly steps for the Marlin Model 80 also apply to the following guns:

Marlin Model 80C   **Marlin Model 80E**

Marlin Model 80DL   **Marlin Model 80G**

Data:	Marlin Model 80
Origin:	United States
Manufacturer:	Marlin Firearms Company
	North Haven, Connecticut
Cartridge:	22 Long Rifle
Magazine capacity:	8 rounds
Overall length:	43 inches
Barrel length:	24 inches
Weight:	6½ pounds

During my early shooting days I owned a Marlin Model 80, and for many youngsters of that time period who wanted a low-priced bolt action it was the rifle of choice. The gun was offered in several sub-models featuring various options in sights and sling loops. A counterpart tube-magazine rifle, the Model 81, has the same mechanical features, except for the magazine and feed system. The Model 80 was made from 1934 to 1971, when it was replaced in the Marlin line by the Model 780.

Disassembly:

1. Remove the magazine. Open the bolt and hold the trigger to the rear while sliding the bolt out the rear of the receiver. The safety must be in off-safe position, of course.

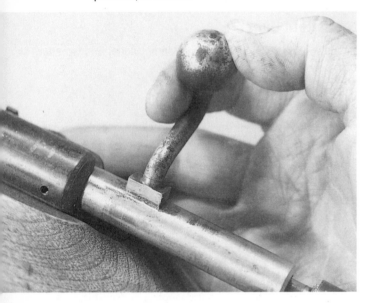

2. Drift out the cross pin in the bolt, just to the rear of the front section.

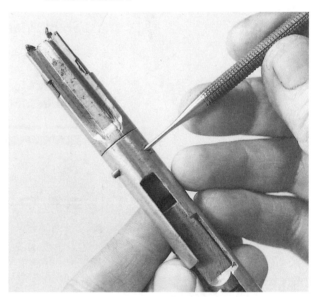

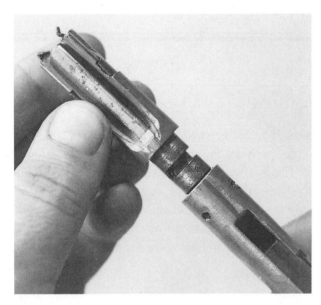

3. Remove the front section of the bolt toward the front.

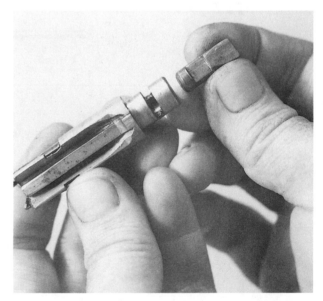

4. Remove the rear firing pin from the front section.

5. Tap the front section to shake out the front firing pin and its return spring, and remove them toward the rear.

6. Insert a very small screwdriver from the front under the left extractor arm, and lever it outward and over toward the right to remove the twin extractor unit. Be sure to lift it only enough to clear, to avoid deformation or breakage.

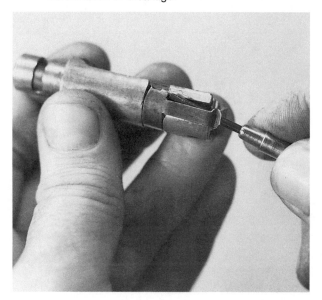

7. Tap the cocking lug pin on the striker knob toward the side, out of its detent notch at the rear of the bolt, to allow the striker to go forward, partially relieving its spring tension. When the striker is forward, it will be in the position shown.

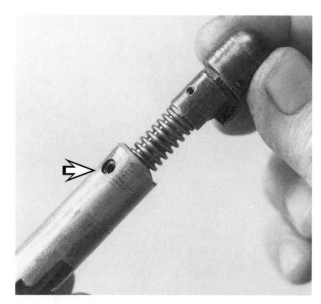

8. Remove the small screw (arrow indicates hole) on the side of the bolt near its rear edge. Remove the striker assembly toward the rear.

9. Grip the forward portion of the striker firmly in a vise, and while keeping pressure on the striker knob, drift out the small cross pin. *Caution: The striker spring is under tension, so control it and release the pressure slowly.* Remove the striker knob, sleeve ring and striker spring toward the rear.

10. Back out the main stock mounting screw, located on the underside at the rear edge of the magazine plate, and separate the action from the stock.

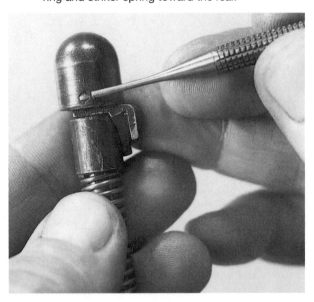

11. The magazine catch hook is retained on the underside of the receiver by a single screw, and is taken off downward.

12. The safety and its positioning spring are retained on the right rear of the receiver by two post screws, and both are removed toward the right.

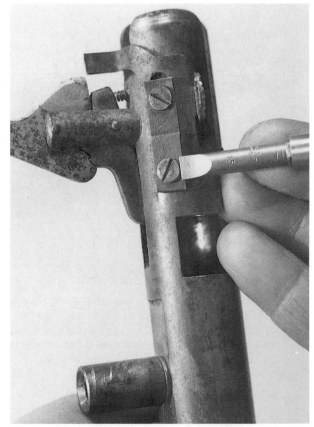

13. The trigger is mounted on a post below the receiver by a cross pin. When the cross pin is drifted out, the trigger and its spring will be released downward. The spring is under some tension, so control the trigger during removal. As the pin is drifted out, be sure the mounting post is well-supported, to avoid deformation or breakage.

14. After the trigger is removed, the sear pin can be drifted out and the sear and its spring removed downward. The same cautions as in the preceding step should be applied.

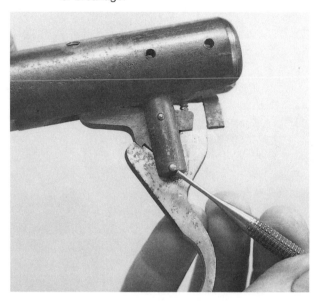

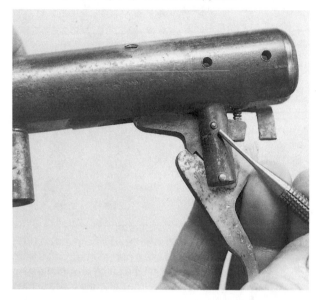

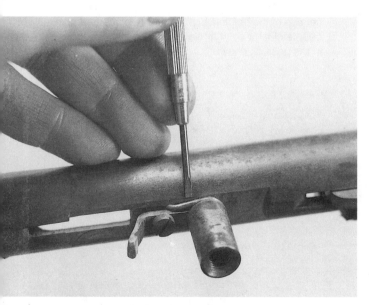

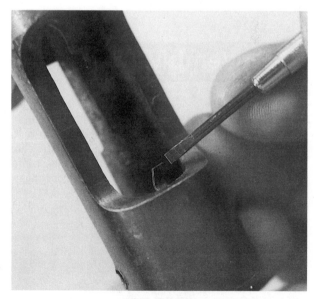

15. The ejector, a part made of round spring-wire, is held in place by the stock screw base, which is threaded into the underside of the receiver. Grip the base firmly with non-marring pliers and unscrew it to release the ejector.

16. Removal of the cartridge guide above the chamber requires removal of the barrel.

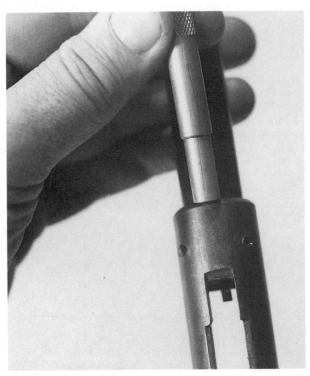

17. A cross pin retains the barrel in the receiver. If the barrel is very tight in the receiver, grip the barrel in a padded vise and use a non-marring drift punch to drive the receiver off the barrel toward the rear. When the barrel is out, the cartridge guide can be lifted from its recess at the top rear of the barrel.

Reassembly Tips:

1. When replacing the striker assembly in the bolt, be sure the threaded hole in the retaining sleeve is aligned with the screw recess in the side of the bolt, and insert a small screwdriver to cam the sleeve into position for insertion of the screw. In this operation, a third hand would be helpful.

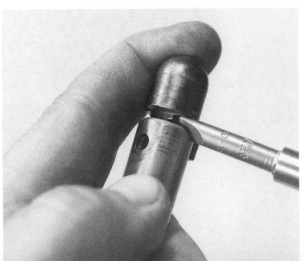

2. When replacing the front section of the bolt, note that the cross-groove in the tail piece and the groove in the rear firing pin must be oriented for passage of the retaining cross pin.

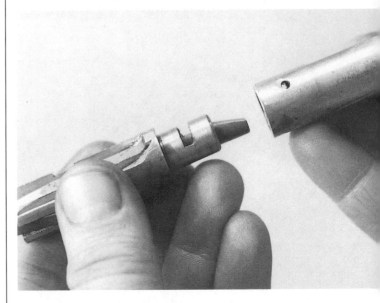

3. Before the reassembled bolt can be reinserted in the receiver, the striker must be recocked. Grip the front section of the bolt in a vise, and turn the bolt handle counterclockwise (rear view) until the cocking lug is in the position shown.

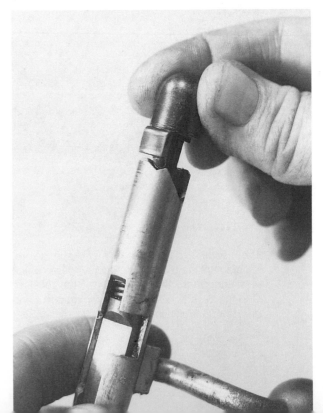

Marlin Model 99M1

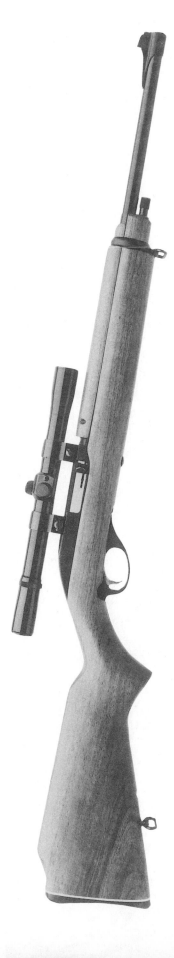

Similar/Identical Pattern Guns

The same basic assembly/disassembly steps for the Marlin Model 99M1 also apply to the following guns:

Marlin Model 99C

Marlin Model 99DL

Marlin Model 99

Marlin Model 99G

Marlin Model 49

Marlin Model 49DL

Marlin Model 60

Marlin Model 989M1

Marlin Model 989M2

Marlin Model 989G

Marlin Model 989MC

Marlin Model 995

Marlin Model 990L

Data:	Marlin Model 99M1
Origin:	United States
Manufacturer:	Marlin Firearms, North Haven, Connecticut
Cartridge:	22 Long Rifle
Magazine capacity:	18 rounds in rifle, 9 in carbine
Overall length:	Rifle-42 inches, Carbine-37 inches
Barrel length:	Rifle-22 inches, Carbine-18 inches
Weight:	Rifle-5½ pounds, Carbine-4½ pounds

The original Model 99 semi-auto was introduced in 1959 and was soon followed by several sub-models—the 99DL, 99C and 99M1, the carbine shown here. The same basic action was later used in the Model 49 and its sub-models, the 989 and the later 990 and 995 rifles. There have been several minor modifications along the way, but the instructions can be applied generally to all of these. The gun was available in both tubular and box magazine types. The gun in the photos is the 99M1 tubular version.

Disassembly:

1. Remove the barrel band retaining screw, located on the right side of the barrel band, and take off the band toward the front. Remove the inner magazine tube.

2. Remove the two screws at the top rear of the handguard and take off the handguard piece.

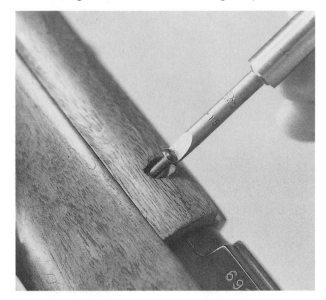

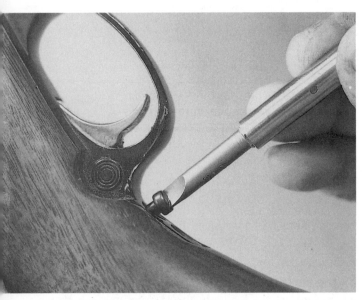

3. Remove the screw on the underside at the rear of the trigger guard the screw nearest the guard. Remove the main stock mounting screw, located on the underside just forward of the trigger guard, and lift the action out of the stock.

4. Removal of the screws at each end of the trigger guard will allow the guard to be taken off downward. The rear screw is a wood screw, and the front screw has a flat internal nut-plate, which may have to be stabilized during removal. The trigger and its spring are retained in the guard unit by a cross pin. Note the position of the spring before removal of the pin, to aid reassembly.

5. Remove the cap screw and screw-slotted post at the rear of the sub-frame, below the receiver. If this assembly is very tight, it may require two opposed screwdrivers to immobilize the post while the screw is taken out.

6. Remove the two opposed screws at the front of the sub-frame below the receiver.

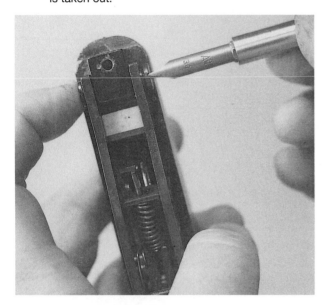

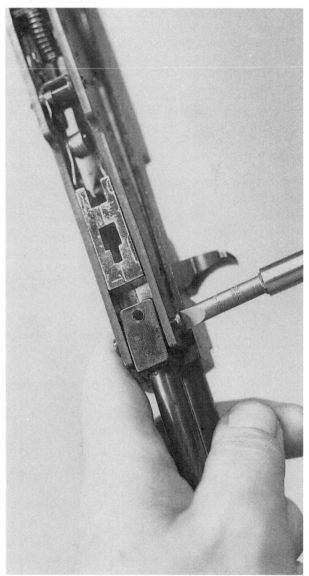

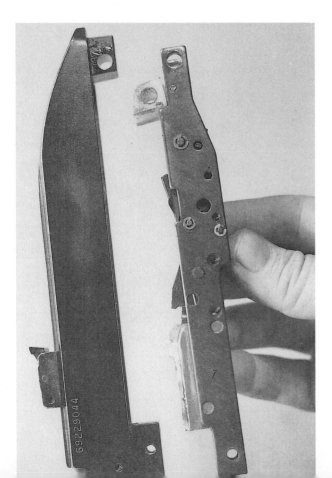

7. Remove the sub-frame downward.

8. Before disassembling the sub-frame, note the relationship of all parts and springs, to aid reassembly. Lower the hammer to the fired position, easing it down. Unhook the right arm of the carrier spring from its resting place on the carrier and ease it downward, relieving its tension. Remove the C-clips from the tips of the hammer/carrier pivot and the sear pivot on the right side only, taking care that the small clips are not lost. Depending on its tightness, it may also be necessary to remove the cross pin at the rear of the sub-frame which retains the recoil buffer. Remove the right sideplate of the sub-frame toward the right. This will allow disassembly of all the internal mechanism parts except the disconnector, which is mounted on the left sideplate on a post retained by a C-clip on the left side.

9. Invert the gun and retract the bolt far enough so that a finger or tool can be inserted in front of it. Lift the front of the bolt away from the inside top of the receiver and remove the bolt handle from the ejection port. Continue to lift the bolt, until its front will clear the underside of the receiver, and take out the bolt, bolt spring and follower. **Caution:** *The spring will be compressed. Control it, and ease its tension slowly.*

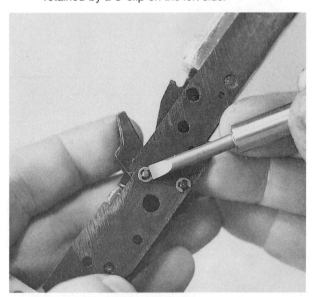

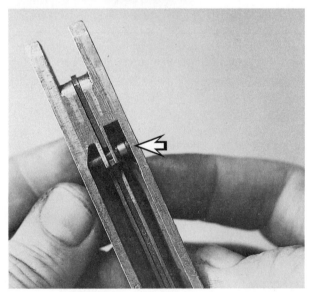

10. The firing pin is retained in the bolt by a cross pin at the lower edge of the bolt. Note that there is also a small roller on the cross pin (arrow), on the right side of the bolt, and take care that this roller isn't lost. When the pin is out, the firing pin can be removed toward the rear.

11. The extractors are retained by vertical pins on each side of the bolt, and these are driven out toward the top. The extractors and their small coil springs are then removed toward each side. **Note:** Keep each spring with its extractor because the springs are not of equal tension. The stronger spring must be put back on the right side.

12. Drifting out the small cross pin in the magazine tube hanger will allow removal of the outer magazine tube toward the front. The hanger can then be driven out of its dovetail cut toward the right. The front sight is retained by a single Allen screw in its top, just to the rear of the sight blade. After the screw is backed out, the sight is removed toward the front. After its large positioning screw on the right side is loosened, the rear sight can be slid off the scope rail in either direction.

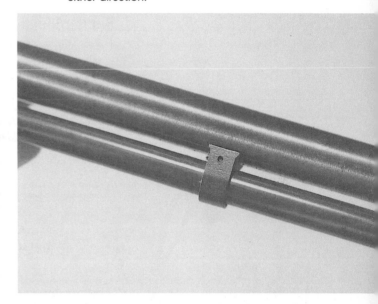

Reassembly Tips:

When replacing the sub-frame in the receiver, be sure the hammer is cocked. There will be some tension from the carrier spring as the sub-frame is pushed into place. Insert the rear screw-post first; then start the two front screws. Do not tighten the screws until all three are in position and started.

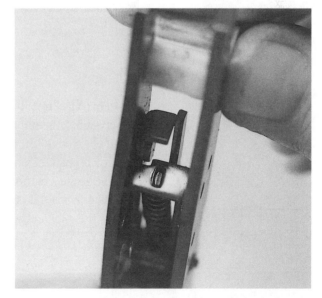

1. When replacing the hammer spring baseplate in the sub-frame, note that there is a notch in one corner of the plate. This must go on the left side at the top, to clear the rear portion of the disconnector.

Marlin Model 782

Similar/Identical Pattern Guns

The same basic assembly/disassembly steps for the Marlin Model 782 also apply to the following guns:

Marlin Model 780   **Marlin Model 783**
Marlin Model 781

Data:	Marlin Model 782
Origin:	United States
Manufacturer:	Marlin Firearms Company
	North Haven, Connecticut
Cartridge:	22 WMR
Magazine capacity:	7 rounds
Overall length:	41 inches
Barrel length:	22 inches
Weight:	6 pounds

The Marlin 780 series is comprised of four guns with identical firing systems, the only difference being in the chamberings and the magazines. The Model 780 and 782 are detachable box magazine guns, chambered for regular 22 and 22 WMR, respectively. The Model 781 and 783 have the same chamberings, with tubular magazine systems. Except for the magazines, takedown and reassembly instructions can be applied to any of the guns in the group. The Model 782 was made from 1971 to 1988.

Disassembly:

1. Remove the magazine. Open the bolt and hold the trigger pulled to the rear while removing the bolt from the rear of the receiver.

2. Turn the end piece counterclockwise (rear view) to drop the striker forward to the fired position. If the end piece can't be turned easily, tap the cam pin out of its engagement with its detent notch at the rear of the bolt.

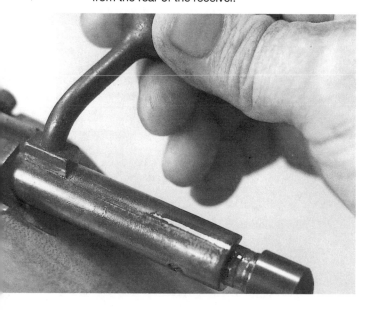

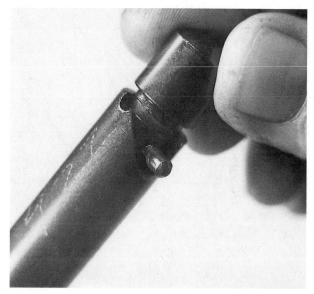

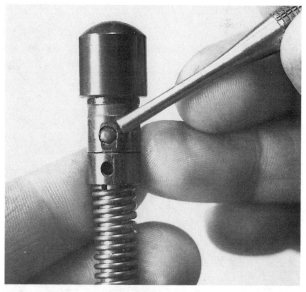

3. Remove the small screw on the side of the bolt near the rear edge. Remove the striker assembly toward the rear.

4. Grip the front of the striker firmly in a vise and drive out the striker cam pin from the knob. **CAUTION:** *Restrain the knob, as the striker sleeve and knob will be forced off when the cam pin is removed. Control them, and ease them off.*

5. Drift out the bolt retaining cross pin.

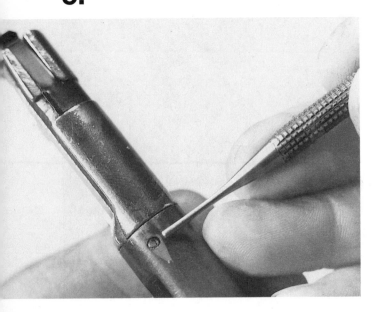

6. Remove the bolt head toward the front.

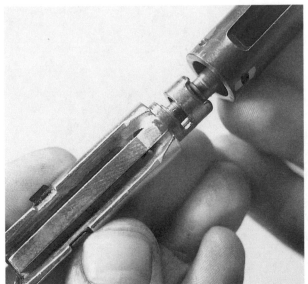

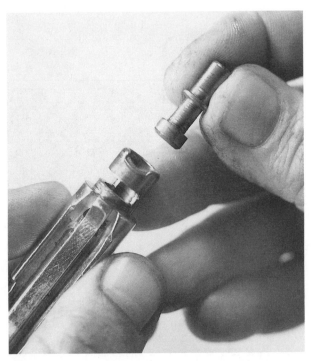

7. Remove the rear firing pin from the bolt head.

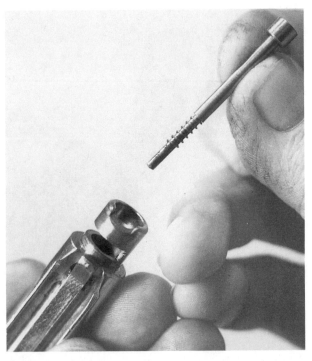

8. Remove the front firing pin and its return spring from the bolt head.

9. Insert a small screwdriver under the left extractor and lift it out of its recess just enough to clear. Turn the screwdriver to lever the extractor clip off the bolt.

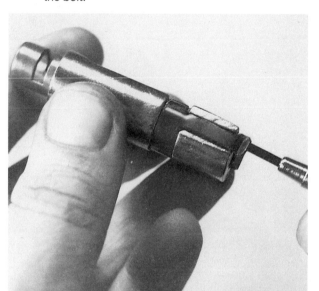

10. Back out the stock mounting bolt, on the underside forward of the magazine plate, and remove the action from the stock. Removal of the small vertical screws at each end of the trigger guard and magazine plate will allow the guard and plate to be taken off downward.

11. Remove the large vertical screw on the underside of the receiver, just to the rear of the magazine guide bar and catch.

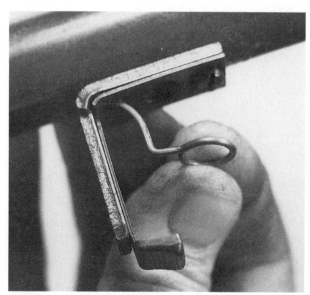

12. Remove the ejector downward and toward the rear.

13. Remove the smaller screw, at the rear of the magazine guide bar and catch base. Remove the guide bar and magazine catch downward. Drift out the trigger cross pin, taking care that the trigger post is well supported.

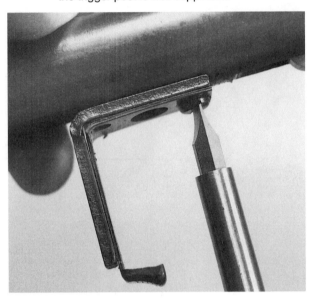

14. Remove the trigger and its spring downward.

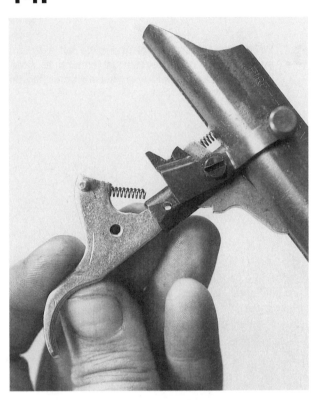

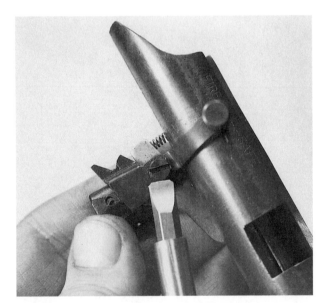

15. Restrain the sear and remove the screw on the right side of the receiver. Remove the safety-lever toward the right.

16. Remove the sear and its spring downward.

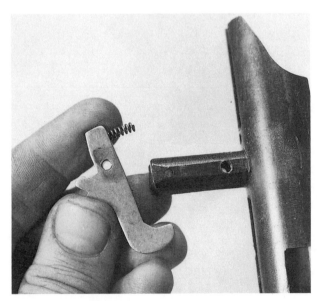

Reassembly Tips:

1. When replacing the bolt head, note that it must be oriented with the retaining cut aligned for insertion of the cross pin. Also, the rear firing pin must be pushed forward as the pin is inserted.

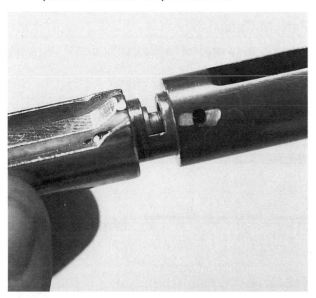

2. When replacing the striker assembly, be sure the screw hole in the striker sleeve is at the top, aligned with the screw recess in the bolt body.

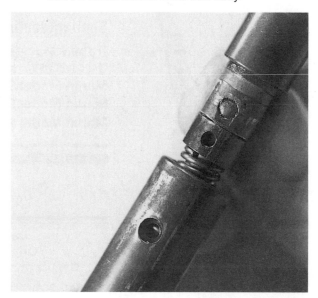

3. The striker must be cocked before the bolt is put back into the receiver. Grip the cam pin with non-marring pliers and turn the bolt clockwise (rear view) until the cam pin engages its notch at the rear of the bolt.

4. Before inserting the bolt, turn the bolt head so its underside aligns with the opening in the bottom of the bolt. Note that there is a guide flange on the left side of the extractor, which must mate with a small groove inside the left wall of the receiver.

Marlin Model 983T

Similar/Identical Pattern Guns

The same basic assembly/disassembly steps for the Marlin Model 983T also apply to the following guns:

Marlin Model 983   **Marlin Model 983S**

Marlin Model 982   **Marlin Model 981**

Marlin Model 980

Data:	Marlin Model 983T
Origin:	United States
Manufacturer:	Marlin Firearms Company, North Haven, Connecticut
Cartridge:	22 Magnum
Magazine capacity:	12 rounds
Overall length:	41 inches
Barrel length:	22 inches
Weight:	6 pounds

The Model 983 series was introduced in 2004, and the original version has a walnut stock. The Model 983T, shown here, has a stock of black fiberglass. There is also a Model 983S, with a stainless steel barrel. The instructions will also apply to several other 98-Series guns, including the 22 Long Rifle versions.

Disassembly:

1. Remove the inner magazine tube. Hold the trigger to the rear, open the bolt, and take out the bolt rearward. Remove the large screw on the underside of the stock. (Note: On the box-magazine versions, it will be necessary to also remove the front trigger guard screw.)

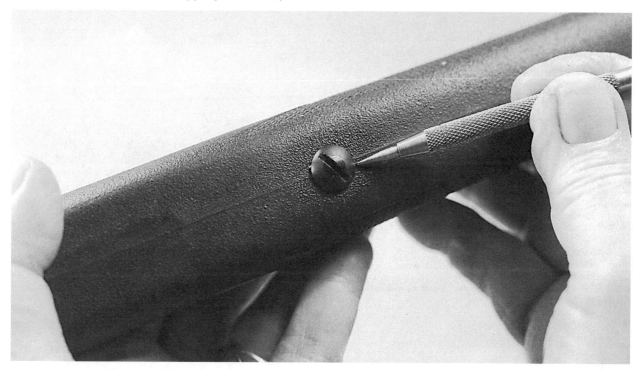

2. Remove the action from the stock.

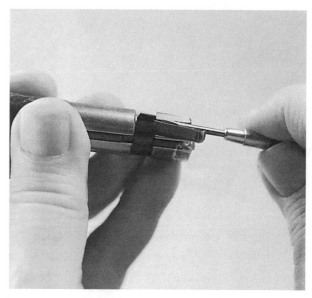

3. If extractor removal is necessary for repair, insert a small screwdriver under the left-side secondary extractor arm and turn the tool to lift the arm out of its recess, as shown.

4. Again, if necessary for repair, the firing pin can now be lifted out of its recess in the bolt. Or, the bolt head may be turned to its exit slot and taken off, which will also free the firing pin return spring for removal.

5. Use a non-marring tool to nudge the striker cam pin out of its detent, allowing the striker to go forward to the fired position.

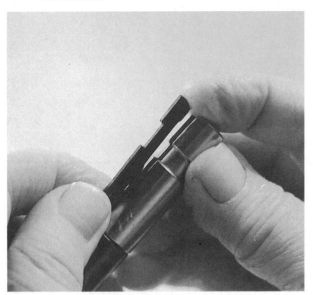

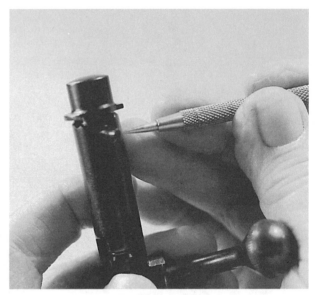

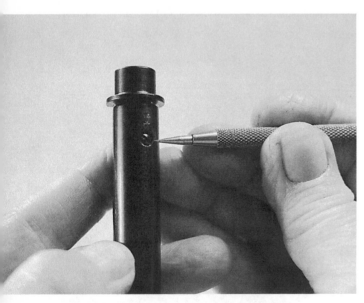

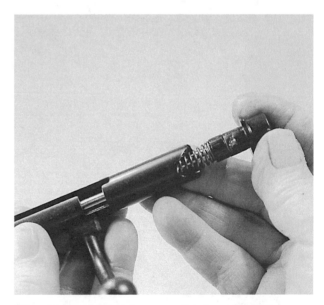

6. Remove the small screw on the side of the bolt body at the rear.

7. Remove the striker assembly from the bolt.

8. Remove the firing pin return spring.

9. Turn the bolt head to its exit point, and remove it from the bolt body. As noted, this can be done earlier, depending on the nature of the repair.

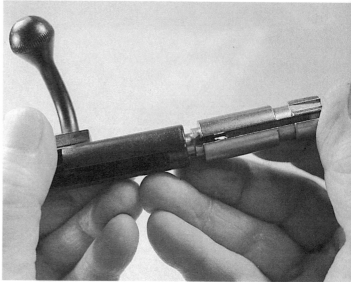

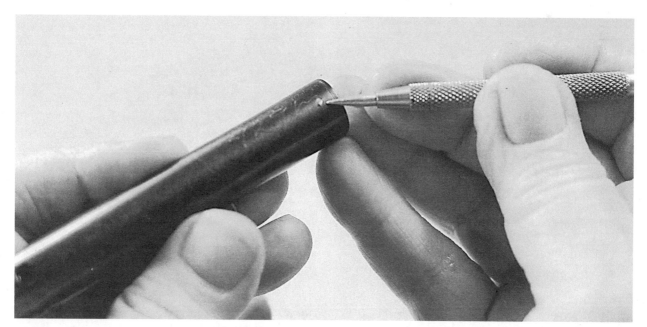

10. If necessary for repair, the bolt head retaining pin can be drifted inward for removal. In normal takedown, it is left in place.

11. The striker assembly can be taken apart by holding the shaft in a vise and drifting out this pin. **CAUTION:** *The strong striker spring will be released.*

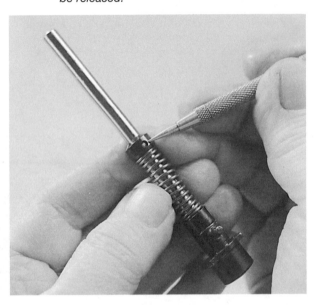

12. Restrain the carrier and its spring, and drift out the carrier pin toward the left.

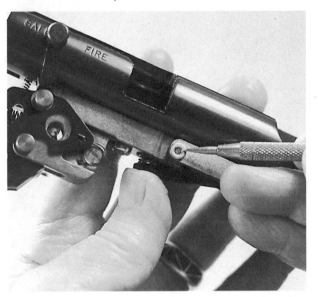

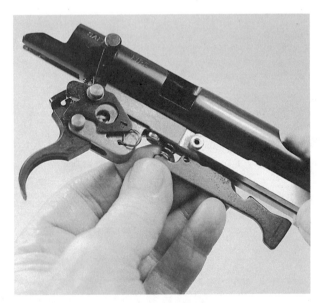

13. Remove the carrier (cartridge lifter) and its spring.

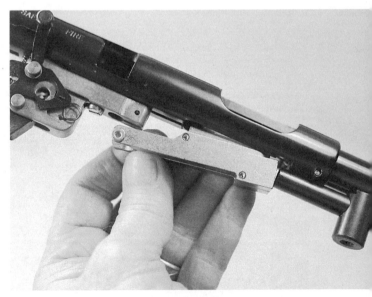

14. Move the cartridge guide slightly rearward, and remove it.

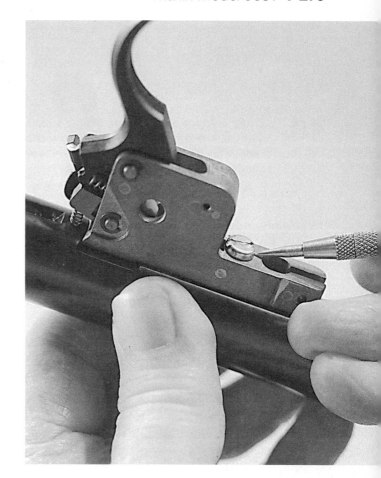

15. Remove the trigger group retaining screw.

16. Remove the trigger group downward. The sear spring will be freed, so take care that it is not lost.

17. If the sear spring is still in place, remove it.

18. Set the safety lever in on-safe (rear) position, and lift out the lower tip of its positioning spring to relieve the tension. The spring is not removed at this time.

19. Use a small screwdriver to remove the C-clip from the end of the safety cross pin. Be especially careful that the small C-clip is not lost.

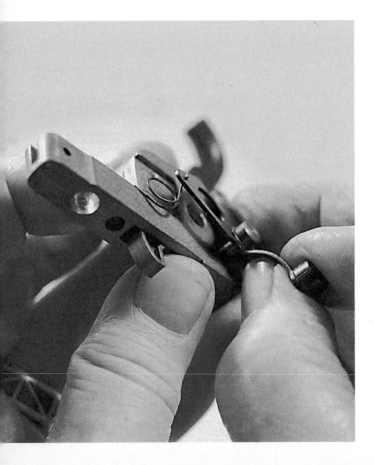

20. Remove the safety lever assembly toward the right. Note that there is a spring-washer under the head of the safety shaft. The positioning spring is easily turned and detached at this time.

21. Detach the trigger spring from its projection on the trigger, and remove it toward the rear.

22. Remove the C-clip from the trigger cross pin.

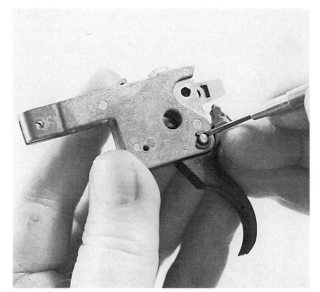

23. Remove the trigger cross pin.

24. Remove the trigger. The sear is also now freed for removal.

25. The outer magazine tube is retained by a cross pin in its hanger, and the tube is taken out toward the front. In normal takedown, it is best left in place. The hanger, the rear sight, and the takedown screw base are all dovetail-mounted, and can be drifted out toward the right.

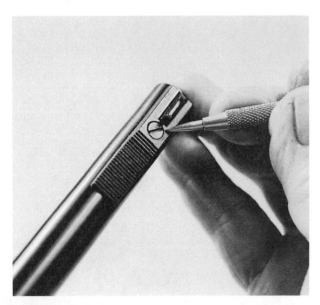

26. The front sight is retained by a vertical screw.

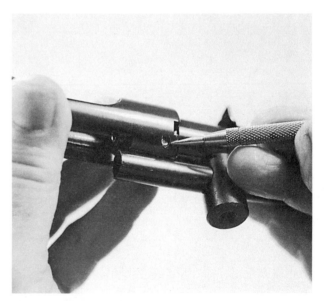

27. The barrel is retained by a cross pin. It is not removed in normal takedown.

Reassembly Tips:

1. When reinstalling the safety, remember that the detent spring must be re-hooked into the lever before it is pushed into place.

2. The firing pin and its return spring are more easily installed before the bolt head is put back into the bolt body.

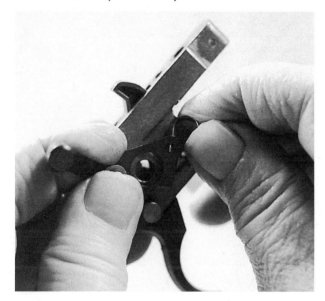

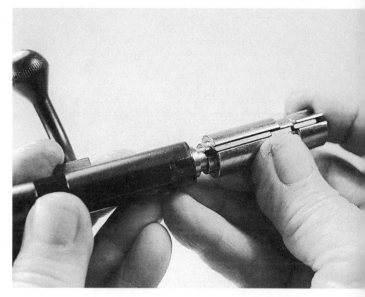

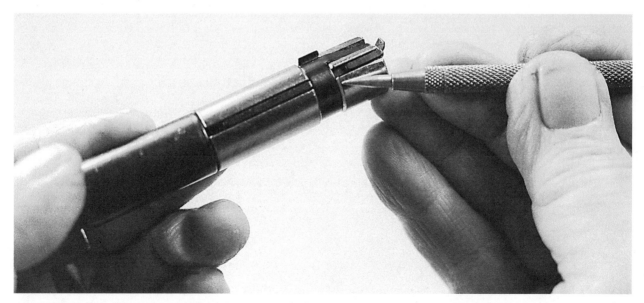

3. When re-installing the extractor unit, have the striker assembly in fired position. This will keep the firing pin forward, so its recess will align with the extractor band.

4. Before the bolt is put back into the receiver, the striker must be in cocked position. A padded vise and a turn of the bolt will do this easily.

5. When reinstalling the cartridge guide, carrier and spring, insert a drift, as shown, to align the parts for reinsertion of the cross pin.

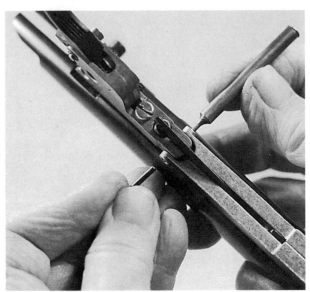

Mitchell AK-22

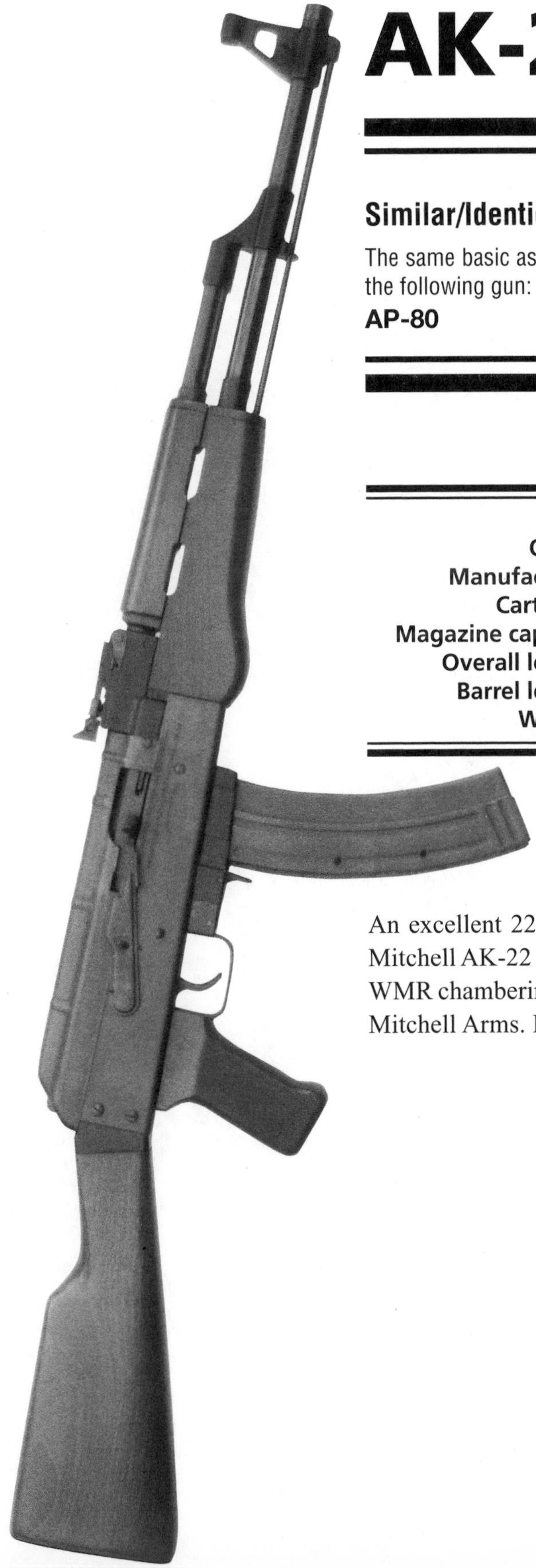

Similar/Identical Pattern Guns

The same basic assembly/disassembly steps for the Mitchell AK-22 also apply to the following gun:

AP-80

Data:	Mitchell AK-22
Origin:	Italy
Manufacturer:	Armi Jager, Turin
Cartridge:	22 Long Rifle
Magazine capacity:	20 rounds
Overall length:	36 inches
Barrel length:	18 inches
Weight:	6½ pounds

An excellent 22 rimfire copy of the famed Russian AK-47 carbine, the Mitchell AK-22 was introduced in 1985. In 1988, it was also offered in 22 WMR chambering. The AK-22 designation was used by the U.S. importer, Mitchell Arms. In Europe, Armi Jager calls it the AP-80.

Disassembly:

1. Remove the magazine and cycle the action to cock the internal hammer. Depress the button at the rear of the receiver, and lift the receiver cover at the rear.

2. Remove the receiver cover, upward and toward the rear.

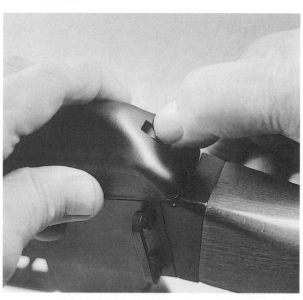

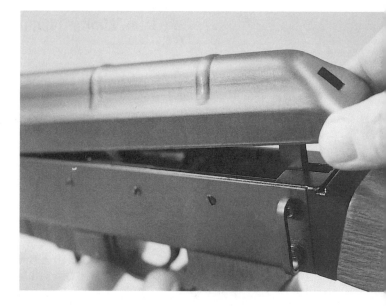

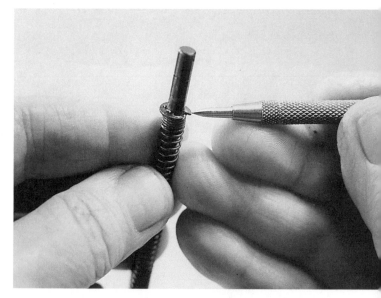

3. Move the recoil spring end piece forward to disengage it from the spring base, and move it to the side. **Caution:** *Keep the spring system under control.* Ease the tension slowly, and remove the spring assembly toward the rear.

4. If removal of the spring from the guide is necessary, pull the spring away from the C-clip and remove the C-clip from the rod. **Caution:** *Control the spring.*

5. Tip the recoil spring base forward, and remove it upward.

6. Move the bolt all the way to the rear, and lift it off upward.

7. Restrain the firing pin, and drift out the roll-type cross pin at the rear of the bolt. The pin does not have to be removed, just drifted far enough to free the firing pin.

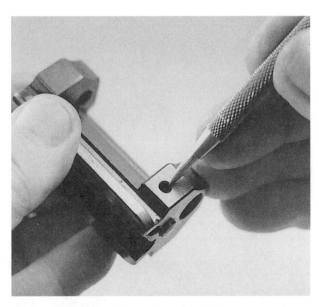

8. Remove the firing pin and its return spring.

9. Insert a small tool to push the extractor plunger toward the rear, and lift out the extractor. **Caution:** *Control the plunger and spring.*

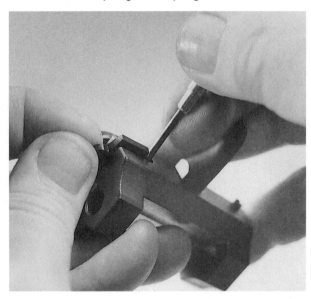

10. Ease the spring tension slowly, and remove the plunger and spring toward the front.

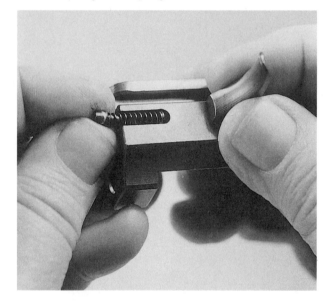

11. Rap the front of the bolt on a non-marring surface to move the retaining plunger forward, and take off the bolt handle toward the right. **Note:** The plunger may come out when the bolt is jarred, so take care that it isn't lost.

12. If the retaining plunger didn't exit in the previous step, use a small tool to nudge it forward for removal from the extractor spring tunnel.

13. To remove the cleaning rod, push it toward the rear, tip it outward, and take it out toward the front. There is a muzzle cap with wrench flats that can be unscrewed, and the front sight base is retained by a roll cross pin and an Allen screw in its underside.

14. If the buttstock needs to be removed, it is retained internally by a large Allen-type screw that requires a long-shanked tool that will hold an Allen bit. For access to this, remove the single Phillips screw at the rear, and take off the buttplate. Disassembly of the action, however, does not require removal of the buttstock.

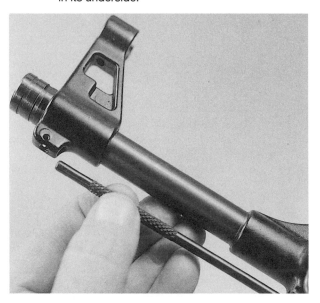

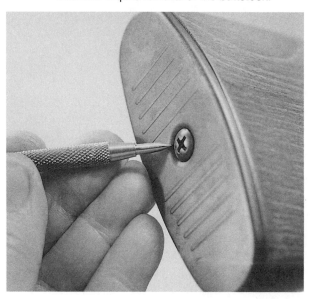

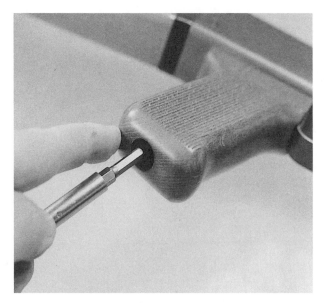

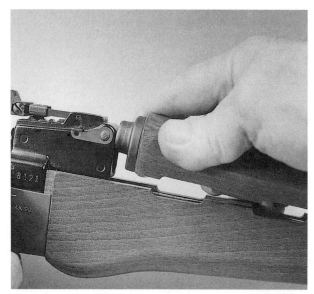

15. Use an Allen bit to remove the screw and washer that retain the handgrip, and take it off downward.

16. Push the upper handguard forward, against the tension of its spring, and tip it upward at the rear for removal.

17. The upper handguard spring is removable by turning it and pulling it out toward the rear. The handguard base can be taken off forward by removing the Allen screw in the sling loop.

18. Restrain the hammer, pull the trigger, and ease the hammer down to fired position. Drift out the trigger guard cross pin toward the left, and take off the trigger guard downward.

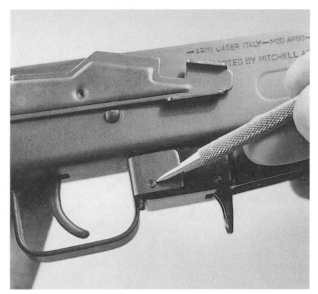

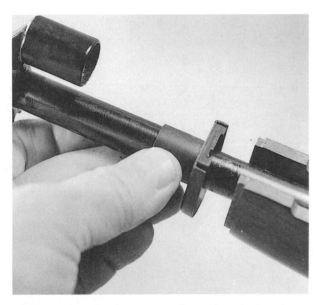

19. Move the forearm cap forward on the barrel.

20. Move the forearm forward, and take it off downward.

21. Remove the screws on each side at the front of the receiver cover.

22. Remove the three screws on the left side of the receiver cover.

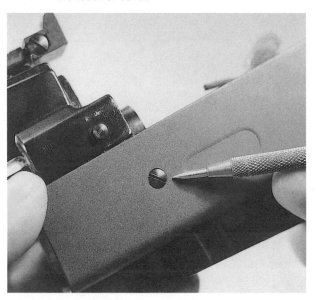

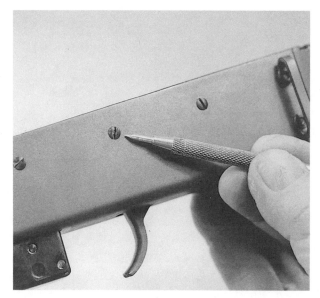

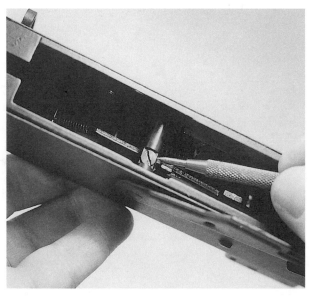

23. Remove the post screw in the safety cross-shaft.

24. Remove the C-clip from the safety cross-shaft, inside the receiver on the right side. **Caution:** *Control the C-clip as it is taken off.* Exert inward pressure on the base of the safety-lever as the C-clip is taken off.

25. Remove the safety-lever toward the right.

26. Remove the two screws on the right side at the rear of the receiver cover. Removal of the screws will release the sling loop on the left side.

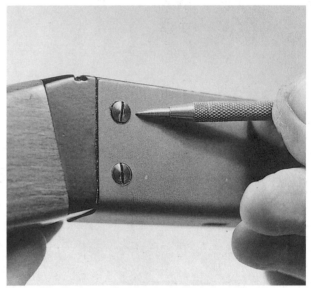

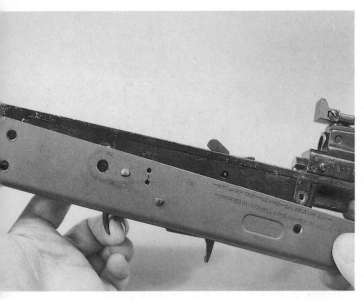

27. Remove the receiver cover downward. The cover will usually be tight, and it may require nudging with a nylon drift to start it. Pull the trigger to clear as the cover is moved downward.

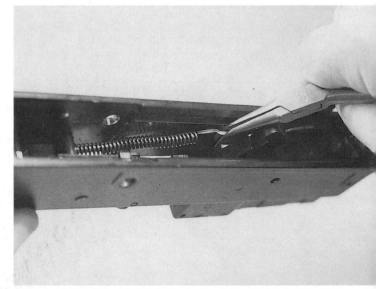

28. Use pliers to grip the hammer spring strut, and carefully disengage it from its recess in the back of the hammer. Tip it upward at the front for removal. **Caution:** *Control the strut and spring.*

29. Push out the hammer cross pin.

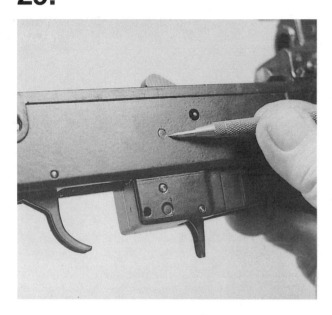

30. Remove the hammer upward.

31. Remove the hammer spring base pin.

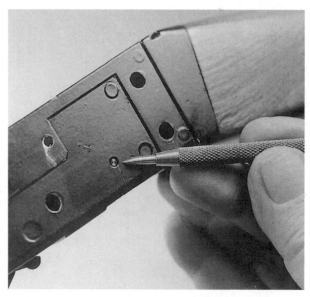

32. Remove the trigger spring cross pin.

33. Push out the trigger cross pin.

34. Remove the trigger assembly upward, moving it slightly rearward to clear it from the sear. The cross pin can be removed to separate the trigger bar from the trigger, and the spring is easily detached from the rear tip of the bar.

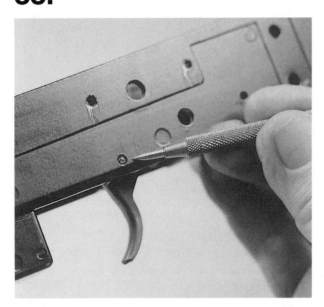

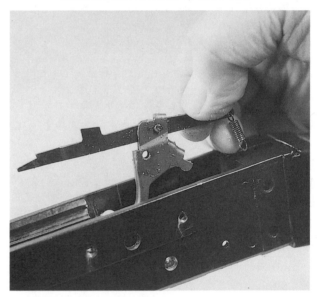

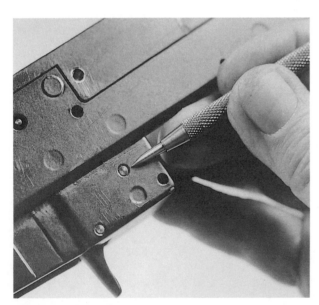

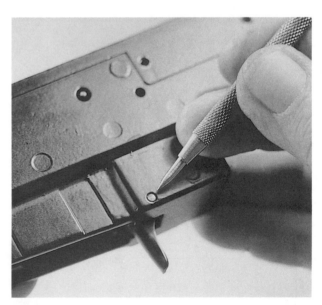

35. Drifting out this cross pin will allow removal of the sear and sear spring. Control the spring as the drift is taken out.

36. Drifting out this cross pin will free the magazine catch and its spring. Control the spring during removal.

37. The ejector and its spring are retained by a cross pin, and these parts are taken out upward.

38. If all parts have been taken off the barrel, and all parts removed from the receiver, removal of this Allen screw will allow the barrel to be driven out of the receiver toward the rear. In normal takedown, it is best left in place. The cleaning rod spring, visible at the front of the receiver, can be taken out of its well if necessary.

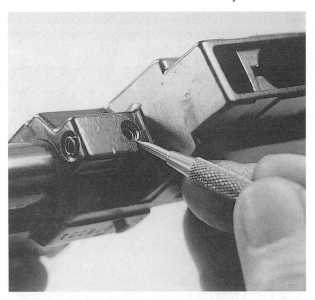

Reassembly Tips:

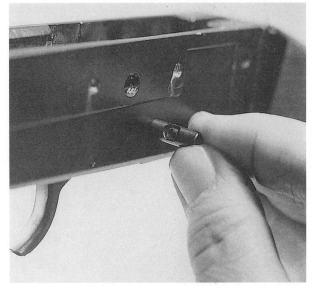

1. When installing the hammer spring base pin, be sure the recess in the pin is oriented toward the front, to accept the rear tip of the spring.

39. The rear sight is retained by a roll-type cross pin. The latch at the front of the sight base is a cosmetic part. If it needs to be removed, the C-clip on the left side is taken off, and the latch is removed toward the right.

2. As the cross pins are replaced, be sure their ends are level with the side of the receiver, to avoid difficulty in replacing the cover.

3. As the cover is pushed back onto the receiver, hook the toe of the trigger in its opening, and depress the trigger as the cover is seated.

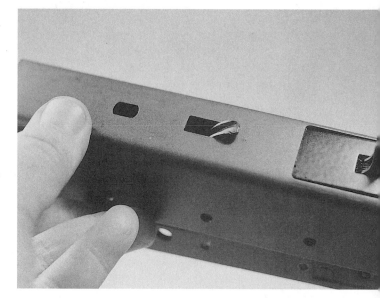

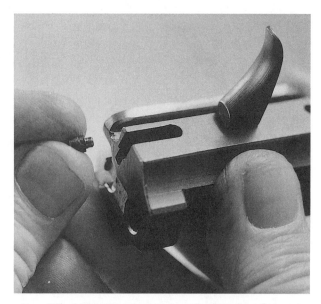

4. When installing the bolt handle retaining plunger, be sure its smaller tip is toward the rear, as shown.

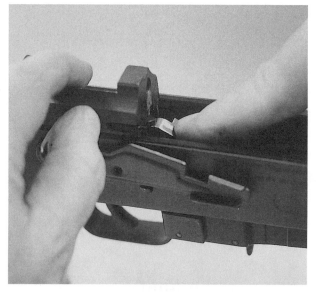

5. As the bolt is pushed back toward the front, it will be necessary to depress the hammer for clearance.

Mossberg Blaze

Data: Mossberg Blaze
Origin: United States
Manufacturer: Mossberg, New Haven, CT
Cartridge: .22 Long Rifle
Magazine capacity: 26 rounds
Overall length: 35.75 inches
Barrel length: 16.5 inches
Weight: 3.5 pounds

The Blaze is a development by Mossberg to produce a rugged, low weight, inexpensive .22 rifle. Several variants exist in different minor configuration patterns and finishes but they are functionally the same. An AK variant called the Blaze-47 is also made but the "shell" is completely different, even though the internals are largely the same. This model wears a Kryptek camouflage pattern and comes with a 26-round magazine, while others are shipped with an 11-round magazine.

Disassembly:

1. There are 16 small phillips head screws on the left side that hold the stock shell halves together. Remove these screws (picture A) and then lift the left shell from the action and right shell (picture B). The sling swivels should be removed at this time as well.

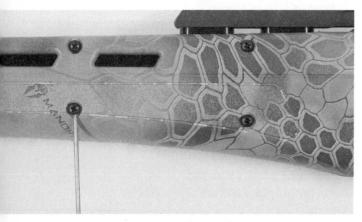

picture A

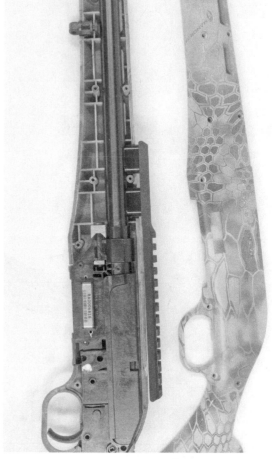

picture B

2. Remove the action from the right side shell.

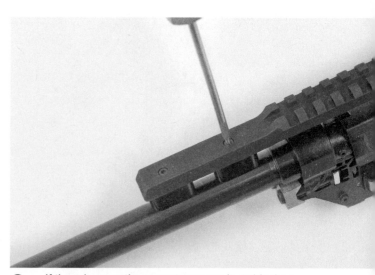

3. If there is an optics mount, remove it at this time.

4. Lift up on the rear of the bolt cover and lift the assembly off the receiver. The charging handle may then fall out to the right. The bolt assembly is easily removed from the cover, as is the recoil spring assembly.

5. Tap out this pin from bottom to top to remove the extractor and spring from the bolt.

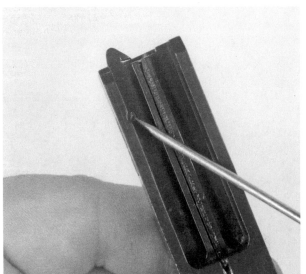

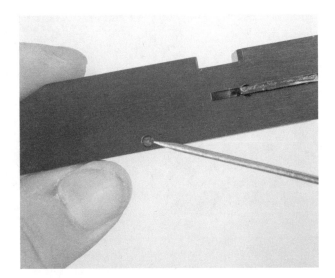

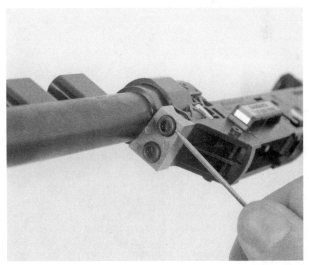

6. Drive out this pin from left to right to remove the firing pin.

7. Remove these bolts and the clamp beneath them to separate the barrel from the receiver. The square nuts that retain the bolts should not be lost.

8. Push out this pin to free the magazine catch and spring.

9. There are five exposed Phillips screws that hold the fire control wall onto the receiver. Remove them. There are two concealed screws beneath some white goop. Remove those too.

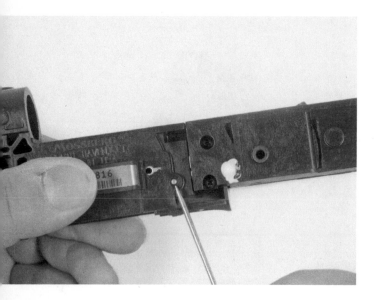

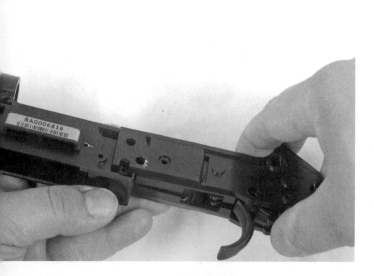

picture A

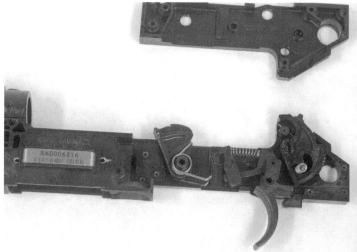

picture B

10. Carefully remove the left receiver wall (picture A). This is a picture of the wall removed but with the parts in place in the receiver right wall (picture B).

11. Remove the hammer and spring.

12. Remove the safety and spring.

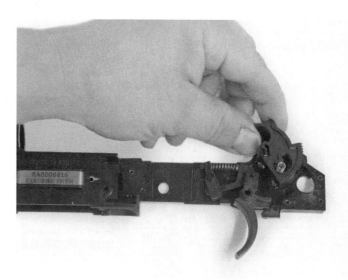

13. Remove the trigger/sear assembly and spring, and the sear pivot pin. It is simpler to remove the spring first. The trigger and connector arm should not be disassembled unnecessarily.

Reassembly Tips:

1. A slave pin will be most helpful when reinstalling the magazine catch. A 3/32" x 1/2" roll pin works well for this step. Note that the curved end of the spring bears against the receiver.

Mossberg Model 44US

Similar/Identical Pattern Guns

The same basic assembly/disassembly steps for the Mossberg Model 44US also apply to the following guns:

Mossberg Model 44   **Mossberg Model 44B**

Data:	Mossberg Model 44US
Origin:	United States
Manufacturer:	O.F. Mossberg & Sons, Inc.
	North Haven, Connecticut
Cartridge:	22 Long Rifle
Magazine capacity:	7 rounds
Overall length:	42½ inches
Barrel length:	26 inches
Weight:	7½ pounds

A slight redesign of the earlier Model 44B, the 44US was primarily used for military marksmanship training during World War II. The one shown in the photos is marked "U.S. Property." Aside from its plain, military-style stock, it is similar to the other Mossberg bolt-action 22 rifles of this time period, and the instructions can be applied generally to most of these. The knowledgeable shooter can see which of our instruction steps apply to his gun. There are many variations of Mossberg mechanisms.

Disassembly:

1. Remove the magazine. Open the bolt, hold the trigger to the rear, and withdraw the bolt from the rear of the receiver. The aperture sight can be pivoted around to the side for clearance.

2. Turn the bolt handle clockwise (rear view) to allow the striker to move forward to the fired position.

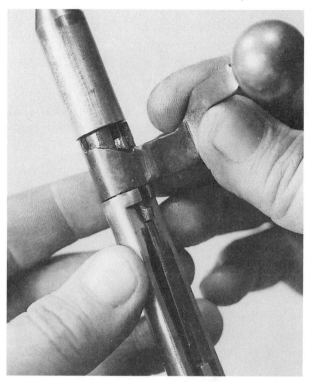

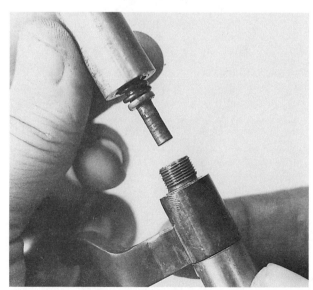

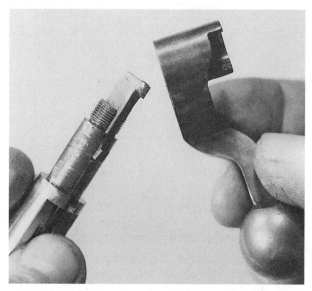

3. Grip the bolt and the rear domed end piece firmly and unscrew the end piece from the rear of the bolt. **Caution:** *The striker spring is under some tension, so keep the end piece under control.* After it is removed, the spring and guide are easily taken out.

4. Move the bolt handle sleeve toward the rear, the striker moving with it. When the sleeve has enough clearance, remove it toward the rear.

5. Remove the striker/firing pin unit from the bolt.

6. The twin extractors can be removed by inserting the tip of a small screwdriver between each extractor and its plunger, pushing the plunger toward the rear, and lifting the extractor out of its recess. **Caution:** *Take care the screwdriver doesn't slip during this operation, and ease the plungers and springs out for removal.*

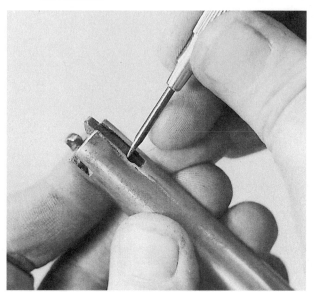

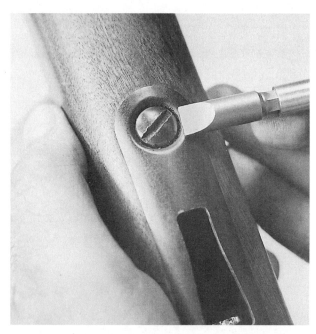

7. The rear sight is removable by taking out the two large screws on the left side, at the rear of the receiver. Further disassembly of the sight is not recommended.

8. Loosen the front sling loop screw and back out the sling loop. The rebated screw shaft will keep the unit on the stock. Back out the main stock mounting screw, located in the forward portion of the magazine plate on the underside, and separate the action from the stock. The barrel band can be taken off only after the front sight is drifted out of its dovetail.

9. Remove the screw at the front of the trigger bracket, on the underside of the receiver. Remove the screw at the rear of the trigger bracket. This screw also is the pivot for the safety-lever.

10. Remove the trigger bracket downward. The safety-lever is easily detached from the rear of the trigger bracket.

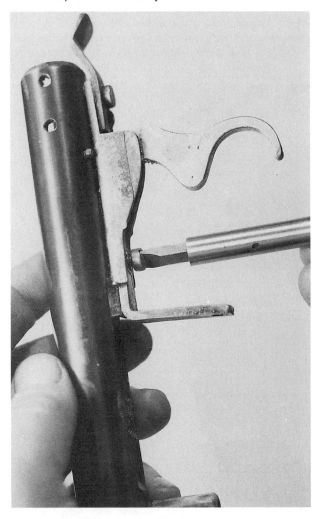

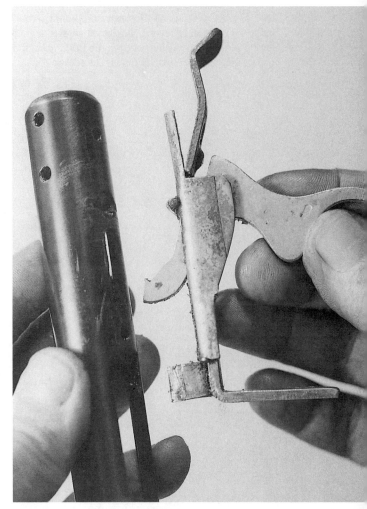

11. The trigger can now be moved forward, and then up out of its slot in the bracket. The cross pin at the top and the spring and plunger at the upper rear are easily detached from the trigger.

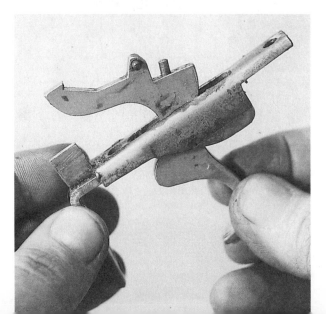

Reassembly Tips:

1. When replacing the trigger and safety system on the underside of the receiver, be sure the cross pin at the top of the trigger is positioned in its groove on the receiver, and install the front screw first. When inserting the safety-lever, use a small screwdriver to lift the trigger spring plunger onto the front tab of the safety-lever before installing the rear screw.

2. When replacing the action in the stock, the barrel ring, or band, must be oriented so its screw hole is at the bottom and aligned with the front sling loop screw.

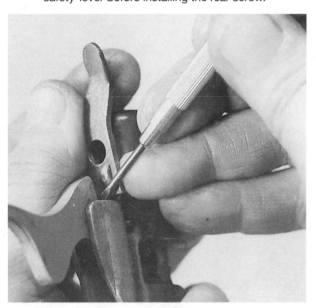

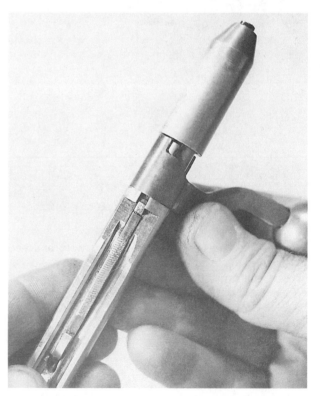

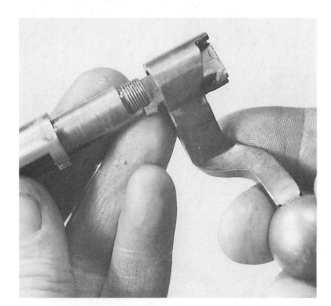

3. When replacing the striker and the bolt handle sleeve, note that the sleeve must be fitted onto the rear of the striker before the striker is fully inserted into the bolt.

4. Before the bolt is reinserted into the receiver, it must be recocked by firmly gripping the forward portion of the bolt and turning the bolt handle counterclockwise (rear view) until the striker lug is brought back to the cocked position, as shown.

Mossberg Model 151M

Similar/Identical Pattern Guns

The same basic assembly/disassembly steps for the Mossberg Model 151M also apply to the following gun:

Mossberg Model 151K

Data:	Mossberg Model 151M
Origin:	United States
Manufacturer:	O.F. Mossberg & Sons
	North Haven, Connecticut
Cartridge:	22 Long Rifle
Magazine capacity:	15 rounds
Overall length:	40 inches
Barrel length:	20 inches
Weight:	7 pounds

With its separate front stock piece giving it a full "Mannlicher" look, the old Model 151M is instantly recognizable, especially to a certain generation of shooters who began using it in the year after World War II. Mechanically, the 151M is similar to the other Mossberg 22 semi-autos, and the takedown instructions can generally be used for several of those, as well. The knowledgeable shooter can see which of our instruction steps apply to his gun. There are many Mossberg mechanisms. The firing mechanism is relatively simple, but there are a few points in total disassembly and reassembly where the amateur could get into difficulty.

Disassembly:

1. Back out the screw on the underside of the front section of the stock, near the muzzle. The screw has a rebated shaft and will stay in the stock piece when it has cleared its threads in the barrel. Remove either of the two screws on the underside of the connector between the front section and the main stock, as shown, and remove the front section forward. The connector band will remain attached to either the stock or the front section, depending on which screw is removed. The upper sling swivel is normally on the band, but on the gun shown it is missing.

2. Back out the main stock mounting screw, on the underside of the stock, forward of the trigger guard, and separate the action from the stock.

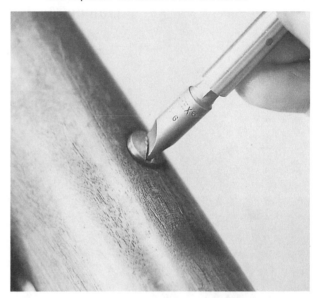

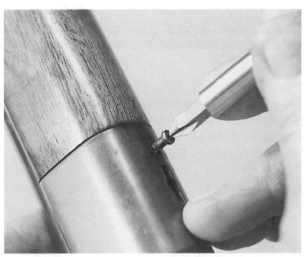

3. Being sure the striker is in fired position, unscrew the receiver end cap and remove it toward the rear.

4. Move the bolt toward the rear until the bolt handle aligns with the larger opening at the rear of its slot in the receiver, and remove the bolt handle toward the right.

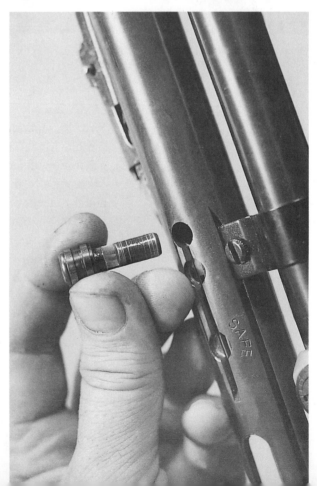

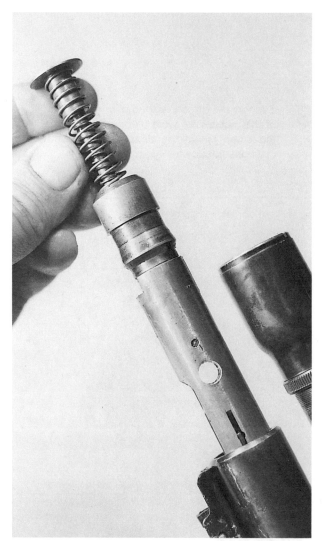

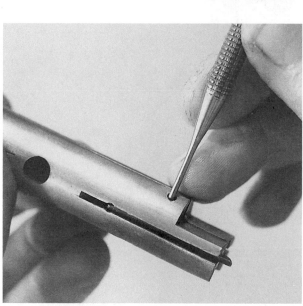

5. Remove the bolt assembly from the rear of the receiver.

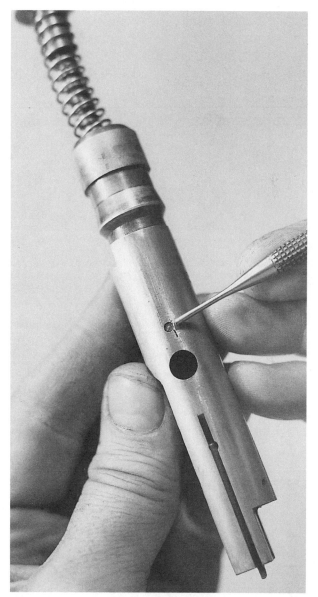

6. Drifting out the cross pin in the bolt, just to the rear of the bolt handle hole, will release the striker and its spring, and the bolt spring and its guide, toward the rear. **Caution:** *Both of these springs are under tension, and this entire assembly will be instantly released when the drift pushing out the cross pin is withdrawn.* Retard the springs and let the tension off slowly.

7. The extractor is retained by a vertical pin on the right side of the bolt near the front. After the pin is drifted out, the extractor and its coil spring are taken off toward the right.

8. The firing pin is retained in the top of the bolt by stake depressions (arrows) in the bolt above a notch near the rear of the firing pin. The stakes are usually not severe, and the firing pin can normally be driven out toward the front, swaging the stake marks as it passes them.

9. Support the disconnector mount on the underside of the receiver to avoid deformation, and drift out the cross pin in the disconnector. Remove the disconnector downward.

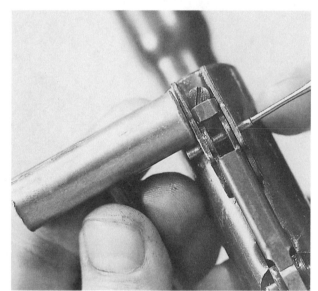

10. Take out the two screws in the disconnector mount. Remove the front screw first and take off the combination sear and disconnector spring. When both screws are removed take off the disconnector mount downward.

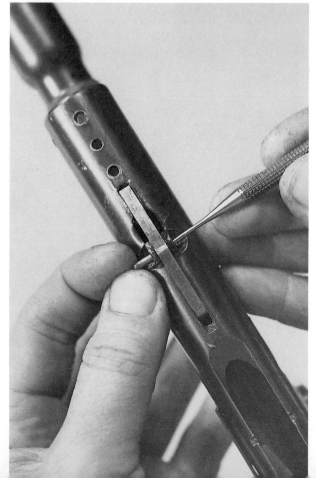

11. Push out the sear cross pin and remove the sear from the bottom of the receiver.

12. To remove the ejector, carefully pry its rear tail out of the vertical recess on the outside left of the receiver, and move the ejector forward; then remove it toward the left.

13. Remove the inner magazine tube. Take out the outer magazine tube retaining spring by removing its screw, located inside the stock well forward of the end of the magazine tube.

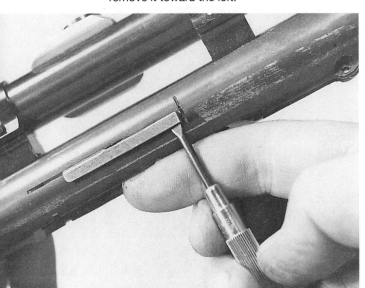

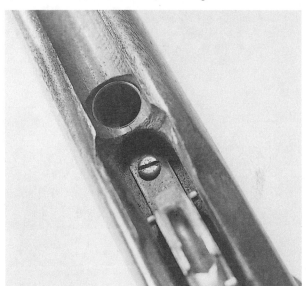

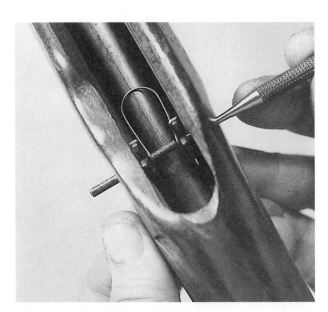

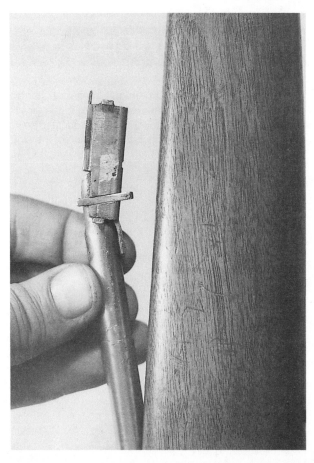

14. Push out the trigger pivot pin, which crosses the stock above the magazine tube, and remove the trigger spring upward.

15. The outer magazine tube assembly can now be moved up and forward, out of the stock, and the trigger taken out upward.

16. The cartridge stop (arrow) is normally powered and retained by a spring which is mounted on the outer magazine tube in the same manner as a pencil pocket clip. To release the cartridge stop, the tail of the spring must be gently pried out of its slot in the tube, and the spring slid back until it clears the stop. The stop is then slid downward off the tube. On the gun shown, an old repair has replaced the stop spring with a blade spring, screw-mounted in the stock well.

Reassembly Tips:

1. When replacing the bolt handle, align the handle hole in the bolt with the rear opening in the slot in the receiver, and be sure the handle is oriented so its cuts correspond with the narrow portion of the slot.

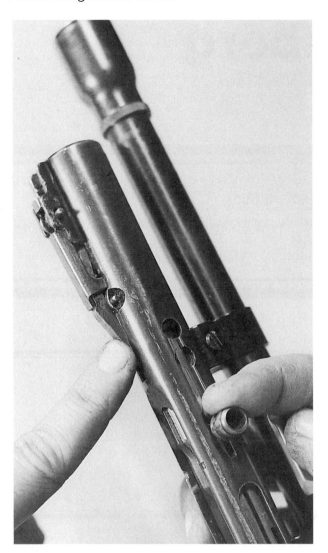

2. When moving the bolt forward, press in the front of the sear to allow the striker to pass, so there will be no tension on the spring.

3. When installing the trigger spring, put it in with its separate ends to the rear. This will allow easy insertion of the pin without tension. When the spring is mounted on the pin, swing each of the separate ends over forward to hook each one around the vertical extensions of the trigger.

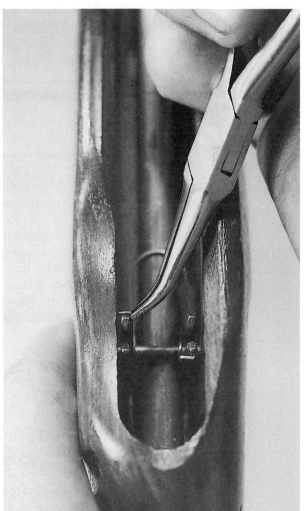

When replacing the outer magazine tube, be sure the angled tip of the retaining spring engages its recess on the underside of the magazine tube before tightening the spring mounting screw. When inserting the tube, use a tool to guide it at the rear, to ensure that it centers in its hole in the buttplate.

Avoid over-tightening the screw which retains the front section of the stock, as this screw has a tendency to break at the head.

4. When replacing the action in the stock, pull the trigger very slightly to be sure its upper extensions properly engage the cross pin in the disconnector.

Mossberg 640K

Similar/Identical Pattern Guns

The same basic assembly/disassembly steps for the Mossberg Model 640K also apply to the following guns:

Mossberg Model 640KS   **Mossberg Model 620K**

Data:	Mossberg 640K
Origin:	United States
Manufacturer:	O.F. Mossberg & Sons
	North Haven, Connecticut
Cartridge:	22 WMR (22 magnum)
Magazine capacity:	5 rounds
Overall length:	44¾ inches
Barrel length:	24 inches
Weight:	6¼ pounds

Marketed as the "Chuckster," the Model 640K was first offered in 1959, the same year the 22 WMR cartridge was introduced. Two other versions were offered, one with fancy wood and several gold-plated parts (the 640KS), and one in single shot only (the 620K). These two were discontinued in 1974, and the regular Model 640K was made until 1986. The instructions can be applied to all three versions.

Disassembly:

1. Remove the magazine, and back out the large screw on the underside in the front tip of the magazine plate. Separate the action from the stock. Removal of the small Phillips screw at the rear of the magazine plate, and at each end of the trigger guard, will allow these parts to be taken off downward.

2. Push the receiver endpiece latch downward, and remove the endpiece toward the rear.

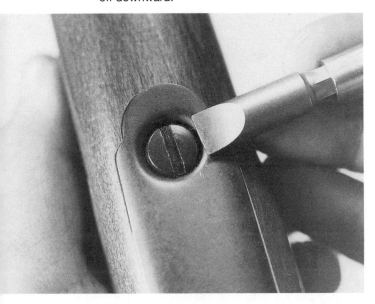

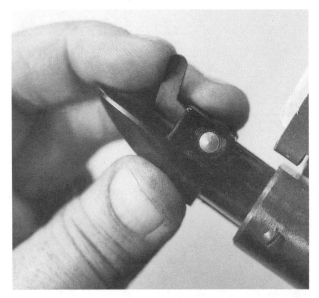

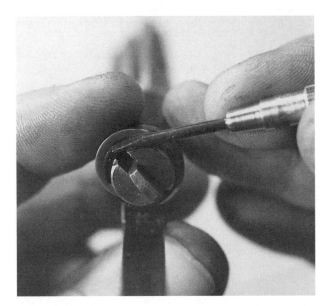

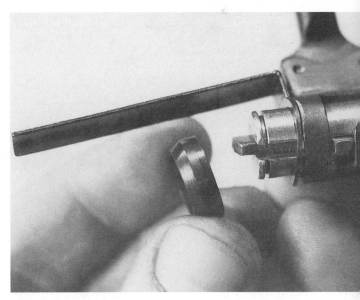

3. Open the bolt, and remove it toward the rear. Remove the C-clip (retaining ring) at the rear of the bolt.

4. Remove the bolt collar from the rear of the bolt.

5. Remove the bolt track cover plate from the rear of the bolt.

6. Remove the bolt handle assembly toward the rear, taking with it the firing pin. Turn the firing pin within the bolt handle until its lug is aligned with the groove inside the handle ring, tip the firing pin, and remove it toward the front.

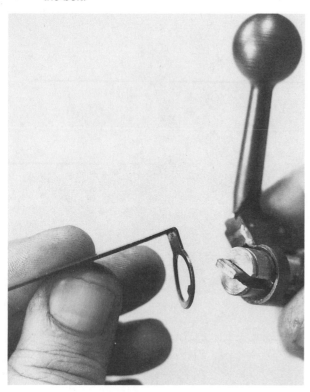

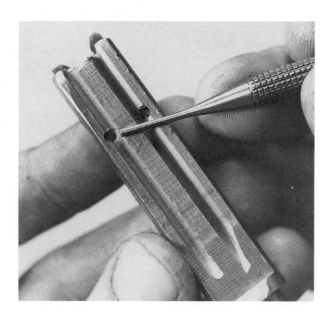

7. The extractors are retained by vertical pins on each side near the front of the bolt. The pins are drifted out upward to release the extractors and their small coil springs for removal toward each side.

8. Insert a tool inside the receiver to restrain the hammer, depress the sear lock on the right side, and pull the trigger. Ease the hammer down to the fired position. Push the hammer spring base out of its recesses in the front of the trigger housing, and remove the base and hammer spring assembly downward. The hammer spring assembly can be taken apart by removing the C-clip behind the base. **Caution:** *The spring is under compression. Control it, and ease it off.*

9. Unhook the rear arm of the sear lock spring from the right bar of the sear, and allow it to spring downward. Remove the spring from its groove in the tip of the hammer post.

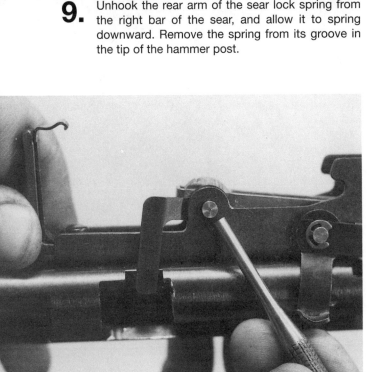

10. Push the hammer pivot pin toward the left. Remove the sear lock downward and toward the front.

11. Restrain the trigger, remove the hammer pivot pin toward the left, and take out the hammer downward. Release the trigger, and allow the sear and trigger assembly to pivot, relieving the spring tension.

12. Remove the C-clip from the cross pin in the top of the trigger, and take out the sear cross pin toward the right. Remove the sear toward the front. Allow the trigger to rotate further, completely easing the tension of its spring. Remove the C-clip from the tip of the trigger pin, take out the pin, and remove the trigger and its spring downward.

13. Remove the C-clip from the end of the safety pivot, and while doing this keep the right side of the gun upward. Push the safety pivot through to the inside, and remove it.

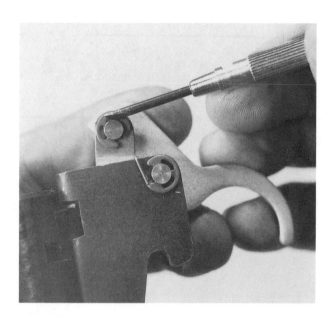

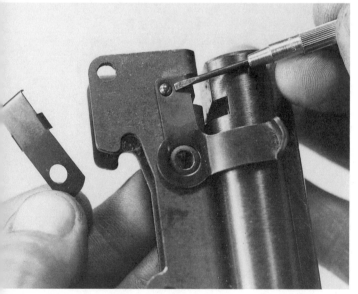

14. Take off the safety positioning spring. This will uncover the safety detent ball, lying in a hole in the safety-lever. Remove the ball, and take care that it isn't lost.

15. The safety-lever can't be taken off until the subframe (trigger housing) is removed. Remove the screw on the underside in the tail of the magazine guide bar and catch. Remove the magazine guide bar and catch downward.

Reassembly Tips:

When replacing the ejector in the receiver, note that the raised projection on the base must be on the left side of the gun. Use a fingertip to hold the ejector in place while installing the screw through the magazine catch and guide bar.

16. The screw just removed also retains the ejector inside the receiver, and this part can now be removed.

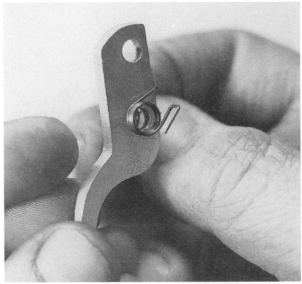

1. When replacing the trigger and its spring, note that the spring is positioned on the trigger as shown.

17. Remove the vertical screw on the inside of the sub-frame at the rear, and take off the sub-frame downward. The safety can now be removed from the top of the sub-frame.

2. When inserting the sear for reattachment to the trigger at the rear, note that the front cross bar goes at the bottom, as shown, when viewed from the front. When the sub-frame is reassembled, the hammer must be recocked before the bolt can be put back into the receiver. Insert a tool through the bolt track, and push the hammer back to the fully cocked position.

3. When replacing the firing pin and the bolt handle, remember that the firing pin must be inserted into the handle ring before the two parts are put back on the bolt.

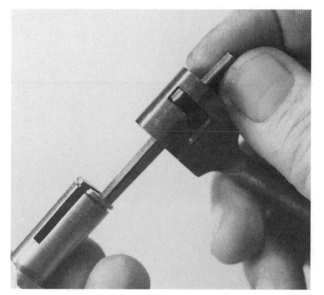

4. Note that the bolt track cover has an inner projection on its mounting ring that fits into the firing pin slot in the bolt, as shown.

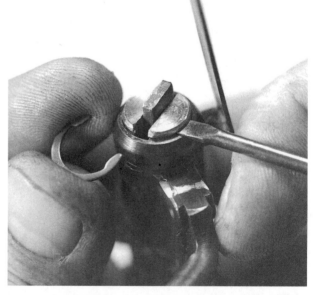

5. When installing the C-clip on the rear of the bolt, use a small screwdriver to compress the cover ring. When installing the receiver end piece, have the bolt at the rear of the receiver, and lift the rear tip of the cover plate onto the end piece as it is moved into place.

Mossberg 702

Similar/Identical Pattern Guns
The same basic assembly/disassembly steps for the Mossberg 702 Plinkster also apply to the following guns:
Mossberg 702 Bantam Plinkster
Mossberg 702 Thumbhole Tipdown

Data:	Mossberg 702 Plinkster
Origin:	United States
Manufacturer:	O.F. Mossberg & Sons, North Haven, Connecticut
Cartridge:	22 Long Rifle
Magazine capacity:	10 rounds
Overall length:	37 inches
Barrel length:	18 inches
Weight:	4 pounds

The Mossberg 702 Plinkster is one of a family of low-priced rimfire rifles introduced to the American market in 2006. The 702 is the semi-automatic offering. Similar models in the Plinkster family are the 802 bolt-action repeater and the 801 Half-Pint Plinkster, a single-shot youth model. The Plinkster is manufactured in Brazil and imported by Mossberg International.

Disassembly:

1. Remove the front takedown screw just in front of the magazine well.

2. Remove the rear takedown screw just behind the trigger guard.

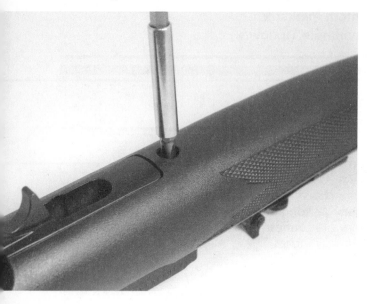

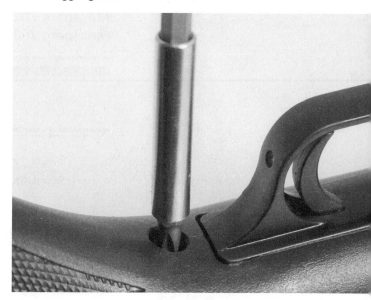

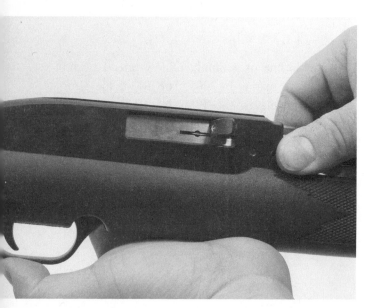

3. Remove the barreled action from the stock assembly by pushing up on the trigger guard from the bottom.

4. Driving out these two roll pins will allow the barrel to be removed from the receiver.

5. Drive out the front fire control retaining pin.

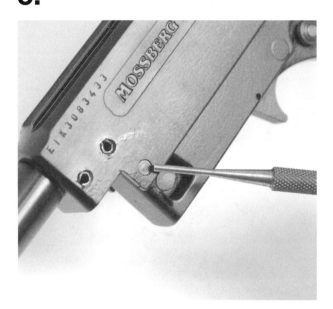

6. While holding the fire control and receiver together, drive out the rear fire control retaining pin.

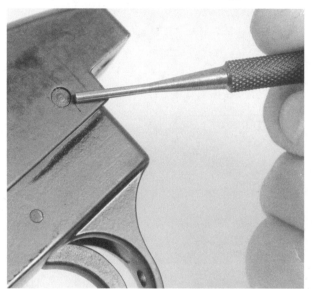

7. The charging handle sits like a saddle on top of the bolt. To remove it, pull the fire control unit down approximately ¼ inch, which will also pull the bolt down. Then lift the charging handle straight up until it touches the top of the receiver. Pull the handle straight out.

8. Use the finger groove end of the charging handle to retract the bolt about ¼ inch and then pull the fire control unit down another inch. Do no pull it all the way out of the receiver.

9. Using your finger to restrain the bolt, pull the fire control unit forward and down out of the receiver.

10. The plastic bolt buffer sits at the rear of the receiver behind the bolt and will fall out when the fire control is removed. The photo shows its orientation in the receiver.

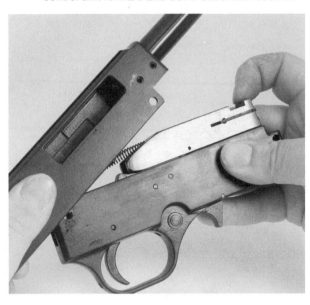

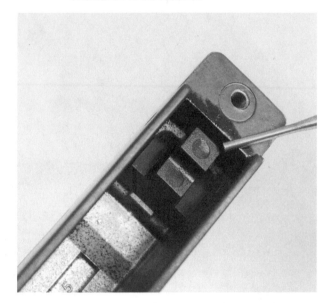

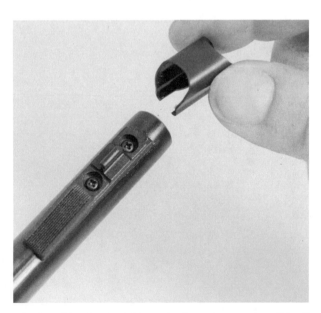

11. The front sight protective cap can be slid off toward the muzzle. The front sight is held onto the barrel by two screws.

12. The rear sight may be taken off of the barrel by the removal of these two screws.

13. The main spring and spring guide can be pulled directly out of the back of the bolt.

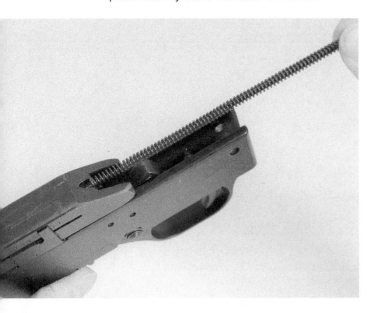

14. Remove the bolt from the fire control by pulling the bolt back off of the feed ramp and sliding it off to the right of the gun.

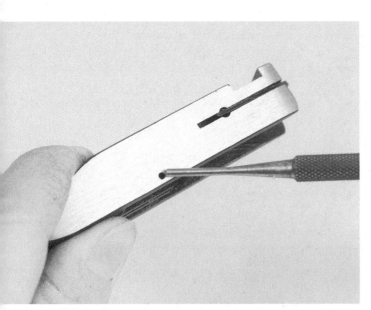

15. Driving out this pin from right to left will free the firing pin.

16. This pin retains the extractor and extractor spring.

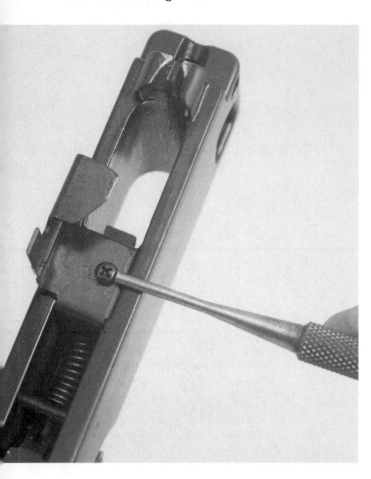

17. Remove this screw to take off the bolt guide.

18. All of the pins in the fire control assembly have splines on one end, however, they might not all be driven in from the same direction. Drive the pins out toward the splines. Drive out this pin to remove the magazine catch, spring and plunger. The magazine catch spring serves a dual purpose, and is also the safety spring. A ball bearing serves as a detent for the safety button and is located behind the safety spring. Do not lose the ball bearing.

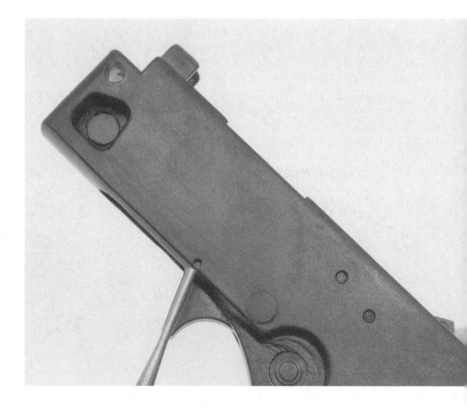

19. Remove the safety button in either direction.

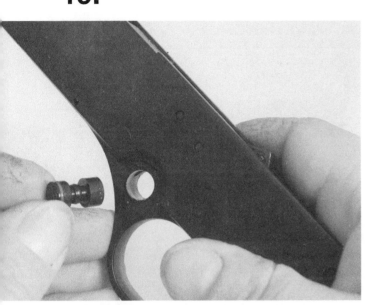

20. Drive the hammer stop pin out from left to right.

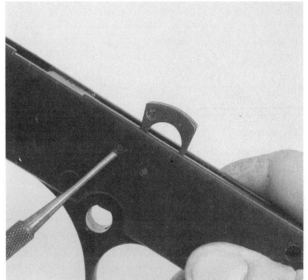

21. With the hammer in the fired position, drive out the hammer pin. Control the assembly while removing it up and to the rear.

22. This pin retains the trigger assembly. The trigger assembly is composed of the trigger, trigger bar, disconnector and trigger return spring. They will promptly fall apart.

Reassembly Tips:

1. This is the proper arrangement of the trigger assembly for installation. Note that the more bent of the two spring legs is arranged to the rear.

2. Use a pair of needle nose pliers to emplace the trigger bar and trigger spring first. When in place, insert the trigger pin far enough to contain the trigger bar.

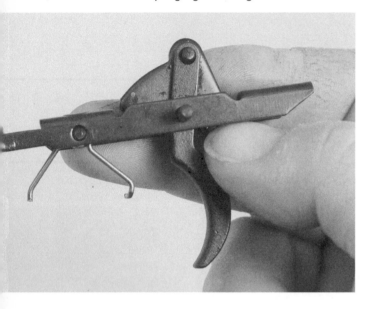

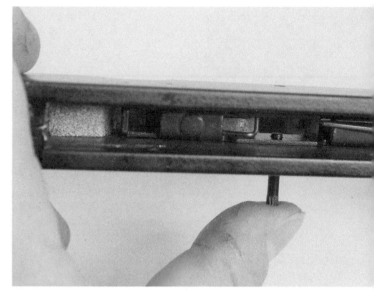

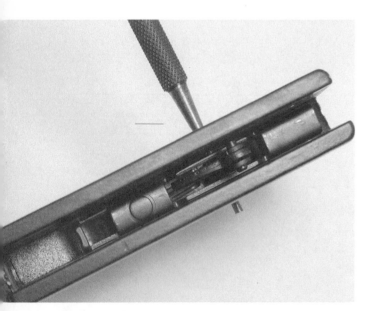

3. Insert the trigger and disconnector assembly and use a punch from the opposite side of the pin to retain the entire assembly. Then drive the pin in to complete the installation.

4. It is necessary to install the safety and magazine catch assemblies before the hammer is installed, as the hammer strut runs through the safety button hole and keeps the button inside the receiver. Insert the safety button, then drop the detent ball into the safety spring hole, followed by the safety spring. Then reinstall the magazine catch.

5. The use of a wire hook to retain the hammer spring will ease the installation of the hammer. The wire can be passed through the receiver and out the front above the magazine catch. With the hammer overcocked, it will allow the wire to be slipped off the strut and pulled out from the front of the receiver.

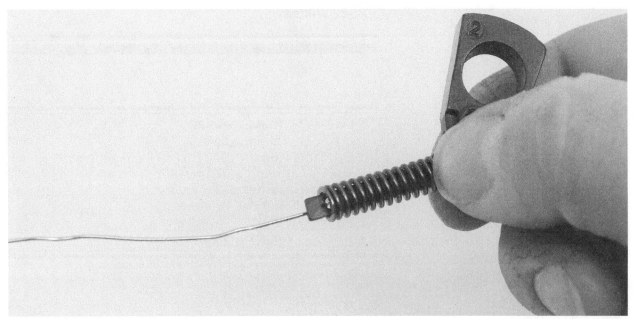

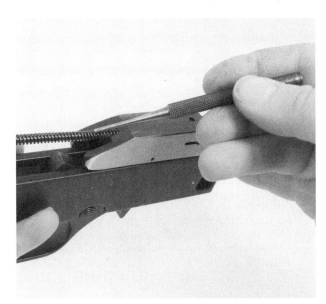

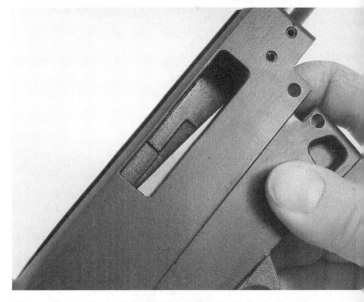

6. When reinserting the combined fire control and bolt assemblies, it is very easy to kink the recoil spring in the location indicated in the photo. When reinstalling, place the spring and guide fully into the rear of the bolt and insert the guide in the hole rather than placing the spring and guide in the receiver and attempting to reinsert the spring into the bolt.

7. Place the bolt buffer into the receiver first and then insert the rest of the bolt and fire control assemblies. In a fashion similar to the disassembly, use your finger to control the bolt as you insert the fire control and bolt assemblies.

Puma PPS22

Similar/Identical Pattern Guns
The same basic assembly/disassembly steps for the PPS22 also apply to the following gun:
PPS22 Wildcat

Data:	PPS 22
Origin:	Italy
Manufacturer:	F.A.P. di PIETTA Giuseppe & C. S.n.c.
Cartridge:	22 Long Rifle
Magazine capacity:	10 rounds
Overall length:	33 inches
Barrel length:	16 inches
Weight:	5 pounds

The PPS is a rimfire rifle with an intentional resemblance to the PPsh submachine guns from the mid 1900's. Like many other firearms, the PPS rifle was designed to have that look of the restricted firearm, yet have the function of the non—restricted.

A simple, yet well-made, piece manufactured by Pietta of Italy, it began to arrive in the United States at the end of 2009, imported by Legacy Sports International. Available in the traditional wood-stocked format, it was also sold with a plastic stock. A more radical model was a "Wildcat" version with front and rear pistol grips and a collapsible stock. Any of these models could be had with a 50-round drum magazine to make the "burp" gun image complete.

Disassembly:

1. Take note that all screws used in this firearm have very shallow slots.

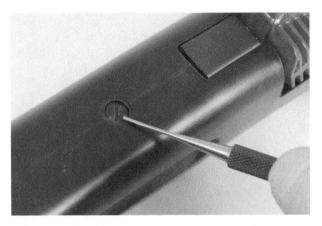

2. Remove the stock screw. Pull the barreled action from the stock.

3. Remove both receiver pin retainer screws and push out both retainer pins. The lower receiver can now be removed from the upper receiver.

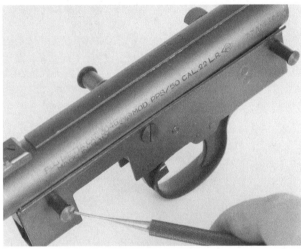

4. Unscrew the ejector screw on the left side. Pull the ejector pin from the right side. The ejector remains captured by the magazine catch pin.

5. Push out the magazine catch pin halfway to remove the ejector. Then pull the magazine catch pin the rest of the way out. Be careful to retain the magazine catch spring and magazine catch as they are under tension.

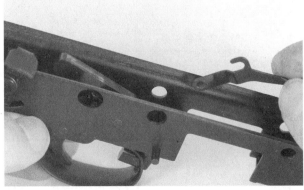

6. With hammer forward, push out the hammer pin and remove the hammer. Be sure to catch the hammer bushings, which are nestled within the hammer spring coils.

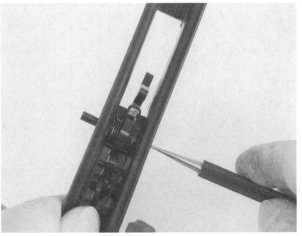

7. The trigger pin and trigger stop pin are both staked in. They should not be removed unless absolutely necessary. Removing the trigger pin will separate the disconnector from the trigger and release the hammer catch tooth (disconnector) and its pin spring.

8. To remove the safety, remove the e-clip from the inside of the right side of the lower receiver. The safety assembly can then be pulled out of the right side and the safety pin and the safety washer can be removed from the safety assembly.

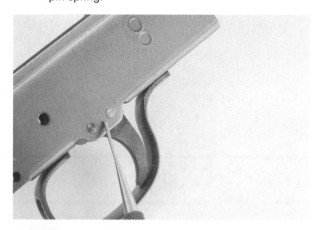

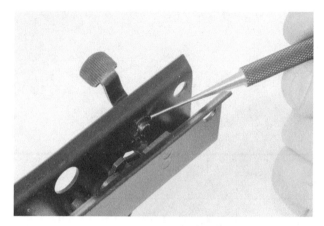

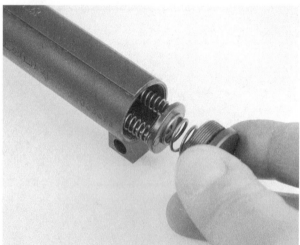

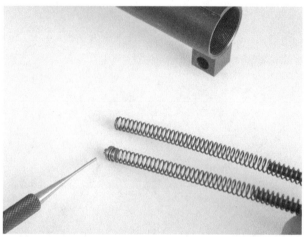

9. Remove the receiver end cap slowly as it is under tension. The buffer spring can be pulled from the receiver end cap.

10. The recoil spring guide and the pair of recoil bolt springs can then be pulled from the back of the receiver. In the front of the left recoil bolt spring is the bolt handle stop.

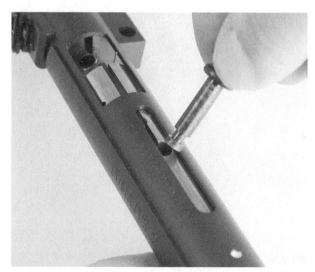

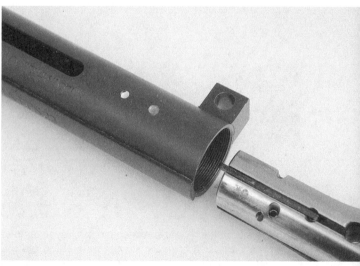

11. Remove the bolt cocking handle.

12. The bolt is now free to slide out of the back of the receiver.

13. Driving out the firing pin retainer will free the firing pin and the firing pin spring.

14. Removing the extractor roll pin will free the extractor and the extractor spring.

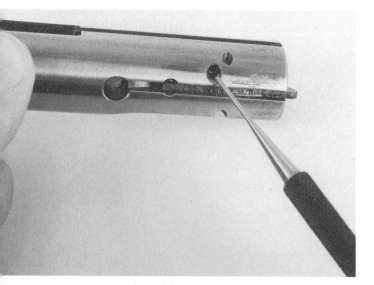

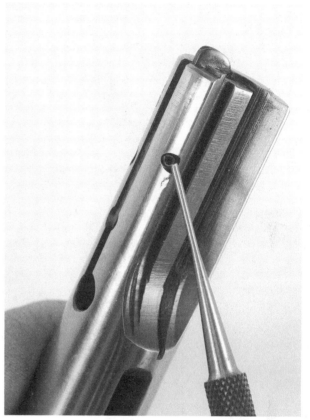

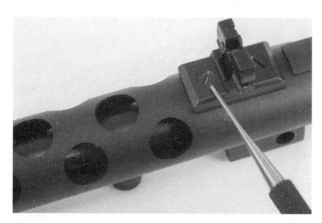

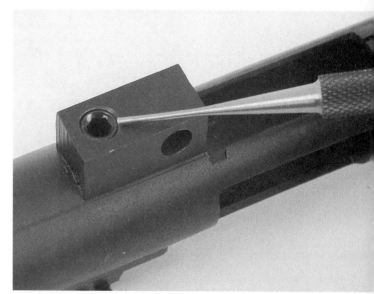

15. For repair or replacement, the front and rear sights can both be removed by unscrewing both retaining screws.

16. If necessary for repair or rebarreling, the barrel can be removed by unscrewing the set screw from the front receiver block, and the barrel can be tapped out toward the front.

Reassembly Tips:

1. The hammer spring also serves as the trigger return spring. The hammer spring pin at the back of the trigger has two grooves. When reinstalling the hammer, make sure that the hammer spring legs go into these notches on the hammer spring pin.

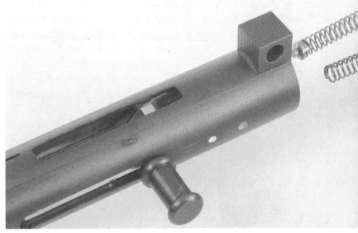

2. Align the bolt using the bolt handle before reinserting the recoil spring guide and springs.

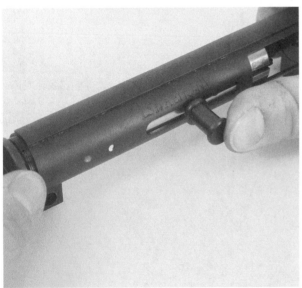

3. When screwing in the receiver end cap, start it in the receiver threads and then operate the action a few times to settle the recoil spring guide. Then finish tightening the receiver end cap.

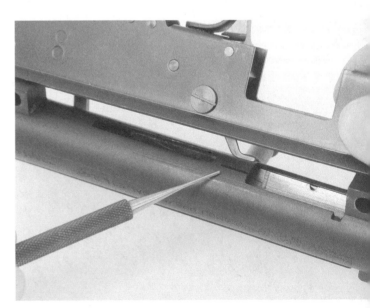

4. When reattaching the lower receiver to the upper receiver, be careful to insert the ejector into the ejector slot on the bottom of the upper receiver as the ejector is easily bent

Remington Model 121A

Similar/Identical Pattern Guns

The same basic assembly/disassembly steps for the Remington Model 121A also apply to the following guns:

Remington Model 121S   **Remington 121S8**

Data:	Remington Model 121 A
Origin:	United States
Manufacturer:	Remington Arms Co. Illion, New York
Cartridge:	22 Long Rifle
Magazine capacity:	14 rounds
Overall length:	41 inches
Barrel length:	24 inches
Weight:	6 pounds

The Model 121A evolved from the earlier Model 12A, and while they are similar, there are numerous mechanical differences. There was also a Model 121S, chambered for the 22 WRF cartridge. A smoothbore version, the Model 121SB, was designed to use 22 shot rounds. The Model 121 guns were made from 1936 to 1954. They were marketed under the trade name "Fieldmaster."

Disassembly:

1. Remove the inner magazine tube and cycle the action to cock the hammer. Set the safety in the on-safe position. With a coin or a specially shaped screwdriver, loosen the takedown screw and pull it out until it stops.

2. Separate the buttstock and trigger group from the main receiver, toward the rear and downward.

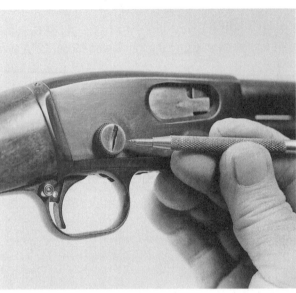

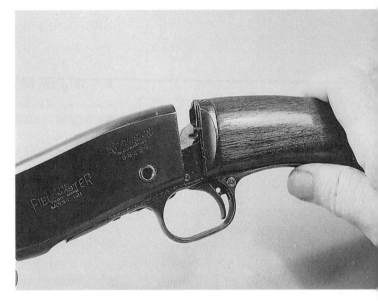

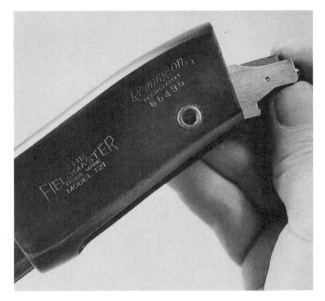

3. Move the action slide all the way to the rear, and tip the protruding rear of the bolt downward.

4. With the bolt held in that position, move the action slide back toward the front, and take out the bolt toward the rear.

5. Drift out the firing pin retaining cross pin.

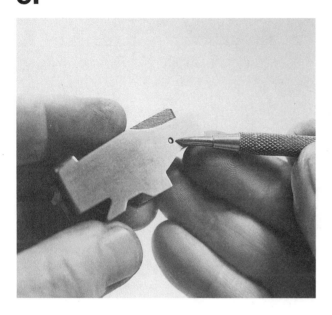

6. Remove the firing pin and its return spring toward the rear.

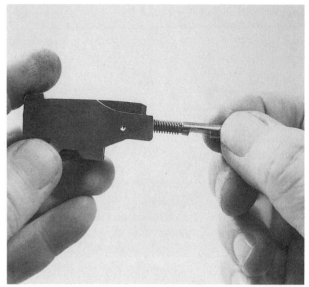

7. Insert a screwdriver between the extractor and its plunger. Depress the plunger rearward, and lever the extractor outward for removal. **Caution:** *Control the plunger and spring, and ease them out.*

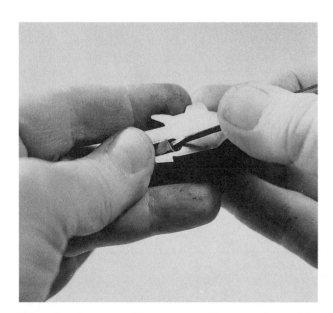

8. Remove the screws on each side of the forend. Note that the screws are retained by lock screws, which must be removed first.

9. Move the forend forward until it is clear of the enlarged portion of the magazine housing.

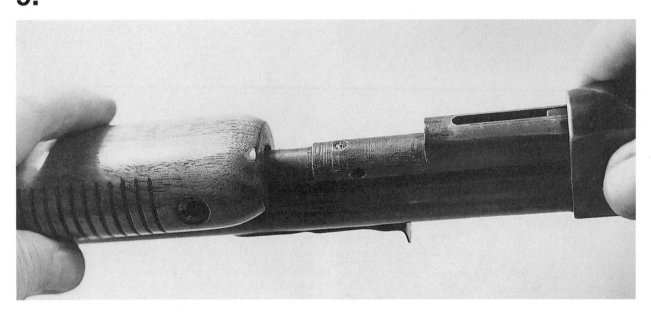

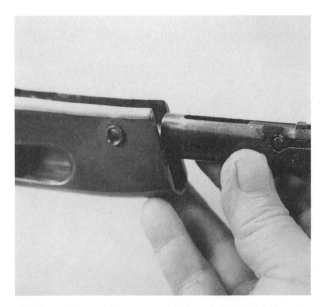

10. Remove the magazine housing toward the rear. The forend will be freed as the magazine housing clears it.

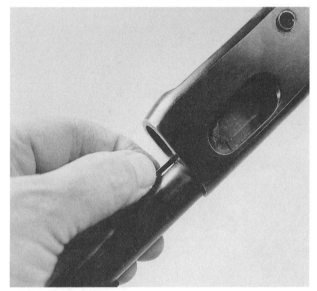

11. Lift the front portion of the cartridge guide and remove it toward the rear. **Caution:** *Lift it only enough to clear its retaining recess.*

12. To remove the magazine hanger, insert a tool or wooden dowel and unscrew it from the barrel.

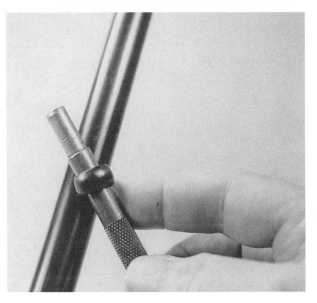

13. Remove the two wood screws that retain the stock buttplate and take it off. With a B-Square stock tool or a long screwdriver, remove the stock mounting bolt.

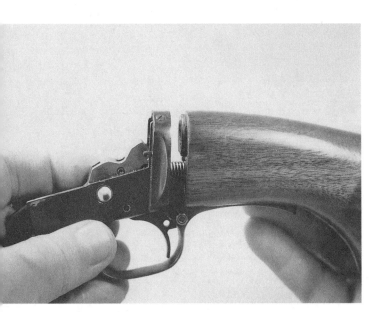

14. Remove the trigger group from the stock.

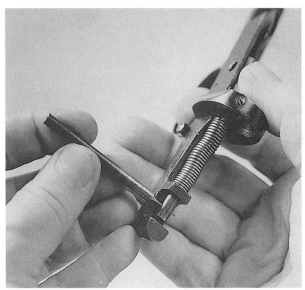

15. Move the safety to off-safe position. Insert a small tool or keeper pin in the cross hole in the hammer spring guide and pull the trigger, easing the hammer forward until the spring is trapped.

16. Use a large tapered drift to push out the hammer and carrier pivot sleeve.

17. Restrain the hammer and remove the tool or keeper pin from the guide. Ease the hammer assembly and carrier out toward the front and upward. **Caution:** *Control the spring.* The guide can be separated from the hammer by drifting out its cross pin, but this is usually staked in place, and it should be removed only if necessary for repair.

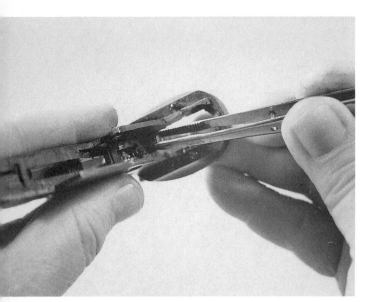

18. Remove the combination trigger and carrier spring and plunger from their well in the top of the trigger.

19. Drift out the trigger pin toward the right.

20. Remove the trigger upward.

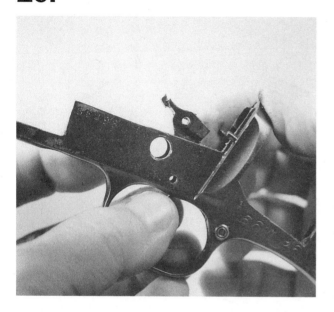

21. Drift out the cross pin that retains the safety detent plunger and spring. **Caution:** *When the drift is withdrawn, the spring will be released, so control it.*

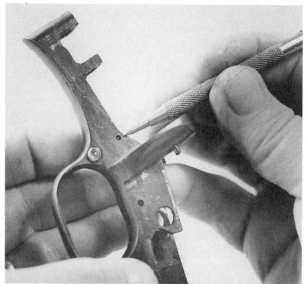

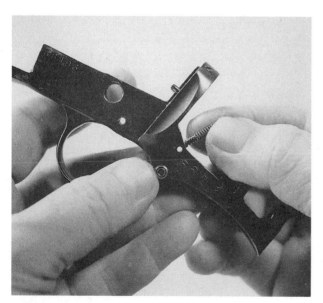

22. Remove the safety detent spring and plunger upward.

23. Remove the safety button toward either side.

24. Depress the carrier trip plunger, and the cartridge stop can be removed toward the rear.

25. Removal of this screw, which retains the carrier trip plunger spring, will allow the spring and plunger to be taken out of the magazine housing.

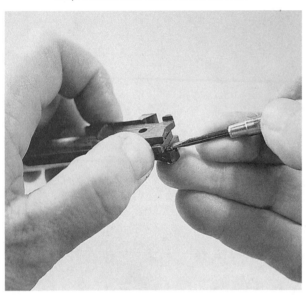

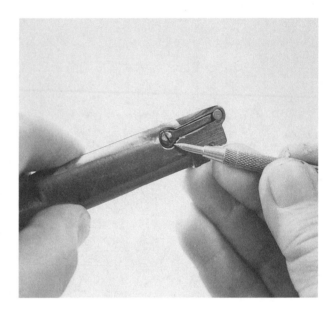

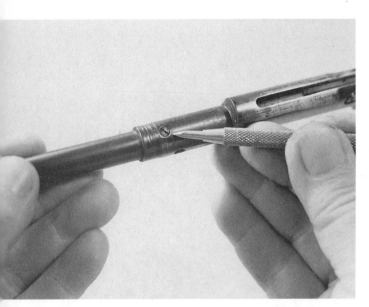

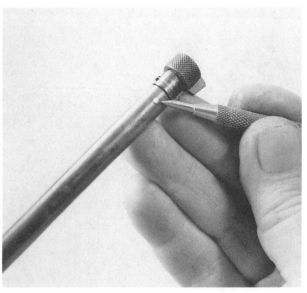

26. The outer magazine tube is screwed into the housing and is also retained by a lock screw. In normal takedown, this system should not be disturbed.

27. The inner magazine tube latch is pivoted and retained by a cross pin in the knob, inside the tube. For access, it is necessary to remove the knob by drifting out the lock pin. In normal takedown, this system is best left in place.

Reassembly Tips:

1. When installing the safety button, be sure the side with the recessed band is on the left, and that the square cut recess is toward the trigger, as shown.

2. When installing the safety plunger and spring, insert a small tool to depress the spring as the cross pin is reinserted.

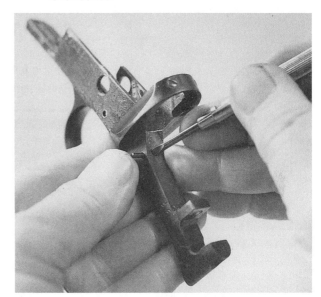

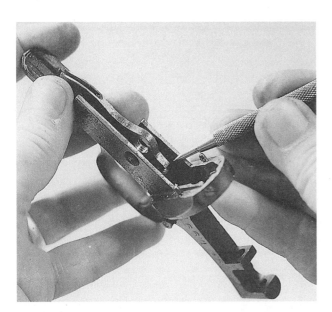

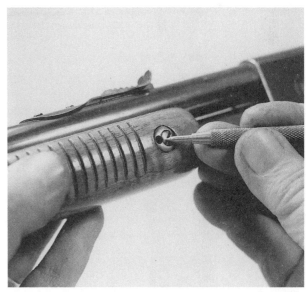

3. When installing the hammer and carrier system, be sure the rear tail of the carrier engages the plunger of the combination trigger and carrier spring. Use the pivot sleeve to hold the carrier in place while the hammer spring is compressed, and use the tool or keeper pin to hold it while the sleeve is removed and reinserted through the hammer and carrier.

4. When installing the forend screws, avoid over-tightening. Turn them until snug; then back them off slightly to install the lock screws.

Remington Model 341P

Similar/Identical Pattern Guns

The same basic assembly/disassembly steps for the Remington Model 341P also apply to following guns:

Remington Model 341A**Remington Model 341SB**

Data:	Remington Model 341P
Origin:	United States
Manufacturer:	Remington Arms Co.
	Bridgeport, Connecticut
Cartridge:	22 Short, Long, or Long Rifle
Magazine capacity:	22 Short, 17 Long, 15 Long Rifle
Overall length:	42¼ inches
Barrel length:	24 inches
Weight:	6½ pounds

The Model 341 was made for a relatively short period, from 1936 to 1940, and the few examples that turn up occasionally on the market are snapped up by those who want an old-style bolt-action 22 with solid steel parts. The gun was offered in three versions: The 341A, with regular open rear sight; the 341P, with a receiver-mounted peep sight; and the 341SB, a smoothbore gun for use with 22 shotshells. The takedown and reassembly instructions apply to all three guns.

Disassembly:

1. If your gun is the Model 341P, with the peep sight, the sight must be either removed or swung up out of the way by taking out the rear mounting screw before the bolt can be taken out of the gun.

2. Open the bolt, hold the trigger pulled to the rear, and remove the bolt from the rear of the receiver.

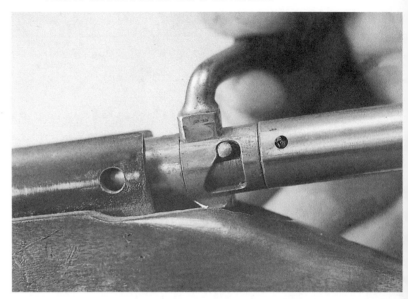

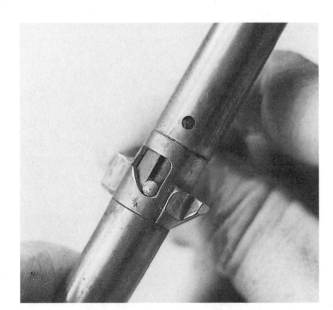

3. Grip the bolt firmly and turn the bolt handle clockwise (rear view) to allow the striker to move forward to the fired position, as shown.

4. Drift out the cross pin near the rear edge of the bolt end piece. **Caution:** *This will release the striker spring tension toward the rear, so control the parts and ease the tension slowly.*

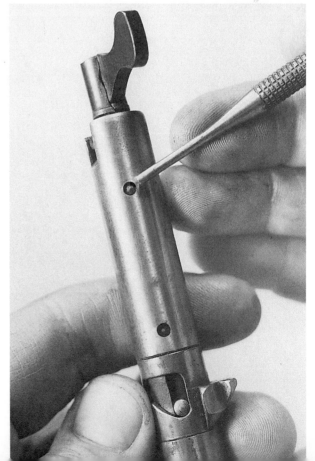

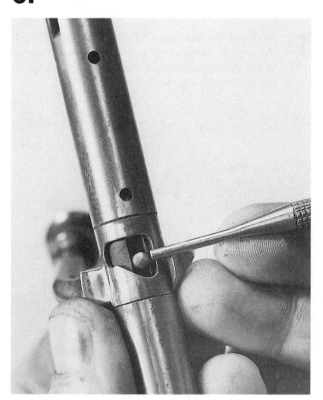

5. Drift out the cross pin just to the rear of the bolt handle sleeve.

6. Push out the cocking cam pin.

7. Remove the striker assembly toward the rear.

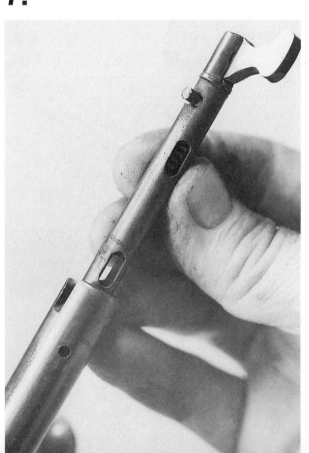

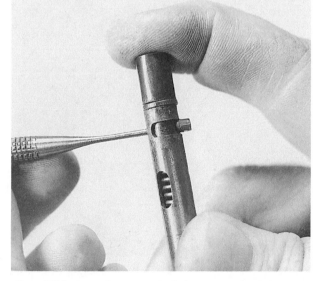

8. With the safety turned all the way to the left, insert a small diameter drift punch through the hole in the side of the striker and drive out the safety cam pin.

9. Remove the bolt sleeve toward the rear. Remove the bolt handle assembly toward the rear. Drift out the cross pin at the front of the bolt that retains the extractor.

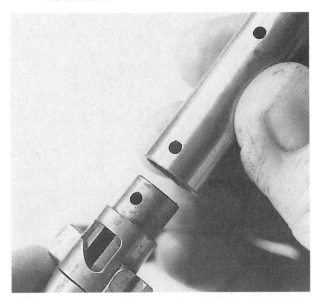

10. Restrain the extractor plunger and spring, and remove the extractor from its recess. Ease out the plunger and spring.

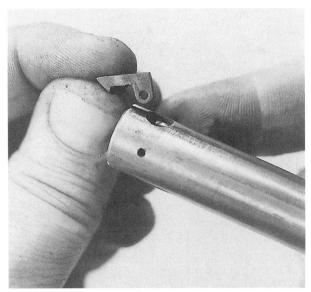

11. The ejector can now be moved toward the rear and then turned toward the side and removed from the interior of the bolt.

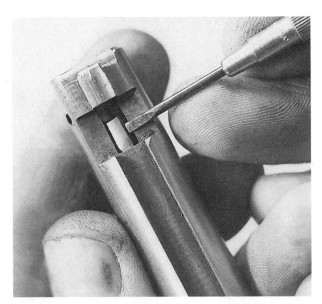

12. Remove the inner magazine tube and take out the large screw on the underside of the stock. Separate the action from the stock.

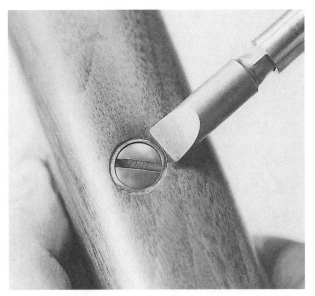

13. Drift out the sear cross pin on the side, near the center of the receiver.

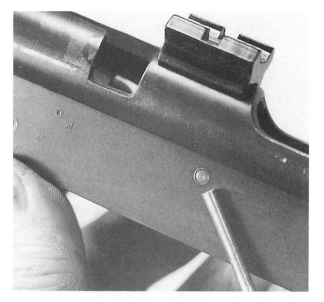

14. This will release the trigger to swing forward, be beyond its normal position, and the trigger spring and plunger can be moved from the upper rear of the trigger.

15. Drift out the trigger and carrier pivot cross pin.

16. Remove the trigger and the attached sear downward. The trigger and sear can be separated, if necessary, by drifting out the connecting cross pin.

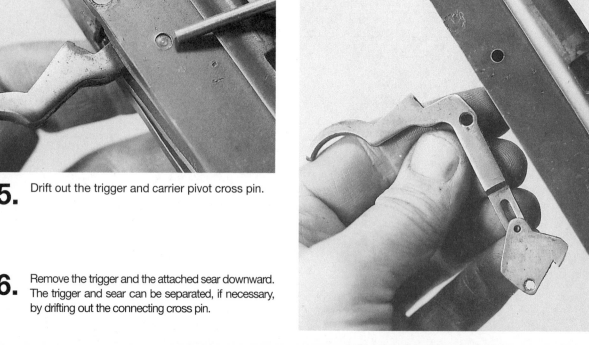

17. Remove the carrier toward the rear. **Caution:** *Take care to restrain the carrier tension plunger, spring and cup on the left side near the front as the carrier emerges from the receiver.*

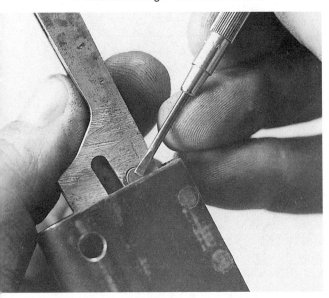

18. Remove the tension plunger, spring and cup from the left side of the carrier.

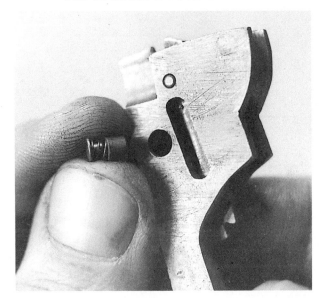

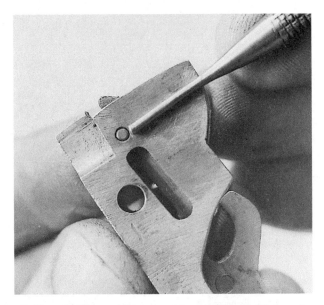

19. Drifting out the cross pin at the front of the carrier will free the cartridge stop for removal toward the front.

20. Backing out the small headless screw on the left side near the front of the receiver will release the outer magazine tube for removal toward the front. The magazine tube loop and spacer screw are both threaded into the underside of the barrel, and can be unscrewed for removal.

Reassembly Tips:

1. The cartridge slide, located inside the carrier, is riveted to a plate, which is hooked into a slot in the bottom of the carrier. **Note:** *The removal of this unit is definitely not recommended in normal takedown.*

2. To avoid damage to the extractor when replacing the cross pin, insert a small drift punch from the other side to align the hole while driving the pin into place.

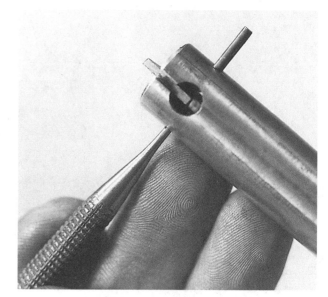

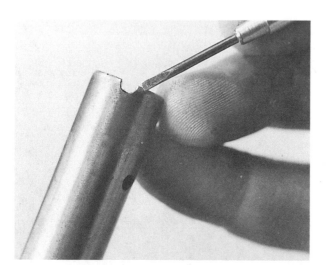

3. When replacing the bolt sleeve on the bolt, note that the small notch at the rear of the sleeve goes on the underside of the bolt.

4. When replacing the rear cross pin in the striker, use a screwdriver from the rear to depress the spring, and insert a drift punch to hold the spring while the pin is started into place. When driving in the two cross pins in the bolt sleeve that pass through the striker, take extreme care to ensure that all parts are in alignment, as it is possible to deform the pins or break the wings of the spring plunger if they are not.

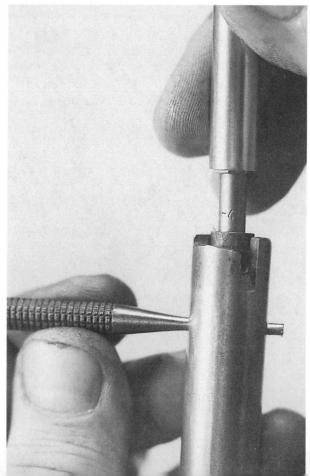

Remington Model 522

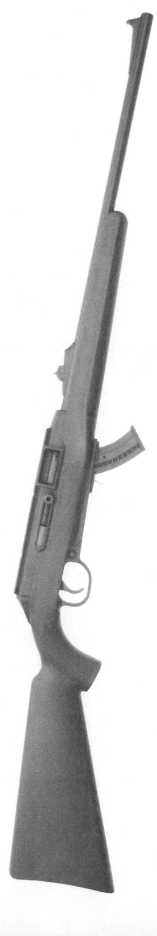

Data:	Remington Model 522
Origin:	United States
Manufacturer:	Remington Arms Company
	Ilion, New York
Cartridge:	22 Long Rifle
Magazine capacity:	10 rounds
Overall length:	40 inches
Barrel length:	20 inches
Weight:	4⅝ pounds

Marketed as the "Viper," the Model 522 was introduced in 1993. With its mostly polymer construction, it fills the gap in the Remington line left by the discontinuance of the Nylon 66. Mechanically, it is more simple than that gun, but it has been designed so that several systems are not routinely dismountable. Operationally, though, it is an excellent and dependable gun.

Disassembly:

1. Remove the magazine, draw the bolt back, and push in the handle to lock the bolt open. Set the safety in on-safe position. Use a 1⅛-inch Allen wrench or bit to remove the front action screw.

2. Remove the Allen screw at the rear of the trigger guard and take the action out of the stock.

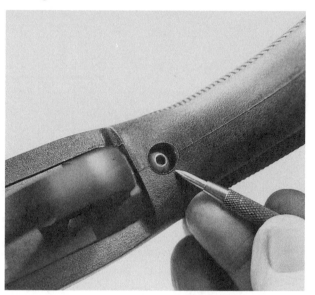

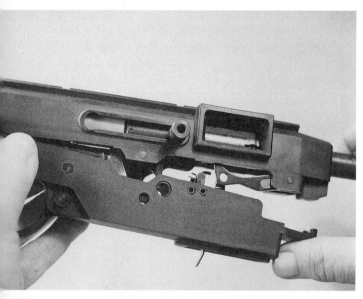

3. Pull the bolt handle outward and ease the bolt forward to closed position. Move the safety to off-safe position. Insert the magazine and pull the trigger to drop the striker to fired position. Remove the magazine. Push the barrel and receiver toward the rear and tip the lower housing downward at the front, as shown. Ease the housing off toward the rear, controlling the tension of the recoil spring and striker spring.

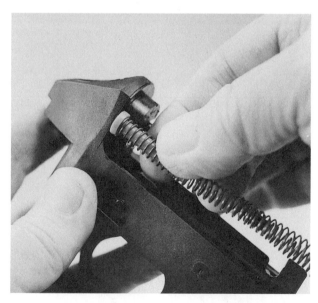

4. Remove the red-colored striker spring and guide toward the right.

5. Remove the recoil spring and its guide toward the left.

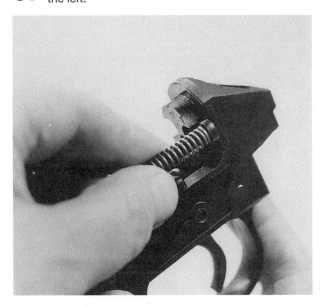

6. Move the bolt all the way to the rear and take out the striker assembly. The combination striker and firing pin unit is retained in the red polymer headpiece by a roll-type cross pin. Except for repair purposes, this system should be left in place.

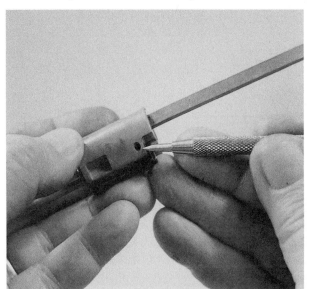

7. Align the bolt handle with its exit space in the track, and remove the handle toward the right.

8. Remove the bolt toward the rear. The striker rebound piece and its spring are retained at the right rear of the bolt by a roll-type cross pin. In normal takedown, this system is best left in place. If removal is necessary, restrain the rebound piece, as the spring is quite strong.

9. To remove the extractor, use a small tool to depress the plunger rearward, and lift out the extractor. **Caution:** *Control the plunger and spring and ease them out.*

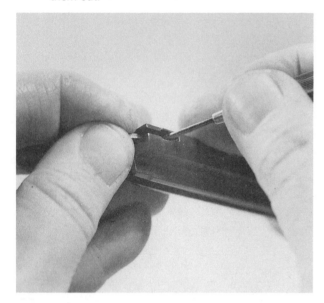

10. The twin sears are pivoted on a pin that goes across the bottom of the receiver. If the sears are to be removed for repair, note their relative positions for reassembly.

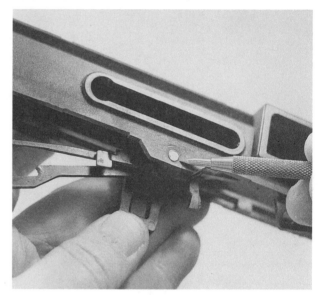

11. On the left side of the receiver, the sear pin is heat-sealed. For removal, the polymer must be softened with a small soldering iron. In normal takedown, this system should not be disturbed.

12. The bolt hold-open device and its spring can be removed by pushing the pin toward the left just far enough to clear the part.

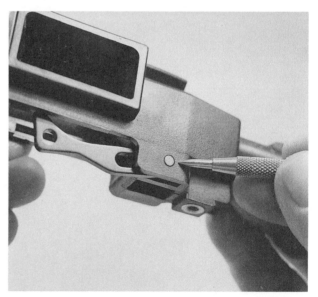

13. If removal of the safety is necessary, insert a tool inside the lower housing to nudge the pin outward. **Caution:** *The safety detent spring and plunger will be released upward.* After the spring and plunger are removed, the safety can be pushed out of its cross-tunnel.

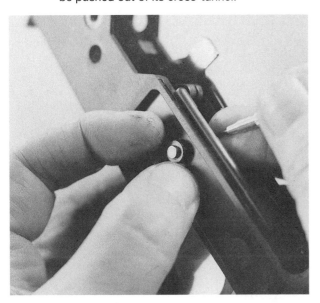

14. Pushing out this cross pin will release the trigger assembly and trigger spring for removal. **Caution:** *The spring will be freed, so control it.* The trigger must be turned during removal to withdraw its forward arm (the magazine safety) from beneath the bridge in the housing. The trigger bar is attached by a cross-screw. If the trigger assembly has been removed (it is still in place here), pushing out this cross pin will release the trigger bar spring for removal. **Caution:** *Control the spring.*

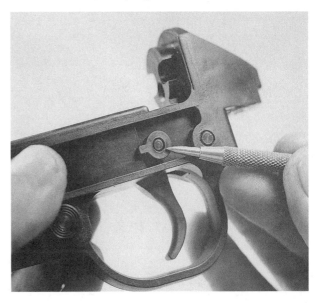

15. The blade-type springs that power the twin sears are heat-locked into a mount in the floor of the lower housing. They are not routinely removable.

16. This small screw secures a bracket plate and the combination ejector and magazine catch. Removal of the screw will free the plate, but because of the heat-sealed bridge, the ejector/magazine catch is not routinely removable.

17. The front sight is retained by a single screw. The rear sight base is retained by two screws. The adjustment slide must be moved for access to the rear one.

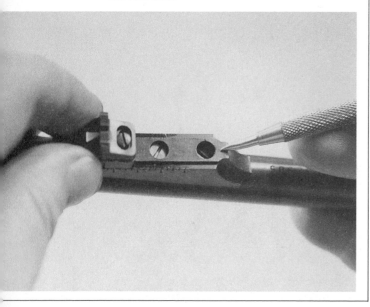

1. When installing the striker spring and the recoil spring, remember that the red-colored striker spring goes on the right, and the black-colored recoil spring guide goes on the left. To help with this, the guide heads are of different sizes.

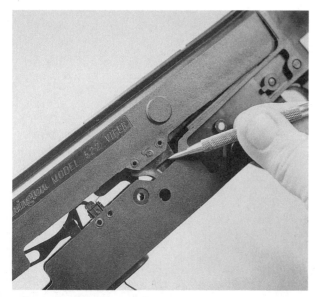

2. With the springs properly engaged, move the lower housing forward and upward until its latch at lower front engages. There is an assembly guide on the left side of the receiver that helps in proper placement.

3. Before the action is put back into the stock, lock the bolt in open position to keep tension on the housing latch. The safety must be in on-safe position when the action is put back in the stock.

Remington Model 550

Similar/Identical Pattern Guns

The same basic assembly/disassembly steps for the Remington Model 550 also apply to the following guns:

Remington Model 550P   **Remington Model 550-2G**
Remington Model 550A

Data:	Remington Model 550
Origin:	United States
Manufacturer:	Remington Arms Company
	Bridgeport, Connecticut
Cartridge:	22 Short, Long, or Long Rifle
Magazine capacity:	22 Shorts, 17 Longs, 15 Long Rifles
Overall length:	43½ inches
Barrel length:	24 inches
Weight:	61¼ pounds

Introduced in 1941, the Model 550 was the first 22-caliber semi-auto to use all three 22 rimfire cartridges interchangeably. It accomplished this with a unique "floating chamber," which allowed the Short cartridge to deliver the same impact to the bolt as the longer rounds. During its time of production, several sub-models were offered: the 550A, 550P, and so on, with different sight options. All of the 550 series guns are mechanically identical, and the same instructions will apply.

Disassembly:

1. Back out the stock mounting screw on the underside of the stock, and separate the action from the stock. If necessary, the stock screw can be removed by moving it out until its threads engage the threads in its escutcheon, and then unscrewing it.

2. Pull the trigger to release the striker, so it will be in the fired position, and unscrew the receiver end cap at the rear of the receiver. If the end cap has been overtightened, there is a large coin slot at the rear of its dome to aid in starting it. Remove the end cap and its attached spring guide, and the bolt spring and striker spring and guide toward the rear. The springs are under some tension, but not so much that the end cap can't be easily controlled. The springs are easily removed from the guide on the end cap, but the hollow guide is not removable. Take care not to lose the collar at the front of the bolt spring.

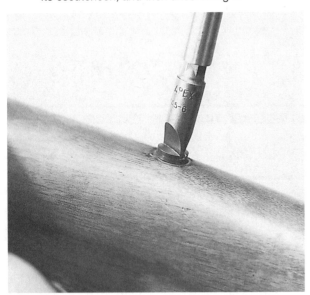

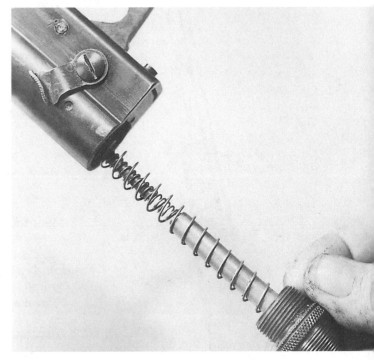

3. Move the bolt all the way to the rear, until the bolt handle aligns with the opening at the end of its track, and remove the bolt handle toward the right.

4. Use a small tool to push the bolt toward the rear, and remove it from the rear of the receiver.

5. Remove the striker (firing pin) from the rear of the bolt.

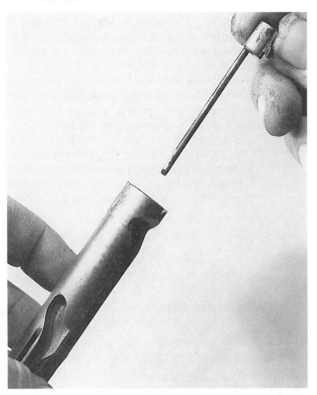

6. Use a small screwdriver to depress the extractor spring plunger, and lift the extractor out of its recess in the bolt. **Caution:** *Take care that the plunger and spring don't get away, as the compressed spring can propel the parts quite a distance.* They are very small and difficult to locate.

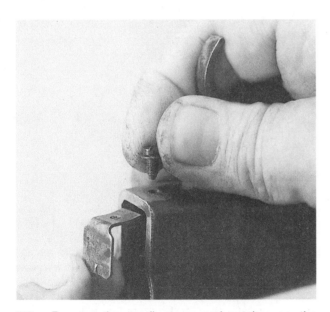

7. Remove the small screw and washer on the underside of the receiver near the rear edge, and take out the L-shaped end cap lockplate.

8. With the safety in the on-safe position, remove the safety screw and take off the safety-lever toward the right. The safety tumbler can then be moved inward and removed toward the rear. As the tumbler is moved inward, the trigger spring will move its plunger upward, so control it and ease its tension slowly. Next, drift out the trigger pin and the trigger limit pin. The trigger will be freed, but can't be removed at this point because of its attached disconnector assembly.

9. Drift out the cross pin in the forward section of the receiver, and remove the carrier assembly and its spring downward. The two leaves of the carrier, the spacer bushing, and the spring are easily separated. This pin also is the sear pivot, and the sear can now be moved forward and taken out downward.

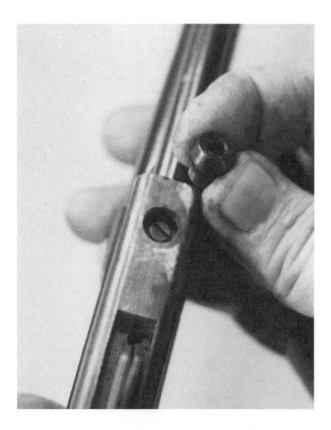

10. Remove the screw-slotted sear spring housing (looks like a large screw head) from the bottom center of the receiver, along with the sear spring it contains. The housing is often found staked in place, and some effort may be required to start it. **Caution:** *Never try to remove the housing while the sear is still in place on its cross pin, or the parts are likely to be damaged.* The trigger assembly may now be moved upward into the receiver, then forward, and out the carrier opening. The disconnector system may be separated from the trigger by drifting out the small cross pin, releasing the disconnector and its spring and plunger. However, the cross pin is usually riveted in place, and during routine disassembly it is best left undisturbed.

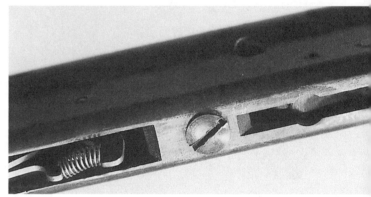

11. Removal of the stock mounting base at the lower front of the receiver will give access to a small screw beneath it. Taking out this screw will allow removal of the outer magazine tube toward the front. This will also release the receiver insert the sub-frame which forms the cartridge guide and allow it to be pushed out toward the rear. The insert is often tight, and may require the use of a hammer and nylon drift to start it. Take care that it is not deformed during removal. The ejector is staked in place in the left wall of the receiver, and no attempt to remove it should be made during normal disassembly.

Reassembly Tips:

1. When replacing the striker in the bolt, be sure its slim forward portion enters its tunnel in the bolt, and that the striker goes all the way forward. This can be checked on the underside of the bolt, as shown.

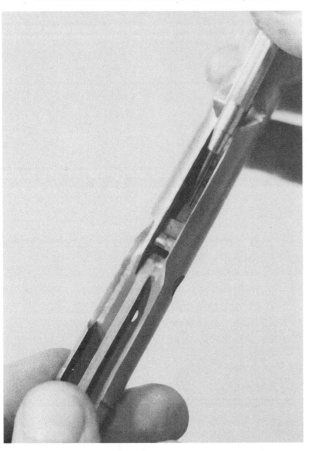

3. Before replacing the receiver end cap, be sure the springs are in the proper order, with the striker spring guide in the front of the spring, and the collar on the front of the bolt spring, as shown.

When installing the sear and sear spring system, put the sear and carrier system in place, and insert a smaller diameter rod or drift through the pin hole to keep them in general position. Then install the sear spring housing, being sure the top of the spring enters its recess in the underside of the sear. Next, move the sear downward and toward the rear, engaging its rear lobe with the collar on the housing. When it is in position, insert the cross pin, pushing out the smaller diameter rod or drift. This is the most difficult point in the reassembly of the Model 550.

2. When replacing the bolt handle, be sure the flat inner tip of the handle is at the top, as shown. Also, be sure the carrier is in its raised position (up at the front) before inserting the bolt in the receiver.

Remington Model 552

Similar/Identical Pattern Guns

The same basic assembly/disassembly steps for the Remington Model 552 also apply to the following guns:

Remington Model 552C   **Remington Model 552BDL**
Remington Model 552GS

Data:	Remington Model 552
Origin:	United States
Manufacturer:	Remington Arms Company
	Bridgeport, Connecticut
Cartridge:	22 Short, Long or Long Rifle
Magazine capacity:	20 Short, 17 Long, 15 Long Rifle
Overall length:	42 inches
Barrel length:	25 inches
Weight:	5½ pounds

The Model 552 was introduced in 1958, and it was intended to be the 22-caliber counterpart of the centerfire Model 742. It does have similar looks and handling qualities, though it's lighter, of course. The gun has been offered in a carbine version with a 21-inch barrel (552C), and a Gallery Special in 22 Short chambering. Currently, only the Deluxe BDL version is being made.

Disassembly:

1. Remove the inner magazine tube and cycle the bolt to cock the hammer. With a non-marring tool such as a brass or bronze drift punch, push out the large cross pin at the rear of the receiver and the smaller cross pin at the center of the receiver. It may be necessary to tap the drift with a small hammer to start the pins out.

2. Remove the trigger group downward and toward the rear.

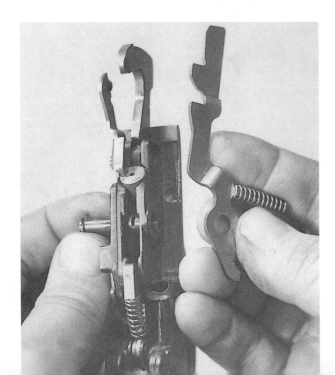

3. Restrain the hammer against the tension of its spring, pull the trigger, and ease the hammer down to the fired position. Remove the small spring clip from the right end of the front cross pin sleeve and push the sleeve out toward the left. This will free the carrier and its spring for removal from the right side of the group. **Caution:** *The carrier spring is strong and is under some tension, so restrain the carrier and ease it off.*

4. Pull the trigger and hold it back to relieve the tension on the rear cross pin sleeve; then push it out toward the left with its spring clip left in place.

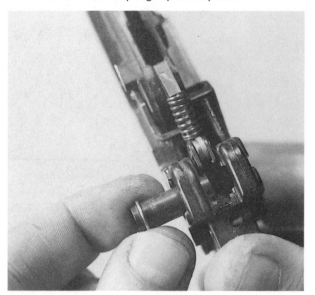

5. Removal of the cross pin sleeve will allow the trigger top to move further to the rear, relieving the tension of the trigger/sear spring. Flex the spring away from its stud on the back of the sear and remove the spring upward.

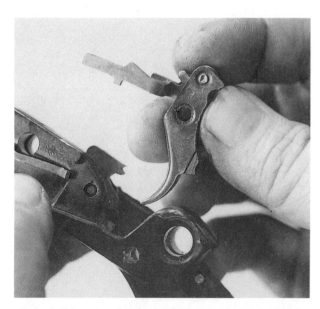

6. Drift out the trigger cross pin and remove the trigger, with its attached connector bar, upward. The two leaves of the connector are riveted at the top of the trigger and removal in normal takedown is not advisable.

7. Insert a small drift punch on the right side of the trigger group, as shown, and push out the sear pivot toward the left. The sear is then removed upward.

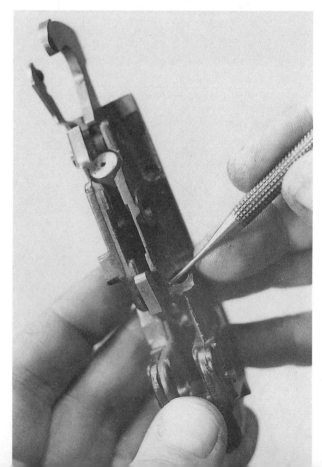

8. Push out the small cross pin at the extreme rear of the trigger group and remove the safety spring and ball upward. The safety can then be slid out toward either side. **Caution:** *The spring is under some tension, so hold a fingertip over the top of the hole when removing the drift punch to control it.* If the detent ball can't be shaken out the top after removal of the spring, wait until the safety is taken out, and then insert a small drift punch from the top and push it out into the safety channel. Take care that this small steel ball isn't lost.

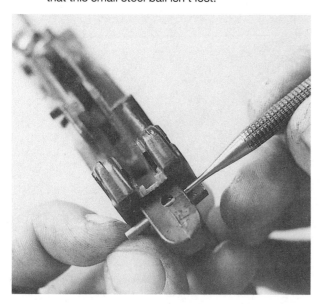

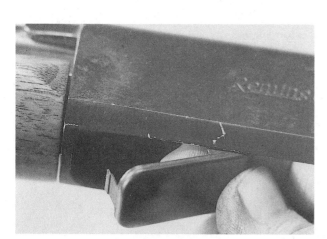

10. Slide the receiver coverplate on the underside about a quarter inch toward the rear, and insert a finger inside the receiver from the rear to tip its front end outward. Pivot it over toward the rear and remove it.

11. With a coin or a specially shaped screwdriver, remove the large screw on the underside of the forend. Move the rear of the forend slightly downward to clear the forward extension of the receiver, and slide the forend forward on the magazine tube. It is not removed at this point.

9. A large cross pin with an enlarged head on the left side pivots and retains both the hammer and the disconnector, and the pin is riveted over a washer on the right side of the trigger group (illus.). Because of the riveting, a drift punch of smaller diameter than the pin body must be used. Be sure the disconnector is well supported when driving out the pin, to avoid damage. **Caution:** *Removal of the disconnector will also release the hammer spring and plunger, so take care to restrain them and ease them out.*

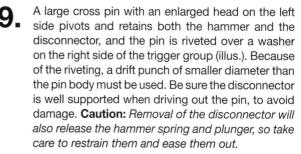

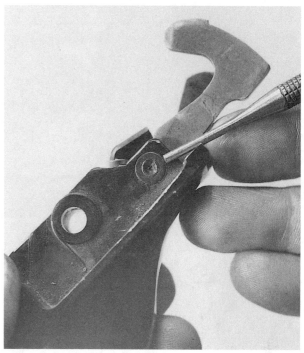

12. Move the barrel assembly forward out of the receiver.

13. Restrain the tension of the bolt spring by holding onto the action bar, and carefully detach the rear vertical lug of the action bar from its recess in the side of the bolt. Remove the bolt toward the rear and ease the action bar forward, relieving the tension of the spring.

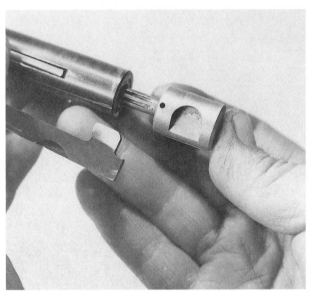

14. Remove the small screw on the underside of the front magazine tube hanger and slide the outer magazine tube out toward the front.

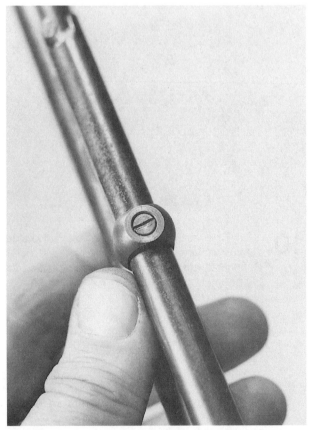

15. Removal of the magazine tube will release the forend piece, action bar and bolt spring to be taken off downward. The front magazine tube hanger has a threaded mounting post and is unscrewed from the underside of the barrel. The steel support piece at the front of the forend can be slid out forward.

16. The firing pin is retained by a small cross pin in the larger rear portion of the bolt, and after removal of the pin it can be taken off upward.

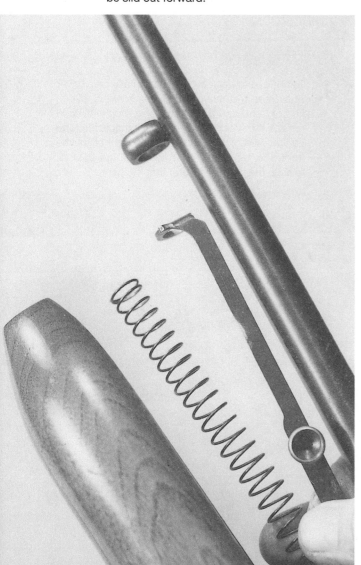

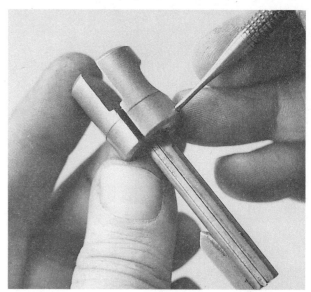

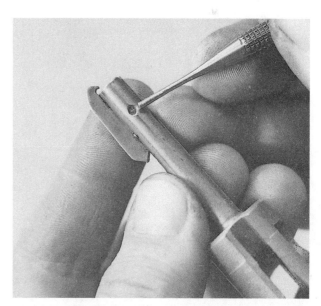

17. After the firing pin is removed, the very short vertical pin that retains the extractor can be driven out, and the extractor and its coil spring can then be taken off toward the right.

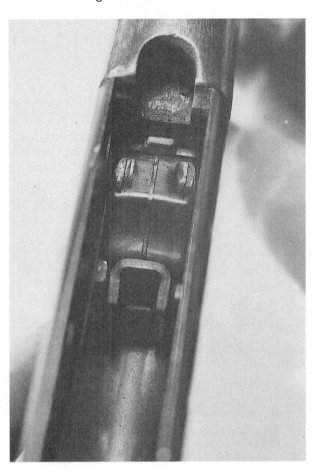

18. Inside the receiver at the rear is a steel bolt buffer and a rubber buffer pad. With the gun inverted, these can be pried upward out of their recess and removed. The stock is retained by a through-bolt from the rear, accessible by removing the buttplate.

19. To remove the ejector, insert a small screwdriver at its rear and move the ejector forward. When its front end can be grasped, tip it outward and remove it toward the left. The rear magazine tube hanger is removed in the same manner as the front one, by simply unscrewing it, and this will release the cartridge ramp that it retains.

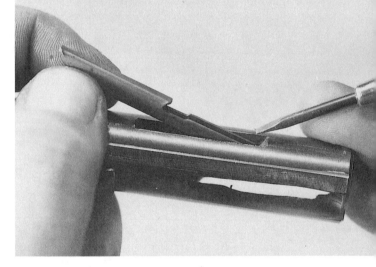

20. The rear sight and the shell deflector are each retained by two small screws. On some Model 552 rifles, the front sight is also retained by two screws. Others have a standard dovetail mount.

Reassembly Tips:

1. When replacing the extractor pivot pin in the slim forward section of the bolt, take care that it does not protrude into the firing pin recess at the top.

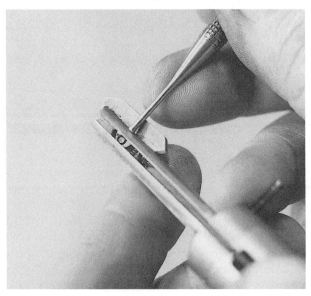

2. When replacing the safety in the trigger group, remember that the side with the red band goes on the left side. When replacing the trigger and its attached connector bars, note that the left connector arm must be installed above the rear tip of the disconnector, as shown.

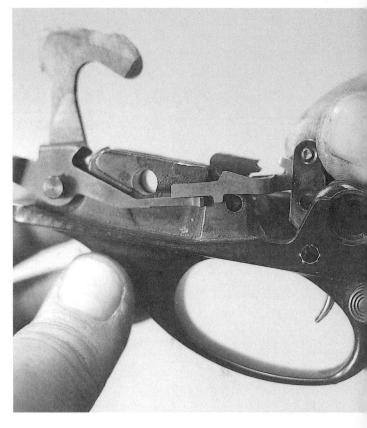

3. Before replacing the barrel assembly in the receiver, put all the components together prior to insertion. The photo shows the proper engagement of the action bar and the bolt. Take care that the lug of the action bar doesn't slip out of its recess in the bolt as the assembly is being slid back into the receiver.

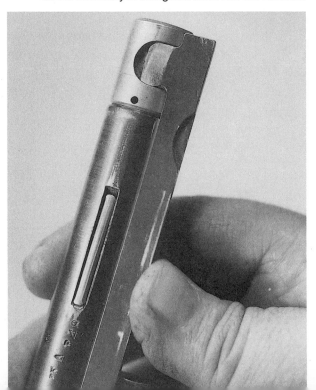

4. To replace the receiver coverplate on the underside, invert the gun and start the plate with its inner surface facing outward. Press it inward, compressing its rear side wings; then swing it over forward until it can be snapped into its retaining grooves.

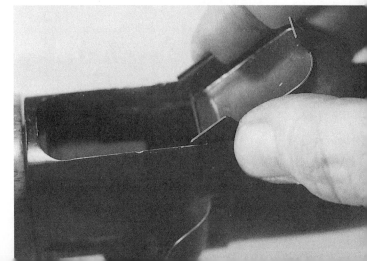

Remington Model 581

Similar/Identical Pattern Guns

The same basic assembly/disassembly steps for the Remington Model 581 also apply to the following gun:

Remington Model 581-S

Data:	Remington Model 581
Origin:	United States
Manufacturer:	Remington Arms Company
	Bridgeport, Connecticut
Cartridge:	22 Short, Long, or Long Rifle
Magazine capacity:	5 rounds
Overall length:	42⅜ inches
Barrel length:	24 inches
Weight:	4¾ pounds

The Model 581 was introduced in 1967 and was made until 1984. For many shooters, it served the same purpose as the 512 and 513 for an earlier generation. The 581 was supplied with a single shot adapter, a useful accessory when teaching youngsters to shoot. It was also available in a left-handed version, the mechanical details being the same.

Disassembly:

1. Remove the magazine, and use a wide, thin-bladed screwdriver to back out the main stock mounting screw on the underside, just forward of the magazine well. Separate the action from the stock. To remove the bolt, open it and move it toward the rear while pushing the safety-lever forward, beyond its normal off-safe position. Withdraw the bolt from the rear of the receiver.

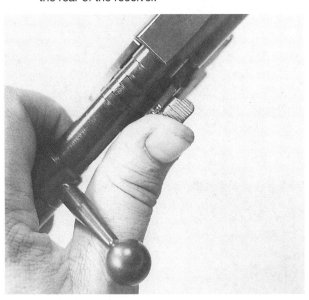

2. Grip the underlug of the striker head, at the rear of the bolt, in a sharp-edged bench vise, and be sure it is firmly held. Push forward on the bolt end piece, against the tension of the striker spring, and unscrew the forward portion of the bolt from the end piece. **Caution:** *The powerful spring is under heavy tension, so control the bolt as the threaded section is cleared.*

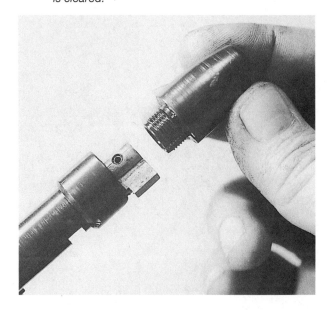

3. Remove the striker and its captive spring assembly from the rear of the bolt. The striker head may be separated from the front portion of the striker by drifting out the roll cross pin. This will release the striker spring with force, so proceed with caution. In normal disassembly, this unit is best left intact. If it is taken apart, take care not to lose the compression washer, located between the spring and the striker head.

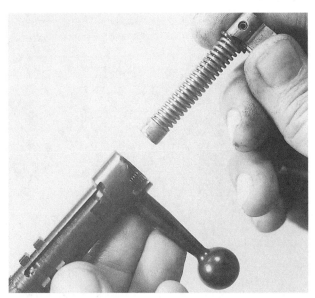

4. A solid cross pin near the forward end of the bolt body retains the breechblock on the front of the bolt. Drifting out the cross pin will allow the breechblock to be taken off toward the front.

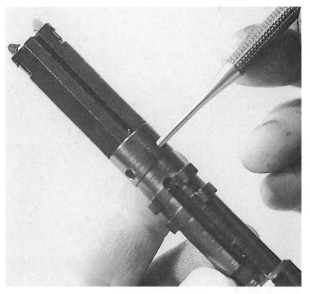

5. Use a small screwdriver to gently pry the left end of the semi-circular spring-clip at the front of the bolt upward. Flexing the left extractor very slightly outward will make insertion of the screwdriver tip easier. Take care to lift the clip only enough to slip it off, as it will break if flexed too far.

6. After the spring clip has been removed, the extractors are easily removed from their recesses on each side, and the firing pin can be taken out of its slot in the top. Note that the extractors are not identical, and each must be returned to the proper side in reassembly.

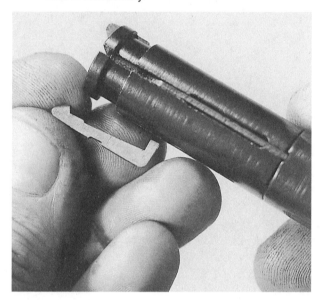

7. The safety-lever is mounted on the trigger housing by its pivot post at the rear and a guide post at the front, and these posts are retained on the left side of the housing by C-clips. Carefully remove the C-clips, guarding against their loss, and take out the two mounting posts toward the right.

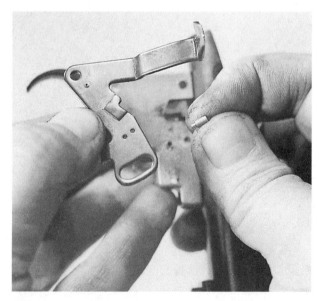

8. Remove the safety-lever toward the right. **Caution:** *As the safety-lever is removed, the safety plunger and spring will be released from their cross-hole in the housing.* Control them during removal, and take them out of the housing. The safety plunger and spring will usually come out of the housing together. If not, it may be necessary to use a small screwdriver to lift out the spring.

9. The large pin at the upper rear of the trigger housing is the sear pivot pin. It is sometimes mistaken for the trigger group retaining pin, and is drifted out in error. This will release the sear within the housing, and the housing must then be removed to replace the sear and its spring in proper order.

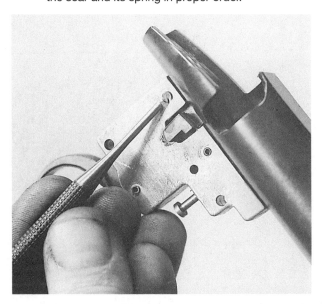

10. The trigger housing retaining pin is a roll pin at the upper center of the housing. Drifting out this cross pin will allow the trigger housing to be taken off downward. When the housing is removed, the bolt stop and its spring can be lifted from their well in the top of the housing, and the sear is easily removed by drifting out its cross pin.

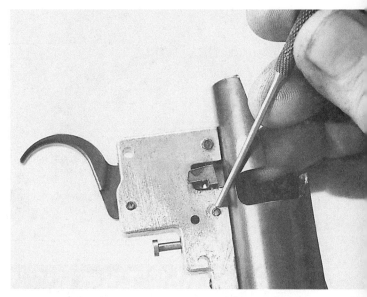

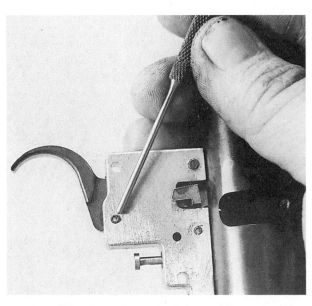

11. The trigger is retained by a roll cross pin at the lower edge of the housing, and is removed downward. The same coil spring powers both the sear and the trigger.

12. The housing tension screw at the extreme front edge of the housing can be backed out if the housing mounting pin is unusually tight, as this will ease tension on the cross pin.

13. Backing out the single screw at the rear of the magazine catch will allow removal of the magazine catch and magazine guide downward. The ejector is an integral part of the magazine guide.

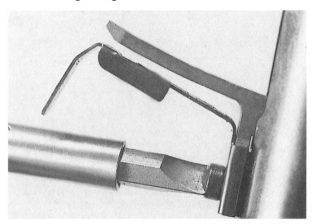

14. Removal of the large screw just forward of the rear sight will allow the sight and sight base to be taken off upward.

Reassembly Tips:

1. When replacing the safety-lever, seat the tip of the safety spring plunger in the larger, dished-out recess on the inside of the lever while pushing the safety into place. In this position, the plunger will be less likely to slip out during installation.

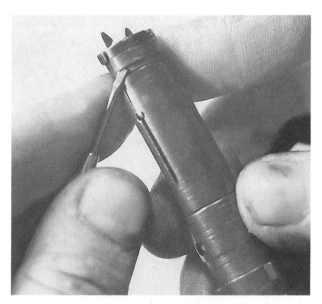

2. When replacing the semi-circular spring clip at the front of the bolt that retains and powers the extractors, note that the small central projection at its top must go toward the front, and its split wing toward the left. Use a small screwdriver to guide its lower end over the extractor as it is pushed into place. When replacing the extractors, note that the one with the sharp break must be placed on the right.

Remington Model 597

Similar/Identical Pattern Guns

The same basic assembly/disassembly steps for the Remington Model 597 also apply to the following guns:

Remington Model 597 Sporter
Remington Model 597SS
Remington Model 597LSS
Remington Model 597 Custom Target
Remington Model 597 Magnum Synthetic

Data:	Remington Model 597
Origin:	United States
Manufacturer:	Remington Arms Company
	Ilion, New York
Cartridge:	22 Long Rifle
Magazine capacity:	10 rounds
Overall length:	38.5 inches
Barrel length:	20 inches
Weight:	5½ pounds

The original Model 597 was introduced in 1997. Since then, there have been several sub-models and special limited-production runs. It has also been offered in 22 Magnum and 17 HMR versions. The one shown here is the Model 597LSS, in stainless steel with a stock of laminated hardwood.

Disassembly:

1. Remove the magazine. Cycle the bolt to cock the internal hammer, and set the safety in on-safe position. Use a 1⁄8-inch Allen wrench to remove the screws at the front and rear of the trigger guard. Note each has a small polymer base, and that the two screws have differing lengths and base shapes.

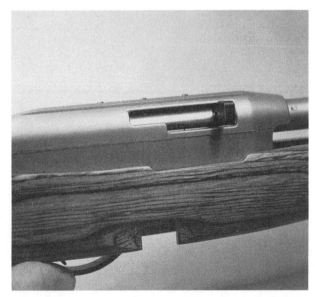

2. Remove the action from the stock.

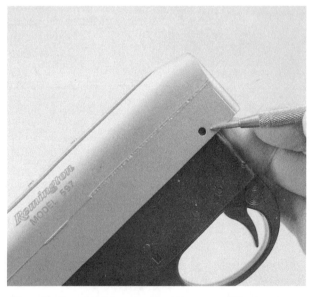

3. Push out the cross pin at the rear of the receiver.

4. Tip the trigger group down at the rear, and remove it.

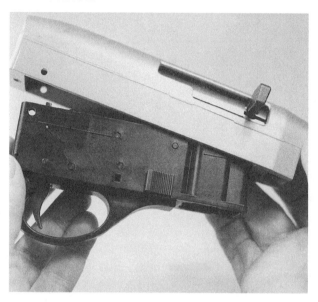

5. With a smaller Allen wrench, remove the two screws at the rear of the receiver.

6. Cycle the bolt a few times, until the bolt spring guides protrude at the rear enough to be grasped. While restraining the spring inside, slowly pull out each guide rod. Control the springs as they are released.

7. Take out the guide rods and springs.

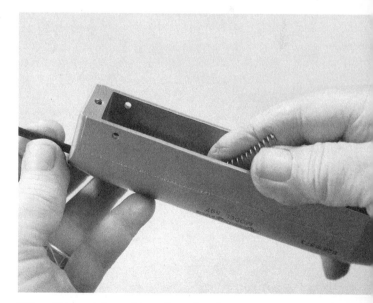

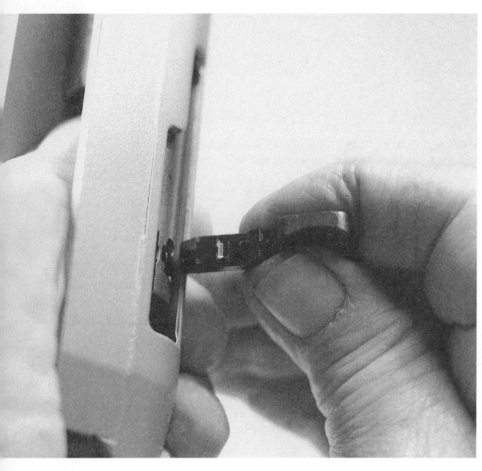

8. Pull the operating handle straight out toward the right.

9. Remove the bolt from the receiver.

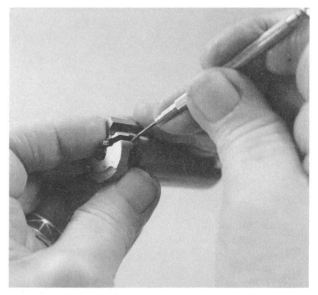

10. If removal of the extractor is necessary, insert a small screwdriver between the extractor and its spring plunger, push the plunger rearward, and tip out the extractor. **Caution:** *Control the plunger and spring, and ease them out for removal.*

11. Drifting out this cross pin toward the right will release the firing pin and its return spring for removal toward the rear.

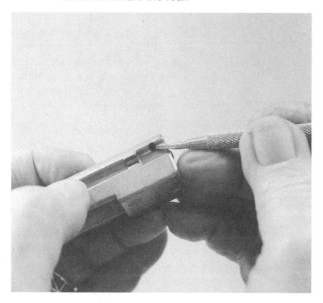

12. If necessary for repair, the bolt handle retainer and its mounting stud can be pried out with a wedge-shaped tool. This system is best left in place.

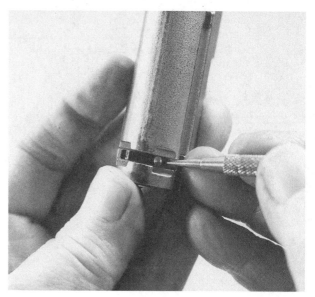

13. The hold-open and its torsion spring can be taken off by prying the headed pin out to the left. In normal takedown, leave it in place.

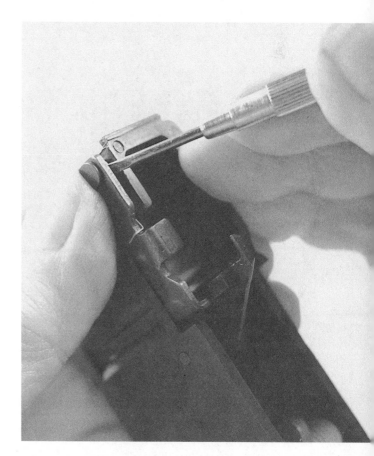

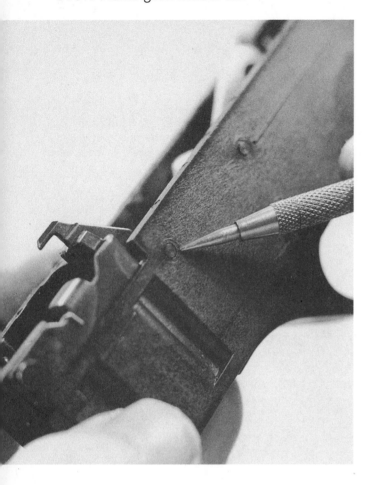

14. The trigger housing is made of polymer, and its depth precludes internal photographs. For these reasons, it is necessary to just show here the takedown sequence, without actual part removal. Drifting out this pin will release the ejector for removal upward.

15. Removal of the magazine catch requires unhooking the torsion spring and extracting a vertical roll-pin. In normal takedown, it is best left in place.

16. If removal of the hammer and its torsion spring are necessary, move the safety to off-safe, restrain the hammer, pull the trigger, and ease the hammer over to fired position. Drifting out this cross pin will allow the hammer and spring to be taken out upward.

17. Assuming the hammer and spring have been removed to allow access, drifting out this cross pin will let the sear be turned over toward the rear and moved to the left for removal. The sear spring can then be taken out.

18. Removal of the trigger-disconnector system will require that first you drift out this pin, to release the expansion-type coil trigger spring.

19. Drifting out this cross pin will allow the trigger and its attached disconnector assembly to be taken out upward. If this system is removed, reassembly will require the use of a special tool to re-attach the trigger spring to its cross pin.

20. For removal of the safety, drift out this small pin and remove the safety spring and detent plunger. **Caution:** *Control the spring.* After the spring and plunger are taken out, the safety button can be moved out toward either side. **Note:** The pin is a roll-type, so use a proper drift.

21. The barrel is retained in the receiver by a clamp arrangement, secured by this Allen screw.

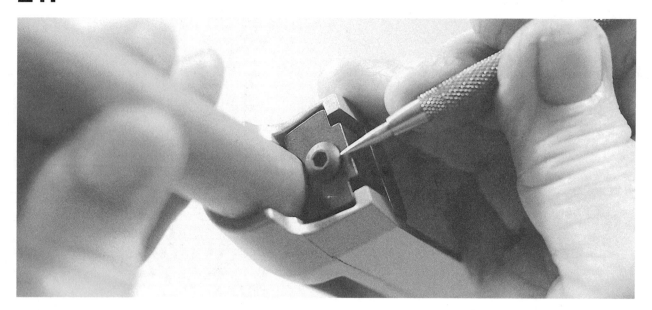

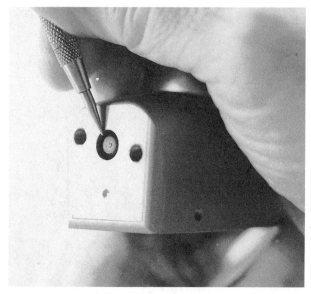

22. If necessary for repair/replacement, the polymer bolt buffer can be drifted forward for removal.

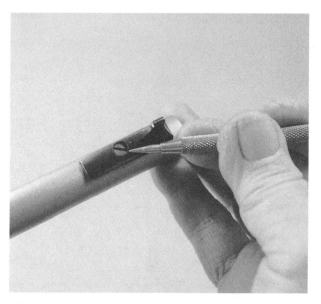

23. The front sight is retained by a vertical screw.

24. The rear sight is retained by two vertical screws. The one to the rear is accessed by taking off the adjustment slide piece.

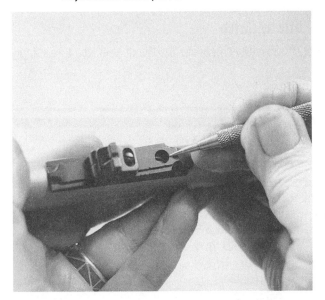

25. The magazine can be disassembled by squeezing its sides at the lower edge and taking off the floorplate. The spring and follower can then be taken out.

Reassembly Tips:

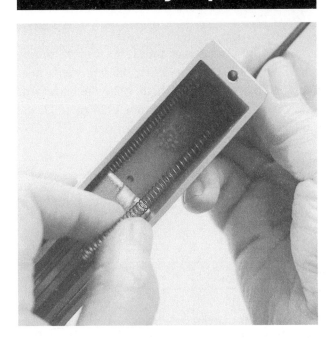

1. When re-installing the bolt springs and guides, insert the guide rods slowly, feeding the spring onto the rod as it is pushed in. Be sure the front tips of the guide rods enter their sockets in the rear face of the barrel. It may be necessary to insert a tool at the front to ensure this. The set screws that retain the guide rods must not be overtightened or the rods will flex and the bolt might not fully close. The set screws should be flush with the outer surface of the receiver.

Remington No. 4

Similar/Identical Pattern Guns

The same basic assembly/disassembly steps for the Remington No. 4 also apply to the following gun:

Navy Arms Baby Carbine

Data:	Remington No. 4
Origin:	United States
Manufacturer:	Remington Arms Company
	Ilion, New York
Cartridge:	22 Long Rifle
Overall length:	37 inches
Barrel length:	22½ inches
Weight:	4½ pounds

One of the premium "boy's rifles" of earlier times, the No. 4 "rolling block" was made from 1890 to 1933. Up to 1901, the gun was a non-takedown design with a fixed barrel. From 1901 to 1926, the barrel was retained by a lever, as on the gun shown here. From 1926 to 1933, the lever was replaced by a large knurled screw with a coin slot.

Disassembly:

1. Turn the barrel latch lever over toward the front, and separate the barrel assembly from the action.

2. The forend is retained on the barrel by a single screw. The front and rear sights are dovetail-mounted.

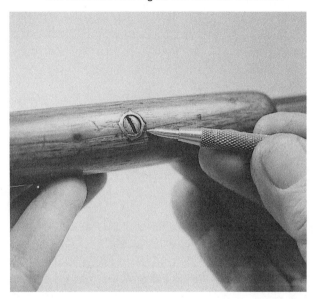

3. Remove the large screw at the end of the upper tang. Take off the buttstock toward the rear. The buttplate is retained by two wood screws.

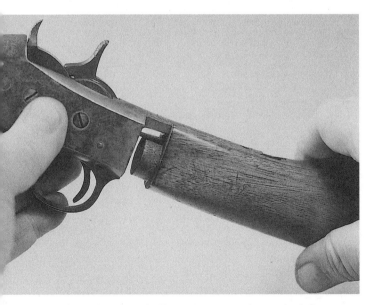

4. Remove the hammer spring screw and take out the hammer spring toward the rear.

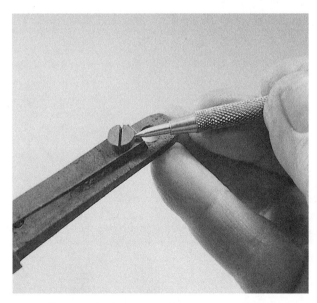

5. Remove the hammer pivot screw. The hammer is not taken out at this time. Remove the breechblock pivot screw.

6. Tip the hammer to the rear and remove the breech block upward. Remove the hammer upward.

7. Drift out the firing pin cross pin. Remove the firing pin toward the rear.

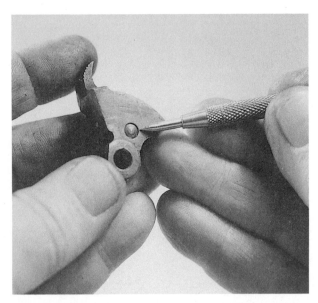

8. Drift out the trigger cross pin and remove the trigger upward.

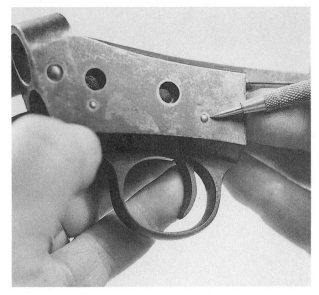

9. Drift out the ejector cross pin. Be sure the barrel latch lever is turned out of the way.

10. Remove the ejector upward.

11. Remove the screw inside, in the floor of the receiver, and take out the combination spring.

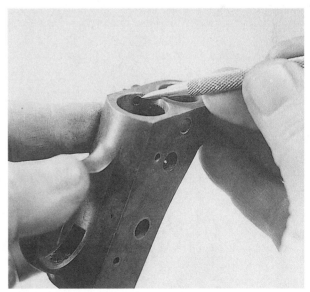

12. Drift out the barrel latch stop pin toward the right.

13. Unscrew the barrel latch from the receiver, turning it clockwise. Note that it has a reverse thread.

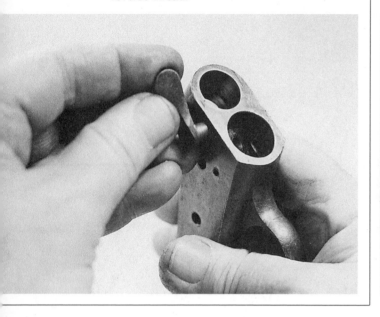

Reassembly Tips:

1. When installing the combination spring that bears on the trigger, ejector and breechblock, turn the screw about halfway in, and reserve tightening until the trigger and ejector are installed. This will make the alignment for cross pin insertion easier. Don't forget to tighten the screw after they are in place.

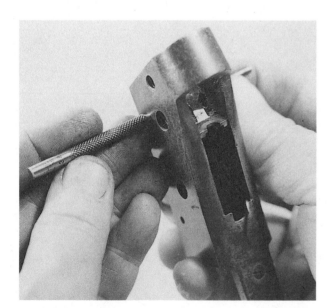

2. Insert a drift to position the trigger and ejector for insertion of the cross pins.

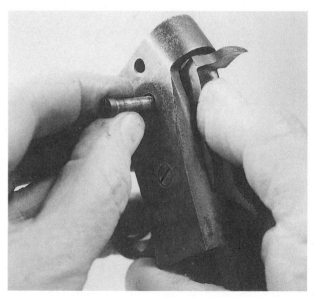

3. Remember that the hammer must be put back in the receiver before the breechblock can be installed. For insertion of the breechblock screw, the block must be pushed down and forward, against the tension of its bearing spring.

Remington Nylon 66

Similar/Identical Pattern Guns

The same basic assembly/disassembly steps for the Remington Nylon 66 also apply to the following guns:

F.I.E. Model GR-8   **Remington Nylon 66MB**

Magtech Model MT-66   **Remington Nylon 66 Bicentennial**

Remington Nylon 66GS

Data:	Remington Nylon 66
Origin:	United States
Manufacturer:	Remington Arms Company
	Bridgeport, Connecticut
Cartridge:	22 Long Rifle
Magazine capacity:	14 rounds
Overall length:	38½ inches
Barrel length:	19⅝ inches
Weight:	4 pounds

Around 1959, when the Remington Nylon 66 first arrived on the scene, many firearms traditionalists sneered at its DuPont Zytel stock/receiver, stamped-steel parts and expansion-type springs. Over the years, though, they found that it works, and keeps working, uncleaned, mistreated, and abused, a tribute to Wayne Leek and the design team at Remington. For those not familiar with its mechanism, though, the Nylon 66 can be a disassembly/reassembly nightmare. The Nylon 66 was discontinued by Remington in 1988, but has been made in South America since then. This later version was marketed by Firearms Import & Export (F.I.E.) as the GR-8, and by Magtech Recreational Products as their MT-66.

Disassembly:

1. Remove the inner magazine tube from the stock. Grip the bolt handle firmly and pull it straight out toward the right.

2. Back out the two cross-screws, located near the lower edge of the receiver cover, and remove them toward the right.

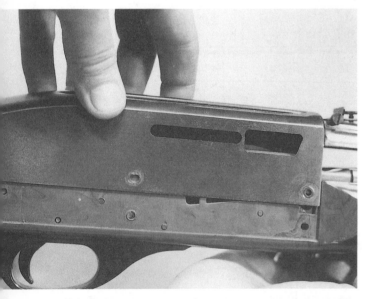

3. Remove the receiver cover assembly upward. The internal cartridge guide spring and the rear sight base are riveted on the cover, and removal is not advisable in normal disassembly.

4. Remove the ejector from its recess in the left side of the receiver.

5. Loosen the large cross-slotted screw on the underside of the stock, just forward of the trigger guard; then push it upward to raise the barrel retaining piece until its upper cross bar clears its recess on top of the barrel. Slide the barrel out toward the front.

6. The front sight is retained on top of the barrel by two screws, one at each end.

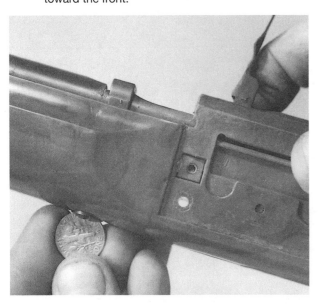

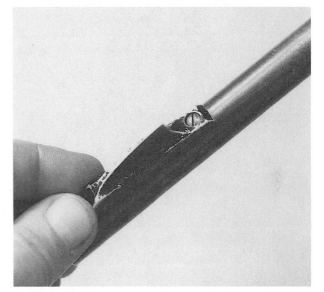

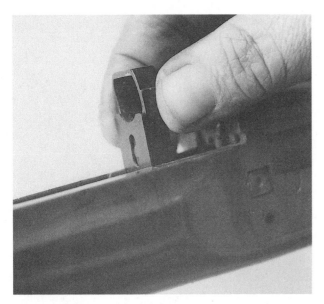

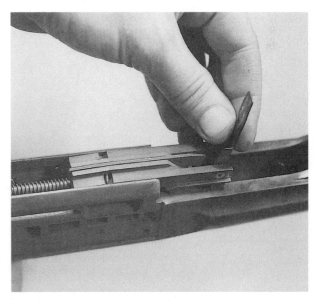

7. Take out the cross-slotted screw from the bottom of the stock, and lift the barrel retainer and its front plate out of their recess in the top of the stock.

8. Be sure the hammer is in its cocked position (at the rear), and the safety in the on-safe position. Grasp the cartridge guide, and move the bolt forward out of its tracks in the receiver. Remove the bolt spring and its guide toward the front.

9. Move the safety to the off-safe position, restrain the hammer against the tension of its spring, and pull the trigger to release the hammer. Ease the spring tension slowly, and move the hammer forward out of its tracks in the receiver. Remove the hammer spring and its guide.

10. Push out the cross pin located in the receiver just above the forward end of the trigger guard (arrow). Tip the trigger guard downward at the front, disengage its rear hook from inside the receiver, and remove the guard downward.

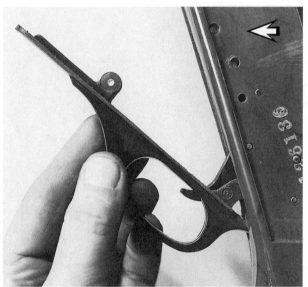

11. Use a small tool to unhook the trigger spring from its groove on the front of the trigger.

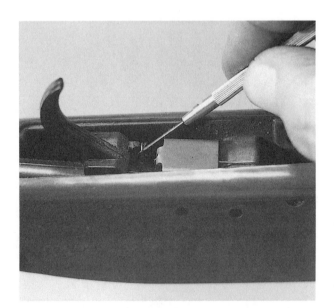

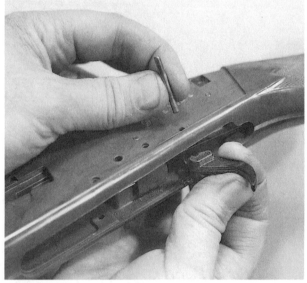

12. Push out the trigger cross pin, and remove the trigger downward.

13. Push out the cross pin just below the ejector recess (arrow), and remove the cartridge stop and its flat spring from the bottom of the receiver.

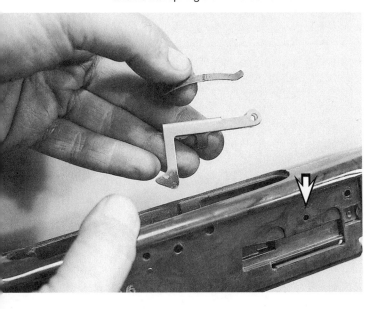

14. Use a tool to push the front of the cartridge feed throat (insert) downward, and tip it out of its recess for removal from the bottom of the receiver.

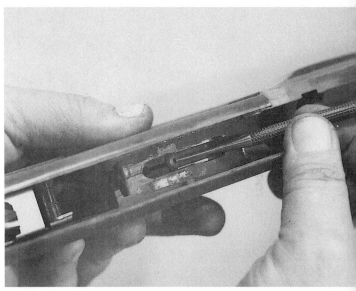

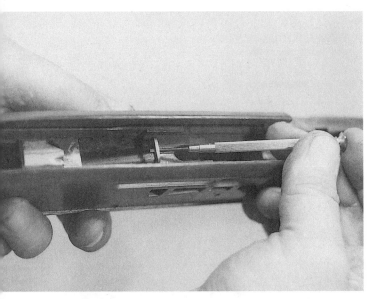

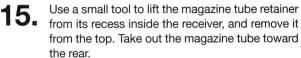

15. Use a small tool to lift the magazine tube retainer from its recess inside the receiver, and remove it from the top. Take out the magazine tube toward the rear.

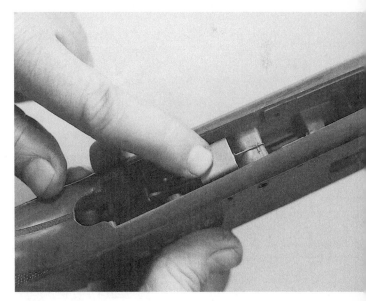

16. Restrain the sear at the top of the receiver against its spring tension, and push the disconnector pivot at the bottom of the receiver to release the sear. Allow the sear to pivot upward, slowly releasing the tension of its spring.

17. Use a tool to disengage the hook of the disconnector pivot spring from the receiver cross-piece at the bottom.

18. Push out the disconnector pivot points, one on each side of the receiver. After one has been removed, the other may be pushed out from the inside, using one of the other cross pins already removed or a drift punch.

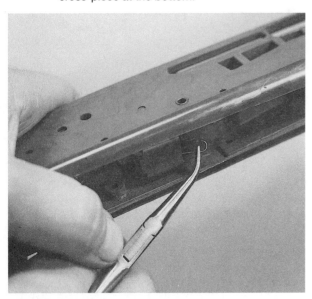

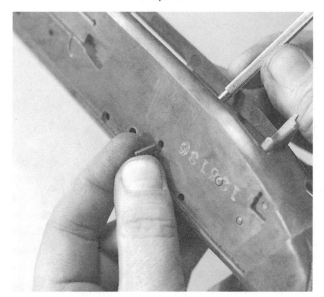

19. Depress the sear slightly to clear the rear arm of the disconnector, and remove the disconnector assembly from the top of the receiver. The disconnector is easily separated from its pivot by squeezing the sides of the pivot inward just enough to detach the lugs from the holes in the disconnector. The springs are also easily detached by turning their ends out of the holes in the parts.

20. Push out the sear pivot pin, and remove the sear and its spring from the top of the receiver (actually, the spring will usually fall from the bottom as the pin is taken out).

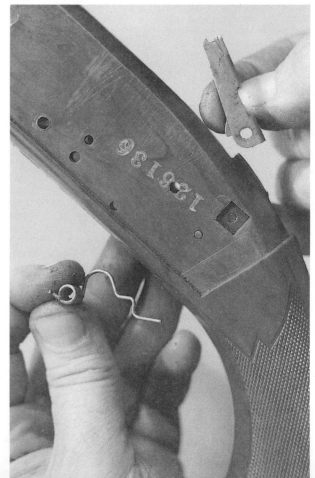

21. Push out the safety-lever cam pin, the last cross pin at the rear of the receiver. This will allow the safety-lever to drop, and the safety and its attached lever can then be removed upward.

22. Use a fingernail or a small tool to move the safety detent spring retaining pin out toward the rear. The pin has a groove at its rear tip to aid removal. The detent spring is not under heavy tension, but it can flip the pin as it is removed, so restrain it with a fingertip during removal. Take out the detent spring and the ball bearing from their hole in the top of the receiver, and take care that the bearing isn't lost.

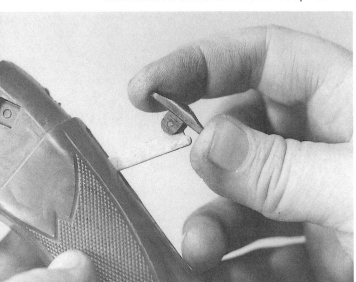

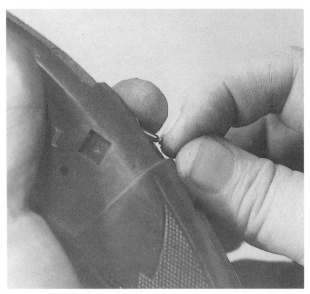

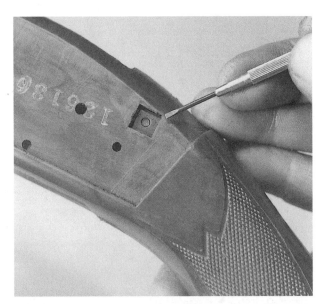

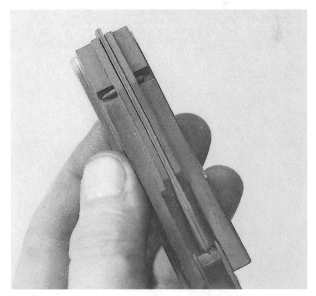

23. The two internal cross screws with square nuts on the left side do not retain parts, and their removal is neither necessary nor advisable during normal takedown.

24. The firing pin is retained in the bolt by a cross pin on top, near the rear of the bolt. The retaining pin is bent down on each side to lock it in place, and one end must be pried upward before the pin is drifted out. The firing pin is then removed toward the rear.

25. Insert a small screwdriver between the rear of the extractor and its plunger, and depress the plunger while lifting the extractor out of its recess. **Caution:** *The spring is under compression, so take care it doesn't get away.* Ease it out, and remove the plunger and spring.

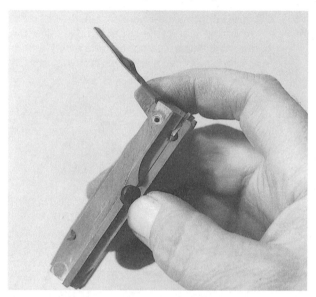

26. A roll pin across the top front of the bolt retains the cartridge guide. Drifting out the pin will release the guide for removal. Be sure to use a roll pin punch to avoid deforming the pin.

Reassembly Tips:

1. When replacing the disconnector assembly, remember that the sear (arrow) must be tipped forward to allow the rear arm of the disconnector to go behind the sear.

2. Remember that the cartridge feed throat ("cartridge insert") must be put in from below. Insert its rear tip first; then swing its front wings upward into the recesses while holding the rear tip in place with a tool, as shown. When the cartridge feed throat is in place, invert the gun so the feed throat will not fall back into the stock before installation of the cartridge stop (the front tip of the stop spring holds the feed throat in place). Installation of the cartridge feed throat is the single most difficult point in the reassembly of the Nylon 66.

3. Do not attempt to install the cartridge stop and its flat spring at the same time. Install the stop, then insert the spring, with its forward end going under the pin (remember, the gun is inverted), and push the spring forward until its indented catch locks on the front edge of the cartridge stop.

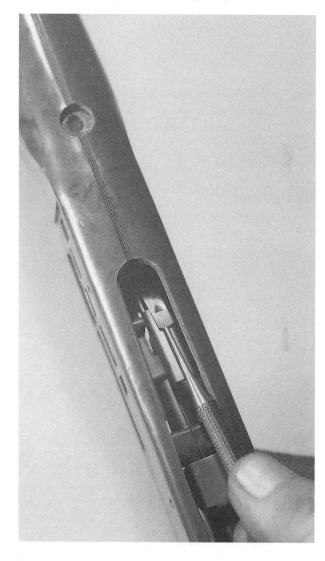

4. When properly installed, the front lip of the sear (arrow) should be under the front cross-piece of the disconnector, as shown.

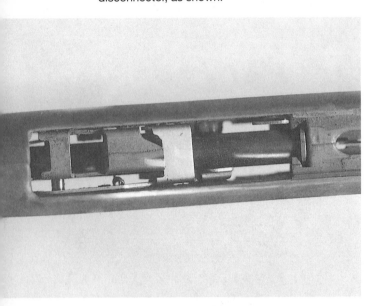

When reinstalling the hammer assembly, it is necessary to use a small tool to depress the sear while holding the trigger back, allowing the hammer to move to the rear. When the hammer is moved back to the cocked position, set the safety in the on-safe position to prevent release of the hammer while the bolt is installed.

When installing the barrel retainer, note that the front plate goes at the front of the retainer, and that the plate has an oblong slot which mates with a stud on the retainer.

Before replacing the receiver cover, be sure the ejector is in place in its recess on the left side. This part is often left out during reassembly, or drops off if the gun is tilted toward the left during replacement of the cover.

Before replacing the cover, be sure the cartridge guide is flipped over forward, to lie on top of the barrel.

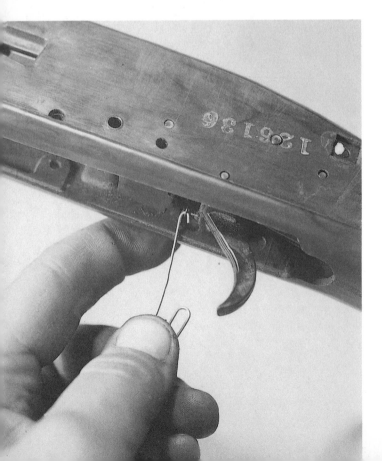

5. It is very difficult to reattach the trigger spring to the front of the trigger without a small hooked tool. The one shown was made from an opened paper clip.

Ruger American Rimfire Compact

Similar/Identical Pattern Guns

The same basic assembly/disassembly steps for the Ruger American Rimfire Compact also apply to the following gun:
Ruger American Rimfire (full size)

Data:	Ruger American Rimfire Compact
Origin:	American
Manufacturer:	Ruger, Mayodan, NC
Cartridge:	.22 Long Rifle, .22 WMR, .17 HMR
Magazine capacity:	10 rounds (.22 LR), 9 rounds (.17 HMR, .22 WMR)
Overall length:	35.75 inches
Barrel length:	18 inches
Weight:	5.4 pounds

Shortly after Ruger released their new American rifle for hunting, they also began producing a rimfire version of that rifle, in similar fashion to the Model 77 and its companion 77/22. These rifles are excellent examples of modern manufacturing, particularly in the ability to make less expensive rifles to maintain sales, with traditionally expensive features such as free floating barrels and adjustable triggers. The stock interestingly comes with two inserts to adjust length of pull and comb height. This model is a Compact, with a 12.5" length of pull and an 18" threaded barrel.

Disassembly:

1. Remove the bolt by opening it and while depressing the bolt stop on the left side of the rear of the receiver, pull the bolt out to the rear.

2. Remove these two bolts, which hold the barreled action into the stock.

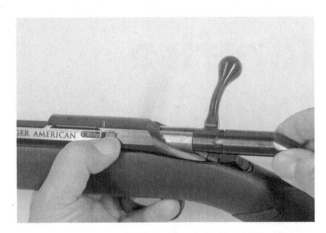

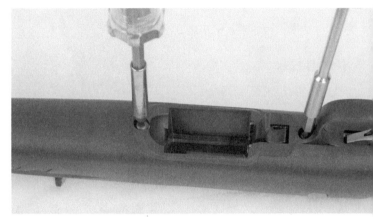

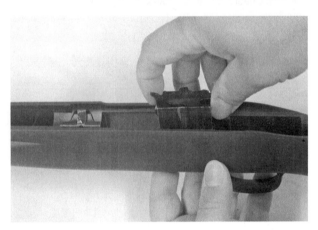

3. The magazine catch/rear receiver block can be pushed up and out of the stock. The front block need not be removed.

4. Push out this pin to free the magazine catch and ejector from the housing.

5. The magazine catch housing and its parts. The ejector on top, the magazine catch and spring, and the pin and magazine catch lever below.

6. Rotate the bolt handle to the closed position. You may need to slightly depress/retract the firing pin's sear engagement arm (picture A). Then push/compress the bolt shroud into the bolt body with your thumb and push out the retaining pin with a punch (picture B).

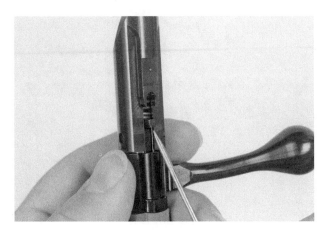

picture A

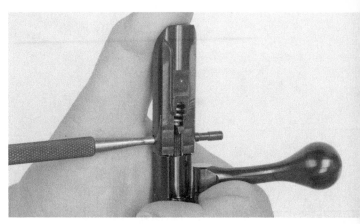

picture B

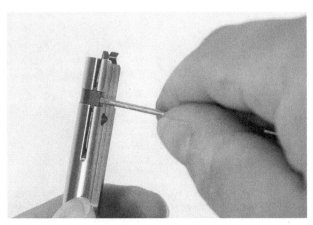

7. When replacing the left trigger housing wall, make sure the spring that is screwed into the left wall, shown at the right in this picture, enters the safety at this location, shown on the left.

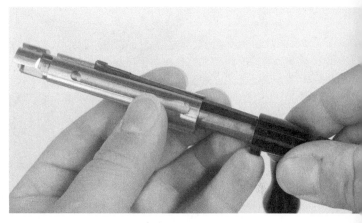

8. The bolt handle and firing pin can now be pulled out of the back of the bolt.

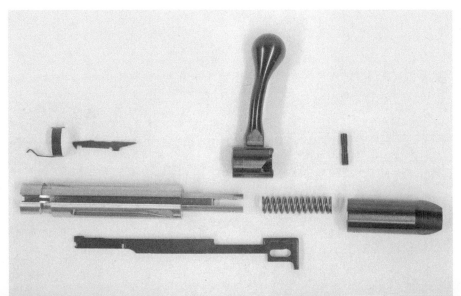

9. The bolt shown stripped.

10. Drive out these two spring pins to remove the trigger housing (picture A). The trigger housing will be free to drop down. There is a black insert at the upper rear of the housing that may fall free at this time (picture B).

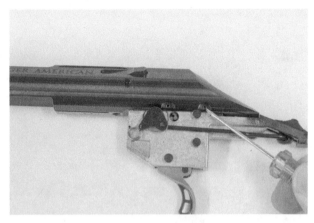

picture A

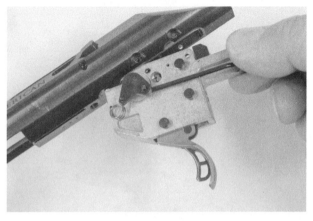

picture B

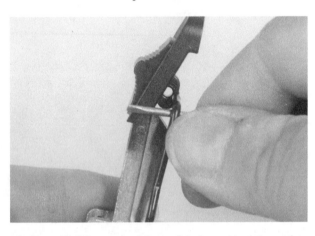

11. Pull the rear of the safety bar out of the safety button. This will free the button to be lifted up and out of the housing.

12. With the rear of the safety bar swinging freely, the left side of the safety drum (attached to the spring) can be pushed slightly to the right, which provides sufficient clearance for the large E-clip on the right side of the housing to be pulled off the safety drum. With the clip free, the drum can be removed out to the left, along with its spring. Do not attempt to remove the spring first or it will likely be damaged.

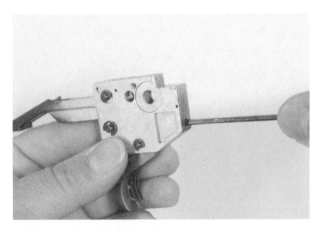

13. Remove the adjustment screw. The spring will not come with it.

14. Tap out this small spring pin, which limits movement of the sear. A spring lies beneath.

15. Remove the three E-clips on the right side of the housing.

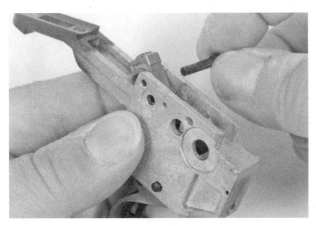

picture A

picture B

16. Remove the top pin to remove the sear (picture A). Then lift out the sear spring (picture B).

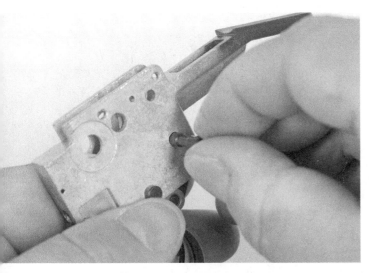

17. Remove the middle pin. This limits movement of the trigger safety insert.

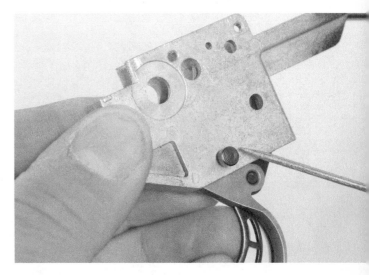

18. Remove the bottom pin to free the trigger assembly.

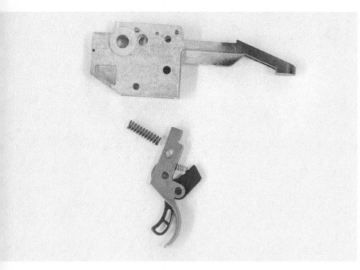

19. The trigger when removed from the housing. There is no need to further disassemble the trigger. The long spring is the adjustment spring that fits into a hole inside the front wall of the trigger housing.

20. The folding rear sight can be removed by drifting it to the right. The front sight is retained by a single screw.

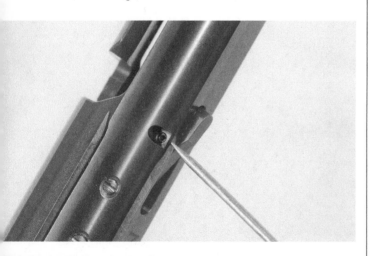

21. Tap out this spring pin to free the bolt stop and spring.

Reassembly Tips:

1. When reinstalling the safety parts, again remember to replace the bar prior to reinstalling the large E-clip. There is insufficient clearance to install the bar after the E-clip has been reseated.

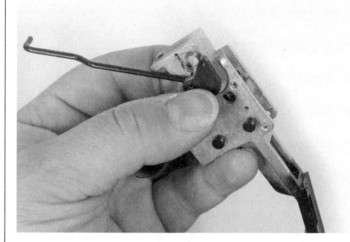

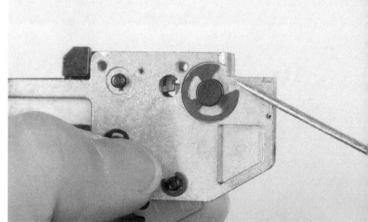

2. The large E-clip, when reinstalled, should be oriented in this fashion (clear of this corner) or it will prevent the installation of the trigger housing into the receiver.

Ruger 10/22

Similar/Identical Pattern Guns

The same basic assembly/disassembly steps for the Ruger 10/22 also apply to the following guns:

Ruger 10/22 Sporter	**AMT Lightning 25/22**
Ruger 10/22 International	**AMT Lightning Small Game**
Ruger 10/22 Deluxe Sporter	**Magnum Research MagnumLite**
Ruger 10/22 Compac	**Ruger 10/22 Target**
Ruger SR-22	

Data:	Ruger 10/22
Origin:	United States
Manufacturer:	Sturm, Ruger & Company Southport, Connecticut
Cartridge:	22 Long Rifle
Magazine capacity:	10 rounds
Overall length:	36¾ inches
Barrel length:	18½ inches
Weight:	5¾ pounds

Since its introduction in 1964, the Model 10/22 has established an enviable record of reliability. Over the past 15 years, I have repaired only one of these guns, and that one had been altered by its owner. Originally offered in Carbine, Sporter and International models, the latter with a full Mannlicher-style stock was discontinued for many years. The gun is again available in all three styles, however, the only differences being in the stock and barrel band. The instructions will generally apply to any of the 10/22 guns.

Disassembly:

1. Loosen or remove the cross-screw at the lower end of the barrel band, and take off the barrel band toward the front. If the band is tight, applying slight downward pressure on the barrel will make it move off more easily.

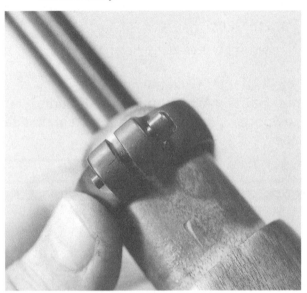

2. Remove the magazine, and cycle the action to cock the internal hammer. Back out the main stock screw, located on the underside just forward of the magazine well.

3. Center the safety halfway between its right and left positions so it will clear the stock on each side, and move the action upward out of the stock.

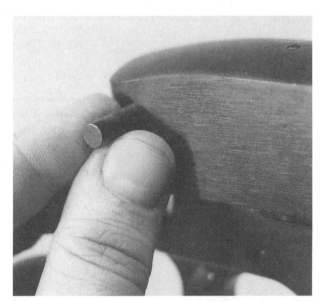

4. When the action is removed from the stock, the bolt stop pin, the large cross pin at the rear of the receiver, will probably be loose and can be easily taken out at this time.

5. Drift out the front and rear cross pins (arrows) that hold the trigger group on the receiver. Then remove the trigger group downward.

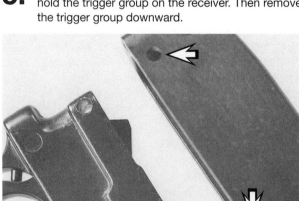

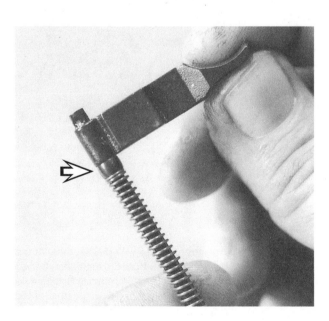

6. If the bolt stop pin was not taken out earlier, it must be removed now. With the gun inverted, move the bolt all the way to the rear and tip the front of the bolt outward, away from the inside roof of the receiver. **Caution:** *Keep a firm grip on the bolt handle, as the bolt spring is fully compressed.* Ease the bolt handle forward, slowly relieving the spring tension, and remove the bolt from the underside of the receiver. Remove the bolt handle and its attached spring and guide rod from the ejection port.

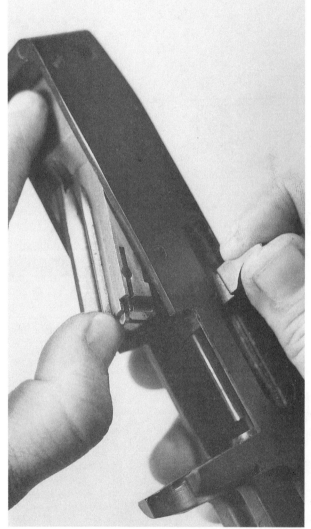

7. The bolt spring guide rod is staked at the forward end, ahead of the bolt handle, and if the stake lumps are filed off for disassembly, a new guide rod may be required. In normal disassembly, this unit is best left intact. If it is taken apart, be careful not to lose the small spacer (arrow) between the spring and the handle at the forward end.

8. The firing pin is retained by a roll cross pin at the upper rear of the bolt. Use a roll-pin punch to drift out the cross pin, and remove the firing pin and its return spring toward the rear.

9. To remove the extractor, insert a small screwdriver to depress the extractor spring plunger, and hold it in while the extractor is lifted out of its recess. **Caution:** *Take care that the screwdriver doesn't slip, as the plunger and spring can travel far if suddenly released.* Ease them out slowly, and remove them from the bolt.

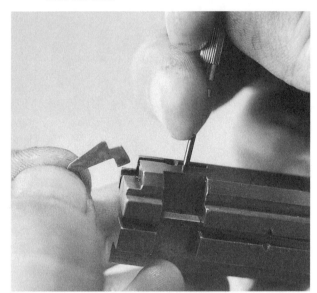

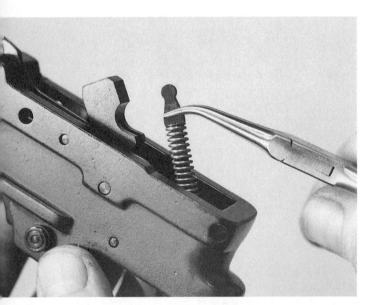

10. Restrain the hammer against the tension of its spring, pull the trigger, and ease the hammer forward beyond its normal fired position. The hammer spring assembly can now be moved forward and upward, out of the trigger group. The hammer spring assembly can be taken apart by compressing the spring and sliding the slotted washer off the lower end of the guide. Proceed with caution, as the spring is under tension.

11. Before going any further with disassembly of the trigger group, carefully note the relationship of all parts and springs, to aid in reassembly. Tip the front of the ejector out of its slot in the front of the trigger group, push out the cross pin at the rear of the ejector, and remove the ejector upward. Note that removal of the cross pin will also release the upper arm of the bolt latch spring.

12. A cross pin at the lower front of the trigger group pivots and retains the bolt latch and the magazine catch lever. The bolt latch is removed upward. Restrain the magazine catch plunger with a fingertip, remove the catch lever downward, and ease the plunger and its spring out toward the front.

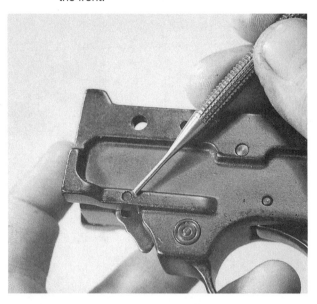

13. Hold the trigger back to remove sear tension from the hammer, and push out the hammer pivot cross pin. Remove the hammer assembly upward. The bolt latch spring encircles the hammer bushing on the right side, and the two hammer pivot bushings are easily removed from the hammer.

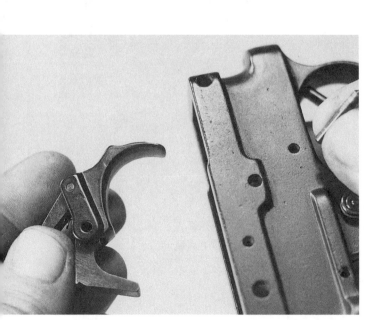

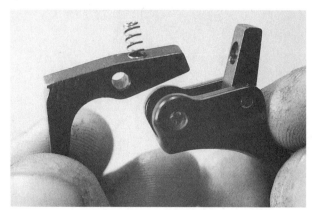

14. Note the position of the sear and disconnector in the top of the trigger before disassembly. Push out the trigger pivot cross pin, and remove the trigger/sear/disconnector assembly upward. As the trigger is moved upward, the trigger spring and plunger will be released at the rear of the trigger guard. Ease them out, and remove them downward and toward the front.

15. The sear is removed from the trigger toward the front, along with the combination sear and disconnector spring. Drifting out the cross pin at the upper rear of the trigger will release the disconnector for removal.

16. Grip the safety firmly with a thumb and finger at each end, and give it a one-quarter turn toward the front; then push it out toward the left. **Caution:** *Insert a fingertip inside the trigger group, above the safety, to arrest the safety plunger and spring, as they will be released as the safety is moved out.*

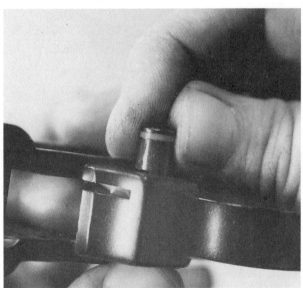

17. In normal takedown, removal of the barrel is not advisable. If necessary, however, use an Allen wrench to back out the two large screws that secure the barrel retainer block and take out the barrel toward the front. If the barrel is tight, grip the barrel in a padded vise and use a nylon hammer to tap the receiver off toward the rear.

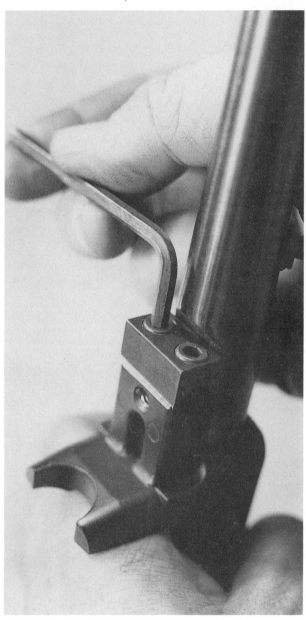

18. Magazine disassembly is not recommended in normal takedown. If it becomes necessary, removal of the screw at the front of the magazine will allow the backplate to be taken off, and the internal parts can then be taken out toward the rear. **Caution:** *Don't remove the spring from the rotor. Carefully note the relationship of all parts to aid in reassembly.*

Reassembly Tips:

1. When replacing the trigger/sear/disconnector assembly in the trigger group, use a slave pin to hold the three parts and the spring in position for reinsertion. The photo shows the parts in place and the slave pin in the pivot hole.

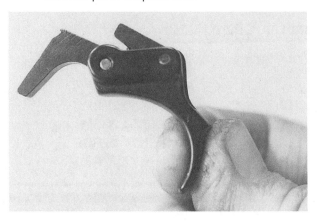

2. When replacing the hammer, its pivot bushings and the bolt latch spring, note that the spring must be on the right side of the hammer, as shown. Be sure the lower arm of the spring engages its notch in the cross-piece of the bolt latch. The upper arm of the spring goes below the cross pin that retains the ejector.

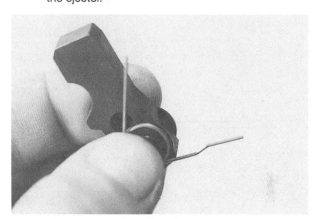

3. When replacing the magazine catch system, remember that the bolt latch must be in place before the catch lever, plunger, and spring are installed. Insert the magazine catch plunger and spring first; then put in the catch lever from below. The upper arm of the lever will hold the plunger and spring in place while the cross pin is inserted. Be sure the cross pin passes through the bolt latch and the magazine catch.

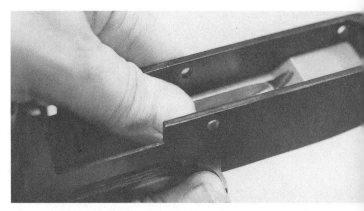

4. When replacing the bolt in the receiver, remember that the bolt handle must be fully to the rear, with the spring compressed, before the bolt can be tipped back into engagement with the handle at the front.

When replacing the action in the stock, be sure the safety is again set between its right and left positions to clear the interior as the action is moved into place.

If the magazine has been disassembled, insert the screw in the magazine body and place the rotor and spring on the screw, with the longer hub of the rotor toward the front. Replace the feed throat, being sure the larger end stud enters its recess at the front. Put the backplate back on the magazine body and hold it in place. Insert the front of the hexagonal-headed magazine nut into the rear of the spring, and be sure the hooked tip of the spring engages the hole in the nut. Turn the nut clockwise (rear view) until the rotor stops turning; then give it an additional 1¼ turns to properly tension the spring. Move the nut into its recess and tighten the magazine screw, taking care not to overtighten.

Ruger Model 77/22

Similar/Identical Pattern Guns

The same basic assembly/disassembly steps for the Ruger Model 77/22 also apply to the following guns:

Ruger 77/22R	**Ruger 77/22RS**
Ruger 77/22RP	**Ruger 77/22RSP**
Ruger 77/22RM	**Ruger 77/22RSM**
Ruger K77/22RP	**Ruger K77/22RSP**
Ruger K77/22RSMP	**Ruger K77/22RMP**

Data:	Ruger Model 77/22
Origin:	United States
Manufacturer:	Sturm, Ruger & Company
	Southport, Connecticut
Cartridge:	22 Long Rifle
Magazine capacity:	10 rounds
Overall length:	39¾ inches
Barrel length:	20 inches
Weight:	5¾ pounds

The original blued-steel and wood-stocked version of the Model 77/22 was introduced in 1983. Six years later, in 1989, the gun was offered in stainless steel with an optional synthetic stock, and also in a 22 WMR version. A beautifully engineered bolt action, the Model 77/22 uses the same magazine and barrel-mounting system as the Ruger 10/22 autoloader.

Disassembly:

1. Remove the magazine and open the bolt. Depress the bolt stop, located at the left rear of the receiver, and remove the bolt toward the rear.

2. Insert a drift through the hole in the underlug of the striker end piece and turn the bolt headpiece to the position shown.

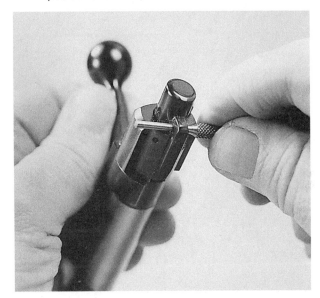

3. After the headpiece is turned, the head of the breechblock pin will be visible in this opening. Use a drift in the aperture on the other side, and push the breechblock pin out. Remove the breechblock toward the front.

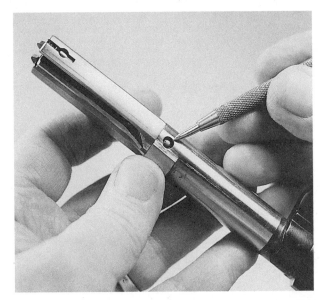

4. The extractors can be removed by using a small tool to push their plungers toward the rear. **Caution:** *Control the plunger and spring on each side, and ease them out.* Keep the extractors separate they are not interchangeable.

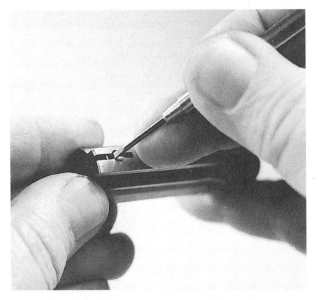

5. Using the drift in the hole in the striker underlug, unscrew the striker assembly from the bolt body. Remove the assembly toward the rear. Note that the firing pin can be detached from its hook at the front of the shaft as it emerges.

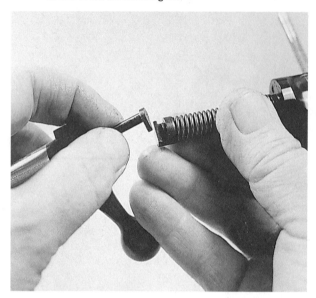

6. While it is possible to use a vise and special jigs to further disassemble the striker system, the factory advises against this. In normal takedown, it is best left intact.

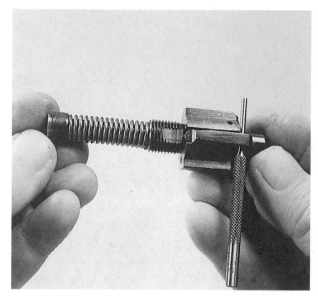

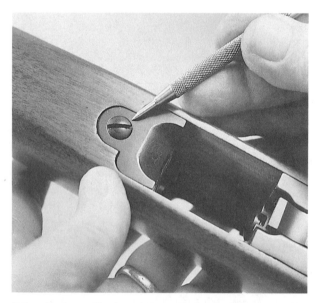

7. Remove the large screw in front of the magazine opening and take off the forward plate.

8. Remove the large screw behind the trigger guard. Tip the trigger guard unit outward to unhook it from the receiver and remove it. Carefully lift the action out of the stock.

9. Restrain the magazine catch plunger and push out the catch lever cross pin.

10. Remove the catch lever downward.

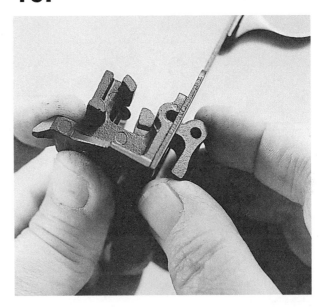

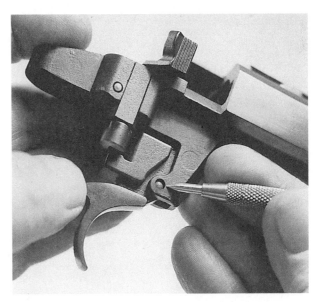

11. Ease the spring tension and remove the plunger and spring toward the front.

12. Restrain the trigger and push out the trigger cross pin.

13. Remove the trigger downward, along with its spring.

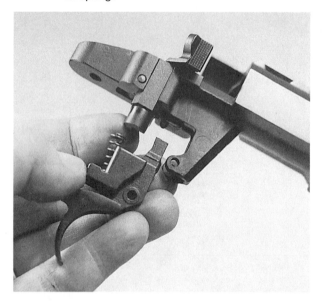

14. Push out the sear cross pin.

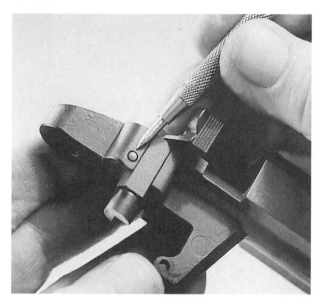

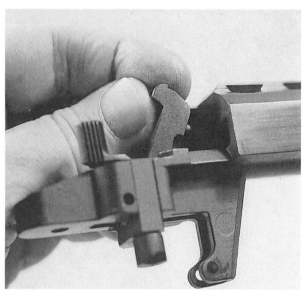

15. Move the sear forward and take it out upward.

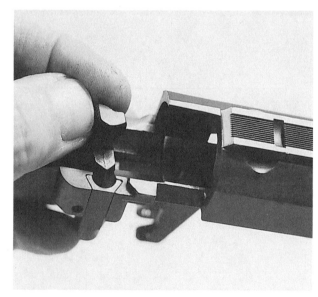

16. Turn the safety-lever until it is in the position shown, over the bolt track.

17. Holding the safety in place at top and bottom, push the safety housing upward. **Caution:** *Keep control of the safety, as the detent plunger and spring will force it outward.*

18. Ease the spring tension slowly and remove the safety toward the right.

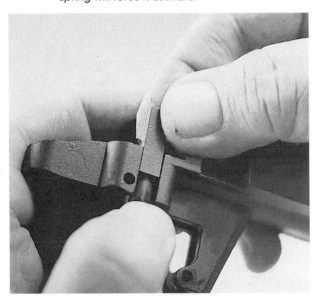

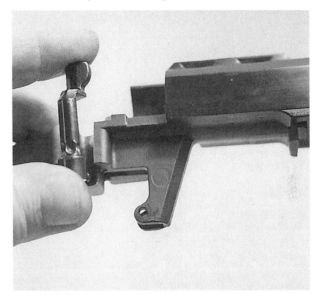

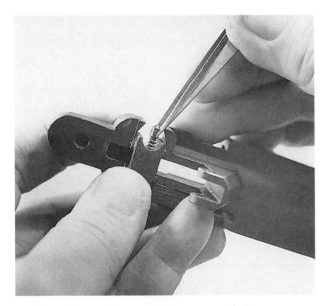

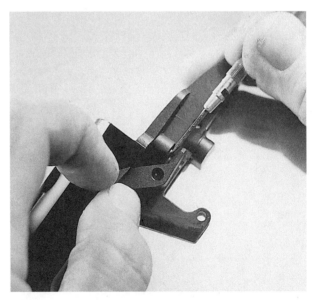

19. Remove the safety plunger and spring.

20. To remove the bolt stop, use a tool to depress the plunger and spring upward and take off the bolt stop toward the left. **Caution:** *Keep the plunger and spring under control, and ease them out.*

21. If barrel removal is necessary, remove the two Allen screws at the front of the receiver, take off the block and remove the barrel toward the front. The front and rear sights are dovetail-mounted.

Reassembly Tips:

1. When installing the safety housing, be sure the recess for the sear cross pin is at the rear, as shown.

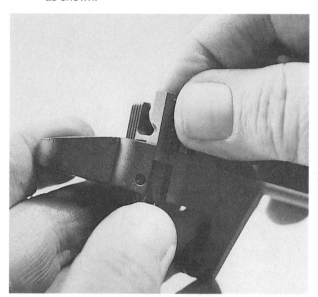

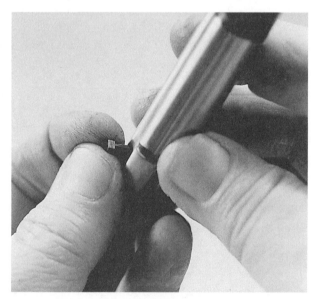

2. When installing the breechblock pin, note that the flats on its head must be oriented to front and rear. Properly installed, the head of the pin must be recessed below the outer surface of the bolt body.

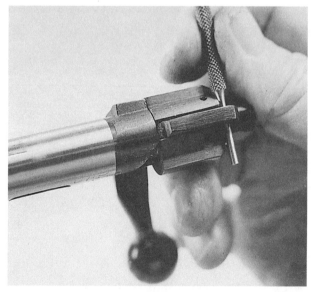

3. Remember to turn the bolt head back to cocked position, as shown, before the bolt is reinserted in the receiver.

Ruger Model 96/22

Data:	Ruger Model 96/22
Origin:	United States
Manufacturer:	Sturm, Ruger & Company
	Southport, Connecticut
Cartridges:	22WMR, 22 Long Rifle, 17HMR
Magazine capacity:	10 rounds (WMR, HMR, 9 rounds)
Overall length:	37¼ inches
Barrel length:	18½ inches
Weight:	5¼ pounds

Along with its centerfire "big brother" in 44 Magnum, the Model 96/22 was introduced in 1996. The 17HMR version arrived in 2002, and the 22LR version was discontinued in the following year. Except for magazine capacity, all versions are mechanically the same.

Disassembly:

1. Open the lever, remove the magazine, loosen the barrel band screw, and take off the band toward the front.

2. Back out the takedown screw until it is free. It will stay in the stock.

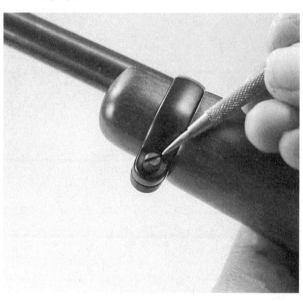

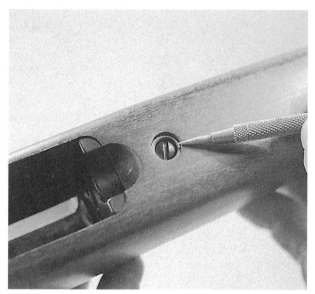

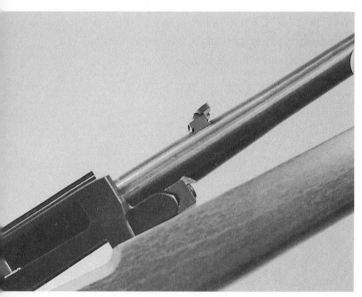

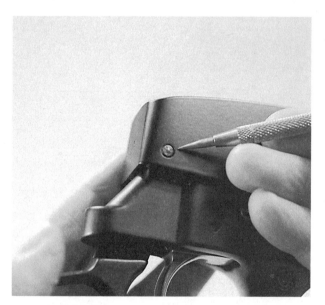

3. Tip the action upward at the front and remove it from the stock. On some guns it will be necessary to move the safety button to a central position to clear the stock opening during removal.

4. Push out the cross pin at the rear of the receiver.

5. Push out the larger cross pin.

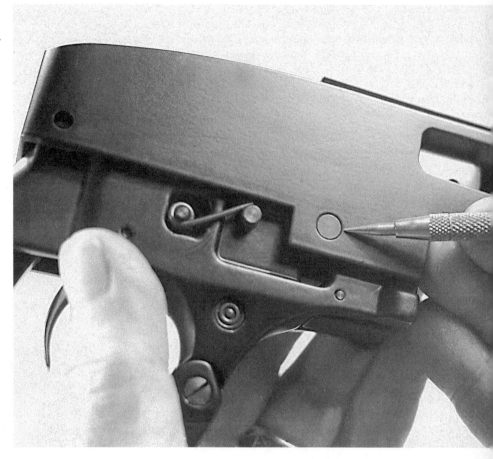

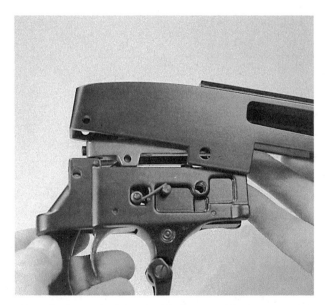

6. Remove the lever and bolt assembly downward.

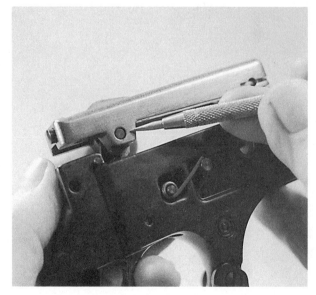

7. Push out the lever-link cross pin, and remove the bolt.

8. If extractor removal is necessary for repair, insert a small tool between the extractor and its plunger to push the plunger and spring rearward, and lift out the extractor. **Caution:** *Control the plunger and spring, and ease them out.* Note the extractors and their springs are not identical, and keep them separate for reassembly.

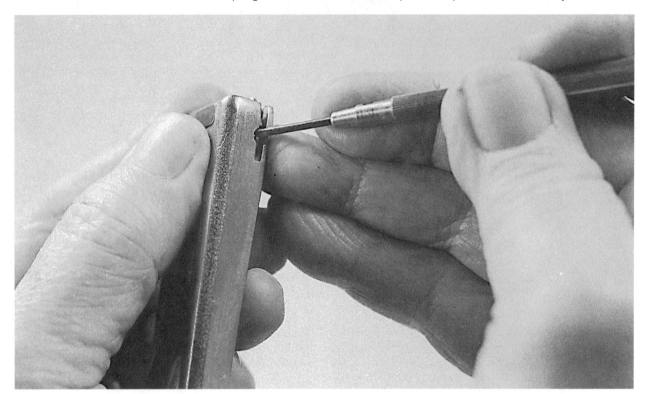

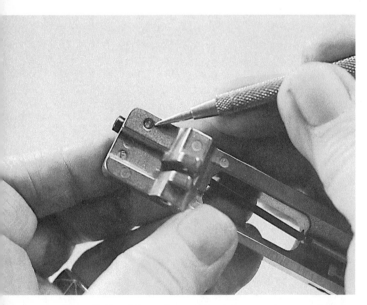

9. If the firing pin and its return spring need to be removed for repair, they are retained by a vertical roll-pin at the rear of the bolt. Use a proper roll-pin drift to avoid damaging the pin.

10. A roll-type pin retains the ejector at the top front of the lever housing.

11. If removal of the magazine catch system is necessary for repair, pushing this pin out toward the right will release the magazine catch and its lever and spring to be taken out downward. Note the relationship of the parts for reassembly.

12. Be sure the bolt link is in upright position, close the lever, and move the safety to off-safe position. Restrain the hammer, pull the trigger, and ease the hammer down to fired position. Use pliers on each side to unhook the forward arms of the hammer springs from their grooves in the hammer cross pin. Ease them downward until their tension is relieved.

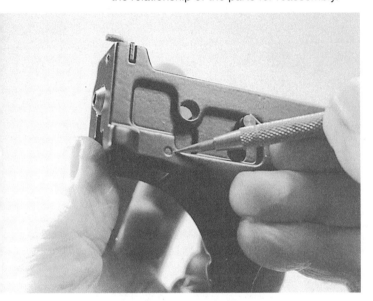

13. Remove the hammer spring support pin.

14. Remove the hammer springs from each side. For ease in reassembly, keep them separate, right and left.

15. Remove the hammer cross pin.

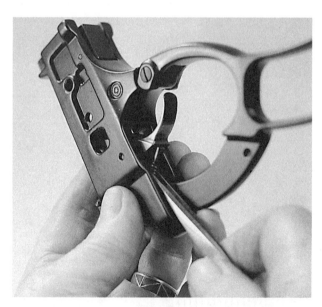

16. Open the lever, move the hammer slightly forward, and take it out upward.

17. Tip the trigger forward, and remove the trigger plunger and spring.

18. Push out the trigger cross pin.

19. Move the trigger assembly slightly forward, and take it out upward. Pushing out the pivot bearing sleeve will release the sear and its coil spring for removal from the top of the trigger.

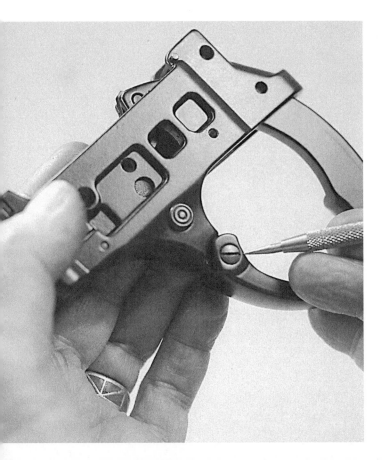

20. Removal of the lever assembly requires opposed screwdrivers, one to hold the pivot post, the other to take out the screw on the left side. After the screw is removed, a slim drift is inserted in the screw hole to nudge the pivot out toward the right, and the lever can then be removed. This system is set tightly in place at the factory, and routine removal is not advisable. If the lever is taken out, the splined cross pin at the top can be drifted toward the right to free the bolt link.

21. If the lever is removed, the lever detent plunger and its coil spring will be released through the indicated opening in the unit. Control them, and take care that they are not lost.

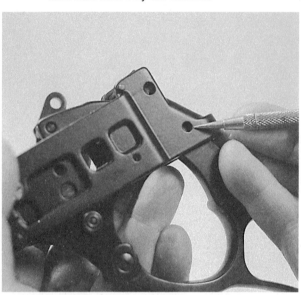

22. Drifting out this cross pin will release the cocking indicator lifter for removal upward.

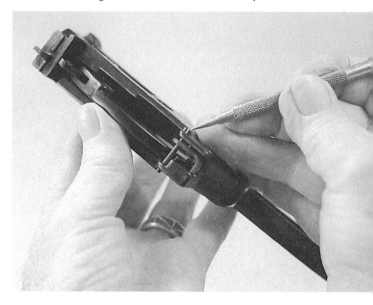

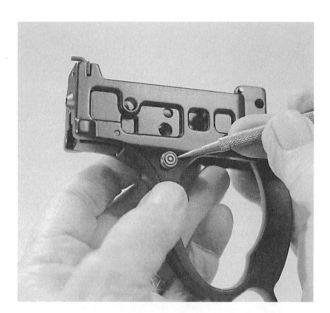

23. If removal of the safety button is necessary for repair, insert a tool from the top to contact the flat on the button, giving it a quarter-turn. It can then be pushed out either side. **Caution:** *The safety detent plunger and its coil spring will be released, so control them.* In normal takedown, leave this system in place.

24. If removal of the cocking indicator is necessary, drifting this roll-pin slightly rearward will release the indicator and its coil spring.

25. The barrel is retained in the receiver by a clamp block and two Allen screws.

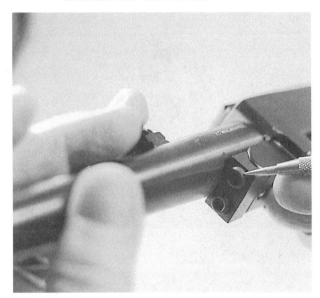

26. The bolt locking bar is staked in place in the receiver, and is not routinely removable.

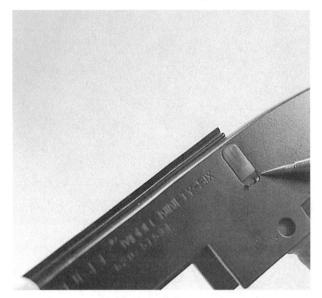

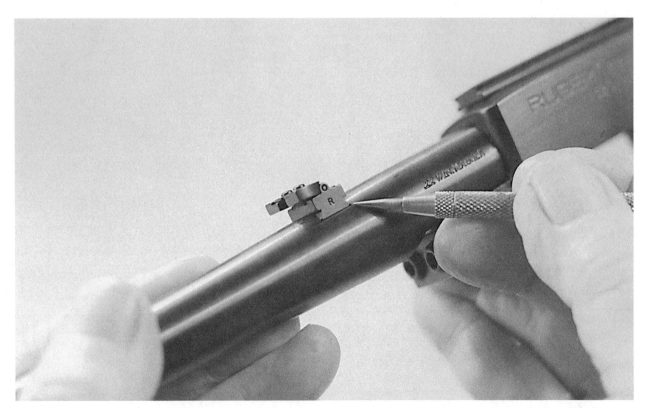

27. The front and rear sights are both dovetail-mounted, and can be drifted out toward the right. Disassembly of the rear sight is not advisable. This advice also applies to the rotary magazine.

Reassembly Tips:

1. When installing the hammer, place it in horizontal position with the lever open and the safety in off-safe position. Hold the trigger to the rear, close the lever, and turn the hammer to vertical position for insertion of the cross pin.

2. As the twin hammer springs are inserted, remember that the shorter arms go inside. Be sure that they enter the recess at the back of the hammer, to contact the bearing pin inside the hammer.

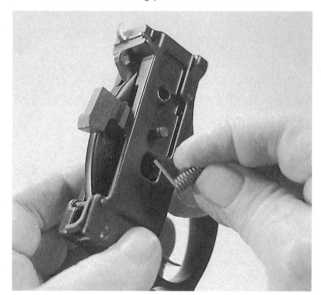

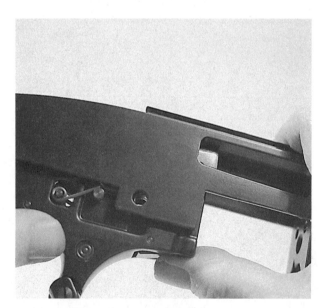

3. Keep the lever assembly level as it is reinserted, to assure the bolt link pin stays in place. Insert the unit until the front edge of the bolt is visible in the ejection port, then replace the cross pins.

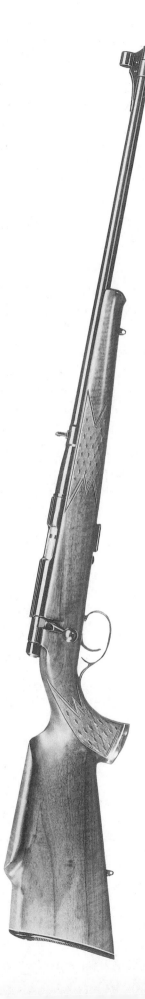

Savage/ Anschutz Model 54

Similar/Identical Pattern Guns

The same basic assembly/disassembly steps for the Savage/Anschutz Model 54 also apply to the following gun:

Savage/Anschutz Model 54M

Data:	Savage/Anschutz Model 54
Origin:	Germany
Manufacturer:	J.G. Anschutz GmbH, Ulm/Donau
	(Imported by Savage Arms
	Westfield, Massachusetts)
Cartridge:	22 Long Rifle
Magazine capacity:	5 rounds
Overall length:	41⅞ inches
Barrel length:	22½ inches
Weight:	¾ pounds

The Anschutz family has been making fine guns in Germany since 1793, and the J.G. Anschutz firm was established in Zella-Mehlis about 1922. In the post-war years, the factory was relocated to Ulm/Donau. From 1966 to 1981, Savage Arms imported an elegant little Anschutz rifle, the Model 54. It cost somewhat more than contemporary guns of its type, but many discriminating shooters felt that the quality was worth the price. The Model 54M is the same, except its chambered for the 22 WMR cartridge.

Disassembly:

1. Remove the magazine and back out the screw on the underside, at the rear of the trigger guard. When the screw is out, flex the trigger guard very slightly to free it from its recess in the stock at the rear, and swing the guard out to the side to give access to the rear vertical screw in the trigger plate. Back out the rear trigger plate screw.

2. Remove the main action screw, located at the center of the trigger plate, just forward of the guard, and separate the action from the stock. The smaller screw at the front of the trigger plate is a wood screw that retains the trigger plate on the stock. With the plate removed, it is possible to take off the guard, if necessary, by turning off its nut on the inside of the plate.

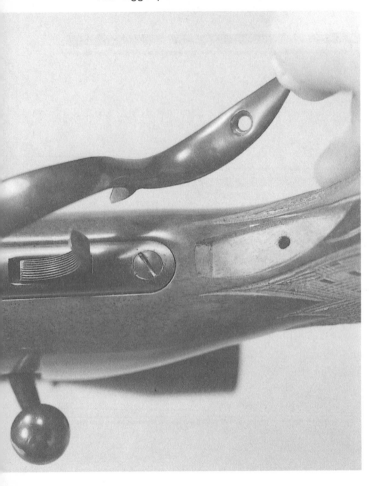

3. To remove the bolt, open it and move it toward the rear while depressing the bolt stop, located on the left side of the receiver, and withdraw the bolt toward the rear. Note that the safety must be in the horizontal off-safe position before the bolt can be opened.

4. Grip the front section of the bolt and turn the safety-lever counterclockwise (rear view) until the striker drops to the fired position. Continue turning the safety until it stops; it can then be taken off toward the rear.

5. The cocking indicator and its spring are held inside the safety dome by an enlarged coil at the rear end of the indicator spring, and the indicator and spring are easily removed by pushing them out toward the front.

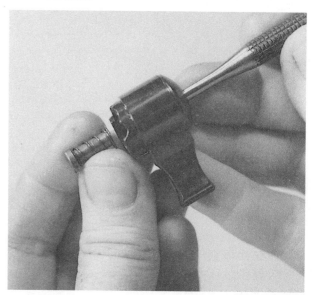

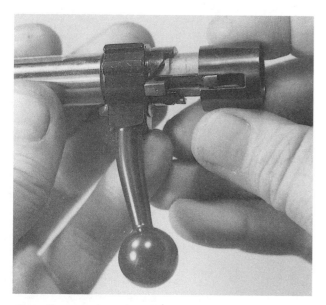

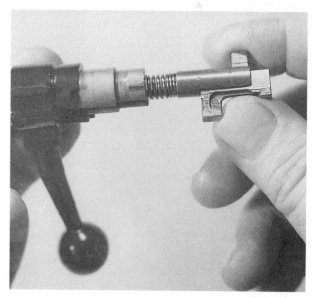

6. Remove the safety sleeve toward the rear.

7. Remove the striker assembly toward the rear.

8. To disassemble the striker assembly, grip the rear of the striker with a strong hand or a padded vise, and push the ridged collar at the front of the spring very slightly toward the rear. Give it a half turn and ease it off toward the front, slowly releasing the tension of the spring. **Caution:** *Control the striker spring.* Remove the collar, spring, and rear spring guide from the striker/firing pin toward the front.

9. After the striker assembly is removed, take off the bolt handle toward the rear.

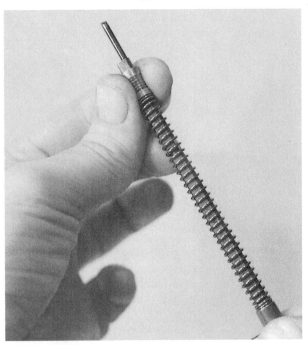

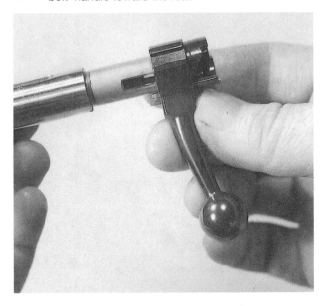

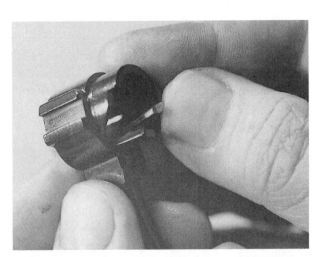

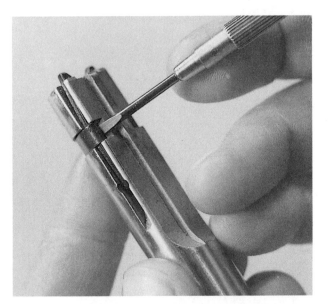

10. To remove the bolt handle positioning plunger and its spring, push the plunger toward the rear and tip its flat rear end inward; then move the part out toward the front of the handle sleeve. Take care not to lose the small coil spring.

11. The extractors are retained on the front of the bolt by a semi-circular spring clip. Use a small screwdriver to pry either end of the clip outward, and ease it off the top of the bolt. The extractors are then easily removed toward each side. Take care to pry the clip only enough to clear the bolt body during removal, as it also is the spring for the extractors, and must not be weakened.

12. The trigger mount is secured at the rear of the receiver by a single vertical screw, and access to the screw head is limited by a rear projection of the mount. An offset or angle-tip screwdriver must be used. Take care not to lose the lock washer under the screw head. Note that it is possible to remove the entire trigger assembly without disturbing the adjustment settings of the trigger spring screw and sear engagement screw. If necessary, these are also easily removed. The nut must be loosened to take out the sear engagement screw at the front. The cross pin can also be driven out, separating the trigger from the mount, but this is usually staked at the ends, so take care not to deform the upper arms of the trigger during removal of the pin. In normal takedown, the assembly is best left intact.

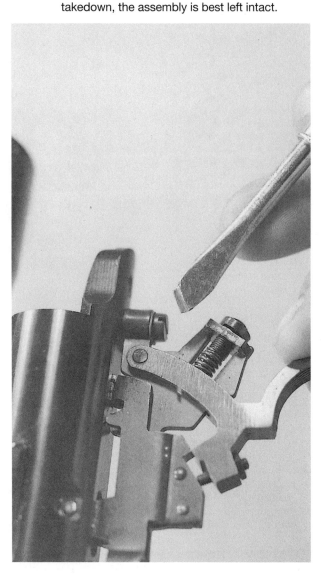

13. The sear is retained on the underside of the receiver by a cross pin and is removed downward, along with its spring, after the pin is drifted out.

14. The bolt stop is retained on the left side of the receiver by a vertical pin. After the pin is drifted out, the bolt stop and its coil spring are removed toward the left.

15. The magazine housing and catch assembly is retained on the underside of the receiver by two large screws at its front and rear. The rear screw is a limited access type and will require the use of an angled-tip screwdriver for removal. The rear screw also secures the internal rear magazine guide and the bolt guide within the receiver. After removal of the screws, the magazine housing and guide are taken off downward, and the bolt guide can be removed from inside the receiver.

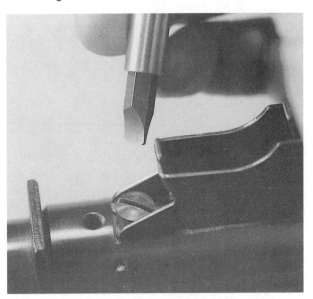

Reassembly Tips:

1. Before the reassembled bolt can be put back into the receiver, it must be recocked. Grip the forward portion of the bolt in a padded vise, and move the bolt handle counterclockwise (rear view) until the striker lug on the underside is in the position shown, and the striker indicator is protruding from the rear of the safety dome. Note that the safety-lever must be in its off-safe position before the bolt handle can be moved.

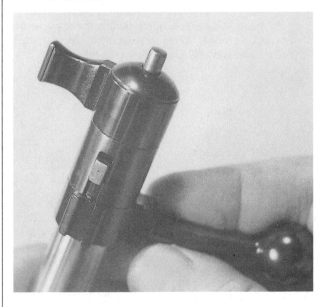

16. The magazine catch and its spring are mounted on a cross pin in the rear of the magazine housing, and the cross pin is usually semi-riveted at the ends. Care must be taken when drifting it out to avoid deformation of the magazine housing and the catch. If the catch and spring don't need repair, they are best left on the housing.

Savage A17

Data:	Savage A17
Origin:	United States
Manufacturer:	Savage Arms, Westfield, MA
Cartridge:	.17 HMR
Magazine capacity:	10 rounds
Overall length:	42 inches
Barrel length:	22 inches
Weight:	5.4 pounds

The A17 is Savage's first semi-automatic rifle designed for shooting the juicy .17 HMR cartridge. Like many of its cousins in the Savage lineup, it comes with an adjustable Accutrigger. Meant for use with optics, it is shipped without sights, and comes with a simple but effective black synthetic buttstock. Unlike other attempts to use .17 HMR in semi-autos, the A17 uses a simple but effective delayed blowback means of operation to control the much higher pressures.

Disassembly:

1. Depress this plunger into the receiver cover and lift the cover off the receiver (picture A). Remove the rear action retaining bolt that lies under the cover (picture B).

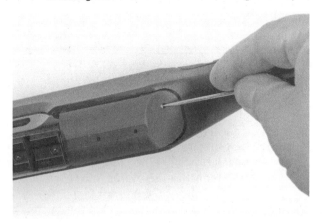

picture A

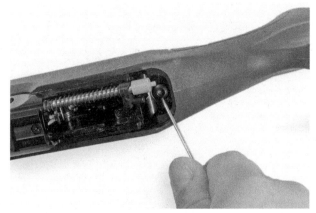

picture B

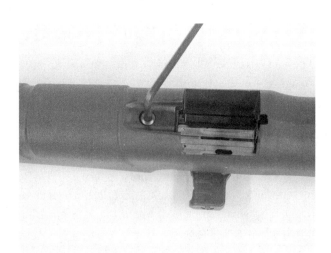

2. Remove the forward action screw from the underside of the handguard, and lift the action out of the stock. The safety button will have to be placed halfway between "safe" and "fire" to clear the stock.

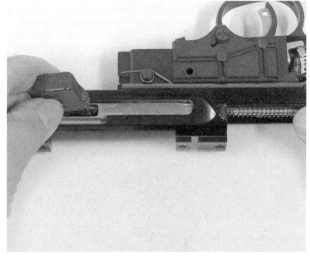

3. Pull the recoil spring to the rear and out, which will also allow the charging handle to be pulled out of the bolt.

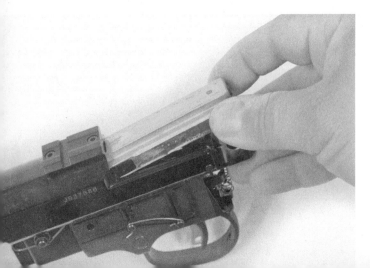

4. Pull the bolt out of the rear of the receiver.

5. Drive out the cross pin at the rear of the receiver (picture A) and then slide the trigger housing forward slightly (picture B). Then the trigger housing can be pulled out of the receiver.

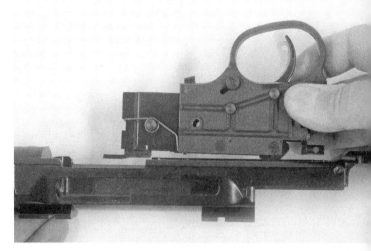

picture A

picture B

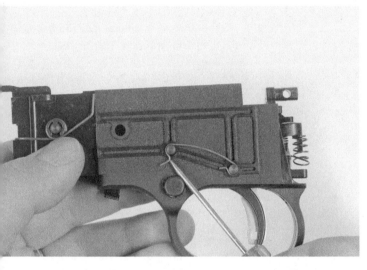

6. Remove this retaining spring, first from the hammer pin, and then unsnap it from the trigger pin.

7. Push out the hammer pin and remove the hammer and hammer spring from the housing.

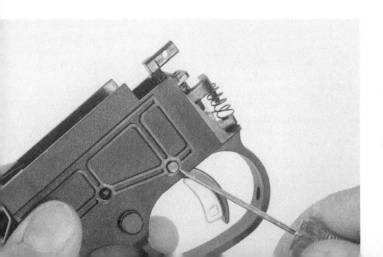

8. Push out the trigger pin.

9. The trigger spring has a tip that projects up and through the trigger housing. Displace the trigger spring by pulling down on the top of the spring (picture A). Then push the trigger assembly forward and then up and out of the housing (picture B).

picture A

picture B

10. Remove this retaining spring clip. Then the disconnector and trigger insert can be removed from the trigger. The spring that connects them can be easily removed by slightly opening the coils by twisting to remove it from the pieces.

11. Remove this spring clip and push the bolt catch pin out to the right. Do not lose the spring and bushing that rest on the pin inside the housing. Then lift the ejector out of the housing to the top. The magazine ejecting spring that wraps around the front of the housing can be removed at this point as well.

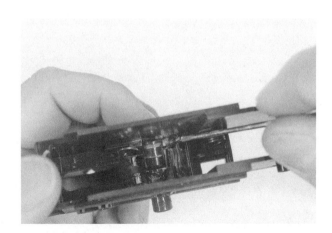

12. Depress the safety spring's forward arch and push the safety button out to the right. The tab on the safety must align with the notch on the right side wall of the housing in order for the safety to be pushed out of the housing.

13. Drive out this pin at the rear of the bolt from bottom to top (picture A). Then push the locking block up (picture B) to allow the firing pin and spring to be removed.

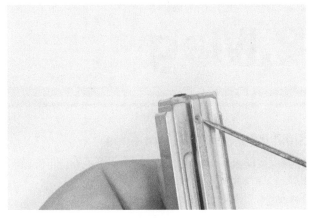

picture A

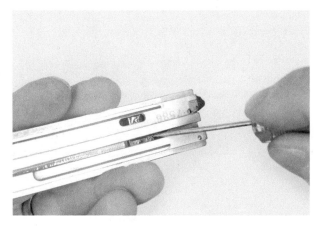

picture B

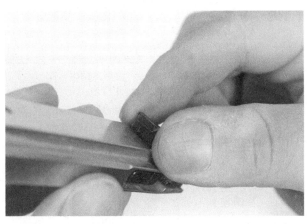

14. Remove the locking block up out of the bolt, and then the locking block cam out to the left.

15. Drive these two pins out to free the extractors. The big one (right side of bolt) has a spring.

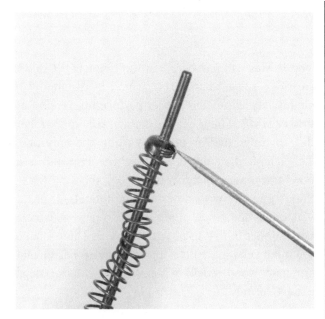

16. The recoil spring assembly can be disassembled by removing this cup, which snaps onto the guide.

Reassembly Tips:

1. When reinstalling the trigger assembly, the rotating tab on the safety must fit inside this notch in the nose of the trigger safety insert. Furthermore, the large retaining spring clip must be arranged in this fashion to allow the trigger to be properly seated.

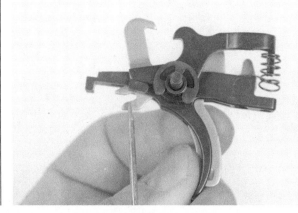

Savage B.Mag

Similar/Identical Pattern Guns

The same basic assembly/disassembly steps for the Savage B.Mag also apply to the following gun:
Savage B.Mag Target

Data:	Savage B.Mag
Origin:	United States
Manufacturer:	Savage Arms, Westfield, MA
Cartridge:	.17 Winchester Super Mag
Magazine capacity:	8 rounds
Overall length:	40.5 inches
Barrel length:	22 inches
Weight:	4.5 pounds

The B.Mag is chambered in the new .17 WSM, a cartridge released in 2014, which is essentially a slightly scaled up and higher performing version of the .17 HMR. The B.Mag is the first rifle to chamber this cartridge and as of this writing the only one. This standard model is very light weight and is a good tromping around in the woods shooting fuzzy things gun. As with other Savage models, it has a version of the Accutrigger and a rotary magazine very similar to that used with the A17. There is also a Target version, with a much heavier barrel and laminate wood stock, which will use these steps almost entirely.

Disassembly:

1. Open the bolt and remove it from the action by depressing the bolt latch and pulling the bolt out to the rear.

2. Remove the magazine. In the front wall of the magazine well is a small latch; from the factory it has a yellow dot on it. Push this latch forward and gently lift up on the front of the magazine well section of the trigger guard to remove it. Do this carefully, as the sides of the magazine well will break easily.

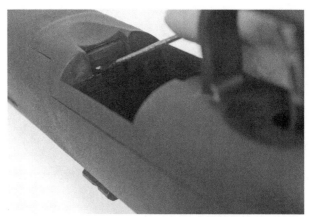

3. Under the trigger guard are the two action screws, one indicated here and the other behind the trigger. Remove them and then lift the action out of the stock.

picture A

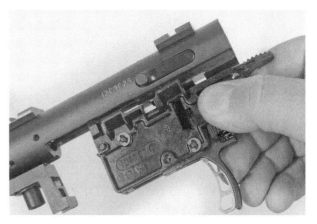

picture B

4. Push out this rectangular bar (picture A) from left to right (in is tapered) and then slide the trigger housing forward into the magazine well to remove it from the action (picture B).

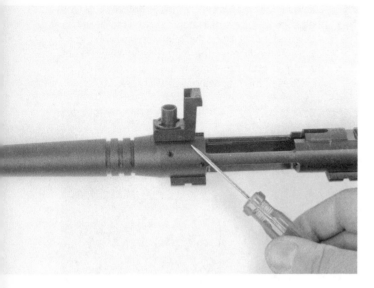

6. Remove this bolt shroud retaining screw and the bolt shroud itself.

5. Unless something needs to be replaced, do not remove this assembly from the receiver.

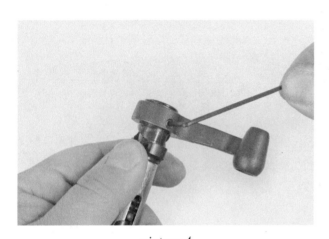

picture A

picture B

7. Remove this set screw in the bolt handle (picture A) and then remove the spring clip from the back of the bolt body (picture B) and pull the bolt handle off the back of the bolt body.

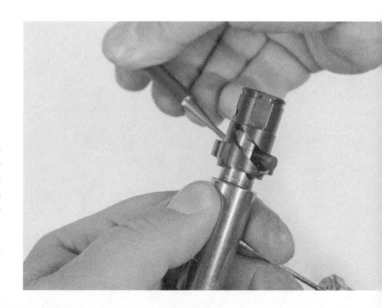

8. The striker spring must be compressed forward to disassemble the bolt. Push the spring assembly forward and use a small screwdriver to hold it in place using the hole in the top of the bolt. The cam pin must be pushed out to either side but the bushing inside the rear of the bolt must be pushed as far forward as it can go (hence the forward compression on the striker spring) while the pin must be most rearward. This will clear the grooved pin from the bushing to be removed from the bolt.

9. Push out the sear engagement pin through the hole in the top of the bolt (picture A) and then remove the firing pin assembly out to the rear of the bolt (picture B).

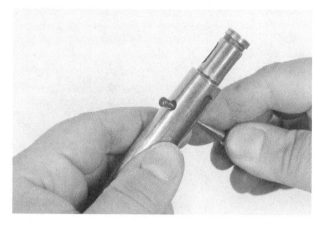

picture A

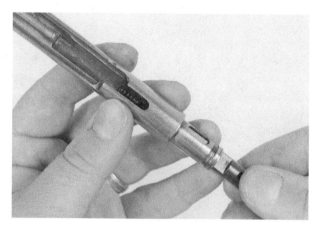

picture B

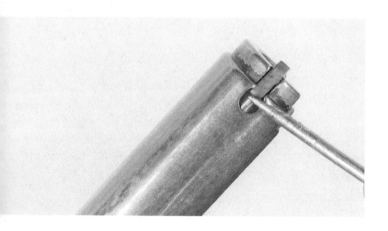

10. Remove the extractor by pulling back on the plunger and rolling the extractor forward and out of the bolt.

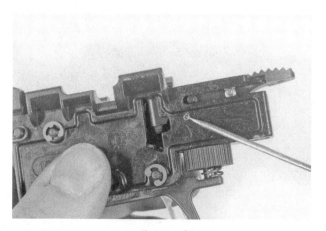

picture A

picture B

11. Drive out this spring pin (picture A). Then pull the safety out to the rear, tilting the back end down as the rear pin clears (picture B) to fully remove it. The pins will fall loose so don't lose them. The detent ball bearing and spring (in a hole in the inside floor of the housing) will be free to fall out of the housing at this time.

12. Remove this spring clip and push the trigger pin out to the right (picture A). Pull the trigger assembly out to the bottom (picture B); include the trigger safety spring in front of the trigger. The adjustment spring and bushing and the trigger safety insert are easily removed at this time.

picture A

picture B

picture A

picture B

13. Remove this spring clip and push out the sear pin to the right (picture A). Then remove the sear and sear spring out through the bottom.

14. Leave the magazine ejection spring in place unless it is broken and needs replacement.

Reassembly Tips:

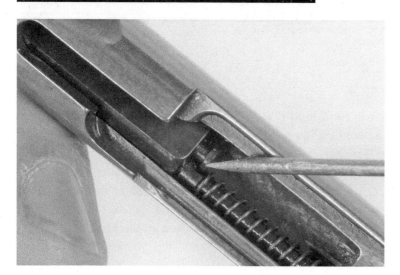

1. There is a notch in the rear of the firing pin that mates with a grooved projection on the front on the striker. These must be joined prior to reinsertion. Put them together at the rear as they are inserted and gently push them forward, making sure to keep the pieces mated properly, until they stop. Then gently roll the firing pin up into its slot and push the striker fully in place with the flat on the bottom matching up with the bottom of the bolt body.

2. The rectangular bar that retains the trigger housing to the receiver is tapered. Note the on the bar arrow and insert the bar in that direction.

Savage Model 63

Similar/Identical Pattern Guns

The same basic assembly/disassembly steps for the Savage Model 63 also apply to the following guns:

Savage Model 63M   **Savage Model 73**

Savage Model 63KM   **Savage Model 73Y**

Data:	Savage Model 63
Origin:	United States
Manufacturer:	Savage Arms Company
	Westfield, Massachusetts
Cartridge:	22 Short, Long, or Long Rifle
Overall length:	36 inches
Barrel length:	18 inches
Weight:	4 pounds

Made between 1964 and 1974, the Model 63 was also offered as the Model 63M, chambered for the 22 WMR round. Another version soon followed, the Model 73, which differed only in having a half-stock rather than the full Mannlicher style of the 63 and 63M. Both guns were offered concurrently during their time of production, and since they are mechanically identical, the takedown and reassembly instructions can be applied to both models, with the exception of details involving the stock of the Model 63.

Disassembly:

1. On the underside of the stock near the muzzle is a small, headless screw in the center of a slotted nut. The inner tip of the screw retains the front sight, and the nut secures the unit to the stock. The nut can be removed with a twin-pointed tool, and the screw will often turn out with it. Or, the nut can be immobilized and the small screw aligned with the slot in the nut, and a wide, thin-bladed screwdriver can be used to back out both at once.

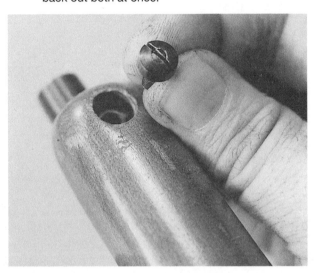

2. Back out the main stock mounting screw, located on the underside of the stock, just forward of the trigger guard, and remove the action from the stock.

3. When the action is out of the stock, the front sight is easily slid off toward the front.

4. Cycle the bolt to cock the internal hammer and remove the vertical screw at the front of the trigger group.

5. Remove the vertical screw at the rear of the trigger group. The head of this screw is not directly accessible, being in a recess at the rear of the guard unit, so it is necessary to use an offset screwdriver, or one with an angled tip, as shown, to remove it.

6. Remove the trigger group downward.

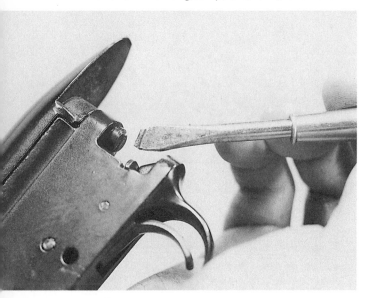

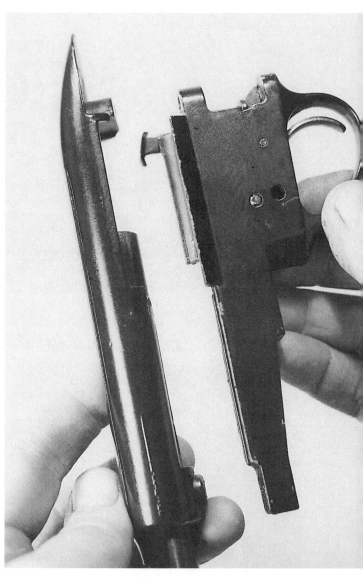

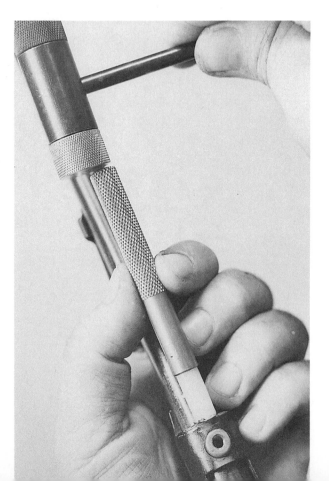

7. Removal of the front trigger group screw will have released the barrel for removal from the receiver, as the tip of this screw enters a recess on the underside of the barrel. Grip the barrel in a padded vise, and use a hammer and nylon drift to gently tap the receiver off the barrel toward the rear.

8. When the receiver has moved a certain distance off the rear of the barrel, it will be possible to lift the bolt assembly out of the underside of the receiver. If only bolt removal is desired, and barrel removal is not necessary, the receiver need not be drifted completely off the barrel.

9. The extractor is retained on the front of the bolt because it acts like a spring clip, its opposed gripping arms riding in a groove around the front of the bolt. To remove the extractor, push against the opposed arms of its spring clip, snapping it off toward the side. It is pushed, of course, from the open side of its clip. Be sure to apply pressure only to its mounting clip, not to its long front arm or tail. Usually, this can be done without tools.

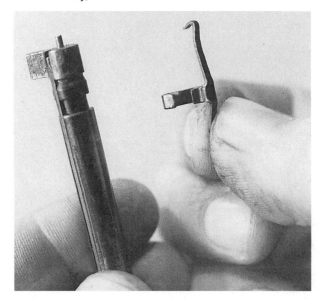

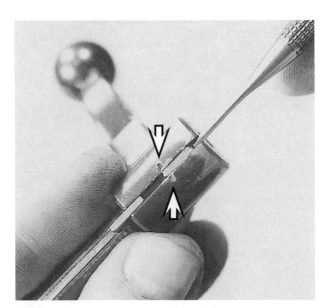

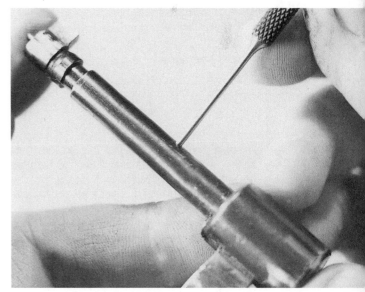

10. The firing pin is retained in its channel in the top of the bolt by stake marks (arrows) in the channel edges over a rectangular recess in the top of the firing pin. The firing pin may be drifted out forward and upward, or out toward the rear, swaging the stake marks aside as it passes.

11. The ejector and its spring are retained by a small roll cross pin at the center of the bolt and are taken out toward the rear.

12. The safety-lever and the bolt safety trip at the front are retained on the right side of the trigger group by separate screws, and are taken off toward the right. Removal of these parts will also release the round spring-wire connector between the levers.

13. The bolt bearing screw is accessible through the main stock screw hole in the underside of the guard unit, and is removed downward.

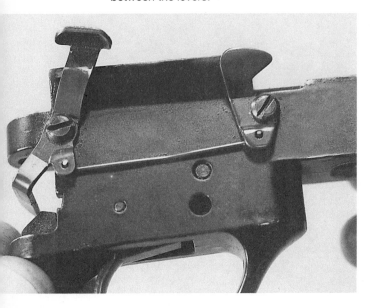

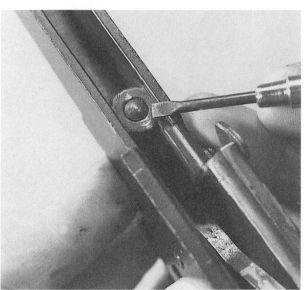

14. Restrain the hammer against the tension of its spring, pull the trigger, and ease the hammer down to the fired position. Drift out the hammer pivot, the larger of the two cross pins, and remove the hammer and the combination hammer and trigger spring upward. Drift out the trigger pivot, the smaller cross pin, and remove the trigger upward, along with the sear, which is mounted in the top of the trigger and pivots on the same pin.

Reassembly Tips:

1. As the receiver is tapped back onto the rear of the barrel, remember that the bolt must be inserted before the barrel and receiver are moved fully into place. The photo shows the optimum position for insertion of the bolt.

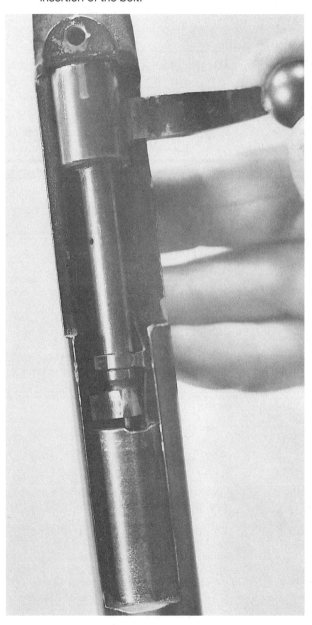

2. When replacing the trigger group on the underside of the receiver, be sure the front screw, the one with the extended tip, is put back in front, and see that the barrel is oriented so the screw tip will enter the recess in the underside of the barrel, locking it in place.

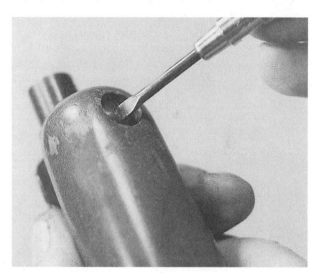

3. When replacing the action in the stock, note that the front sight must be slid onto the muzzle before the action is seated, so the protrusion on its underside will enter its well in the stock. The sight screw and nut may be turned into place together; then the small center screw may be turned separately for any adjustment necessary to snug the unit in place.

When replacing the sear and trigger assembly, be sure both the sear and trigger are properly aligned with the cross-hole in the trigger group before inserting and driving in the cross pin. If there is difficulty, a slave pin can be used.

When replacing the extractor on the bolt, note that it is snapped into its groove upward, so the operating arm of the extractor will lie on the right side when the bolt is in the receiver.

Savage Model 64F

Similar/Identical Pattern Guns

The same basic assembly/disassembly steps for the Savage Model 64F also apply to the following guns:

Savage Model 64FSS (Stainless)
Savage Model 64F Camo
Savage Model 64G

Data:	Savage Model 64F
Origin:	United States
Manufacturer:	Savage Arms, Inc.
	Suffield, Connecticut
Cartridge:	22 Long Rifle
Magazine capacity:	10 rounds
Overall length:	40 and 41 inches
Barrel length:	20 and 21 inches
Weight:	5½ pounds

The latest in a long line of Savage 22 autoloaders, the Model 64F was introduced in 1990. A deluxe wood-stocked version, the Model 64G, arrived in 1996, and a heavy-barrel model in 2002. All of the sub-models are the same mechanically.

Disassembly:

1. Remove the magazine. With an Allen wrench of the proper size, take out the screws on each end of the magazine plate, and note that each has a washer.

2. Remove the action from the stock.

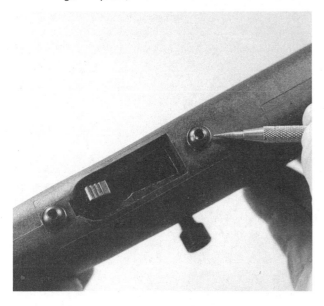

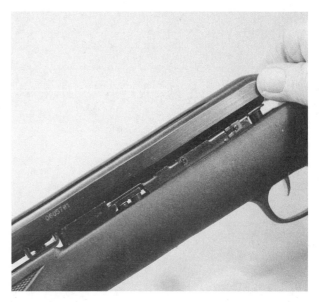

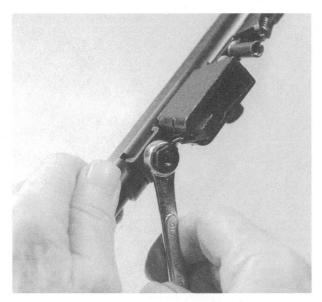

3. To remove the bolt, the barrel must be taken out of the receiver. Use a 7/16 wrench to take off the front stock-mounting stud, and remove the barrel clamp.

4. Use the cocking handle to lock the bolt in open position. Use a non-marring tool (a nylon drift or a block of wood) to nudge the receiver rearward off the barrel, then remove the barrel toward the front. Take care that the slim ejector, mounted in the rear of the barrel, is not damaged.

5. The ejector is mounted in a recess on the left side of the barrel and is staked in place. If removal is necessary for repair, it can be drifted out to the left. In normal takedown, the ejector is best left in place.

6. Restrain the bolt, disengage the hold-open, and ease the bolt forward to closed position. Pull the trigger to drop the striker to fired position. Move the bolt forward in the receiver to the point shown, placing the cocking handle in the ejection port. Turn the handle to free it, and remove it toward the right.

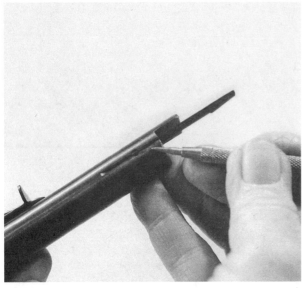

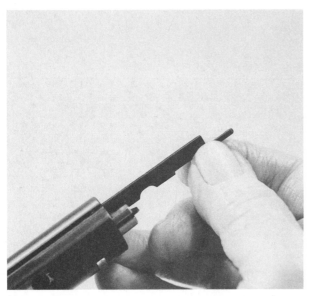

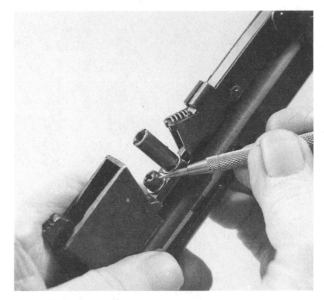

7. Remove the firing pin.

8. If it is necessary to remove the bolt from the receiver, you must first take off the magazine housing assembly. Remove the Phillips screw and its lock-washer, and the rear stock-mounting stud just to its rear, with its lock-washer.

9. Move the magazine housing slightly rearward, and take it off downward. Drifting out the cross pin at the front of the housing will allow removal of the magazine catch and its torsion spring.

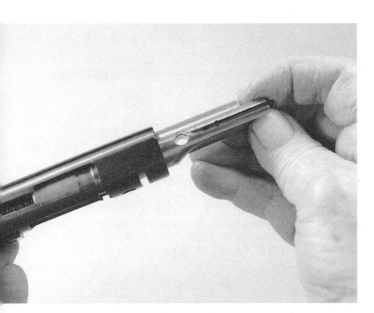

10. Remove the bolt and striker assembly from the receiver toward the front.

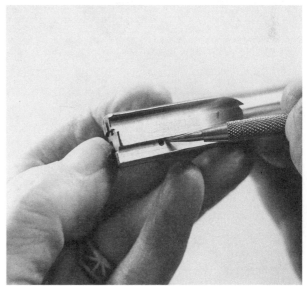

11. The extractor and its coil spring are retained in the bolt by a vertical roll-pin which is drifted out upward. Be sure to use a proper roll-pin drift, to avoid damaging the pin. Control the spring.

12. The striker and recoil spring assembly in the bolt body are not routinely dismountable.

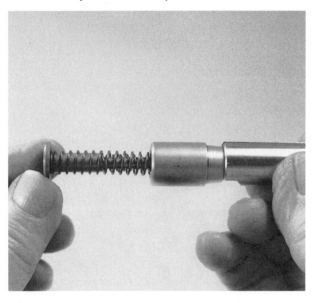

13. Remove the large post-screw at the rear of the trigger group, along with its lock-washer.

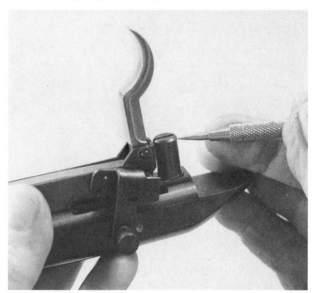

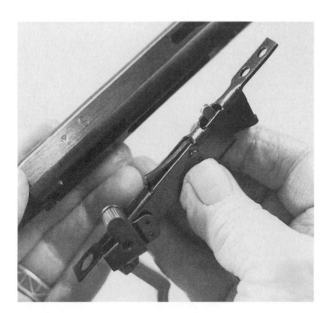

14. Remove the trigger group downward.

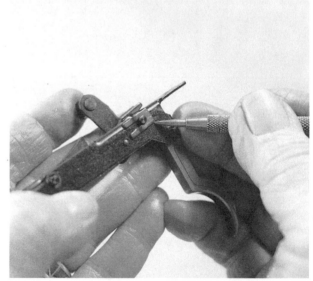

15. Pushing this spring-clip off rearward will allow the safety lever to be taken off toward the right. The safety detent plunger and its coil spring will be released, so take care they are not lost. If the safety is removed, the large pin that connects the trigger to the trigger-bar/disconnector can be taken out toward the right. Except for repair, disassembly of the trigger group is not advisable.

16. Removal of the C-clip on either side will allow the sear and its torsion spring to be taken out upward. Control the spring, as the cross pin is removed.

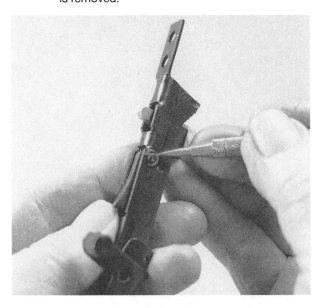

17. The trigger cross pin is also retained by a C-clip on each side. If the large connector pin at upper rear has been previously removed, removal of the trigger pin will allow the trigger to be taken out downward. Note that the trigger-bar/disconnector and its front-mounted coil spring can be removed only after all other parts are out of the trigger group.

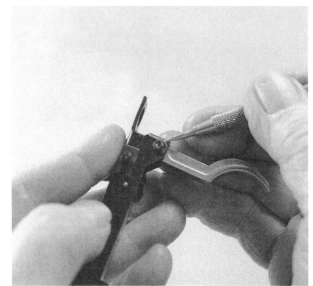

18. The front and rear sights are dovetail-mounted, and can be drifted out toward the right.

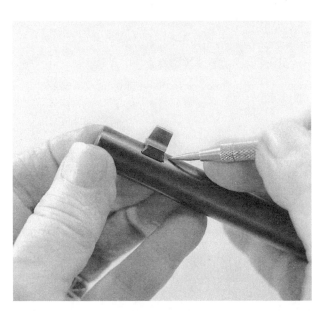

19. The magazine can be disassembled for cleaning by sliding the floorplate off toward the rear. **Caution:** *The follower spring will be released.* As the plate is put back in, it will be necessary to use a very slim tool to depress the spring at the front.

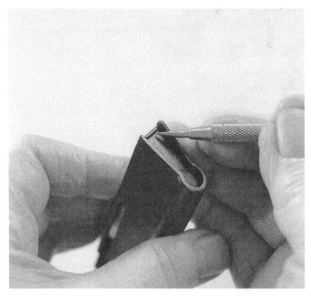

Reassembly Tips:

1.

2.

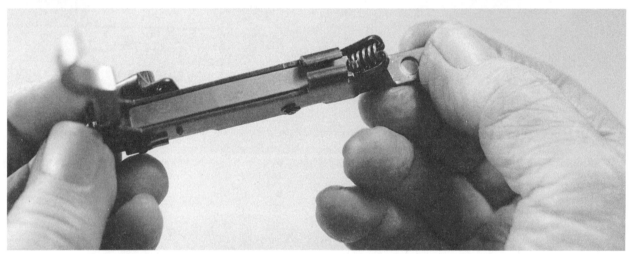

3. If the trigger group has been disassembled, these three views of the properly-assembled unit may be helpful (nos. 1, 2, and 3).

4. As the barrel is being put back into the receiver, be sure to again lock the bolt open, and remember that the ejector must align with its recess in the bolt, as shown. For illustration, the parts are outside the gun here.

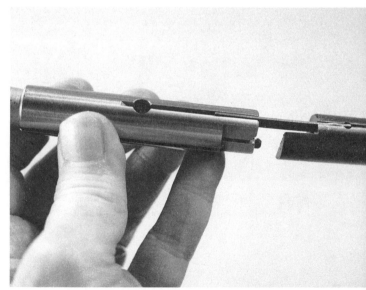

Savage Model 72

Similar/Identical Pattern Guns

The same basic assembly/disassembly steps for the Savage Model 72 also apply to the following gun:

Savage-Stevens Model 74

Data:	Savage Model 72
Origin:	United States
Manufacturer:	Savage Arms Company
	Westfield, Massachusetts
Cartridge:	22 Long Rifle
Overall length:	37 inches
Barrel length:	22 inches
Weight:	4½ pounds

The Model 72 was marketed as the "Crackshot." There was an earlier Stevens gun with that name, but this little rifle is not similar. Actually, it is an updated version of the popular "Favorite." Briefly, there was a Model 71, which differed in some mechanical details. The Model 74, made from 1972 to 1974, was a lower-priced version with a round barrel. The Model 72 was produced from 1972 to 1987.

Disassembly:

1. Remove the two buttplate screws and take off the stock buttplate. Use a B-Square stock tool or a long screwdriver to unscrew the stock mounting bolt and remove the stock from the receiver.

2. Remove the forend screw and take off the forend.

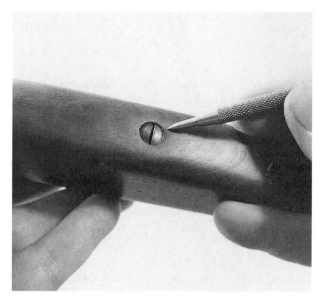

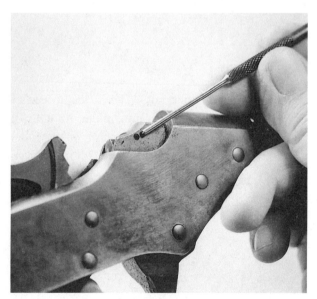

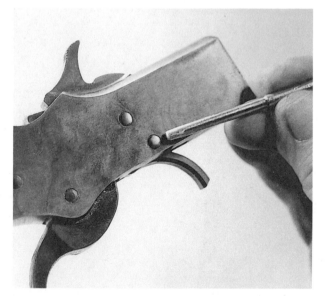

3. If only the firing pin needs to be removed for repair purposes, it can be taken out, along with its return spring, by drifting out the roll-type cross pin in the breechblock.

4. Open the action and drift out the trigger cross pin toward the right. On these large pins, use a bronze drift of suitable size to avoid marring the heads of the pins.

5. Remove the trigger and its spring downward, detaching the trigger from the hammer block loop, which will be stopped by its cross-piece. Take out the hammer block upward.

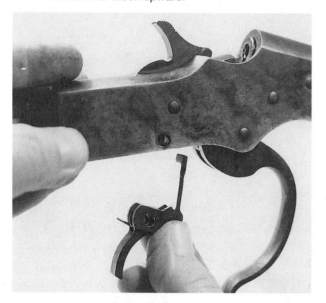

6. The hammer block and trigger spring are shown in their relative positions here.

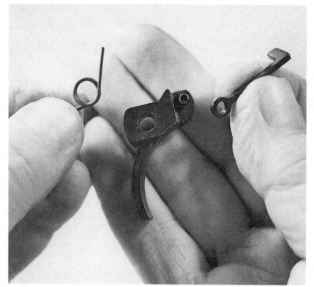

7. Removal of the trigger pin will have released the tension of the hammer spring. Drift out the hammer cross pin toward the right.

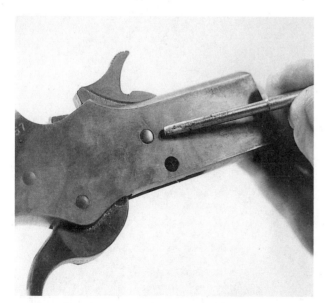

8. Remove the hammer and its spring upward. Note that the spring may fall out the lower opening as the hammer is removed.

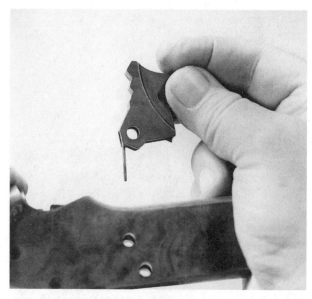

9. Drift out the lever pivot cross pin.

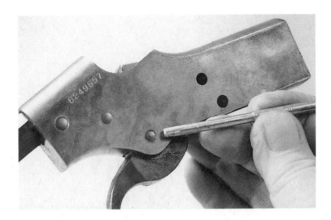

10. Drift out the breechblock pivot pin.

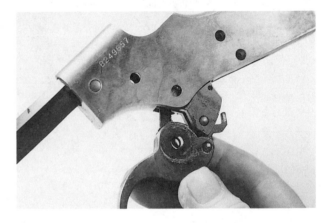

11. Remove the lever and breechblock assembly downward.

12. Remove the ejector from the front of the lever.

13. Drift out the breechblock link pin and separate the breechblock and link. If the firing pin has not been previously removed, drift out its roll-type pin and remove the firing pin and its spring toward the rear.

14. The link can be removed from the lever by drifting out this cross pin. **Caution:** *In Model 72 and Model 74 guns, there is a link tension plunger and spring in the lever under the link, and these will be released when the pin is removed, so control them.*

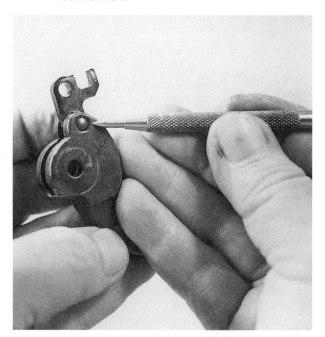

15. The barrel is retained by a large cross pin that is drifted out toward the right. The receiver is then driven off the barrel shank, using a hardwood buffer to prevent marring. In normal takedown, the barrel is left in place. The sights are drifted out of their dovetails toward the right.

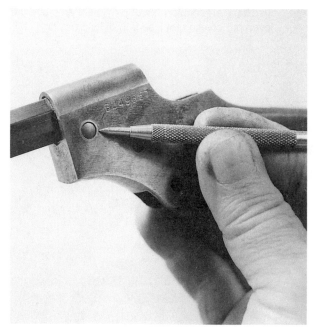

Reassembly Tips:

1. When installing the breechblock and lever assembly, be sure the ejector is replaced in the front of the lever in the proper orientation, as shown. Also, be sure the top of the ejector engages its recess below the chamber.

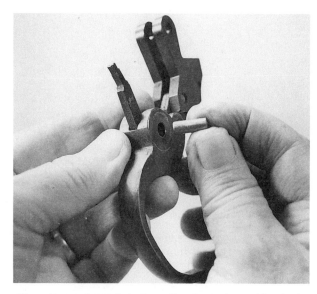

2. Use a slave pin to keep the ejector in position in the lever during reassembly.

3. Insert the breechblock pivot pin first; then move the lever into position for insertion of its cross pin.

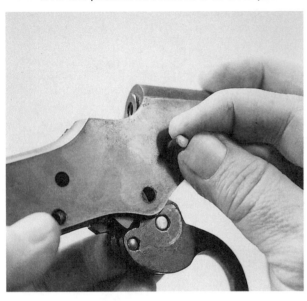

4. When installing the trigger spring, note that the longer arm of the spring goes toward the front, as shown.

5. Use a slave pin to retain the trigger spring during reassembly and be sure the loop of the hammer block engages the post on the trigger.

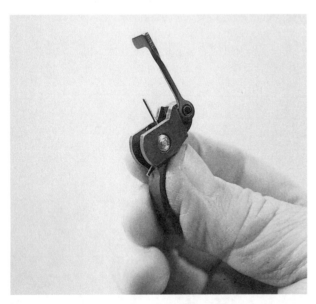

6. With the hammer pulled back, the hammer block is inserted at the top, its cross-piece lying in the "hook" at the back of the link. Its lower loop will protrude as shown to engage the post on the trigger.

Savage Mark II

Similar/Identical Pattern Guns

The same basic assembly/disassembly steps for the Savage Mark II also apply to the following guns:

Savage Mark II BV, Camo   Lakefield Mark II
Savage Mark II GY (Youth)
Savage Mark II GL (Left-Hand)
Savage Mark II FSS (Stainless)

Data:	Savage Mark II FXP
Origin:	United States
Manufacturer:	Savage Arms, Inc.
	Suffield, Connecticut
Cartridge:	22 Long Rifle, 17 Mach 2
Magazine capacity:	10 rounds
Overall length:	39½ inches
Barrel length:	20½ inches
Weight:	5½ pounds

With the Savage Mark II series of guns, introduced in 1990, there is a choice of wood or synthetic stock and regular blued steel or stainless. In 2004, the 17 Mach 2 chambering was added. Through all of the versions, the mechanism has remained the same, and the instructions will apply.

Disassembly:

1. Remove the magazine, and open the bolt. Hold the trigger to the rear, and remove the bolt. With an Allen wrench of the proper size, back out the front screw on the underside of the stock. When resistance is felt, stop. The screw will stay in the stock.

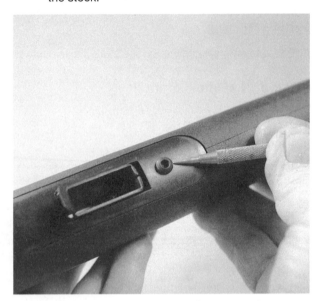

2. Remove the screw at the rear of the magazine plate, and its washer.

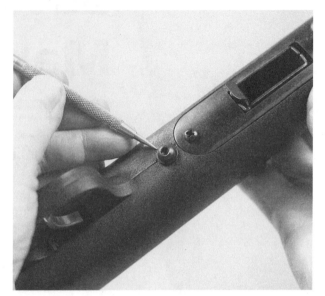

3. Remove the action from the stock.

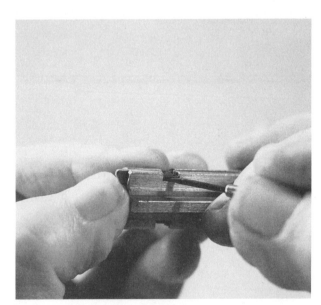

4. If removal of the extractors is necessary, push the left extractor slightly outward, and insert a small tool to gently pry the spring band off upward. The band must be lifted enough to clear the shoulder-notch. **Caution:** *Control the spring band as it is taken off.* Both extractors will be freed to be lifted out of their recesses. Note that the extractors are not identical, and keep the left and right separate for reassembly.

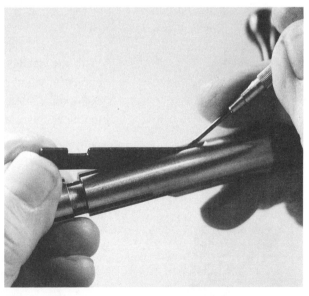

5. Taking off the spring band will also free the firing pin for removal.

6. The front and rear sections of the bolt, and the striker system, are not routinely dismountable.

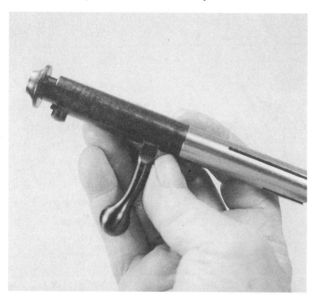

7. The action parts are very tightly set in place at the factory and routine removal is not advisable. For cases where takedown is absolutely necessary, we will show the sequence. The forward stock stud retains the front of the magazine housing.

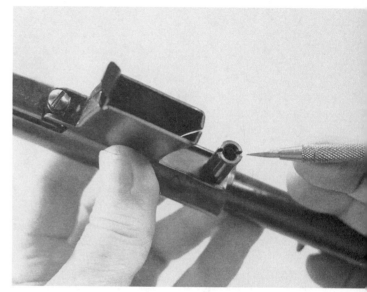

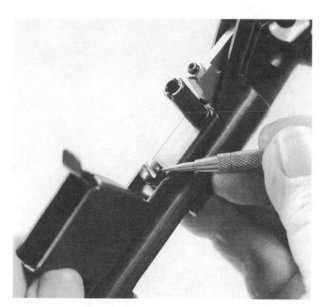

8. If the front stud has been removed, taking out this screw and its lock-washer will allow the magazine housing and the magazine catch to be moved out toward the front.

9. Assuming that the magazine housing and catch have been removed, removal of the rear stock stud and its lock-washer and spacer will allow the bolt guide to be taken off downward.

10. If the previous steps have been taken, removal of the large post-screw at the rear will allow the trigger group to be taken off downward.

11. The sear adjustment nut has been set at the factory and secured with sealant. It should not be disturbed.

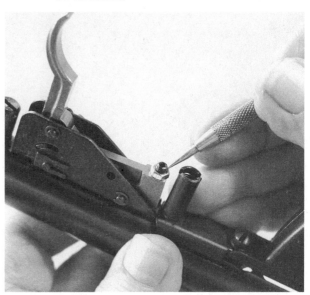

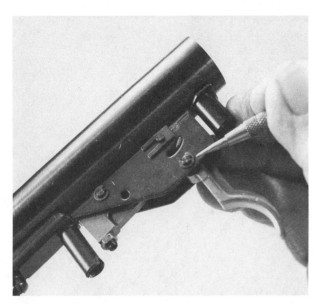

12. The sear and trigger cross pins are retained in the trigger group by C-clips, and the safety cross pin by a sliding spring-clip. Removing the clips will allow the pins to be taken out toward the right, and the parts can then be removed, along with their attendant springs. In normal takedown, this system is best left in place.

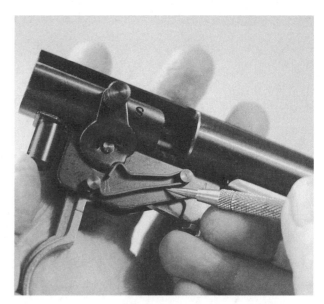

13. The safety detent spring can be taken off its posts only after the safety is moved toward the left.

14. The front and rear sights are dovetail-mounted, and can be drifted out toward the right. The barrel is retained in the receiver by a single cross pin.

15. While it is possible to pry the magazine floorplate outward at the front and slide it off forward, some deformation is likely to occur. It is best left in place.

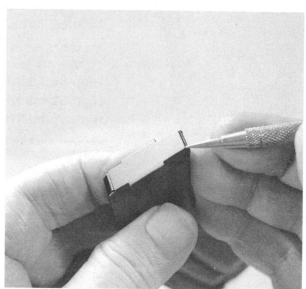

Reassembly Tips:

1. When installing the extractor spring band, take care to keep it under control. Hook it first into the right extractor, as shown, then push it down and across. Be sure the firing pin is in forward position.

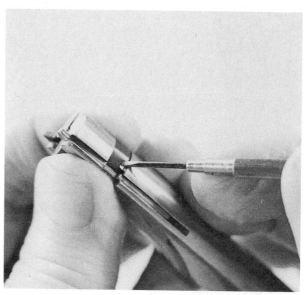

2. It will be necessary to insert a small tool under the spring band on the left side, to lift and guide it onto the left extractor.

Sears Model 25

Similar/Identical Pattern Guns

The same basic assembly/disassembly steps for the Sears Model 25 also apply to the following guns:

High Standard A-102 Sport King
High Standard A-102 Sport King Carbine
High Standard A-102 Sport King Deluxe

Data:	Sears Model 25
Origin:	United States
Manufacturer:	High Standard Firearms
	Hamden, Connecticut
Cartridge:	22 Short, Long, Long Rifle
Magazine capacity:	22 Short, 17 Long, 15 Long Rifle
Overall length:	43¾ inches
Barrel length:	22¼ inches
Weight:	5⅝ pounds

Made for Sears, Roebuck & Company by High Standard, this gun was also marketed by High Standard under their own name as the "Sport King" Model A-102. The sear/disconnector system has elements of the old Savage Model 6 and Stevens Model 87, with the bolt staying open between shots until the trigger is released. The gun was discontinued around 1976, but apparently a lot of them were sold, by both Sears and High Standard, because they are frequently seen.

Disassembly:

1. Remove the inner magazine tube and back out the stock mounting screw, located on the underside of the stock. Separate the action from the stock.

2. Pull the trigger to drop the hammer to the fired position and unscrew the receiver end piece, taking it off toward the rear.

3. Move the bolt to the rear, and remove the hammer assembly from the rear of the receiver. This includes the hammer and the captive hammer and bolt springs and their guide rod. This unit can be disassembled, but the guide rod ends are riveted to contain the unit, and disassembly might require that a new guide and rod be made.

4. Align the bolt handle with the opening at the rear of its track in the receiver, and remove the handle toward the right.

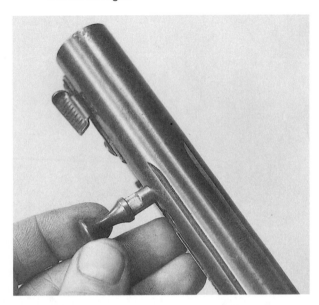

5. Use a small tool to push the bolt toward the rear until it can be grasped and taken out of the receiver.

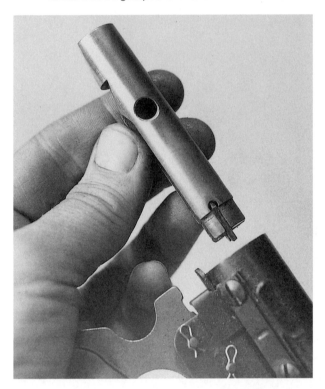

6. Lift the firing pin straight up out of its slot in the top of the bolt.

7. To remove the twin extractors, insert a small screwdriver to depress the plunger, and lift each extractor out of its recess toward the side. **Caution:** *Take care that the screwdriver doesn't slip, as the compressed springs can drive the plungers quite a distance. Ease them out.*

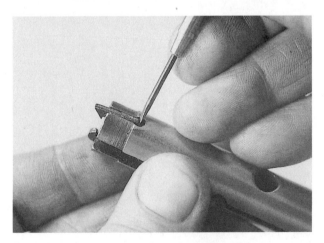

8. Use a small screwdriver to detach the rear hooks of the carrier spring from their notches on the front of the sub-frame. Move the rear arms of the spring outward, and allow them to move toward the rear, partially relieving the tension.

9. Detach the carrier spring from the ends of the carrier pivot on each side and remove the spring.

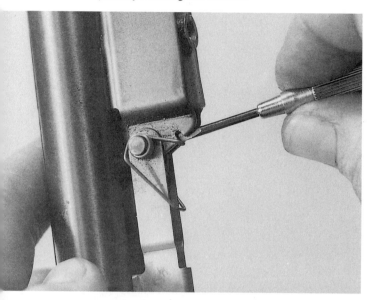

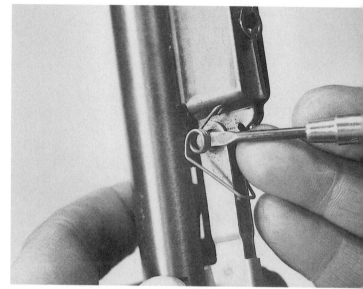

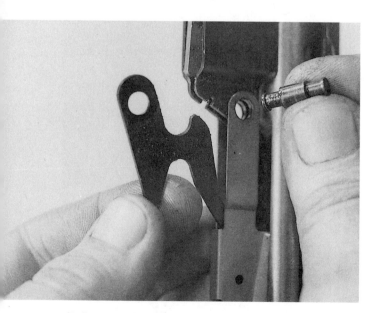

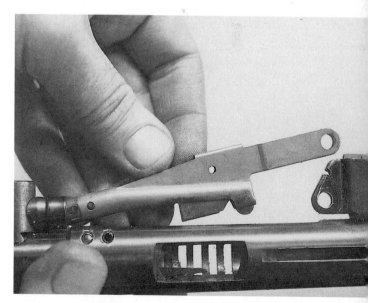

10. Remove the carrier pivot and take out the carrier downward.

11. The cartridge feed throat can now be moved toward the rear, tilted downward at the rear, and taken off.

12. The safety catch and its positioning spring are retained on the right rear of the receiver by two post screws, and these are taken out to allow removal of the spring and safety toward the right.

13. Take off the spring clip on the tip of the trigger pivot, and push the pin out toward the opposite side.

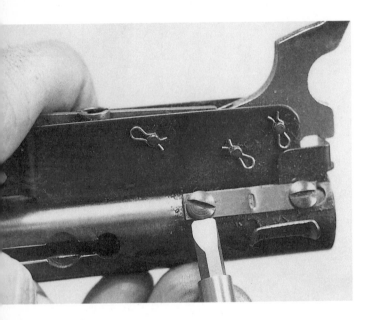

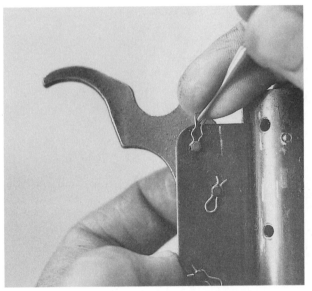

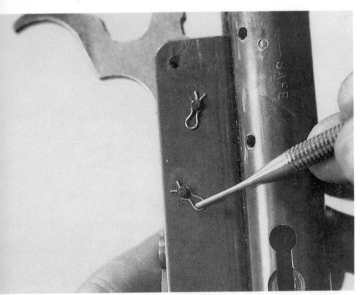

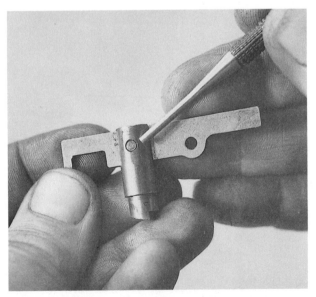

14. Take off the spring clip on the tip of the trigger bar pivot, and take out the pin toward the opposite side. **Caution:** *Keep pressure on the underside of the bar while removing the pin, to control the pressure of the springs, and ease it out.* Remove the bar and disconnector assembly downward.

15. Drifting out the cross pin in the disconnector will allow it to be separated from the bar. **Caution:** *There is a strong coil spring mounted inside the part, so control it when drifting out the pin.*

16. Remove the trigger and sear assembly downward. Note that the other cross pin retained by a spring clip is a stop pin for the trigger and does not have to be removed.

17. Drifting out the cross pin at the front of the trigger will allow separation of the sear from the trigger. **Caution:** *Ease out the compressed spring mounted inside the sear. Also, take care that the front wings of the trigger are not deformed during removal of the pin.*

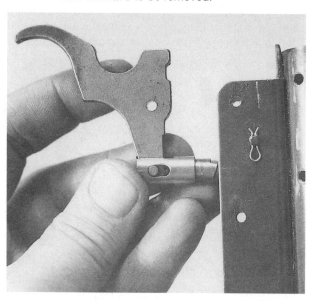

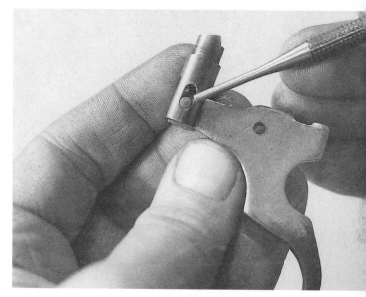

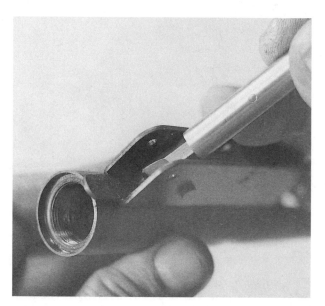

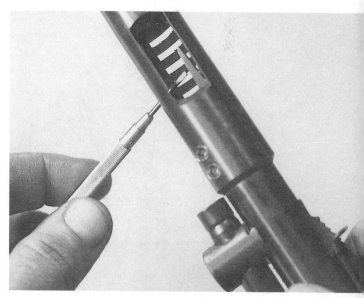

18. The sub-frame, the trigger and sear housing, is retained on the underside of the receiver by two vertical screws; when these are taken out it is removed downward.

19. The cartridge guide, mounted inside and above the chamber, is removable only when the barrel is taken out. There is also a small coil spring mounted in a recess in the roof of the receiver, above the guide.

20. The barrel is retained by two large roll cross pins. Use a roll pin punch to drift these out; then grip the barrel in a padded vise and use a non-marring punch to drive the receiver off the barrel toward the rear. The outer magazine tube is staked in place inside the rear loop (the stock mounting stud), and removal is not recommended except for replacement of a damaged unit. If necessary, the tube can be driven out toward the front using a large wooden dowel as a drift to avoid damaging the tube mouth.

Reassembly Tips:

1. When replacing the carrier spring, use small sharp nosed pliers to grasp the rear arms of the spring and guide them into their notches in the sub-frame.

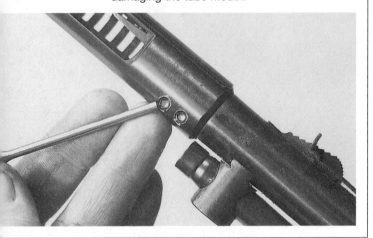

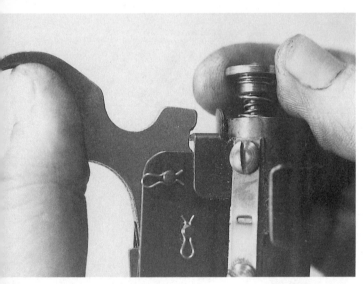

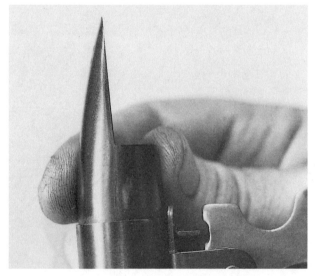

2. When replacing the bolt, pull the trigger to ease insertion in the receiver. Also, when replacing the hammer assembly, pull the trigger to allow the hammer to move forward to fired position to facilitate replacement of the receiver end piece.

3. When replacing the end piece, tighten it by hand only, no tools; then back it off until it is in the position shown to mate with the stock.

When replacing the barrel in the receiver, take care that the small spring above the cartridge guide is not deformed as the barrel and attached guide are slid into place.

Sears Model 31

Similar/Identical Pattern Guns

The same basic assembly/disassembly steps for the Sears Model 31 also apply to the following gun:

Sears Model 34

Data:	Sears Model 31
Origin:	United States
Manufacturer:	High Standard
	Hamden, Connecticut
Cartridge:	22 Short, 22 Long Rifle
Magazine capacity:	25 Shorts, 17 Long Rifles
Overall length:	41¾ inches
Barrel length:	23¼ inches
Weight:	5½ pounds

Made for Sears, Roebuck & Company by High Standard, the Model 31 was marketed under the "J.C. Higgins" brand name. Its appearance was unusual in one area: long, slim panels extended from the forend back along each side of the receiver. As an option, the gun could be supplied with a tape-measure-style nylon web sling, which was mounted inside the buttstock. The gun was later redesigned to become the Model 34, but the internal mechanism was essentially the same, and the instructions generally can be used for either gun.

Disassembly:

1. Remove the inner magazine tube, cycle the bolt to cock the hammer, and set the safety in the on-safe position. Remove the cross screw located near the rear tip of the wooden side panels which cover the receiver.

2. Pull the rear of the trigger group downward, move the unit slightly toward the rear, and remove it downward.

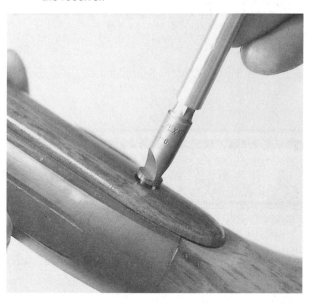

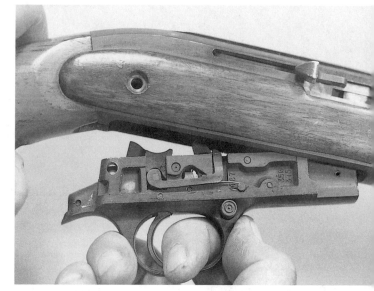

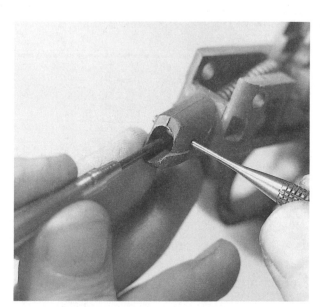

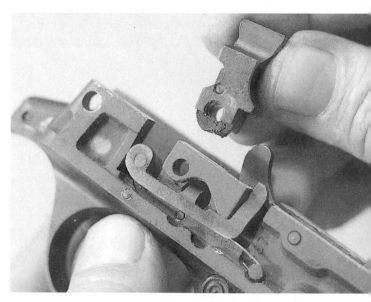

3. Release the safety, restrain the hammer against the tension of its spring, and pull the trigger. Ease the hammer down to the fired position. Use a small drift punch to push out the small cross pin at the extreme rear of the trigger group, and remove the hammer spring and its guide toward the rear. **Caution:** *The spring is under tension, even with the hammer at rest.* Removal of the pin will be easier if a small screwdriver is inserted at the rear to exert pressure on the spring, and this will also help in easing it out.

4. Push out the hammer pivot pin and remove the hammer from the top of the trigger group.

5. Disengage the disconnector spring from its groove in the bottom front of the disconnector and remove the disconnector toward the right. The spring is mounted on a cross pin, and the pin and spring are easily removed toward the right.

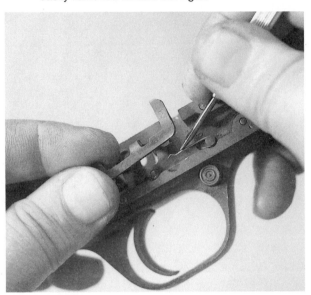

6. Drifting out the sear pivot pin toward either side will allow removal of the sear and its spring upward. Before removal, note the relationship of the sear and its spring to aid reassembly.

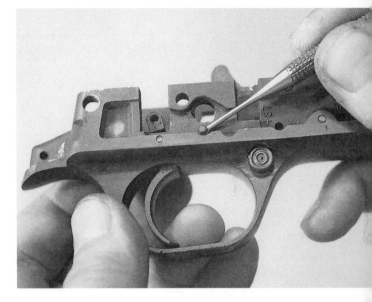

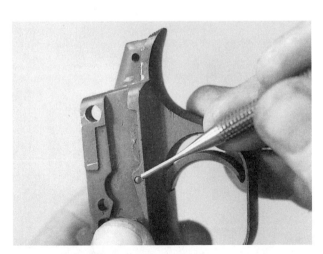

7. Drift out the trigger cross pin and remove the trigger and its spring upward.

8. Insert a drift punch of very small diameter, or an opened paper clip, into the tiny hole in the underside of the safety cross-piece on the left side to depress the safety positioning and retaining plunger and spring. While holding the plunger in, use the drift to turn the safety slightly (about a quarter turn) in either direction, and remove the safety toward the left. When the safety clears the plunger and spring they will be released, so restrain them and ease them out.

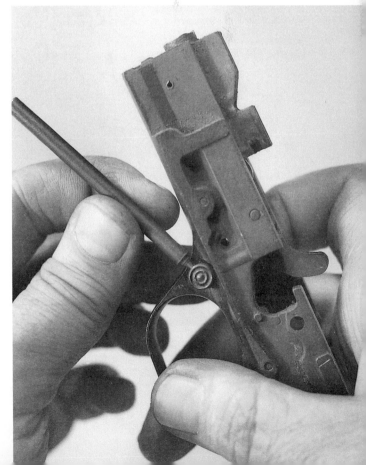

9. Push out the carrier pivot pin toward either side and remove the carrier upward. The carrier is under some tension from the spring below it, but not so much that it can't be easily controlled.

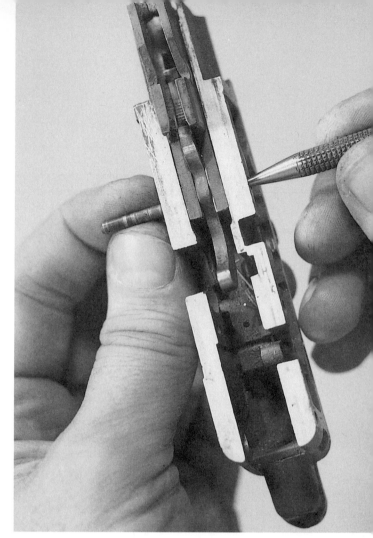

10. Use a roll-pin punch to drift out the small cross pin at the front of the trigger group and remove the two sides of the cartridge guide upward.

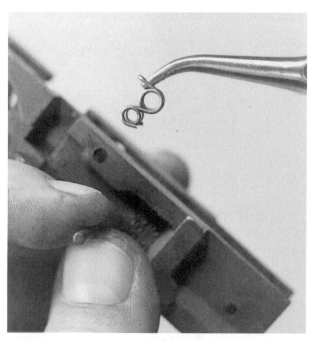

11. Push out the cross pin at the lower edge of the trigger group, just forward of the guard, and remove the carrier spring upward. Before removal, note the way the spring is installed on the pin, to aid reassembly.

12. Invert the gun and retract the bolt all the way to the rear to clear the ejector. Lift the front of the bolt away from the inside top of the receiver, and slide the cocking handle forward; then remove it from the ejection port.

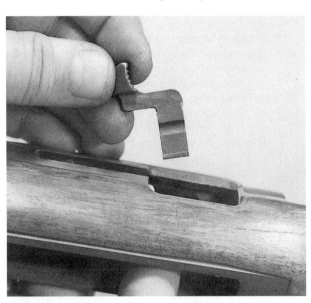

13. Continue tipping the front of the bolt outward until it clears the inner edge of the receiver; then ease it out, releasing the spring tension slowly. Take out the bolt spring and its guide.

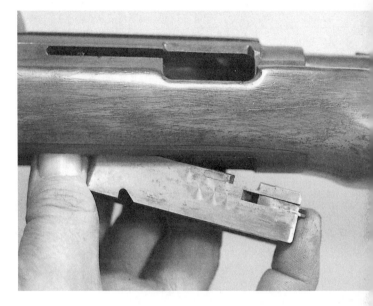

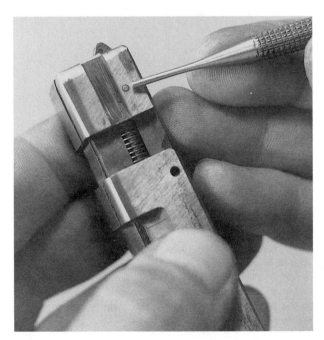

14. The extractor and its coil spring are retained by a vertical pin at the right front of the bolt. Remove the pin by drifting it out toward the top, and take out the extractor and its spring toward the right.

15. The firing pin is retained by a vertical pin at the left rear of the bolt, and this pin must be removed upward. The firing pin and its spring are then taken out toward the rear.

16. The ejector is staked in place inside the left wall of the receiver and should not be removed except for replacement of a broken part. If this is necessary, it can be drifted out downward, alternating the drift point to each end of the ejector as it is struck. Backing out the large screw on the underside of the forend will allow the forend and its integral side panels to be taken off downward. The magazine tube is retained by a cross pin through the tube hanger, and the tube is taken out toward the front. The buttstock is attached by a through-bolt at the rear, accessible after removal of the buttplate. If the gun has the reel-type sling, the reel must be lifted out to give access to the stock bolt.

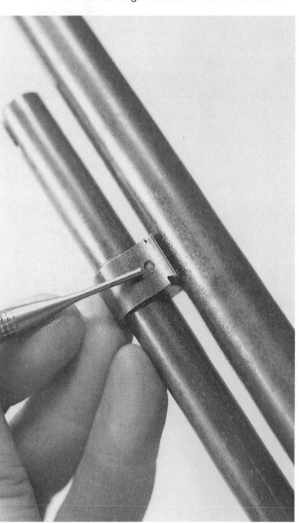

Reassembly Tips:

1. The most difficult reassembly operation is replacement of the carrier spring and carrier. In this photo they are shown assembled outside the trigger group to show the proper relationship of the carrier spring and the small notch on the underside of the carrier. When replacing the carrier, be sure the cross bar of the spring is at the top. Insert the carrier pin through one side of the trigger group wall and one side of the cartridge guide, up to the carrier space. Be sure the small notch in the underside of the carrier engages the cross bar of the spring. Push the carrier down and forward, slightly compressing the spring, until the pivot pin can be pushed through the hole in the carrier and on to the other side. When properly installed, the carrier should move with an audible snap between its raised and lowered positions.

Install the sear, hammer and disconnector in that order, to ensure that the inner arm of the disconnector is in proper engagement with the side tab of the sear. When installing the sear, be sure the right-angled tip of the forward arm of the sear spring engages properly with its shelf on the inside right wall of the trigger group.

SIG 522 Classic

Similar/Identical Pattern Guns

The same basic assembly/disassembly steps for the SIG 522 Classic also apply to the following guns:

SIG 522 SWAT

Data:	SIG 522 Classic
Origin:	United States
Manufacturer:	SIG SAUER, Inc., Exeter, New Hampshire
Cartridge:	22 Long Rifle
Magazine capacity:	26 rounds
Overall length:	35⅛ inches
Barrel length:	16½ inches
Weight:	6½ pounds

The SIG 522 is another rifle designed to roughly duplicate the feel of a full-powered, centerfire rifle, yet in a rimfire package. The SIG 550, a rifle manufactured in Switzerland and imported in small numbers, was reintroduced in the United States as the SIG 556 early in 2006. This rifle proved popular in various iterations in law enforcement and home defense markets. The 522 capitalizes on the popularity of the 556, looking and handling like the 556, but firing 22 Long Rifle ammunition.

Unlike other 22 copies of centerfire rifles, whose receivers are almost universally made of some type of plastic product or possibly aluminum forgings, the SIG 522 utilizes a thick-walled extruded aluminum upper receiver into which the barrel is secured. This makes for a very rigid and tough, yet cheap-to-produce action. It also uses the commonly available Atchisson/Ciener style of magazines.

Disassembly:

1. Push out both the front and rear takedown pins. Remove the lower receiver from the upper receiver.

2. Pull the bolt assembly all the way to the rear until it stops. Pull out the charging handle with a slight jiggle.

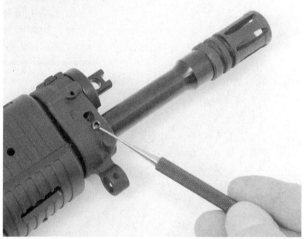

3. Remove the bolt from the receiver.

4. Remove the gas block set screw. The front sight block assembly can be pulled off the front. Upper and lower handguard assembly can be pulled off toward the front. Remove the lower handguard from the upper handguard by pulling to the rear to unlock it, and down.

5. To remove the muzzle device, unscrew it from the barrel. However, it is not necessary to remove the muzzle device in order to disassemble the rifle.

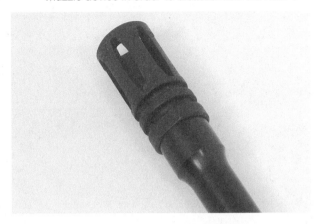

6. The storage tube can be removed from the front sight block by pushing it forward. However, the plastic latches that hold the tube in the front sight block will wear out quickly, and it is not necessary to remove it from the gun for disassembly. The tube plug can be removed by pulling it straight out.

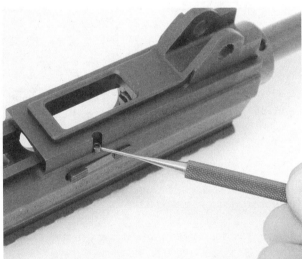

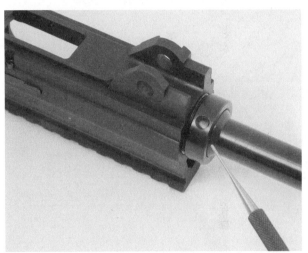

7. The bolt stop and the bolt stop spring can be pulled from the receiver by removing this screw.

8. Using a spanner wrench to remove the barrel nut allows the barrel to be pulled from the front of the receiver.

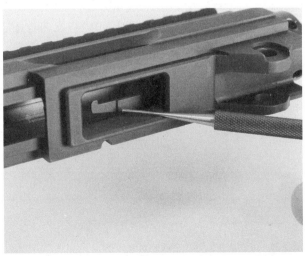

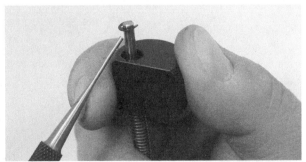

9. The ejector is retained in the barrel by the receiver. Removing the barrel from the receiver will allow the ejector to fall out.

10. The recoil spring guide is retained on both ends with a spring clip. Removal of either clip will allow the recoil spring assembly to be disassembled. This spring is compressed, so secure it as the clip is removed. Once the spring is no longer under compression, the buffer and spring can be removed from the guide and the guide can be removed from the bolt. There is a small washer inside the bolt that the spring bears upon.

11. Driving out this pin will free the firing pin and the firing pin return spring. Remove them to the rear.

12. To remove the extractor, use a small flat-edged screwdriver to push the extractor plunger back into its hole, and remove the extractor by pulling it forward, "wrapping" it around the front of the bolt.

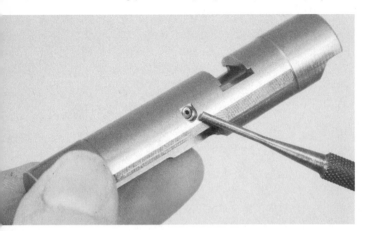

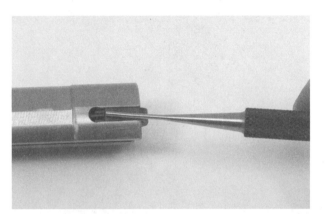

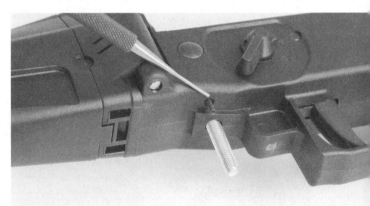

14. The rear takedown pin plunger and plunger spring are retained by the pistol grip and will fall free when the pistol grip is removed. The rear takedown pin can now be pulled from the receiver.

13. Remove the pistol grip screw. Do not lose the pistol grip nut, which is inside the pistol grip.

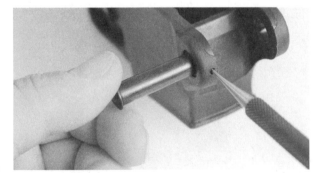

15. The front takedown pin is removed by inserting a punch into the hole in the front of the receiver, pressing in and rotating the pin as the punch is withdrawn. This deactivates the plunger. The front takedown pin can now be pulled out of the receiver to the right side. Place a thumb over the hole to prevent the plunger and spring from entering orbit.

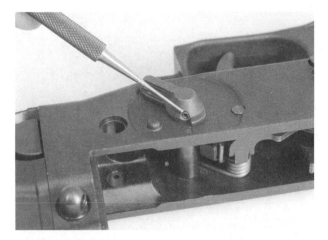

16. With the hammer in the fired position, drive out the safety lever spring pin from the left side safety lever and remove the safety lever from the safety shaft.

17. Rotate the safety so that the right side safety arm is pointing up and push the safety shaft out of the receiver to the right. Note that there are two springs exerting pressure on this shaft.

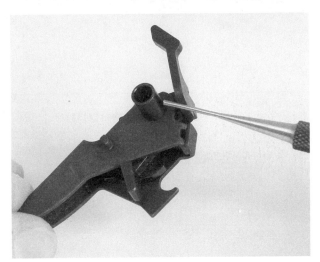

19. Removal of the trigger bushing will free the disconnector, sear and sear spring from the trigger.

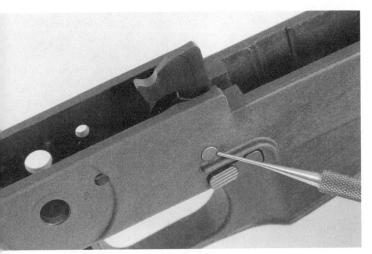

21. Push the hammer pivot pin out. This will allow the hammer and hammer spring to be removed from the receiver.

18. Push out the trigger pivot pin. This frees the trigger assembly and trigger spring to be removed from the receiver.

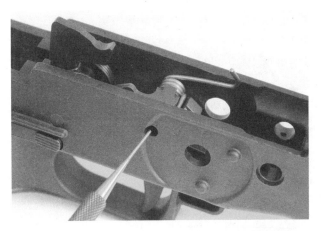

20. The long arm-like safety detent spring retains the hammer pivot pin in the receiver. Push the back tip down to the bottom of the receiver and lift the entire spring straight up, detaching it from the hammer pivot pin. Slightly jiggling the spring as it is lifted might help in freeing the spring from the hammer pivot pin.

22. To remove the magazine catch, use a punch to depress the right magazine catch into the right side of the receiver until it bottoms out. Using another punch, push out the magazine catch pivot pin towards the bottom of the receiver. It will push out easily and the left magazine catch can be removed from the right magazine catch and spring. Pull the right catch and spring from the right side of the receiver.

23. To remove the folding buttstock, drive out the folding stock hinge pin and pull the stock from the receiver. Do not lose the folding stock disc spring.

24. This slider lock secures the buttstock to the inner stock piece. To remove the buttstock from the inner stock piece, pull this slide lock back, push in the stock adjustment lever until it stops and pull the stock piece off to the rear.

Reassembly Tips:

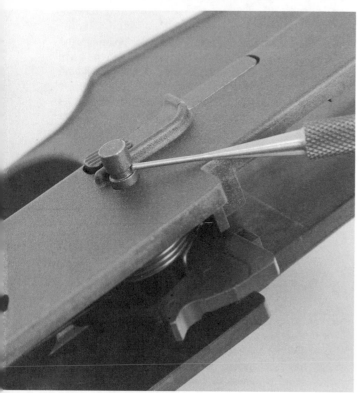

1. When reinserting the hammer and trigger pivot pins, the grooves on the pins should be oriented to the left of the receiver.

2. The small arm of the trigger spring should be placed here, behind the disconnector. The large diameter of the trigger bushing should be to the left of the trigger. The trigger spring sits on the small diameter to the right of the trigger. It is vital to place the small-coiled sear spring correctly under the squarish section just behind the small arm of the trigger spring. If the spring is not pushing directly against the underside of this surface, the sear might not reconnect to the hammer after firing.

Smith & Wesson M&P 15-22

Similar/Identical Pattern Guns
The same basic assembly/disassembly steps for the M&P 15-22 also apply to the following guns:
Smith & Wesson M&P 15-22 Performance Center
Smith & Wesson M&P 15-22 MOE
Smith & Wesson M&P 15-22 CA

Data:	Smith & Wesson M&P 15-22
Origin:	United States
Manufacturer:	Smith & Wesson, Springfield, Massachusetts
Cartridge:	.22 Long Rifle
Magazine capacity:	25 rounds
Overall length:	33 ¾ inches extended, 30 ½ inches collapsed
Barrel length:	16 inches
Weight:	5 ½ pounds

One of the interesting side effects of the modern sporting rifle phenomenon is the production of like models in rimfire calibers. The M&P 15-22 is such an example, produced in conjunction with the Smith & Wesson's M&P line of semi-automatic centerfire rifles, introduced in 2009. These rifles, based on the AR-15, are very popular, and with rising costs in ammunition and production, the alternative of shooting rimfire ammunition through a largely similar (or otherwise identical in some cases) rifle for training purposes has great appeal. One of many similar models from many companies, the M&P 15-22 is perhaps the best seller of them all and for good reason. It is lightweight, accurate enough for training or plinking and has a very simple, solid method of operation. Furthermore, it shares many parts in common with its .223 Rem. big brothers, and handles in a closely similar fashion as well. While a special wrench is necessary to change the barrel or handguard, the rest of the rifle is very simple to maintain and its ability to mount a large variety of optical sights brings it a great benefit as well.

Disassembly:

1. Pull out the rear takedown pin. Rotate the upper open from the lower.

2. Pull out the front pivot pin to detach the upper from the lower.

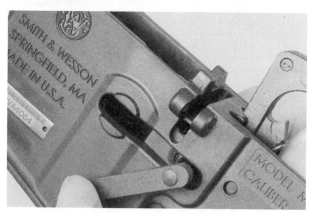

3. To remove the bolt catch, drive the bolt catch roll pin forward or backward out of the bolt catch. The bolt catch will fall out as will the bolt catch buffer and the bolt catch buffer spring.

4. Depress the magazine button until it bottoms. Then rotate the magazine catch counterclockwise until it can be removed from the receiver. Remove the button and the magazine catch spring from the right side of the receiver. Gently release the magazine catch button as it is under spring tension.

5. With the hammer in the fired position, drive out the hammer pin in either direction.

6. Drive out the trigger pin and remove the disconnector from inside the slot in the trigger. The trigger will now float in the receiver but will not be removable until the selector is removed.

7. Unscrew the pistol grip screw, which is accessed from the bottom of the pistol grip. As the pistol grip comes off, the selector detent and spring and the rear pivot pin detent and spring can be accessed.

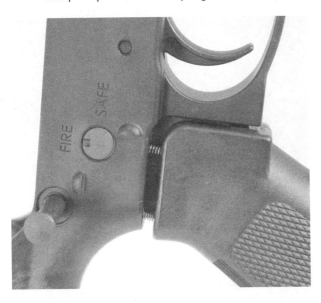

8. Remove the selector from the lower receiver. The trigger can now be removed.

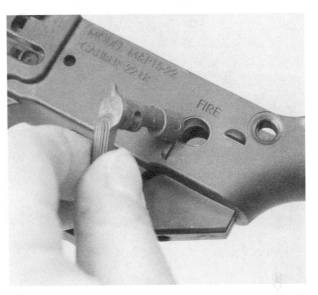

9. The front pivot pin can be removed by using a 1/16th-inch punch. Push it through the small hole in the front of the pivot pin to depress the detent. Use the punch to rotate the pivot pin out of alignment with the detent, then pull the pivot pin out of the receiver. Catch the detent and spring as they will jet out of the receiver.

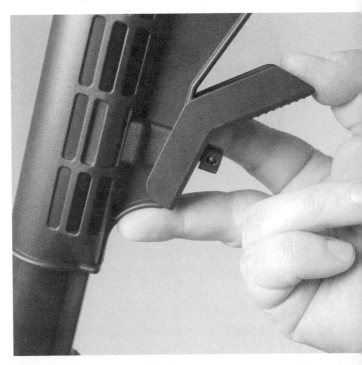

10. To remove the butt stock, pull down on the rear of the stock lever and pull the stock off of the receiver. To access the storage compartment in the receiver extension, pull out the rubber plug.

11. The iron sights are retained by thumb screws. Disassembly of the rear sight is not recommended unless something is broken.

12. Pull the charging handle and bolt back and out of the gun together.

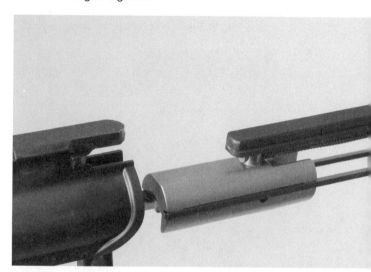

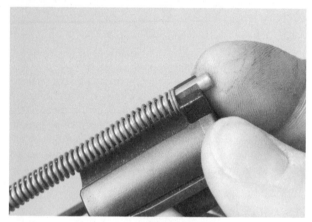

13. Push the bolt slightly back on its rails to allow the clearance slot on the spring guide to clear the ears at the rear of the bolt assembly. Control the spring as it is under compression. Pull the rear of the bolt assembly off of the bolt.

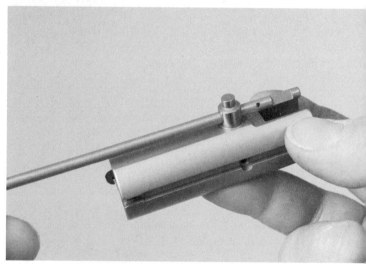

14. The spring guide can be pulled out from the front of the bolt.

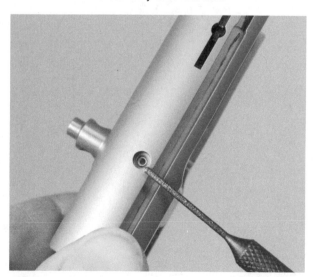

15. Driving out this pin will free the guide rod housing, the firing pin and the firing pin spring.

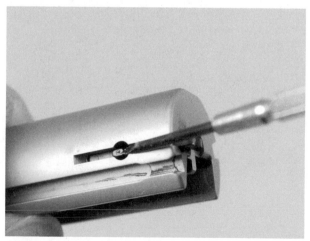

16. To remove the extractor, pull backward on the extractor detent and pull the extractor from the bolt. Control both the extractor detent and spring as they are under compression.

17. The ejector is part of the barrel assembly. The hand guard and barrel are retained by a castle nut. A special wrench will be needed to remove this nut. It is not recommended that this be done unless the ejector needs to be replaced.

18. The handguard and the cap is retained by four prongs. Depressing these prongs and pushing them forward will detach the endcap from the handguard. If removal of the handguard or barrel is necessary, a special barrel nut wrench is required to unscrew the barrel nut. The handguard will come off the front and the barrel can be removed by pulling it back through the receiver.

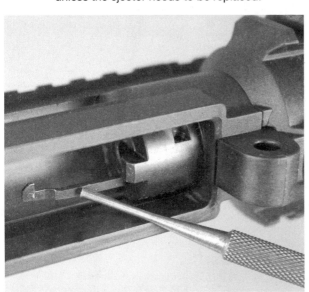

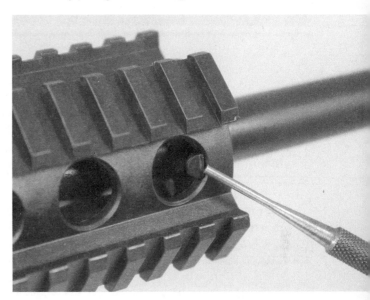

Reassembly Tips:

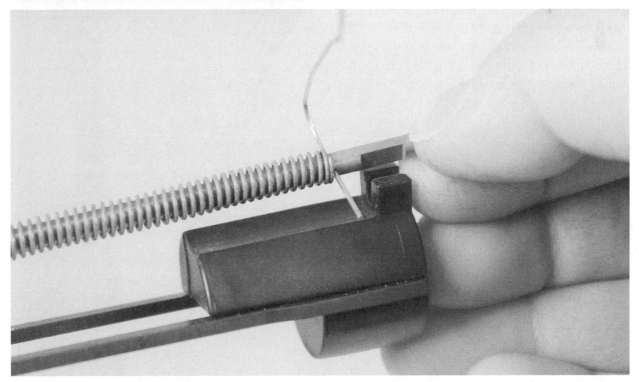

1. When reinstalling the spring and guide rod to the bolt, shove a paperclip through the hole in the guide rod to hold the spring partially compressed. Once the guide rod is in place, pull out the clip.

Stevens Favorite

Data:	Stevens Favorite
Origin:	United States
Manufacturer:	J. Stevens Arms & Tool Company
	Chicopee Falls, Massachusetts
Cartridge:	22 Long Rifle
Overall length:	36½ inches
Barrel length:	22 inches
Weight:	4 pounds

The little Stevens Favorite was certainly well-named. After its introduction in 1889, it became the most popular "boy's rifle" of all time, and lasted through 46 years of production. The gun was simple and reliable, a single shot with a lever-actuated falling block. In 1915, it was redesigned, the most notable internal changes being in the ejector and hammer spring. These differences will be noted in the instructions. The gun covered here is the early model, made prior to 1915.

Disassembly:

1. Back out the barrel retaining screw, located just forward of the lever on the underside of the gun. On guns made after 1915, the head of the screw will be a knurled piece, rather than a ring.

2. Remove the barrel and forend assembly forward.

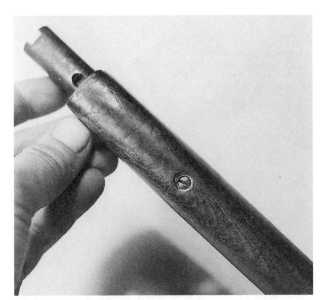

3. The forend is held on the underside of the barrel by a single screw.

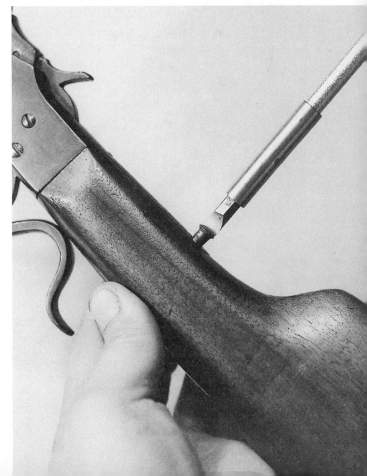

4. Remove the screws at the rear tip of the upper and lower receiver tangs to release the stock for removal. Remove the stock toward the rear. If the stock is very tightly fitted, it may be necessary to bump the front of the comb with the heel of the hand or with a soft rubber hammer.

5. The screw that retains the hammer spring can be reached through the stock screw hole in the upper tang. Remove the hammer spring screw and take out the spring toward the rear. On the post-1915 guns, the hammer spring will be a heavy coil with an internal hammer strut and a base sleeve at the rear, which bears on a groove in the head of a large screw in the lower tang. On these guns, grip the sleeve firmly with pliers and move it forward, and then upward to clear the base screw. After the hammer spring is removed, in both models, the screw which retains the trigger spring will be accessible. For this screw, use either an offset screwdriver or a screwdriver with the tip cut to an angle.

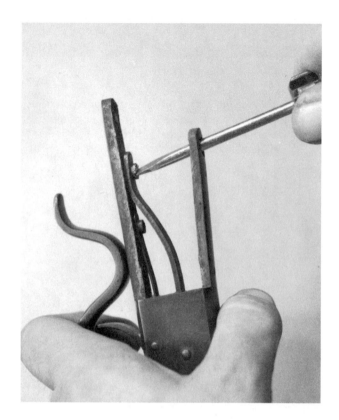

6. Taking out the hammer and trigger pivot screws will release the hammer for removal upward and the trigger for removal downward.

7. Remove the lever pivot screw, located at the lower edge of the receiver.

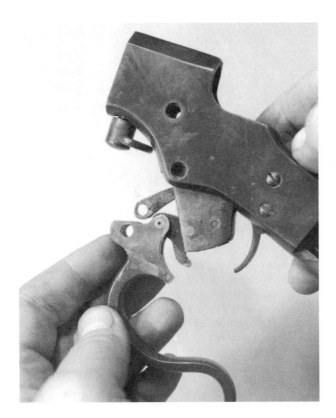

8. Remove the breechblock pivot screw.

9. Remove the lever and breechblock assembly downward. The ejector, which is retained by the lever pivot screw, will also come out at this time.

10. The ejector on the later model guns is different from the one shown. On the post-1915 guns, it has a front lobe which contains a plunger and spring, the plunger bearing on the breechblock pivot. The plunger is staked in place, and removal in routine disassembly is not advisable. Drifting out the upper cross pin in the breechblock will release the firing pin for removal toward the rear. The lower cross pin holds the link to the breechblock, and the pin at the top of the lever retains the lever on the link.

Reassembly Tips:

1. When replacing the lever and breechblock assembly in the receiver, be sure the ejector is in the position shown, with its cartridge rim recess and firing pin groove toward the rear. Also, be sure the link is in the position shown, with its hooked beak downward and pointing toward the rear.

When replacing the lever and breech block assembly in the receiver, the forward arms of the breechblock should be inserted into the bottom of the receiver first; then the breechblock is tipped into position.

On both models, insert the breechblock pivot screw first; then insert the lever pivot screw, being sure it passes through the lower loop of the ejector. On the later guns, it will be necessary to use a small tool to center the ejector loop while inserting the screw, holding it against the tension of its plunger and spring.

Stevens-Springfield Model 53A

Similar/Identical Pattern Guns

The same basic assembly/disassembly steps for the Stevens-Springfield Model 53A also apply to the following guns:

Stevens-Springfield Model 53
Stevens-Springfield Model 053

Data:	Stevens-Springfield Model 53A
Origin:	United States
Manufacturer:	Savage Arms Company
	Chicopee Falls, Massachusetts
Cartridge:	22 Long Rifle
Overall length:	38¼ inches
Barrel length:	21 inches
Weight:	4 pounds

Savage Arms completed a purchase of the old Stevens firm in 1936, and Stevens continued to make guns in the original Chicopee Falls factory as a subsidiary of Savage. The "Springfield" brand name should not be confused with the U.S. Springfield Armory. The Model 53, 53A, and 053 differed only in sight options and stock configurations. The guns were made from 1935 to 1948.

Disassembly:

1. Hold the trigger to the rear, open the bolt and remove the bolt toward the rear.

2. Back out or remove the action mounting screw located on the underside of the forend. Remove the action from the stock.

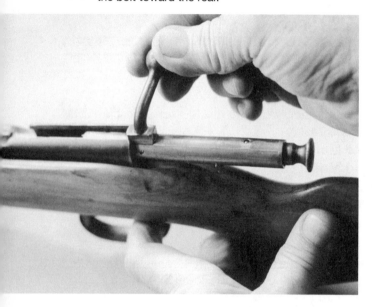

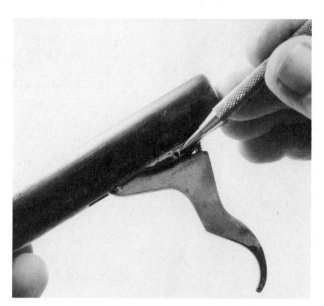

3. Two wood screws retain the trigger guard on the stock. An angled or offset screwdriver will be necessary for the screw at the front, inside the guard. The stock buttplate is also retained by two wood screws.

4. The trigger is retained by a cross pin. Drift out the pin and remove the trigger downward. The coil trigger spring can then be removed from its well at the rear of the trigger.

5. Unscrew and remove the knob at the rear of the bolt.

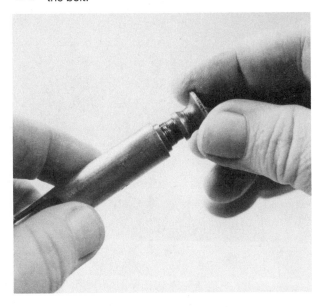

6. The striker rebound spring will likely come off with the cocking knob. If not, it is retrieved from inside the bolt.

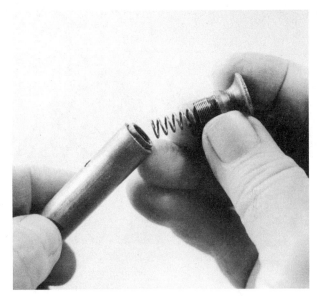

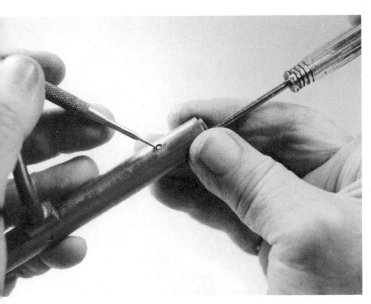

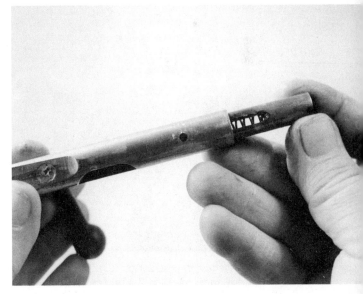

7. Insert a screwdriver at the rear to slightly depress the striker spring, and push or drift out the retaining cross pin. Take care that the pin is not canted during removal.

8. Remove the striker assembly toward the rear. The spring is easily removed from inside the striker.

9. Drift out the firing pin retaining pin located just below the bolt handle. Remove the firing pin and its return spring toward the rear. **Caution:** *The spring is under tension.*

10. Drift out the extractor cross pin and remove the extractor and its plunger and spring. **Caution:** *The spring is under tension, so restrain the extractor as the drift is removed.*

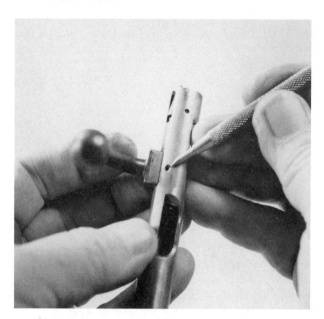

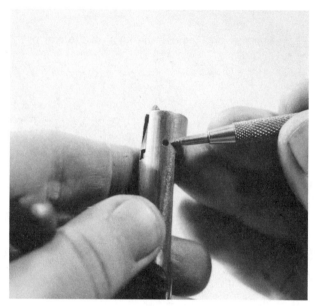

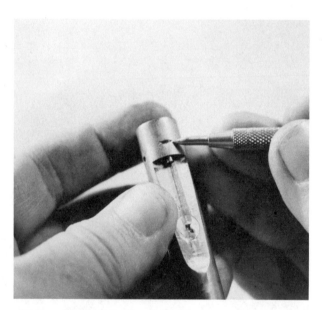

11. The ejector is retained by a recess in its shaft and a stake mark on the underside of the bolt. If removal is necessary, the part is driven out, ironing the stake mark. In normal takedown, it is best left in place.

12. The stock mounting post and the front and rear sights are dovetail-mounted on the barrel. If removal is necessary, they are driven out toward the right.

13. The barrel is retained in the receiver by a cross pin. In normal takedown, this is left in place. If barrel removal is necessary, drift out the pin and use a wood block to move the receiver off the barrel.

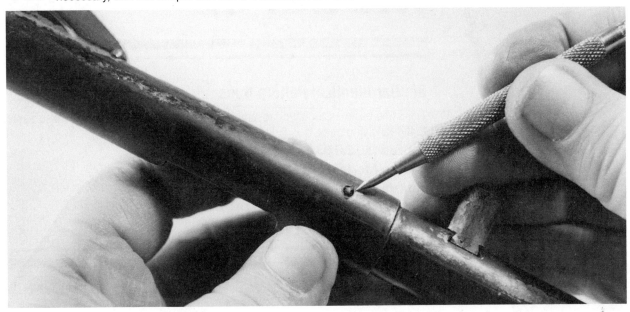

Reassembly Tips:

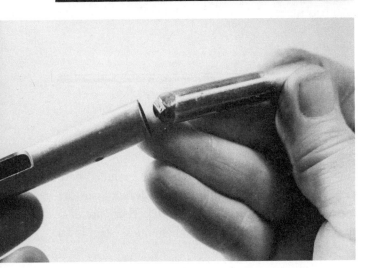

1. When replacing the striker in the bolt, be sure the sear contact notch is on the underside, as shown.

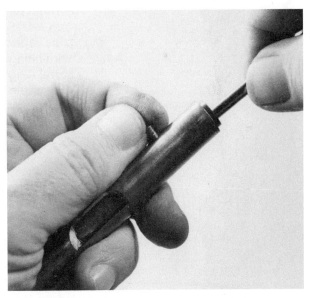

2. When replacing the striker assembly cross pin, insert a tool at the rear to compress the spring, keeping its rearmost coil in front of the pin.

Taurus Model 63

Similar/Identical Pattern Guns

The same basic assembly/disassembly steps for the Taurus Model 63 also apply to the following guns:

Taurus Model 63 Stainless
Taurus Model M73 (.22WMR)
Taurus Model M73 Stls.
Taurus Model M173 (.17HMIR)
Taurus Model M173 Stls.

Data:	Taurus Model 63
Origin:	Brazil
Manufacturer:	Taurus International, Miami, Florida
Cartridge:	22 Long Rifle
Magazine capacity:	10 rounds
Overall length:	39½ inches
Barrel length:	22 inches
Weight:	5½ pounds

The excellent Taurus copy of the Winchester Model 63 is included here *(along with that rifle)* because there are some slight differences in the takedown. The Taurus Model 63 was introduced in 2003. There are also versions in 22WMR and 17HMR, and in all of them stainless steel is an option. Mechanically, they are all the same.

Disassembly:

1. Remove the inner magazine tube from the stock. Cycle the bolt to cock the hammer and set the safety in on-safe position. Back out the take-down screw at the rear of the receiver until it is free (it will stay in the frame). If the screw is very tight, it has a coin-slot.

2. Move the butt stock and frame rearward and downward for removal. If the gun is new or otherwise very tight, it may be necessary to bump the trigger-guard with a hand or rubber hammer to start it. It can also be loosened by opening and releasing the bolt several times.

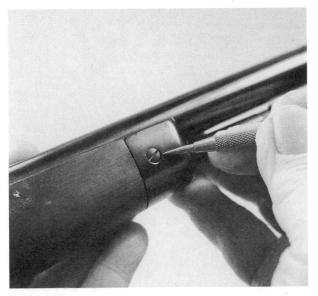

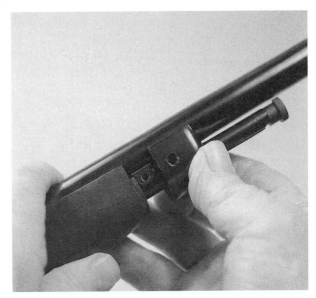

3. Remove the screws on each side of the forend cap.

4. Move the forend cap off toward the front. The cocking plunger assembly (Taurus: "action slide") will come off with the cap.

5. The spring is easily removed from inside the plunger shaft. If the plunger must be separated from the cap, drifting out this pin will allow the knob to be taken off and free the shaft for removal rearward.

6. Keep the forend tightly to the rear to avoid damaging the wood at the front, and push out or drift out the cap base. After the base is taken out, the forend is removed toward the front.

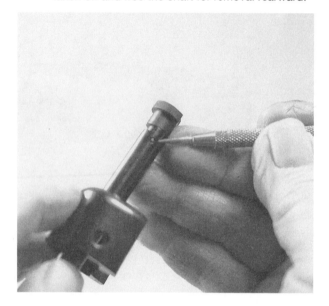

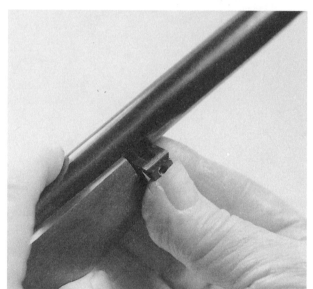

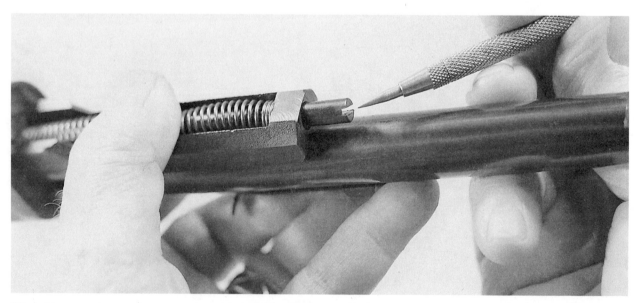

7. Unscrew the recoil spring guide rod. **Caution:** *Restrain the spring as the guide rod is slowly removed, and ease out the spring.*

8. Move the bolt assembly rearward to clear the ejector, then downward and rearward for removal. The ejector, mounted inside the receiver on the left side, can be drifted out toward the front, but only after barrel removal. In normal takedown, this is not done.

9. If extractor removal is necessary for repair, insert a small tool between the extractor and its plunger, depress the plunger and spring rearward, and tip out the extractor. **Caution:** *Control the plunger and spring, and ease them out.*

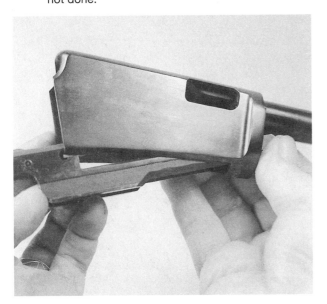

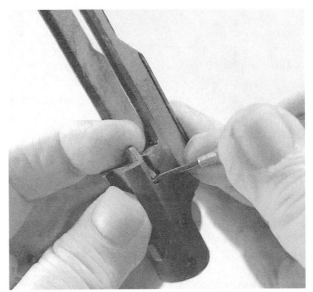

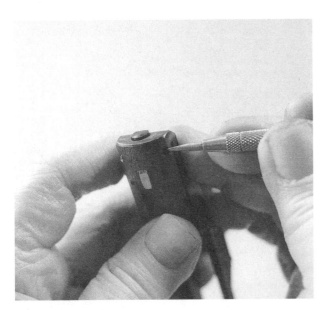

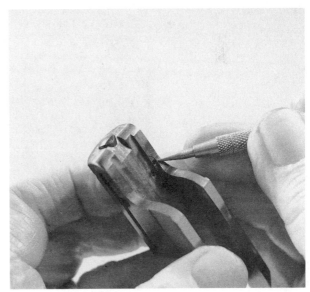

10. The firing pin and its return spring are retained by a cross pin at the top rear of the bolt.

11. If the Taurus safety-lock system needs to be taken out for repair or replacement, it is retained by this vertical pin. An opening on the left side of the bolt then allows the unit to be pushed out to the right. The pin is drifted out upward.

12. If the takedown screw must be removed, it is retained in the frame by this cross pin.

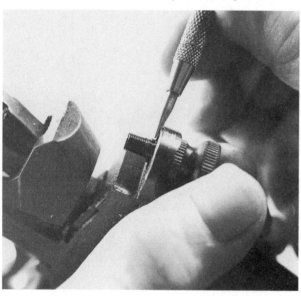

13. The takedown screw detent plunger and its coil spring can be taken out (after removal of the screw) by drifting out this cross-pin. **Caution:** *Control the plunger and spring.*

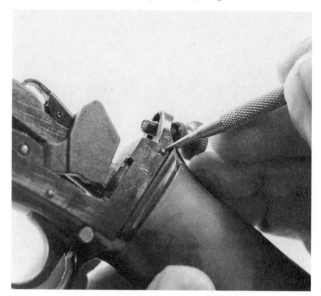

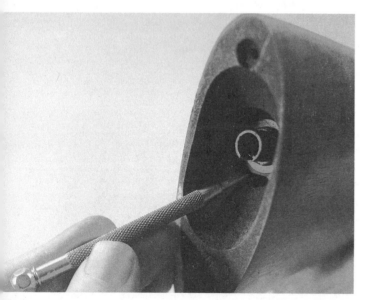

14. In normal takedown, removal of the buttstock is not advisable. If it must be done, the buttplate is taken off, and the large nut that retains the stock will require a ⅞-inch (or 23mm) socket wrench with very thin walls. If the safety has to be accessed, its detent plunger and spring are retained at lower rear by the buttstock.

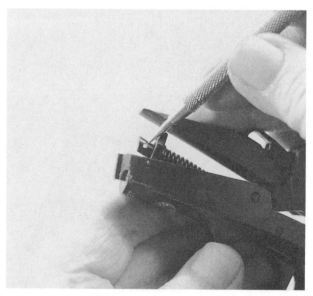

15. If hammer removal is necessary, insert a small pin through the hole in the hammer spring guide, then ease the hammer down to trap the spring.

16. With the spring trapped, drifting out this cross pin will free the hammer spring base.

17. Drifting out the hammer cross pin toward the right will free the hammer and its spring, guide, and base for removal toward the front. If this assembly is to be taken apart. **Caution:** *Control the spring.*

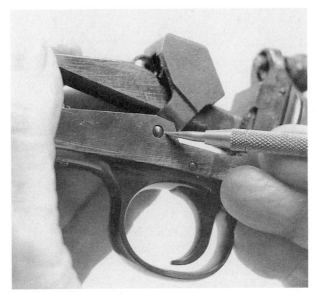

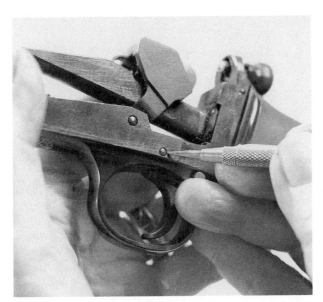

18. If the hammer system has been taken out, drifting out this cross pin will allow the trigger, sear, and sear spring to be removed. Reassembly of this unit will require the use of a slave pin. Note that the torsion-type trigger spring at the rear is easily accessible only if the buttstock has been removed.

19. The cartridge stop (Taurus: "ammunition retainer") and its coil spring can be removed by drifting out this cross pin toward the right. Note that the pin is riveted, and should not be routinely removed. The cartridge guide and outer magazine tube ("feeder assembly") are not routinely removable.

20. The front and rear sights are dovetail-mounted, and can be drifted out toward the right.

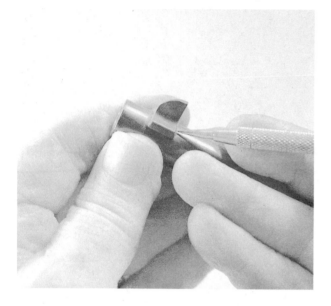

21. The inner magazine tubes can be disassembled by drifting out the lock-pin and taking off the knob, but in normal takedown it is best left intact *(see note at end of Tool Section)*.

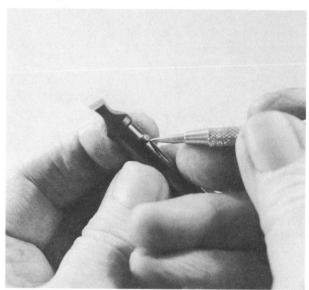

Reassembly Tips:

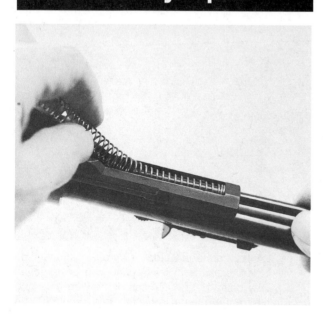

1. When reinstalling the recoil spring, feed the spring onto the guide as the rod is slowly inserted. As the last of the spring is put in, a screwdriver blade is helpful in compressing it. Be sure the guide rod is properly aligned before screwing it into the receiver. When the guide is in place, its rear tip should be even with the inside of the receiver.

Thompson/ Center Classic

Similar/Identical Pattern Guns

The same basic assembly/disassembly steps for the Thompson/Center Classic also apply to the following guns:

T/C Benchmark Target

T/C R55

T/C Silver Lynx

Data:	Thompson/Center Classic
Origin:	United States
Manufacturer:	Thompson/Center Arms
	Rochester, New Hampshire
Cartridge:	22 Long Rifle
Magazine capacity:	5 and 8 rounds
Overall length:	32½ inches
Barrel length:	23 inches
Weight:	4½ pounds

The T/C Classic arrived in 2000, and is well-named, with match-grade barrels and high-quality construction. It was soon followed by a heavy-barrel target version (2003), stainless steel in 2004, and the R55, in 17 Mach 2 (2005). Takedown for routine cleaning is easy, but beyond that the amateur should not proceed.

Disassembly:

1. Remove the magazine. Cycle the action to cock the internal hammer, and set the safety in on-safe position. Remove the screws at each end of the trigger guard assembly. Note they are of differing lengths.

2. Remove the trigger guard unit.

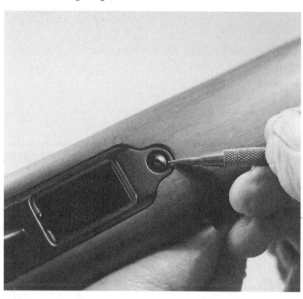

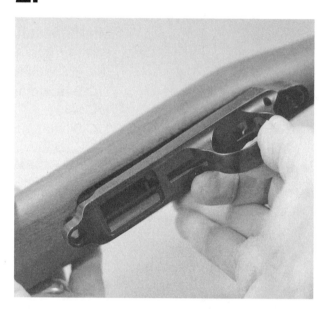

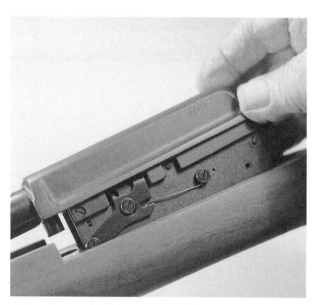

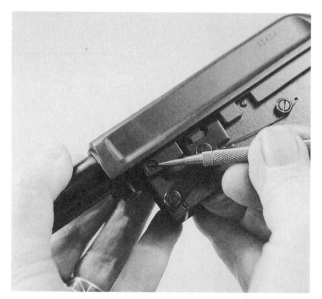

3. Remove the action from the stock.

4. Remove the four screws (two on each side) that retain the trigger group (T/C: "fire control assembly").

5. Remove the trigger group from the receiver.

6. Move the bolt to mid-position, keep inward and rearward pressure on the bolt handle, and lift out the bolt.

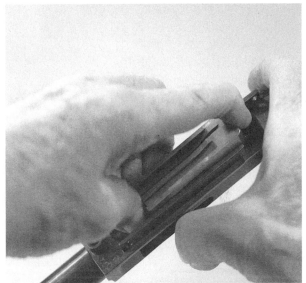

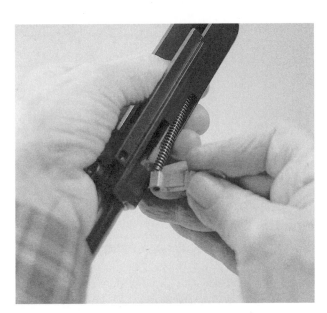

7. Keeping rearward pressure on the handle to control the spring, tip the handle out the ejection port and slowly relax the spring tension. Remove the handle.

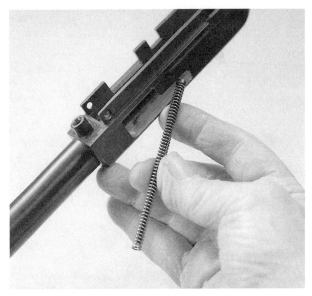

8. Remove the bolt spring and its guide. Note the polymer buffer inside the rear of the receiver is not routinely removed.

9. The extractor and its coil spring are retained by a vertical pin that is easily pushed out. Control the spring.

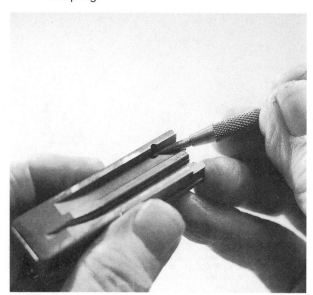

10. The firing pin and its return spring are retained in the bolt by a roll-type cross pin. Use a proper roll-pin drift to avoid damaging the pin.

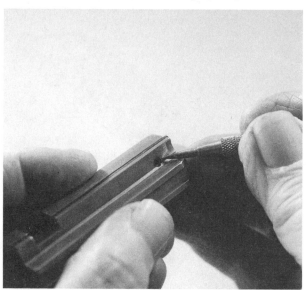

11. If the bolt hold-open must be removed for repair, taking out the pivot screw and guide screw, and their bushings, will free it. The spring arm is easily detached from its recess.

12. The shaped torsion spring that is the ejector is retained on the inside of the unit by a screw that is accessible through the indicated opening.

13. Removal of the magazine catch and its coil spring require separation of the two sides of the trigger group, and this is not routinely done.

14. Depressing the hammer slightly will move the safety to off-safe position. You may then restrain the hammer, pull the trigger, and ease the hammer down to fired position. This will give access to the area behind the hammer for cleaning. The hammer and its torsion spring are not routinely removable, as this requires separation of the two sides of the trigger group. If the hold-open spring has to be taken off for repair purposes, removal of this screw and its bushing will free the spring.

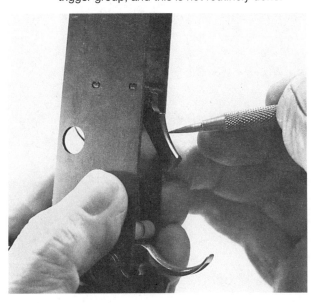

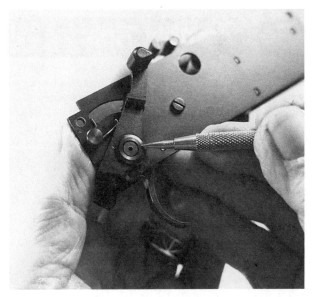

15. This C-clip retains the pin that mounts the safety spring on the right side.

16. This Allen screw retains the safety lever bushing. The cross-shaft behind it is also the trigger pivot. Removal of this system is not advisable.

17. The front sight is retained by a vertical screw. The rear sight has two, the rearmost accessible by taking off the adjustment slide.

18. The magazine can be disassembled by depressing the button in the floorplate and sliding the floorplate off toward the front. **Caution:** *Control the spring, and take out the lockplate, spring, and follower.*

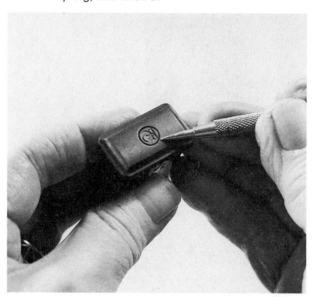

Reassembly Tips:

If the hammer has been uncocked, it should be recocked and the safety put in on-safe position before reassembly.

Thompson/Center Hotshot

Data:	Thompson/Center Hotshot
Origin:	United States
Manufacturer:	Thompson/Center Arms, Rochester, New Hampshire
Cartridge:	22 Long Rifle
Magazine capacity:	5 rounds
Overall length:	30 inches
Barrel length:	19 inches
Weight:	3 pounds

Many manufacturers have introduced rifles meant for the younger shooter. The Hotshot is Thompson/Center's entry. Very similar in outward appearance, it is somewhat smaller than its big brothers, the Encore and Contender, and is approximately three quarters their size. However, function is the same, and young shooters would have no problem growing into one of the larger T/C rifles in later years. New in 2010, the Hotshot is distinctively inexpensive and easy for young shooters to operate. Camouflaged models were also introduced in hunting style and in pink.

Disassembly:

1. Remove the two forend screws and pull off the forend.

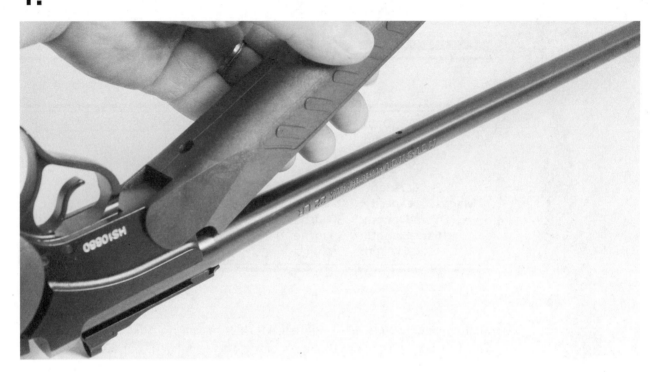

2. Break open the action and drive out the pivot pin from left to right. The right end of the screw is splined and it must be reinstalled from the right.

3. Removing these two screws will release the barrel lug and extractor from the barrel.

4. To remove the grip cap, remove the two grip cap screws.

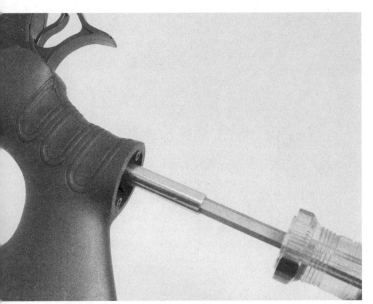

5. Remove the stock screw from inside the pistol grip to release the buttstock from the frame.

6. Drive out the front most of the three frame pins from left to right to release the trigger guard.

7. At the back of the frame, the trigger guard locking spring can be pulled out from the bottom.

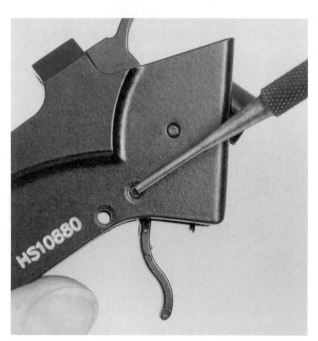

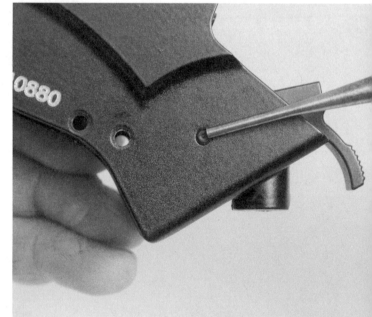

8. Drive out the middle pin from left to right to release the trigger. The latch spring and plunger will fall out of the hole when the trigger is removed. Some models have two trigger guard springs, others one. Pull them from the rear of the frame after the trigger guard has been removed.

9. Drive out the hammer pin from left to right to remove the hammer and hammer spring. The hammer has two plastic bushings. Removing the pin will allow them to fall free from the frame. Remove the hammer by pulling it out from the top of the frame.

10. Remove this screw to take out the bolt face.

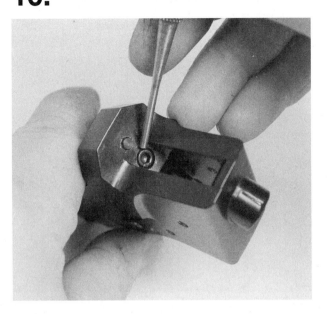

11. The bolt face contains the firing pin and firing pin spring, which are loose. The hinge at the bottom of the breech face can be removed by pushing out this hinge pin.

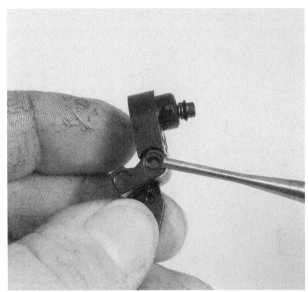

Reassembly Tips:

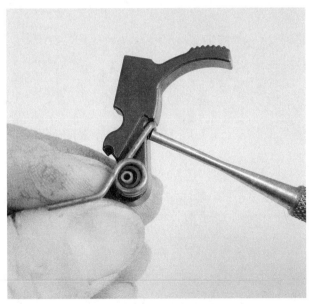

1. Note the proper orientation of the hammer spring on the hammer. The use of a slave pin to reinstall the internal parts is highly recommended.

2. The hammer, trigger, trigger guard pins and the large hinge pin all have splines on the right side. These pins must be inserted from the right to the left.

3. The latch spring and plunger ride in a channel cut into the right side of the receiver. Place them in this channel and push them straight up into their hole.

4. The trigger guard spring(s) and trigger guard are arranged as shown in the photo, displayed outside the frame for clarity. The center arm of the spring is arranged forward and down. This center arm is placed inside the rear of the trigger guard when both are installed in the frame, acting to keep the trigger guard forward.

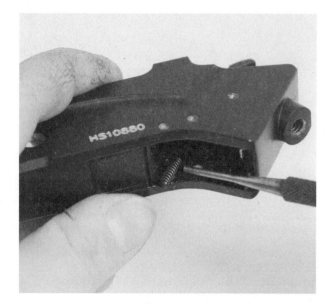

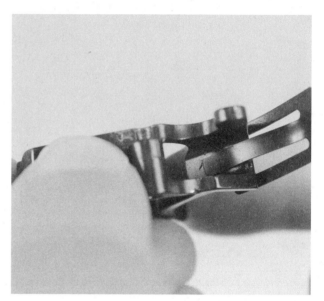

5. Shown here is the proper orientation of the trigger return spring to the trigger guard pin. It rests on top of the trigger guard pin inside the receiver. The trigger guard pin is shown in the trigger guard solely to display the correct placement of the spring. The pin would have to be removed for the trigger guard to be fully installed.

U.S. Springfield Model 1922 M2

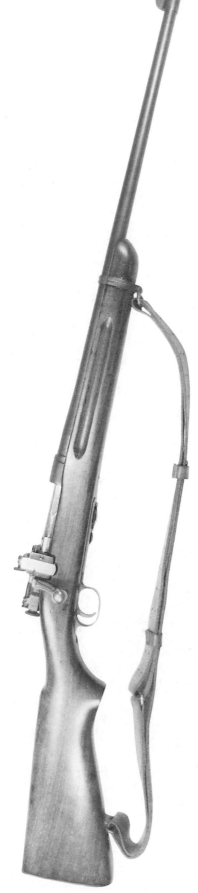

Similar/Identical Pattern Guns

The same basic assembly/disassembly steps for the U.S. Springfield Model 1922 M2 also apply to the following gun:

U.S. Springfield Model 1922 M1

Data:	U.S. Springfield Model 1922 M2
Origin:	United States
Manufacturer:	Springfield Armory
Cartridge:	22 Long Rifle
Magazine capacity:	10 rounds
Overall length:	43.7 inches
Barrel length:	24 inches
Weight:	8.90 pounds

The Model 1922 M2 was the final version of a target rifle designed and made at Springfield Armory and used initially for military marksmanship training. A number of these guns were later furnished to educational institutions and sold to NRA members in cooperation with the DCM. The original 1922 rifle was modified to produce the 1922 M1 and 1922 M2 guns, and the earlier guns were usually changed by the Armory as they came in for repair. The earlier guns are different mechanically, especially in the bolt assembly. The final M2 version is the one covered here.

Disassembly:

1. Remove the magazine. Set the bolt stop lever, located at the left rear of the receiver, on its central position, just a few degrees above horizontal. Withdraw the bolt toward the rear.

2. Drift out the cross pin in the stock, just forward of the barrel band.

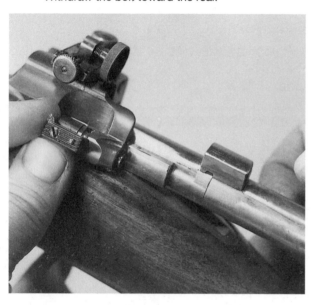

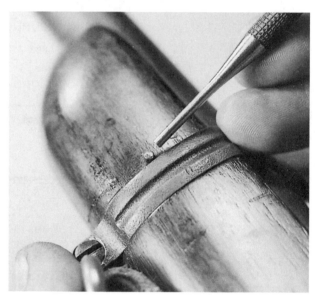

3. Remove the cross-screw at the bottom of the barrel band and take off the sling loop downward. The band can now be moved off toward the front.

4. Use a drift punch tip to depress the magazine floorplate latch, accessible in a hole at the rear of the plate. While holding the catch in, move the plate toward the rear; then take it off downward.

5. Remove the vertical screw on the underside at the front of the trigger guard unit. Remove the vertical screw on the underside at the rear of the trigger guard and separate the action from the stock. The trigger guard unit can now be taken off downward. The floorplate latch and its spring are retained on the inside of the guard unit by a cross pin and are removed upward.

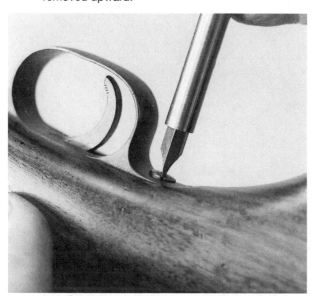

6. To remove the rear sight, first turn out the knurled knob on the right side at the front of the sight until it stops; then push it toward the rear and hold it there while sliding the sight upward out of its base. It can be taken completely off, or just moved until it exposes the screw covered by the sight slide, near the scale marker.

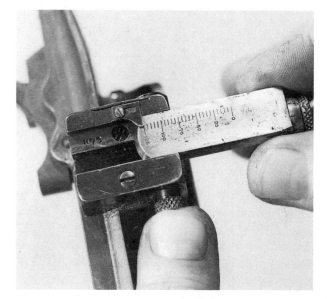

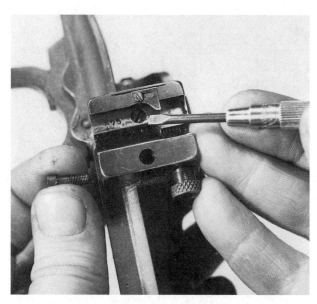

7. Remove both of the mounting screws, the short one inside the slide track, and the longer one in the forward portion of the sight, and take off the sight base toward the right. Further disassembly of the rear sight is not recommended in normal takedown.

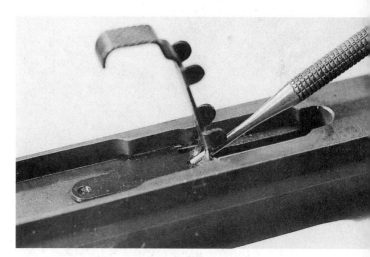

8. The magazine catch is tempered to be its own spring, and is mounted on the underside of the receiver by two forward side projections which are slid into recesses on each side. To remove it, use a small screwdriver to very slightly lift its rear tail, to clear the locking dimple from its recess, and place a drift punch against the end of the slot in the front of its base, next to the receiver. Tap the unit toward the rear until its side projections clear their slots in the receiver, and remove the magazine catch. **Caution:** *Apply pressure* **only** to the mounting base plate, and **not** to the lower extension of the catch, or it may be deformed or broken.

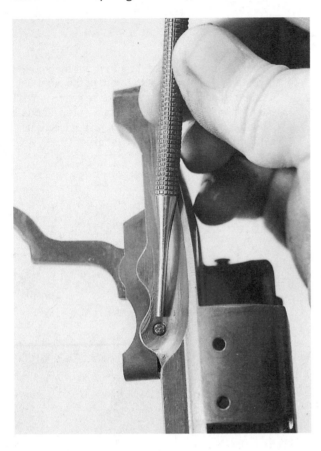

9. Push out the sear pivot pin toward the left, the side on which it has a large, nail-like head.

10. Remove the sear and the attached trigger downward, along with the coil spring mounted in the front of the sear. Drifting out the cross pin in the sear will allow separation of the trigger from the sear.

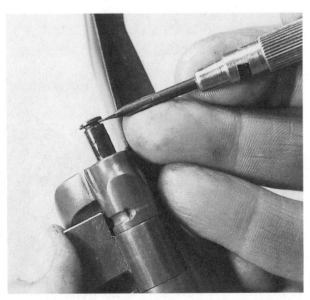

11. To remove the bolt stop, first back out the small screw in the serrated outer edge of the stop lever. After the screw is removed, withdraw the bolt stop pin toward the rear, using a fingernail or tool in the cannelure provided at its rear tip. During this operation, have the bolt stop turned up to the locked position, and exert slight downward pressure on it to restrain the plunger and spring mounted inside the stop lever. When the pin is out, the bolt stop can be taken off toward the left. Take care not to lose the small spring and plunger.

12. Grip the bolt firmly and pull back the striker knob until the safety can be turned up to vertical position, halfway between the on-safe and off-safe positions. This is more easily done before taking the bolt out of the receiver. Press the bolt sleeve lock inward, hold it in, and turn the rear section of the bolt counterclockwise (rear view), unscrewing the rear portion from the bolt body.

13. When the middle lug on the bolt body has turned sufficiently to clear the lug on the bolt head from its internal recess, the bolt head can be taken off toward the front.

14. Continue turning the rear section until its threads clear the bolt body, and withdraw the rear assembly from the body of the bolt. During this operation, take care not to disturb the safety-lever, as it is holding the lower lug of the cocking piece out of engagement with the rear of the bolt body.

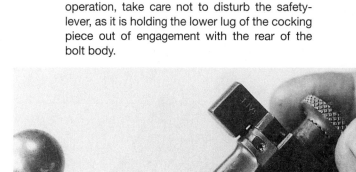

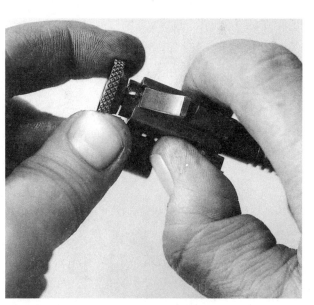

15. Grip the firing pin section of the striker in a padded vise, taking care to exert no side pressure that might break it. While holding the bolt sleeve against the tension of the striker spring, release the safety and keep the sleeve pressed down, away from the striker knob. Slowly release the tension, allowing the sleeve to move back against the knob, as shown.

16. With the front section still gripped in a padded vise, exert downward pressure on the bolt sleeve, slightly compressing the striker spring, and unscrew the cocking knob ("firing pin nut") from the rear tip of the striker shaft. **Caution:** *Keep the bolt sleeve under control, against the compressed spring. When the knob is off, slowly allow the sleeve to move off, releasing the tension of the spring.*

17. Remove the bolt sleeve and the striker spring from the rear of the striker shaft.

18. Remove the cocking piece from the rear of the bolt sleeve. The round-wire nut tension spring is mounted in the rear of the cocking piece and is easily taken out toward the rear.

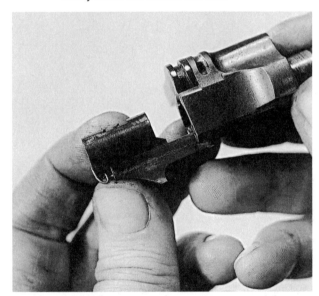

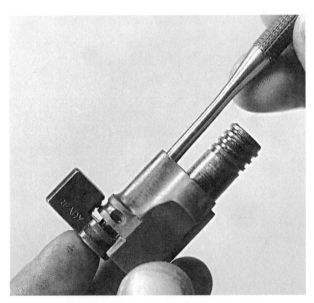

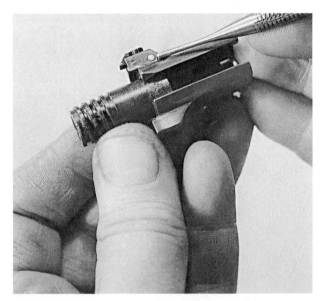

19. To remove the safety from the bolt sleeve, turn the lever up to central position and use a drift punch against the front tip of its pivot shaft, as shown, to nudge it out toward the rear. **Caution:** *As the small plunger and spring inside the safety-lever clear the rear top of the sleeve, they will be released downward. Restrain them, and take care they aren't lost.*

20. A vertical pin on the left side of the bolt sleeve retains the lock plunger and its spring. The pin is drifted out upward, and the plunger and spring are taken off toward the left.

Reassembly Tips:

21. The ejector is retained on the left side of the bolt head by a very small vertical pin, requiring a small diameter drift punch. When drifting out the pin, keep a fingertip over the hole at the front of the ejector, to restrain the coil spring housed inside it, as this will be released as the ejector is removed.

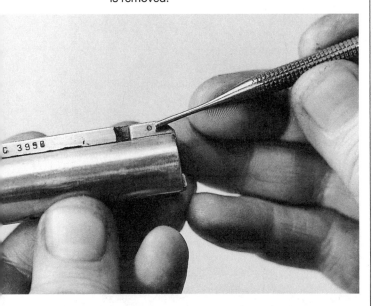

1. When replacing the extractor in the bolt head, place it in position over its recess and press it inward and toward the rear, with a fingertip centered on the arch of its back. This can usually be done without tools.

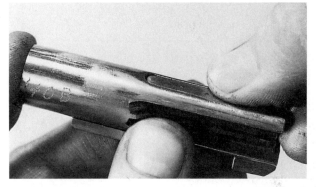

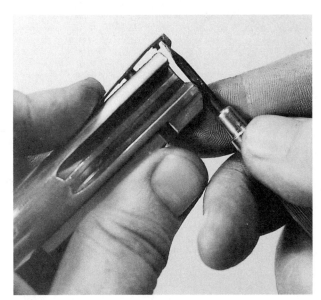

22. The extractor is its own spring. Insert a small screwdriver under its forward beak, and very carefully lift it just enough to clear its underlug from its well in the bolt head; then move it toward the front and off. Use extreme care, as replacement parts for this gun are virtually impossible to find.

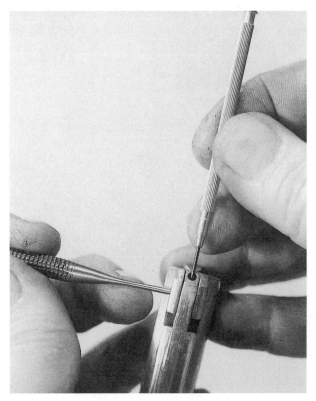

2. When replacing the ejector in the bolt head, use a very small screwdriver to depress the internal spring while the pin is driven back into place, to avoid possible damage to the spring.

3. When replacing the bolt head, remember that this must be done before the final turn of the bolt sleeve at the rear. Place the bolt head in position; then complete the turn of the bolt sleeve and allow the bolt lock to snap into its notch.

4. When the bolt is inserted into the receiver, the bolt stop must be in its open position and the bolt lug must be at the top. Once the front section is inserted, the lug is easily oriented by just turning the bolt handle.

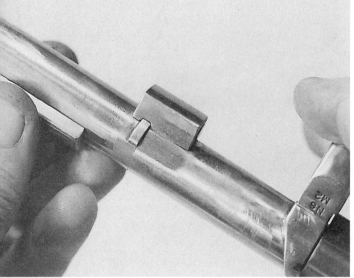

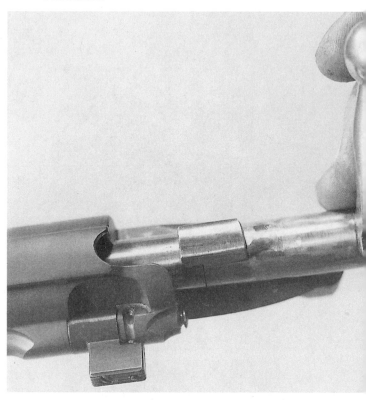

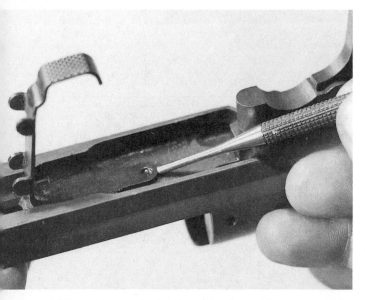

5. When replacing the magazine catch, start it into its side tracks; then use a drift against its rear tail, next to the underside of the receiver, to tap it into place. *Do not exert any pressure on the lower extension of the catch, or it may be deformed or broken.*

Walther G22

Data:	Walther G22
Origin:	Germany
Manufacturer:	Carl Walther, GmbH, Germany
Cartridge:	22 Long Rifle
Magazine capacity:	10 rounds
Overall length:	29½ inches
Barrel length:	20 inches
Weight:	6 pounds

Walther has been the source of many firearms of note. The G22 rifle is another interesting example. The bullpup-style rifle has yet to gain popularity in this country, even though the concept has existed for many decades. Fortunately, the G22 is a bullpup that seems to have found a niche and many have been sold in the U.S. Left-handed shooters like it because it has the ability to be switched to left-hand operation in a few minutes, allowing any lefty to operate it safely and comfortably. The greatest benefit is, of course, the use of a barrel length that in a more traditional rifle design would make the overall rifle length significantly longer.

Disassembly:

1. Remove the magazine. Next, loosen this bolt.

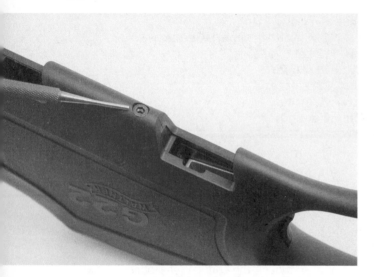

2. Drive out the transverse pin just in front of the safety.

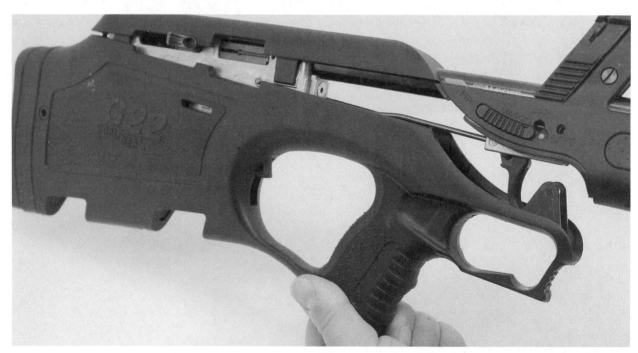

3. Lift the barrel and action assembly from the stock.

4. Removing the two stock screws will allow the rubber butt pad to be removed and the spacers to be inserted or removed from the stock.

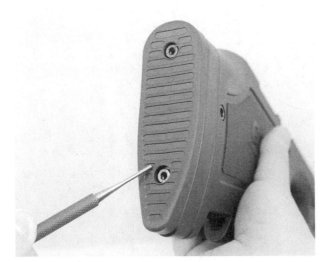

5. Pull off the cheek piece, allowing the two port covers to fall free.

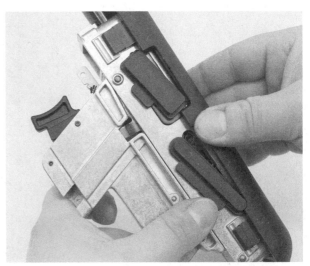

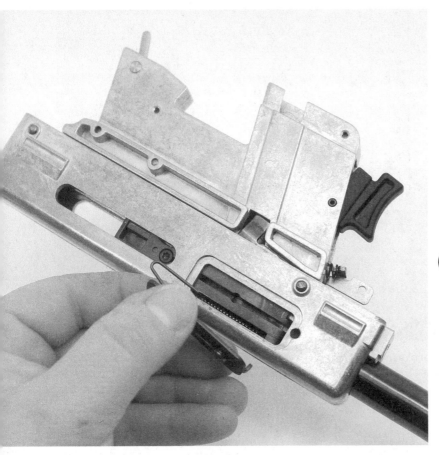

6. Remove the ejector assembly.

7. Remove the two screws just below the optic rail. The screws are not identical. The rear screw is slightly longer.

8. Pull the rear sight straight back and remove it from the gun.

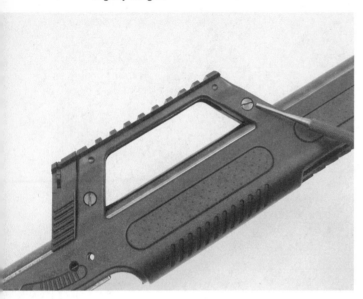

9. Remove the spacer from the front of the optic rail.

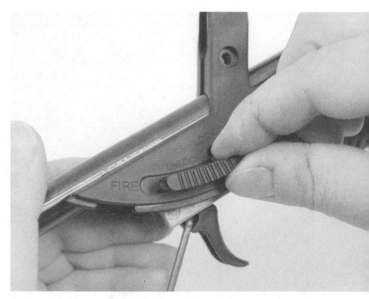

10. Gently work the safety lever panels loose from both sides. They are connected by two through-pins, which might come out when you remove the buttons.

11. Remove the set screw beneath the front sight assembly to remove the assembly straight off the front. Do not twist or rotate the front sight assembly in any way.

12. The handguard assembly can now be pulled off the barrel.

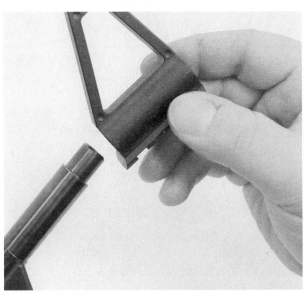

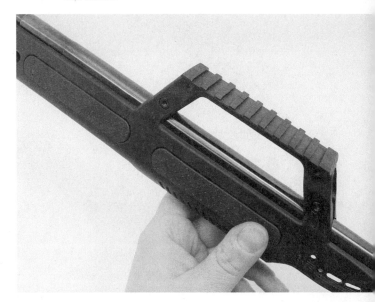

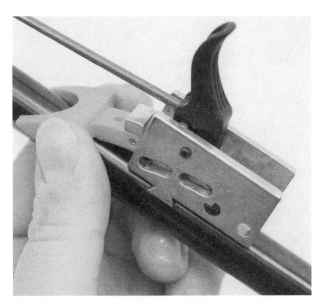

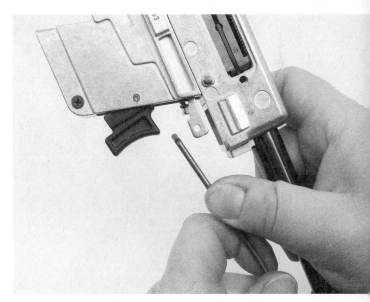

13. Gently and slowly, with the action upside down, pull out the safety indicator to the rear. A small ball detent and detent spring will fall out. Do not loose these parts.

14. Remove the trigger bar from the trigger. Unhook the trigger rod from the fire control housing.

15. Remove the trigger from the trigger housing by removing this pin.

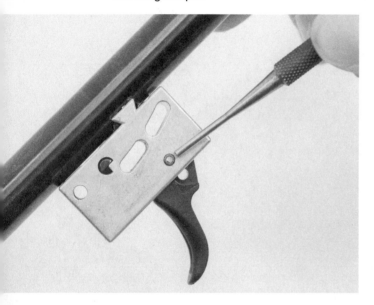

16. Pry this spring arm slightly forward to remove the trigger lock. The spring is staked in. Do not remove it unless necessary for repair.

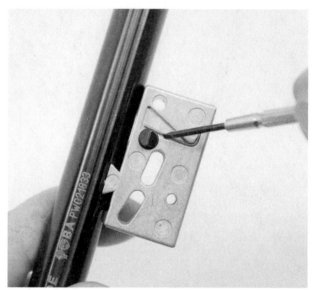

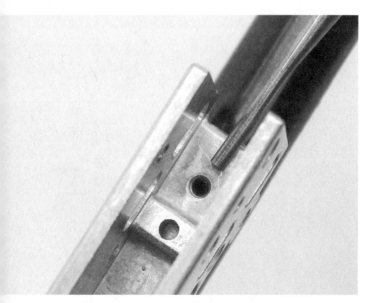

17. The trigger housing is dovetailed into the barrel. Loosening this set screw and driving the housing out to the right will remove it from the barrel.

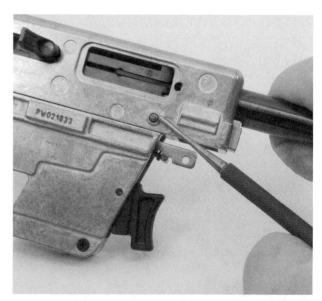

18. Drive out the front action pin, which is just below the front of the ejection port and the rear action pin, which is at the rear bottom corner of the receiver. This will free the fire control assembly with the magazine well from the receiver.

19. As you remove the fire control assembly, place a finger over the bolt stop on the left side as it becomes visible. Once free of the receiver, its spring will cause it to fall free.

20. It is necessary to remove the magazine catch to separate the two halves of the fire control assembly. Drive out this pin to remove the catch and its spring.

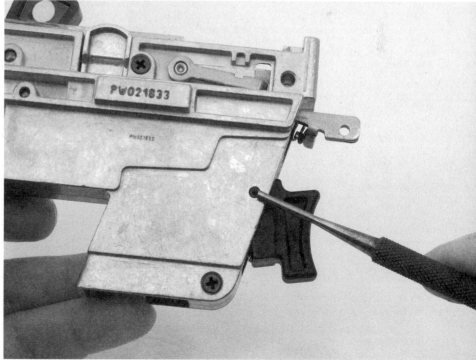

21. Carefully remove the trigger return spring as it is heavily compressed.

22. Remove the four Phillips screws from the right side while holding the two halves together.

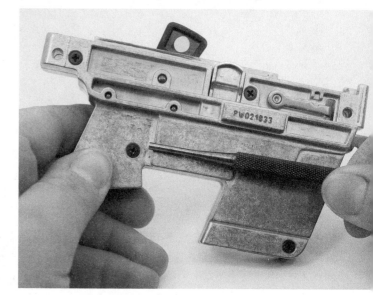

23. Place the fire control so that it is lying on its left side and slowly remove the right side from it. As seen in the photo, place a thumb over the hammer strut.

24. On the inside of the right half, use pliers to grasp the spring at the bottom of the disconnector and pull it out. Place your finger below to catch the spring as it pops out.

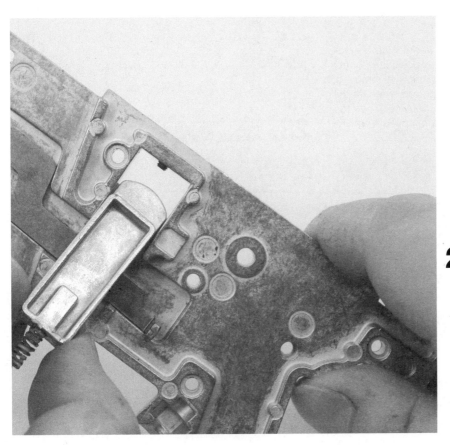

25. Pull the disconnector out and down. The disconnector holds the trigger bar into the right half. Removing the disconnector will also free the trigger bar. There is a small set screw at the top of the disconnector slot which controls the height of the disconnector. Do not remove or adjust it unless necessary.

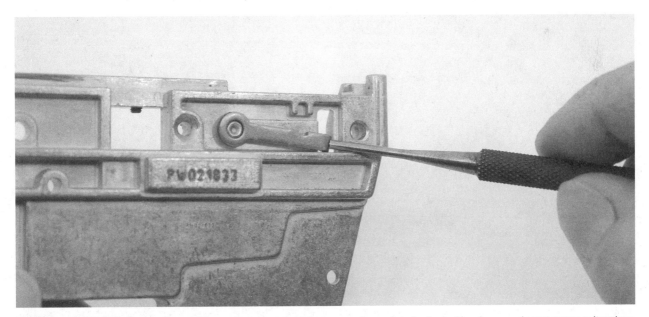

26. Remove the magazine safety spring. However, the magazine safety is riveted in place so do not remove it unless replacement is necessary.

27. The sear spring is quite powerful. Use a small screwdriver to pry it from its position. Control it as it will travel far. With the tension removed, the sear can be pulled straight up. Then lift the hammer assembly from the housing. The stop and the spring can then be removed from the hammer strut.

28. The hammer strut pin is splined and it is not necessary for removal except for repair.

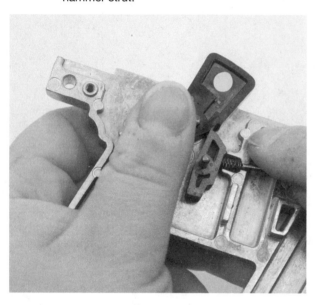

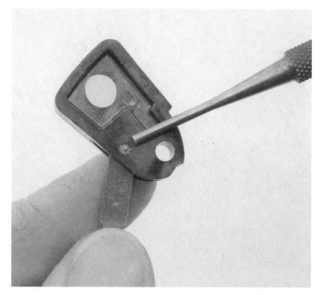

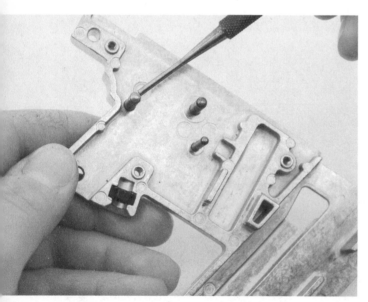

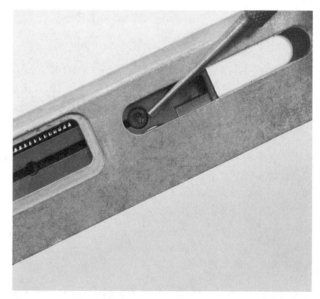

29. The rear support pin indicated in the picture can be removed. However, the sear and hammer pins are staked in. They do not need to be removed unless they need to be replaced. The small nut at the bottom can also be removed.

30. On the side of the receiver opposite of the bolt handle is a socket screw that holds the bolt handle in the bolt. Remove this screw to remove the bolt handle.

31. To remove the bolt assembly, gently tap the receiver upon your palm and the rear buffer area of the bolt assembly will slide down from its perch. Stop it from coming all of the way out into your palm as the springs will pop loose. From this point, pull out the assembly in a controlled fashion by slightly compressing it and then easing the spring tension as it is removed.

32. Driving out this pin will free the extractor and extractor spring. Please note that these parts can be installed on the left side of the bolt to allow the rifle to be set up for left handed use.

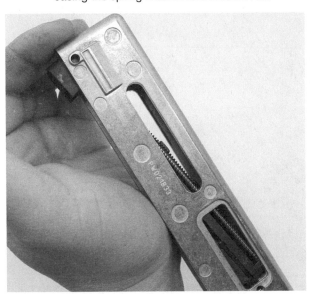

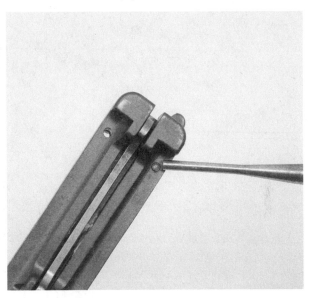

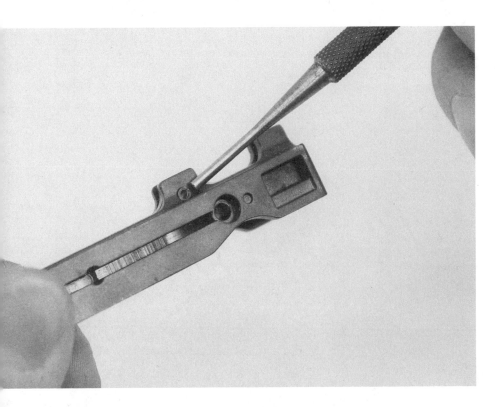

33. Driving out this pin will free the firing pin and the firing pin return spring below it.

34. The barrel can be removed from the receiver by removing this screw and its retention plate.

Reassembly Tips:

1. It will be necessary to reassemble the bolt assembly as one unit. Partially compress the springs and then insert them both into the holes on the top front of the bolt.

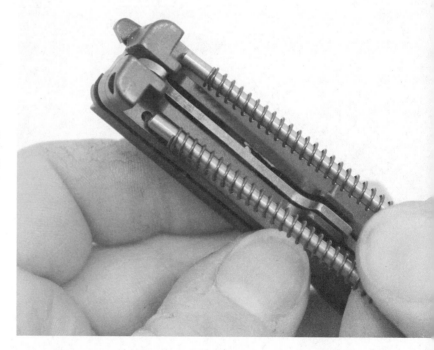

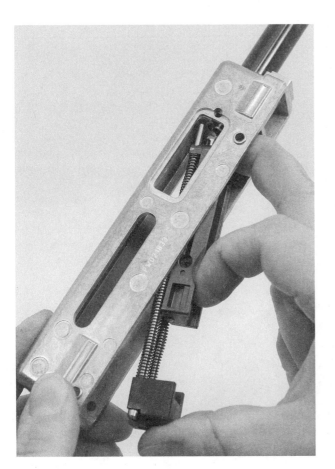

2. With the bolt assembly captured and slightly compressed, insert the front of the bolt into position first and then rotate the rear up and into the back of the receiver.

3. When placing the two fire control halves together, the hammer should be forward (uncocked). This will relieve tension from the spring allowing the spring seat to better align with its hole in the left side housing.

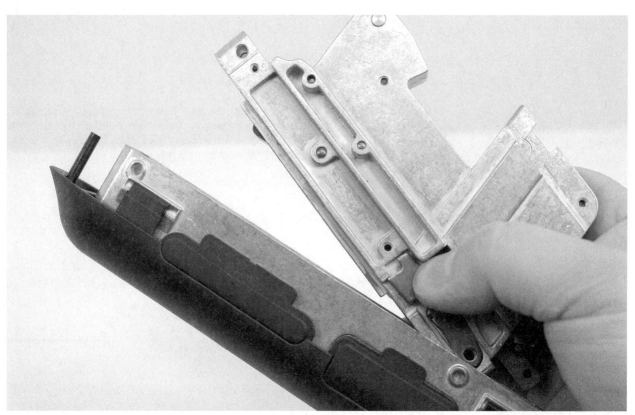

4. The hammer must be cocked in order to place the fire control back into the receiver. The bolt stop will also need to be held in place in order to place the housing in the receiver.

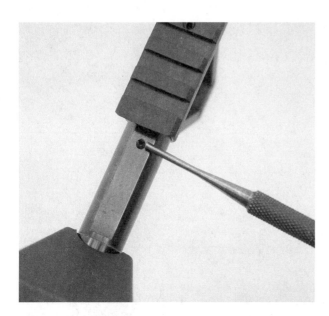

5. When reinstalling the front sight, note that there is an alignment flat in the bottom of the barrel that keeps the sight in place. The dimple in the flat is where the set screw inserts to lock the front sight on the barrel. This dimple must be aligned with the set screw hole. Do not overtighten this screw as it will easily strip out the threads in the plastic front sight.

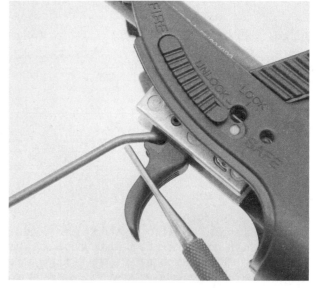

6. The curved down portion of the trigger rod goes toward the front with the straightened portion to the rear. Note that it is possible to install this rod backwards.

Weatherby Mark XXII

Similar/Identical Pattern Guns

The same basic assembly/disassembly steps for the Weatherby Mark XXII also apply to the following gun:

Weatherby Mark XXII Tube Magazine

Data:	Weatherby Mark XXII
Origin:	United States
Manufacturer:	Weatherby, Inc.
	South Gate, California
	(Made under contract in Japan)
Cartridge:	22 Long Rifle
Magazine capacity:	5 and 10 rounds in box magazines,
	15 rounds in tubular magazine model
Overall length:	42¼ inches
Barrel length:	24 inches
Weight:	6 pounds

The Mark XXII had the classic Weatherby look and, in addition to its fine fit and finish, it had several unique features. One was a selector lever that allowed the gun to be used as a single shot, with the bolt remaining open after firing until released by the lever. With the lever in its other position, the gun would function as a normal semi-auto. There were two versions of the Mark XXII, the only difference being in the magazine systems—one had a tubular magazine, and the other, shown here, had a detachable box type. The Mark XXII was made from 1963 to 1989.

Disassembly:

1. Remove the main stock mounting screw, located on the underside, forward of the magazine well. Remove the screw at the rear of the trigger guard on the underside and lift the action straight up out of the stock. It should be noted that it is possible to take off the barrel and receiver unit alone by pushing out the large takedown pin at the rear of the receiver toward the left, and moving the barrel/receiver unit forward and upward, but this will leave the trigger group subframe in the stock. After the two screws are taken out, the trigger guard unit can be taken off downward.

2. Push out the cross pin at the rear of the receiver toward the left and remove it.

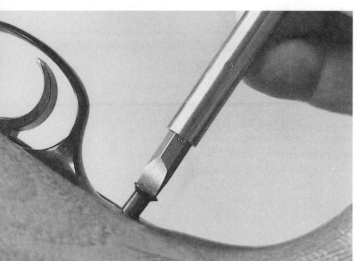
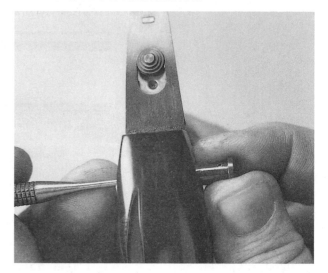

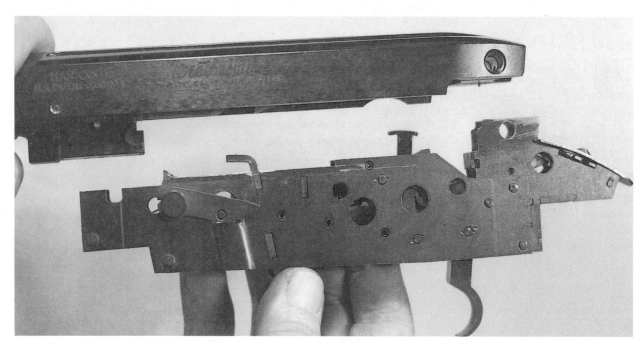

3. Move the trigger group about ⅛-inch toward the rear and remove it downward.

4. Before any disassembly of the trigger group, hold the hammer against its spring tension, pull the trigger and ease the hammer down to the fired position. The selector lever on the right side of the group is retained by a large C-shaped spring clip. Carefully slide the clip off downward and remove the selector lever toward the right.

5. The pivot and mounting stud for the single shot bolt catch is retained inside the group by a C-clip. Use a small screwdriver to slide the clip off upward, and take care that it isn't lost. There is an access hole on the left side through which the clip can be reached. The bolt-catch piece is then removed toward the right, along with its pivot-post, unhooking its spring at the front. The torsion spring is held in the group by a roll cross pin.

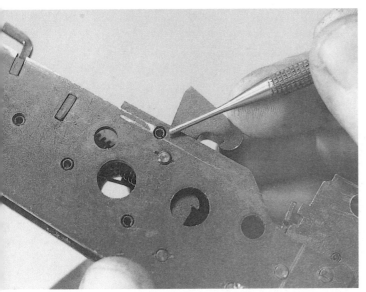

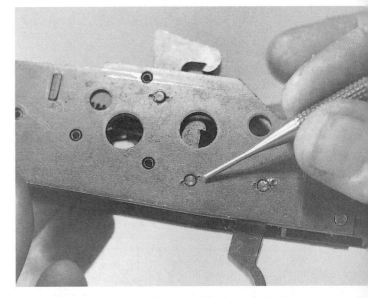

6. Set the hammer on its first step, and drift out the roll cross pin just forward of the hammer at the top edge of the group. Restrain the hammer, pull the trigger to release it and let it go forward beyond its normal down position, relieving the tension of the hammer spring. Drifting out the solid pin just below the roll pin, the hammer pivot, will allow removal of the hammer and its spring and guide upward.

7. The sear is retained by a solid pin near the lower edge of the receiver. Drifting out this pin will allow removal of the sear and its spring downward.

8. The trigger is retained by a cross pin just to the rear of the sear pin. The trigger and its attached sear bar and spring are removed downward. The coil trigger spring will be released as it clears its plate at the rear of the trigger, so restrain it and take care that it isn't lost.

9. Drifting out a small roll pin at the rear of the trigger group will allow removal of the safety bar toward the front. **Caution:** *The safety bar plunger and spring will be released upward as the bar is moved out, so restrain them against loss.* The rear portion of the safety, the button and indicator plate, are not easily removable, as this would require taking off the staked tang plate. This is not advisable in normal takedown.

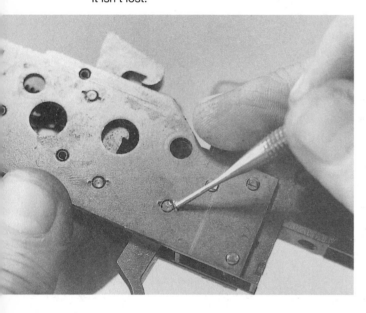

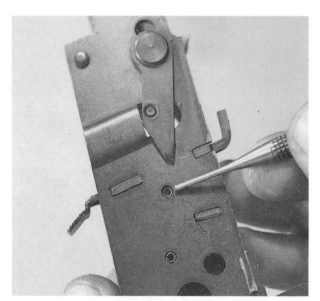

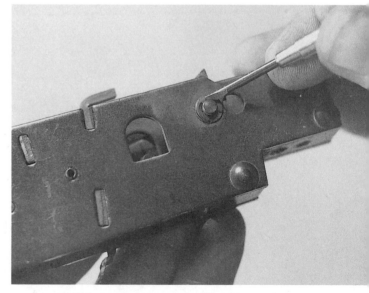

10. The magazine catch and its spring are retained by a roll cross pin. Note the relationship of the spring and the catch before removal, to aid reassembly. The catch and spring are removed downward. The ejector is staked in place between the riveted sideplates of the trigger group and is not removable in normal takedown.

11. The bolt hold open device is retained by a C-clip on the right side of the group, the clip gripping the end of its cross-shaft. Note that there is also a small washer under the C-clip, and take care that it isn't lost. The hold open is removed toward the left.

12. Firmly grasp the bolt handle and pull it straight out toward the right.

13. Invert the gun and move the bolt slowly toward the rear. Lift the front of the bolt enough to clear the receiver, and ease the bolt out forward, slowly relieving the tension of the bolt spring. **Caution:** *Control the compressed spring.* Remove the spring and its guide from the rear of the bolt.

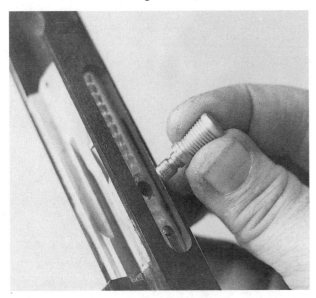

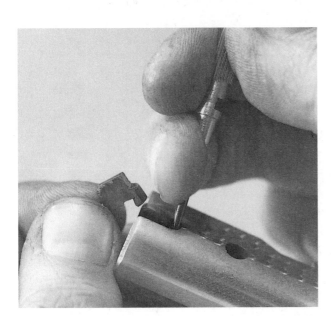

14. Use a small screwdriver to depress the extractor spring plunger, and lift the extractor out of its recess at the right front of the bolt. **Caution:** *Do not allow the screwdriver to slip, as the small plunger and spring will travel quite a distance if suddenly released.*

15. The firing pin is retained by a vertical roll pin located at the left rear of the bolt, and the firing pin and its return spring are removed toward the rear.

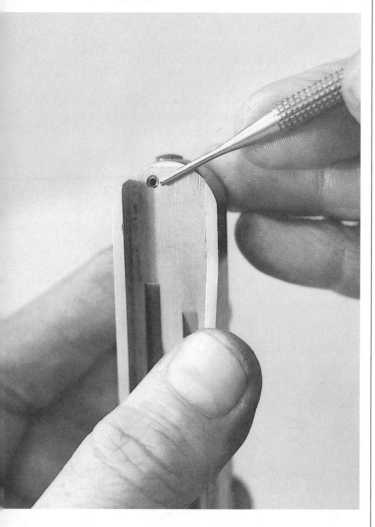

1. When replacing the single shot bolt-catch on the right side of the trigger group, remember to hook the torsion spring under its forward end. The spring may be installed first, and then its end moved out, downward and up to hook it under the part.

When replacing the large takedown cross pin at the rear of the receiver, be sure it is inserted from left to right. Otherwise, the stock will block its removal when the rifle is fully reassembled.

Winchester Low Wall

Similar/Identical Pattern Guns

The same basic assembly/disassembly steps for the Winchester Low Wall also apply to the following gun:

Winchester High Wall

Data:	Winchester Low Wall
Origin:	United States
Manufacturer:	Winchester Repeating Arms Co.
	New Haven, Connecticut
Cartridge:	22 Long Rifle
Overall length:	42 inches
Barrel length:	26 inches
Weight:	8 pounds

Designed by John Moses Browning, the Winchester single shot rifle was made from 1885 to 1920. It was chambered for a long list of cartridges, both rimfire and centerfire. The heavier rounds were in the version popularly called the "High Wall," with the receiver fully enclosing the breechblock. A later takedown version of the gun had a torsion-type spring on the hammer axis, but was otherwise mechanically the same.

Disassembly:

1. Remove the rear wood screw from the lower tang. Remove the stock retaining screw from the upper tang. Remove the buttstock toward the rear.

2. Remove the forend retaining screw. Remove the forend downward and toward the front.

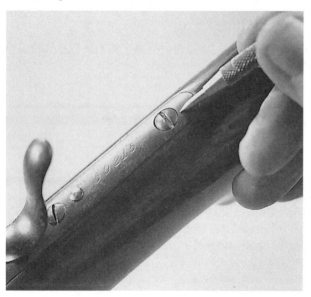

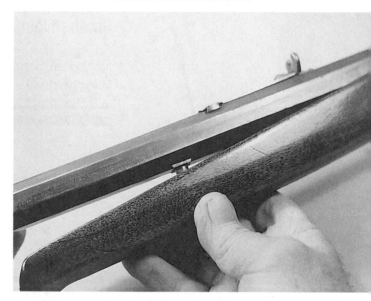

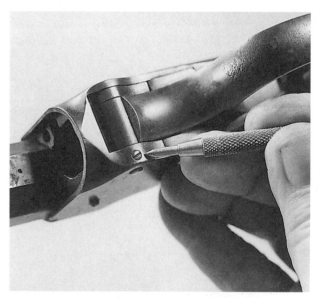

3. Remove the hammer spring retaining screw. **Note:** In the gun shown, the spring and screw are non-original replacements. The spring is normally longer and heavier and is attached to a dovetail-mounted base. Remove the hammer spring toward the front.

4. Remove the lever pivot lock screw.

5. Push or drift out the lever pivot toward the right.

6. Remove the breechblock and lever assembly downward. The ejector will fall free as the assembly clears the receiver.

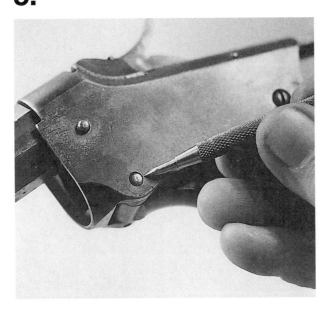

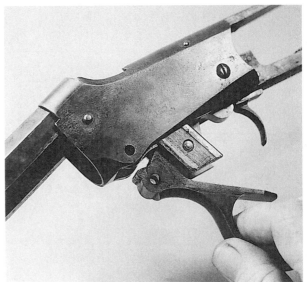

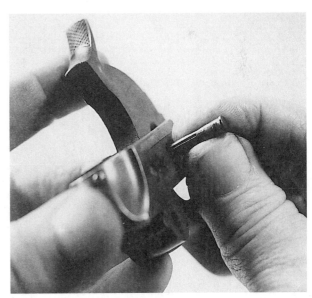

7. The hammer pivot is locked by a tempered split end that resembles a screw slot. This must be driven out toward the side that has the solid end of the pin. A regular drift may start it out, but if not, it may be necessary to make a V-tip tool to compress the ends of the pin.

8. After the tip of the pin is compressed and freed, drift out the hammer pivot. This will allow the hammer to be removed from the breechblock.

9. Push out the lever pin and separate the lever from the breechblock.

10. Push out the lever link pin and remove the link.

11. Remove the firing pin retaining screw. **Note:** In the High Wall version, the firing pin is retained in the breechblock by a cross pin.

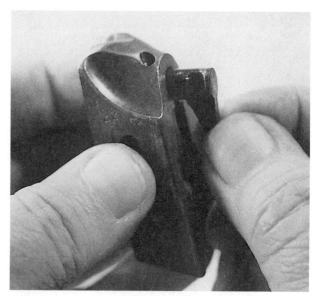

12. Remove the firing pin toward the rear.

13. Remove the screws on each side of the receiver that retain the lower tang unit. **Note:** Keep these in order, right and left, and they will fit better on reassembly.

14. Remove the lower tang assembly toward the rear. This unit will likely be tight and may require a nudge with a nylon drift. If so, be sure the drift is against a shoulder of the tang, and not the trigger, or the trigger pivot could be bent.

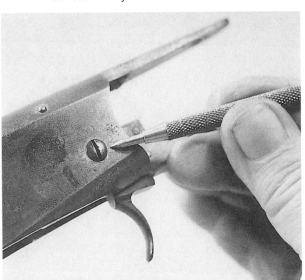

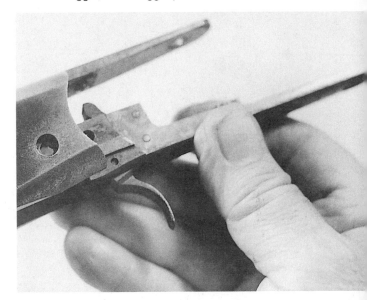

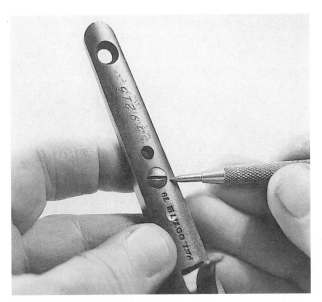

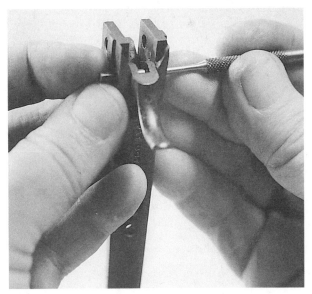

15. Remove the sear knock-off spring retaining screw and take out the spring.

16. Push out the trigger pin and remove the trigger downward.

17. Push out the sear knock-off pin and remove the sear knock-off. When the sear knock-off is taken out, take care that the trigger contact pin is not lost, as it is often loose. The lower pin in the tang unit is the trigger stop pin, and it is not removed in normal takedown.

18. In most guns the sear spring will be retained by a screw in this location. The gun shown has a filler screw at this point.

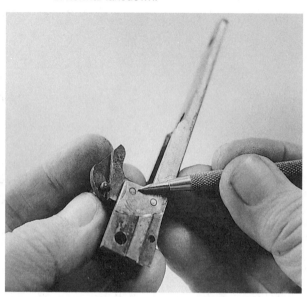

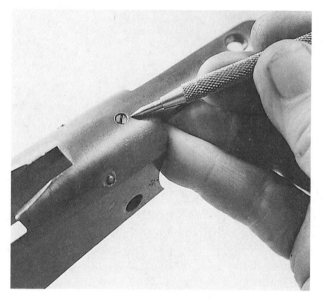

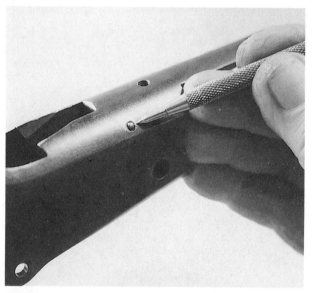

19. In our subject gun, the sear spring screw is located inside the upper tang. Remove the screw and take out the sear spring.

20. Drift out the sear cross pin. Take care not to mar the curved top of the receiver.

21. Removal of the pin will free the sear to be taken out downward.

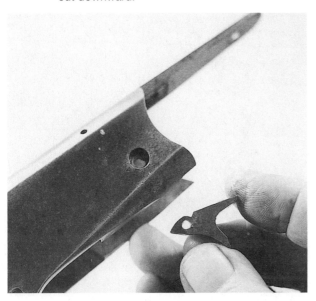

22. The barrel is threaded into the receiver and is also secured by a large cross pin. In normal takedown, this is left in place.

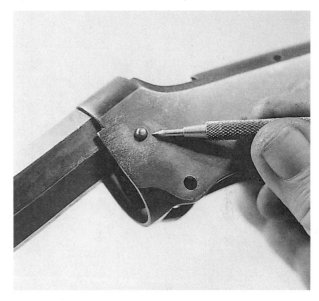

Reassembly Tips:

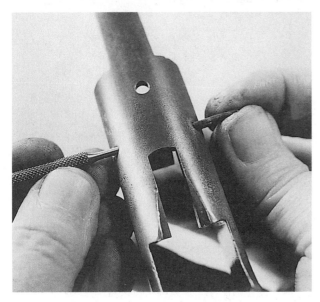

1. When replacing the sear, be sure it is properly oriented with the crescent-shaped surface toward the front (see step 21 in takedown). Insert a drift to hold the sear in position while the cross pin is started.

2. When replacing the sear knock-off spring, be sure its front tip goes under both of the cross pins, as shown.

3. As the tang is pushed into place, use a finger inside the receiver to depress the sear to clear the sear knock-off. Be sure the tang is positioned properly for entry of the two screws. If the first screw does not go in and engage easily, adjust the tang position.

4. If the link has been removed from the lever, be sure it is installed with its lobe toward the rear, as shown.

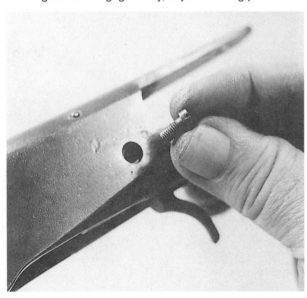

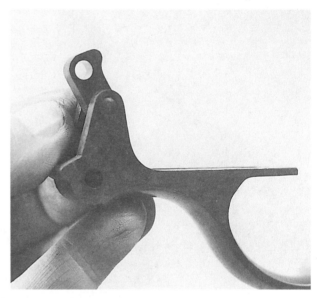

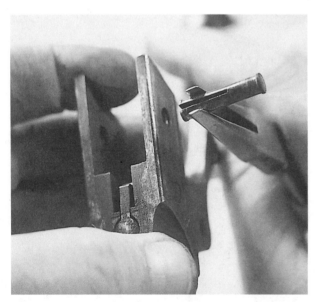

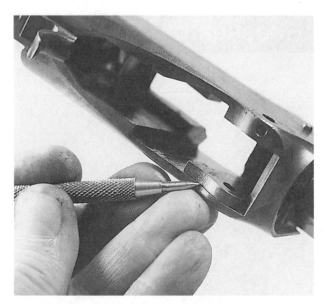

5. To restart the split-end hammer pivot, squeeze the end with pliers as it is inserted.

6. Before the breechblock and lever assembly is reinserted, place the ejector in position in the receiver, as shown.

Winchester Wildcat

Similar/Identical Pattern Guns
The same basic assembly/disassembly steps for the Winchester Wildcat also apply to the following gun:
Winchester Wildcat Target/Varmint

Data:	Winchester Wildcat
Origin:	Russia
Manufacturer:	Tulsky Oruzheiny Zavod
Cartridge:	22 Long Rifle
Magazine capacity:	10 rounds
Overall length:	38⅜ inches
Barrel length:	21 inches
Weight:	4½ pounds

In 2007, Winchester Repeating Arms began importing a bolt-action rifle into the United States based upon a rifle already available in Europe. The European rifle, the TOZ-78, bears a clear parentage, in fact, both rifles were manufactured in the Tula Arms factory in Russia. A surprisingly accurate rifle, it was obtainable with a hunter/sporter-type barrel taper or as a dedicated large-contour heavy barreled target rifle. The stock was made of beach and was stained to a walnut color.

Both models were equipped with a crisp two-stage trigger that was easily match quality. Furthermore, the target model had a user-adjustable trigger, a virtually unheard of feature for a rimfire rifle. Street prices were comparable to any similar domestically manufactured rifles and they proved popular as a result. But alas, it was not popular enough, and the rifle was plagued with an insufficient supply of spare parts. Importation was discontinued in 2009.

Disassembly:

1. Remove the magazine. Open and pull the bolt back. The trigger retains the bolt in the receiver. With the safety on "fire" and the bolt open, hold the trigger back and pull the bolt out of the back of the receiver.

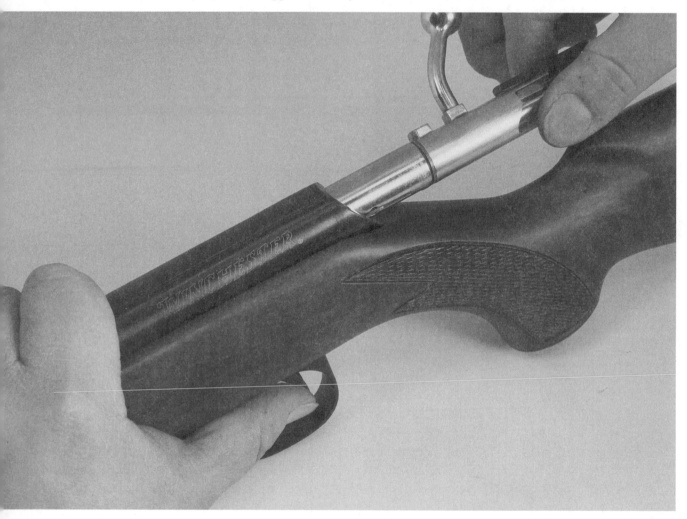

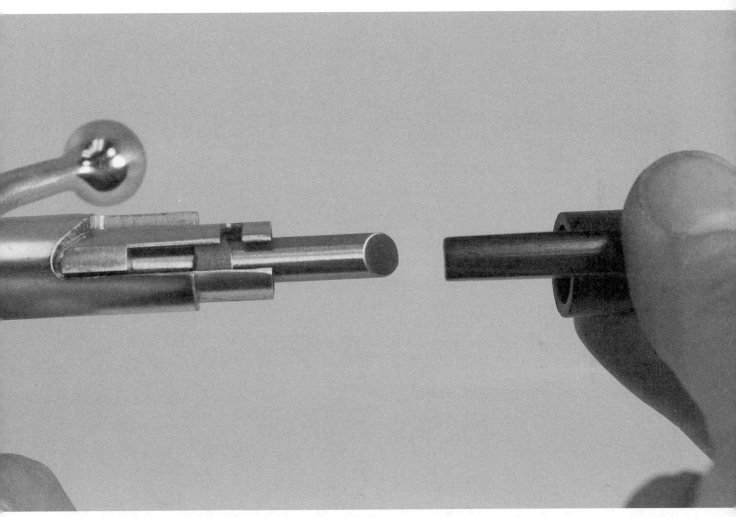

2. The bolt end cap can be removed by twisting it counterclockwise, as if it were being unscrewed. This unlatches the bolt end cap from the bolt and it can be slipped off the rear of the bolt. Note the latch's slot in the back of the bolt body.

3. Pull the firing pin out of the rear of the bolt.

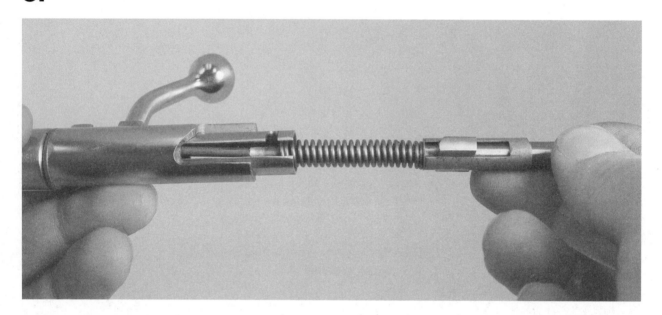

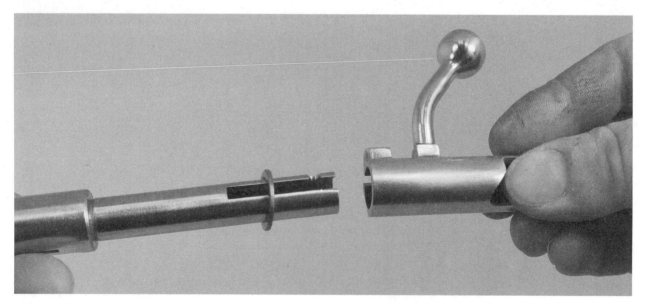

4. Pull the bolt handle sleeve and the thrust washer off the rear of the bolt.

5. Driving out the two extractor retaining pins will free the extractors and the extractor springs. Control them as they are compressed. Note: the extractors are not identical.

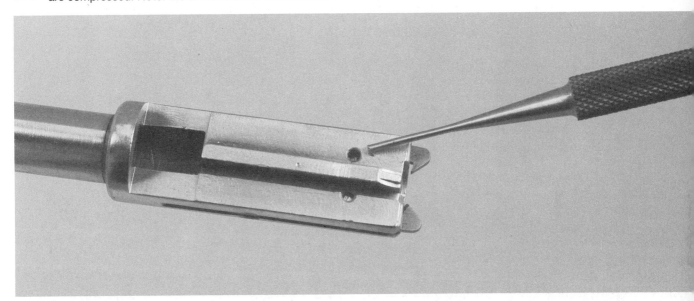

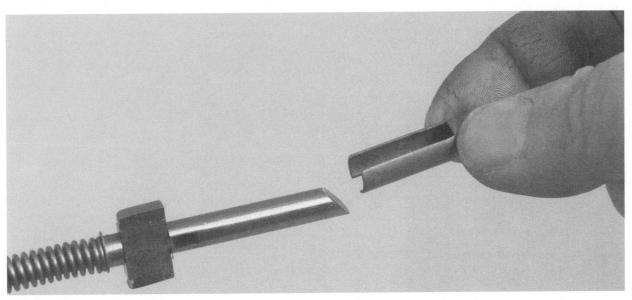

6. To disassemble the firing pin assembly, pull the cocking element retainer from the rear of the firing pin. The rectangular cocking element will likely fall out.

7. The firing pin spring and washer are retained by this pin. Compressing the firing pin spring and pushing this pin out will free the firing pin spring and washer.

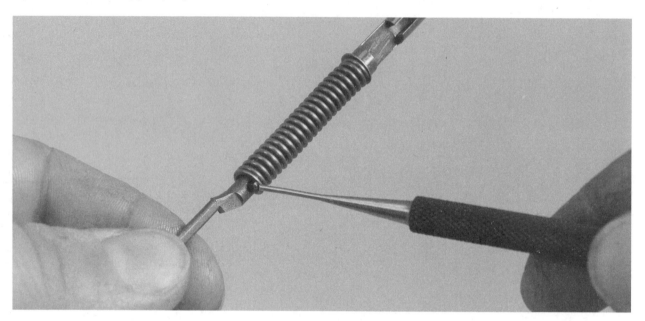

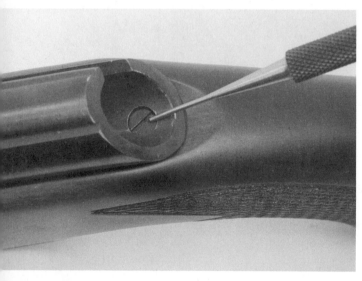

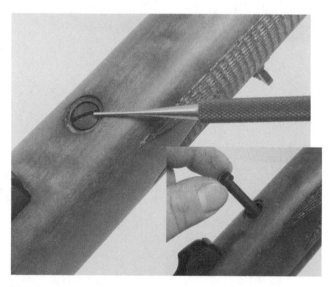

8. To remove the action from the stock, unscrew the rear stock screw.

9. Unscrew the front stock screw until the action can be lifted from the stock.

10. Use a small pliers to remove the safety spring on the left side of the trigger housing.

11. Remove the front and rear trigger housing screws and the screw retainer plates. The trigger housing will now be freed from the receiver.

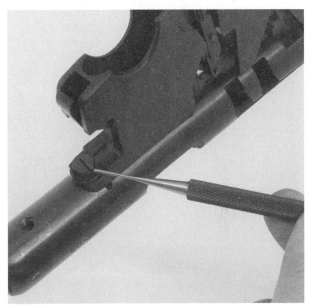

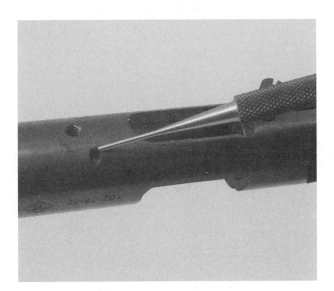

12. The barrel can be removed for replacement by driving out the barrel retainer pin.

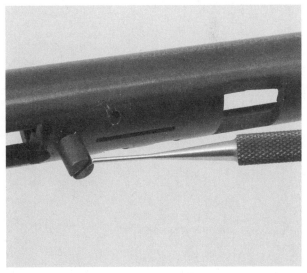

13. Unscrewing the bolt rail retaining screw will free the bolt guide ways from the front bottom of the receiver.

14. The front and rear sights are dovetailed and should be driven out to the left side if necessary for replacement or adjustment.

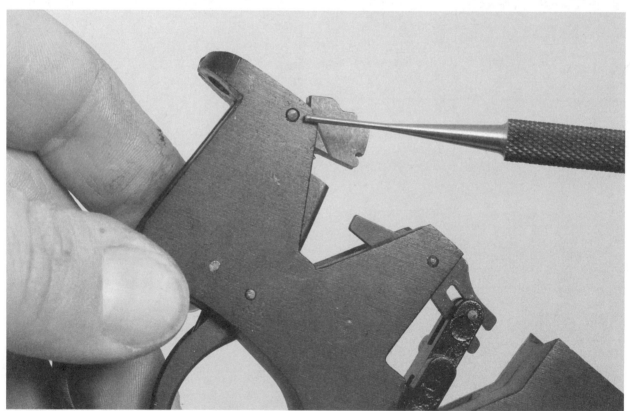

15. Drive out the sear pivot pin to remove the sear and sear spring.

16. Drive out the safety arm pivot pin to remove the safety arm.

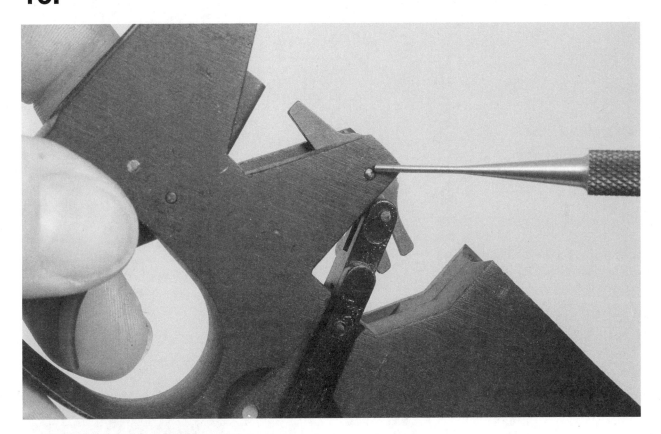

17. Drive out the safety lever pivot pin to remove the safety lever. The shorter pin at the top of the safety lever doesn't need to be removed as it functions only as a guide pin for the safety arm.

18. Drive out the trigger return spring pin to remove the trigger return springs and thus release the spring tension from the trigger.

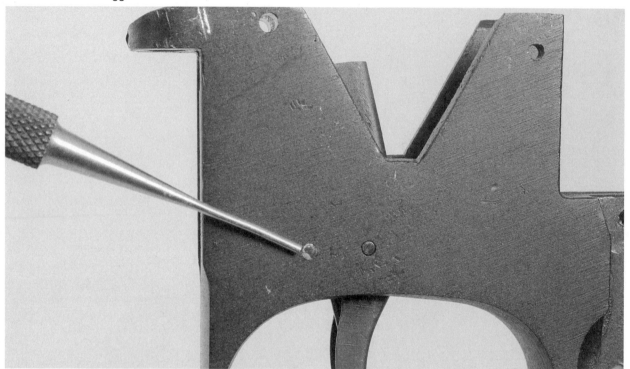

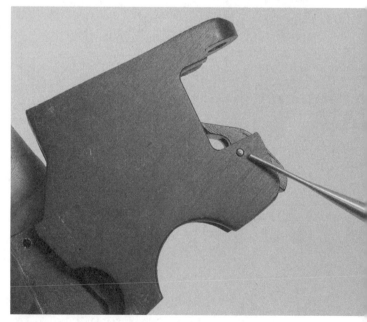

19. Drive out the trigger pivot pin to remove the trigger. The trigger is composed of an inner and outer piece and two bushings and removing this pin will also separate these four pieces.

20. Drive out the magazine catch pivot pin to remove the magazine catch and spring.

Reassembly Tips:

1. The extractors are different. The sharper, more acute hook is the one on the right and the duller extractor goes on the left.

2. When reinstalling the cocking element, the notch should be oriented to the bottom and to the front. This is the sear notch. There is a little tab on the rear of the cocking element that fits into a notch on the left side of the firing pin.

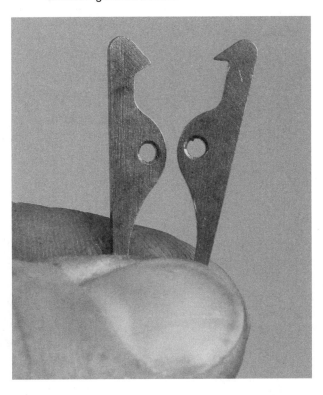

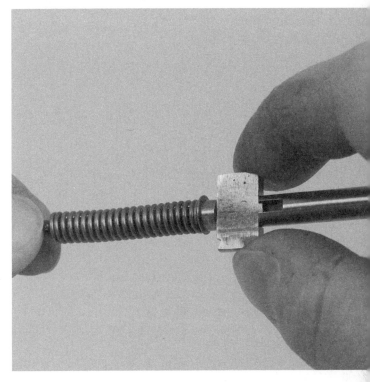

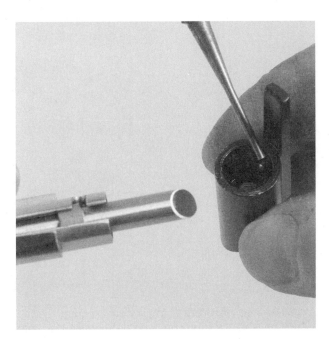

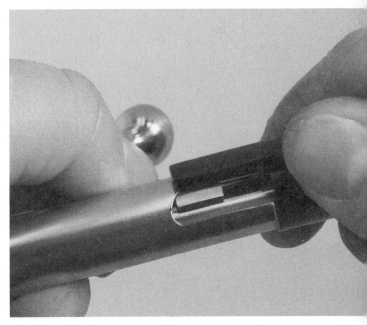

3. Note the small pin on the inside surface of the bolt end cap. This pin will track into the slot on the rear of the bolt.

4. Place the bolt end cap onto the rear of the bolt and align its pin in the cut running the length of the rear part of the bolt, push slightly to compress the firing pin spring and then rotate the bolt end cap clockwise to run the pin into the slot on the bolt.

5. Continue turning clockwise to cock the bolt before returning it to the receiver.

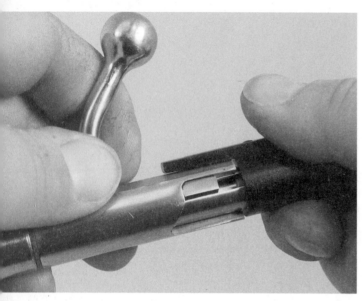

6. The slot on the bottom of the receiver is for the safety arm. The safety arm must fit into this slot before the rest of the trigger housing can be mounted.

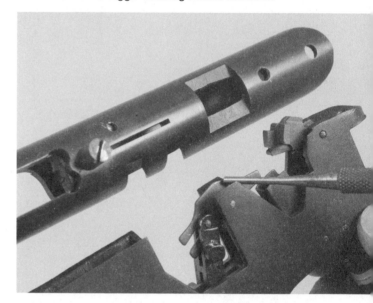

7. When reinstalling the trigger housing to the receiver, use a string, twisty tie or other means to hold the trigger in the pulled position, giving the sear clearance to lower. This will keep the sear from being held high in the housing, which prevents proper reassembly.

8. Be sure the safety spring is installed correctly with the straighter arm up and the more curved arm down. Place the curved lower arm into the safety lever. Then bend the long arm into the divot in the receiver.

Winchester Model 61

Similar/Identical Pattern Guns

The same basic assembly/disassembly steps for the Winchester Model 61 also apply to the following gun:

Winchester Model 61 Magnum

Data:	Winchester Model 61
Origin:	United States
Manufacturer:	Winchester Repeating Arms
	New Haven, Connecticut
Cartridge:	22 Short, Long, or Long Rifle
Magazine capacity:	20 Short, 16 Long, 14 Long Rifle
Overall length:	41 inches
Barrel length:	24 inches
Weight:	5½ pounds

A sleek little slide-action "hammerless" gun, the Model 61 had a virtually infallible feed system, with the cartridge rim firmly guided up a T-slot in the bolt face from the moment of leaving the magazine. This system was also used in the Model 9422 lever-action rifle. Made from 1932 to 1963, the Model 61 was also offered in 22 WRF chambering, and for a short time, just before it was discontinued, in 22 WMR. Internal mechanisms are the same, and the instructions will apply to any of these.

Disassembly:

1. Remove the inner magazine tube and cycle the action to cock the internal hammer. Use a coin or a specially shaped screwdriver to back out the takedown screw, located at the rear of the receiver on the left side.

2. When the takedown screw has moved a short distance to the left, clearing its seat in the receiver wall, separate the front and rear sections of the gun, moving the rear section toward the rear and downward.

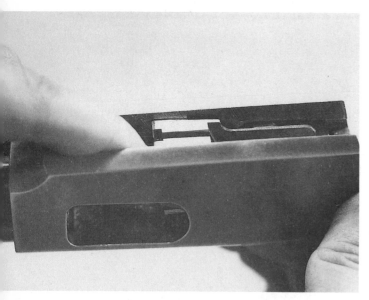

3. With the front section of the gun inverted, move the breechblock (bolt) all the way to the rear and depress the retaining spring, located in a slot inside the right wall of the receiver. Move the bolt forward and upward, disengaging its side lug from the action slide bar; then move the bolt toward the rear.

4. Remove the bolt from the rear of the receiver.

5. To begin disassembly of the bolt, drift out the vertical pin in the left lower front that retains the feed extractor and its transverse coil spring. The pin should be driven out downward using a very small diameter drift punch to start it. Its upper end is within a recess on the bolt, so it can't be drifted straight out. After starting, it usually comes out easily.

6. The ejector and its spring are retained on the left side of the bolt by a vertical pin which is driven out upward, its lower end being within the same recess as the one described in step 5. The ejector and its spring are moved out forward. Note that the ejector must be removed before the firing pin can be taken out.

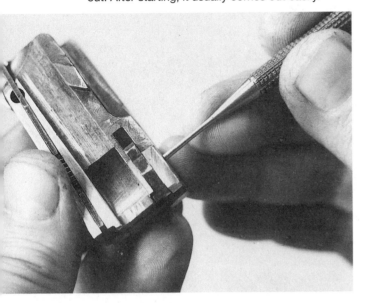

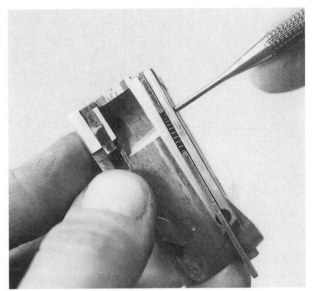

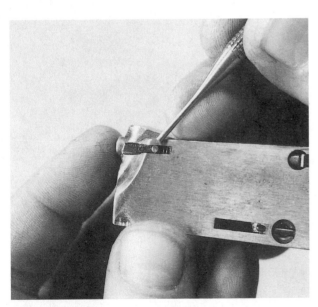

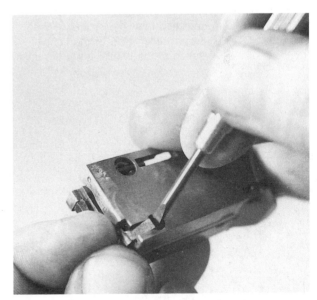

7. The firing pin is retained by a cross pin at the upper rear of the bolt, and the pin is also the compressor for the firing pin return spring on the right side. The pin is fixed into the body of the firing pin itself, rather than into the bolt. After the ejector is removed, the firing pin cross pin is driven out toward the left, and the firing pin and its spring are removed toward the rear.

8. To remove the extractor, use a small screwdriver to depress and hold the extractor spring plunger, and lift the extractor out of its recess toward the right. **Caution:** *Take care that the tool holding the plunger doesn't slip, and ease out the plunger and its spring.*

9. The carrier plunger and its spring are retained on the right side of the bolt by a lengthwise pin which is drifted out toward the front. **Caution:** *As the pin clears the coil spring housed within the plunger, the spring will be released, so restrain it and ease it out.* The plunger is easily moved out of its recess toward the right.

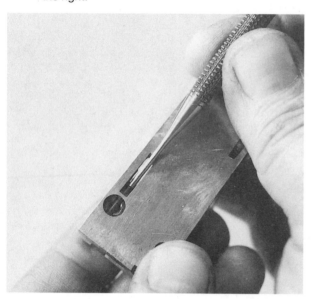

10. Drift out the cross pin in the rear magazine tube hanger loop and remove the outer magazine tube toward the front.

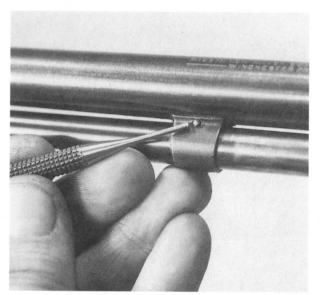

11. With the magazine tube removed, the action slide bar and its handle are easily tilted out toward the side and detached from the receiver. Removal of the screws on each side of the handle will allow separation of the handle from the action slide piece.

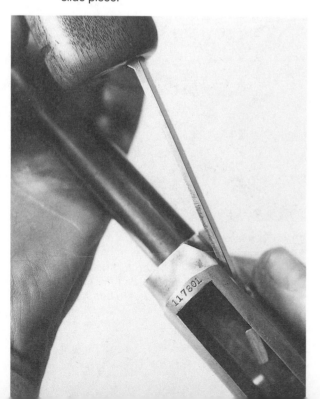

12. Push the cartridge stop housing out of the receiver toward the front.

13. The cartridge stop is retained in the housing by a vertical pin, but this should not be removed in normal disassembly. If it is absolutely necessary for repair, take care when drifting out the pin that the side block of the housing is well supported, or it can be deformed.

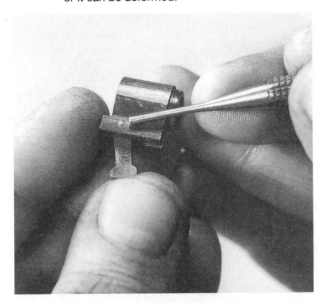

14. Remove the buttplate and use a B-Square stock tool or a long screwdriver to take out the stock mounting bolt. Take off the stock toward the rear.

15. If removal of the takedown cross-screw becomes necessary, use a very slim drift punch to drive out the small cross pin that transverses its shaft on the right side, just at the edge of the threaded section.

16. With the hammer in the cocked position, insert a small pin or drift punch tip through the transverse hole in the rear tip of the hammer spring guide. Restrain the hammer, pull the trigger and ease the hammer forward until the pin or drift rests against the rear of the frame, trapping the spring.

17. Depress the action slide lock to clear the left end of the hammer pivot and drift out the hammer pivot pin. This pin is also the pivot for the carrier. Note the relationship of these parts before removal.

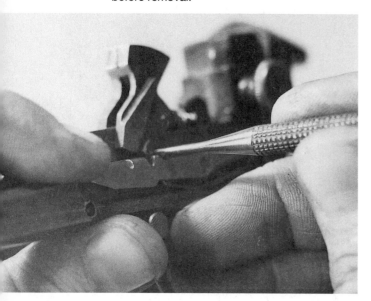

18. Restrain the hammer against the tension of its spring and carefully remove the pin or drift from the hole in the rear tip of the spring guide. Ease the hammer off forward and upward, along with its guide and spring. The spring is easily removable from the guide, but the cross pin that attaches the guide to the back of the hammer is usually riveted in place, and in normal takedown it is best left on the hammer.

19. Remove the carrier upward and toward the rear, disengaging the tip of its frame-mounted torsion spring from the slot and cross pin in the lower lobe of the carrier. Do not lift the carrier straight up or move it forward during removal, or the spring will be deformed. The spring is retained in the frame by a cross pin, located just forward of the guard. Note its position inside the frame before removal.

20. Drift out the trigger cross pin, move the trigger toward the rear to clear the inner projection of the slide latch, and remove the trigger upward.

21. Removal of the trigger pin will also free the hammer catch/slide latch lever, and it can be tipped down at the front, moved toward the rear, and taken out the rear opening of the frame. The clearances here are close, and some maneuvering of the part will be required.

22. The slide lock can now be moved off its post toward the left, then moved out toward the front. Take care not to lose the round-wire spring mounted in a vertical hole in its underside.

23. With the safety in off-safe position, insert a very small drift into the hole in its top, inside the frame, and tip the drift punch over toward the front of the unit, turning the safety to disengage its positioning plunger from the detent cuts on the underside of the safety. The safety can now be tapped out toward the left side. **Caution:** *As the safety clears the plunger and spring mounted below it, they will be released.* Restrain them, and ease them out.

Reassembly Tips:

1. When replacing the trigger, slide latch lever/hammer catch, and slide latch system, insert the latch lever first, then the trigger and its spring, and push the trigger pin only halfway across the frame. With the latch lever/hammer catch still loose, move the slide latch in toward the rear, being sure the rear tip of its spring goes *beneath* the side stud on the latch lever, and the rear tip of the latch *above* the stud. When the latch is back on its stud, the lever can be moved into alignment, and the trigger cross pin driven into place.

2. When installing the carrier, grip the rear arm of the carrier spring with sharp-nosed pliers, and hold it in raised position while fitting it into the slot in the lower lobe of the carrier, on top of the cross pin. The carrier is then moved forward and downward until its pivot hole is aligned with the cross pin hole in the frame, and the tension of the spring will hold it in place until insertion of the hammer.

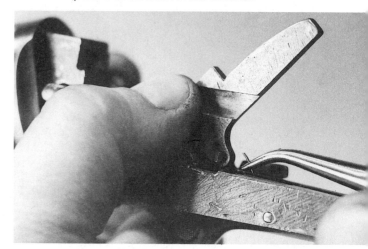

3. Place the hammer in general alignment with the cross pin hole, and insert a drift punch of smaller diameter than the pin, just to hold the hammer in place while aligning the rear tip of the guide and the spring with the hole at the rear of the frame in the vertical spring baseplate. When the tip of the guide rod can be inserted through the hole in the plate, put a pin or drift tip through the transverse hole in the guide, just as in takedown, to trap the spring while the hammer pivot pin is driven through the hammer and carrier.

4. When replacing the carrier plunger, note that the rounded portion of its inner tip must be oriented toward the bottom of the bolt, as shown.

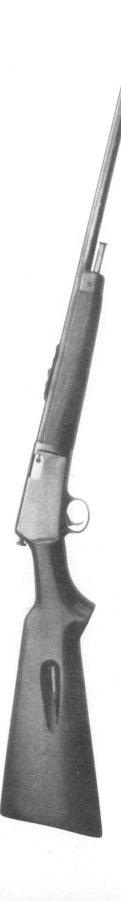

Winchester Model 63

Similar/Identical Pattern Guns

The same basic assembly/disassembly steps for the Winchester Model 63 also apply to the following gun:

Winchester Model 1903

Data:	Winchester Model 63
Origin:	United States
Manufacturer:	Winchester Repeating Arms Co.
	New Haven, Connecticut
Cartridge:	22 Long Rifle
Magazine capacity:	10 rounds
Overall length:	39½ inches
Barrel length:	20 and 23 inches
Weight:	5½ pounds

The original gun of this design, the Model 1903, was chambered for a special cartridge, the 22 Winchester Auto. It was made in this form from 1903 to 1932. The Model 63, in 22 Long Rifle, was made from 1933 to 1958. Very early guns will have the 20-inch barrel and pedal-type latch on the takedown knob that were carried over from the 1903 model. Otherwise, mechanically, the two models are practically identical.

Disassembly:

1. Use a coin or a specially shaped screwdriver to loosen the takedown screw at the rear of the receiver. After it is freed, the serrated knob is easily turned by hand. Back it out until it is stopped by its internal pin. **Note:** If you have a Model 1903, or a very early Model 63, the knob will have a pedal-type latch below it which must be depressed to allow turning.

2. Separate the buttstock and trigger group assembly from the receiver, moving the assembly straight toward the rear. Tight fitting may require the use of a rubber mallet for initial separation.

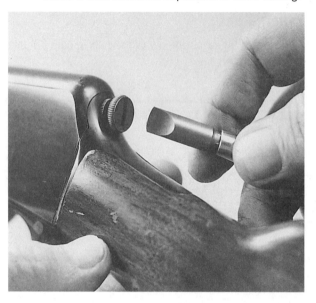

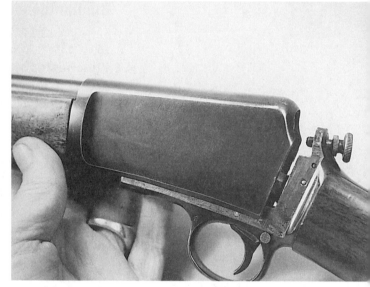

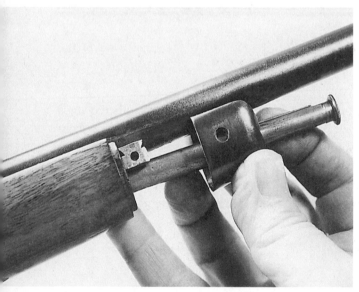

3. Remove the two screws, one on each side, that retain the forend cap. Remove the forend cap and cocking plunger assembly toward the front. The plunger spring is easily removed from inside the plunger. The knob is retained on the plunger by a cross pin.

4. Keep the forend snugged to the rear to avoid damaging it and carefully drift the forend cap base out of its dovetail toward the right. Use a brass or nylon drift to avoid damaging the screw-hole threads. Remove the forend toward the front.

5. Unscrew and remove the recoil spring guide rod. **Caution:** *Restrain the spring as the rod is taken out.*

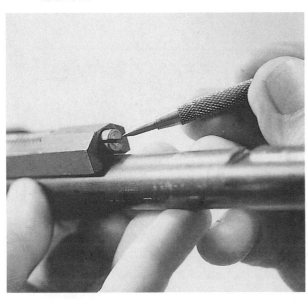

6. One method of controlling the spring during removal of the guide rod is shown here.

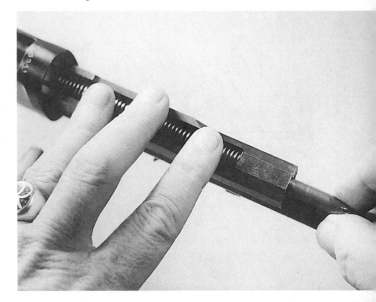

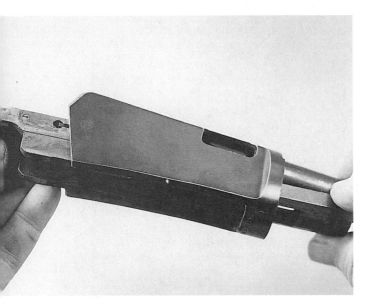

7. Move the bolt assembly rearward and take it out of the receiver.

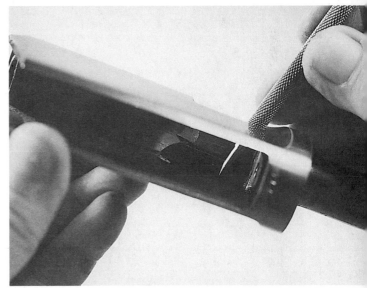

8. The ejector is retained by a single screw inside the left wall of the receiver, and the screw is accessible through the ejection port. In normal takedown, this is best left in place.

9. Restrain the firing pin and push out the firing pin retaining cross pin.

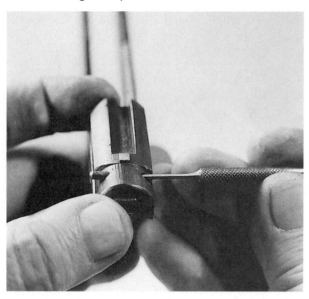

10. Remove the firing pin and its rebound spring toward the rear.

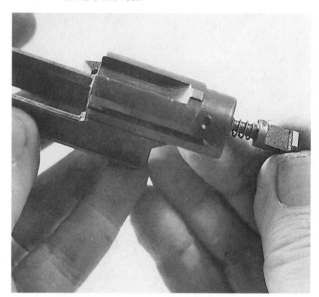

11. Remove the extractor plunger stop screw.

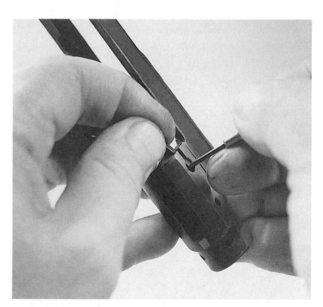

12. Insert a small tool between the extractor and its plunger, and depress the plunger toward the rear. Lift out the extractor. **Caution:** *Control the plunger and its compressed spring.*

13. Remove the inner magazine tube. Take out the two buttplate screws and remove the buttplate.

14. The best way to remove the stock mounting nut is to alter a ⅝-inch deep socket, cutting away its edge to leave two projections that will engage the slots in the nut. Removal can also be done this way: Use an angled drift punch to break the nut loose.

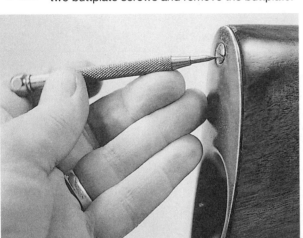

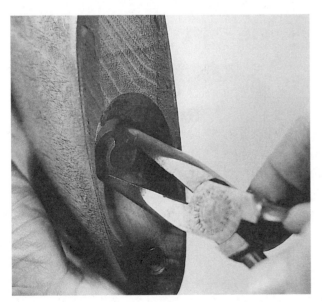

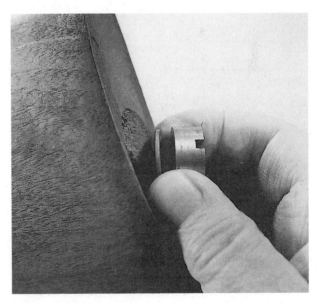

15. Once the nut is freed, an opened sharp-nosed pliers can be used to unscrew it.

16. Remove the stock mounting nut and its washer toward the rear.

17. Remove the buttstock toward the rear.

18. Remove the safety detent plunger and spring toward the rear.

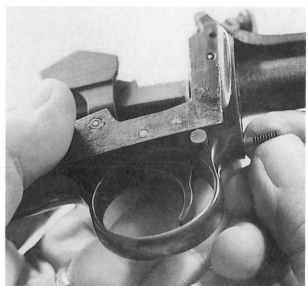

19. Retract the hammer slightly until the cross-hole near the tip of the spring guide is accessible, and insert a small pin to trap the hammer spring. Ease the hammer back forward.

20. Drift out the hammer spring base lock pin.

21. Tip the hammer spring base to the side until its upper portion stops against the frame. This will free it from its recess.

22. Drift out the hammer pivot pin.

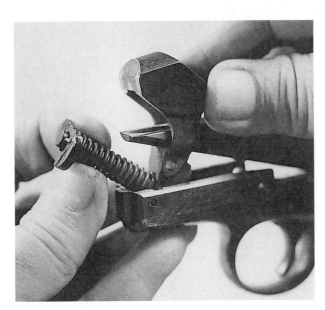

23. Remove the hammer and spring assembly toward the front. Pressing the spring base against a slightly opened vise and removing the keeper pin will allow the base and spring to be taken off the guide. **Caution:** *The spring is under tension.* The guide pivot pin can also be removed to take the guide off the hammer.

24. Drift out the trigger cross pin.

25. Take out the sear and its spring from inside the trigger group.

26. Turn the trigger downward into the guard for removal.

27. Use a tool to push the trigger spring out toward the front, into the receiver, for removal. **Caution:** *Lay a shop cloth over the lower receiver to arrest the spring as it is freed.*

28. Remove the safety button toward either side.

29. If removal of the takedown screw is necessary, determine the smaller end of the cross pin in its tip, and drift that end to push it out. The knob/screw can then be taken off rearward.

30. If you have removed the takedown screw, then drifting out this pin will release the takedown screw lock plunger and its spring for removal upward. **Caution:** *The spring is under tension.*

31. The cartridge stop and its spring can be removed from the magazine housing by pushing out this cross pin. Take care that the small coil spring is not lost.

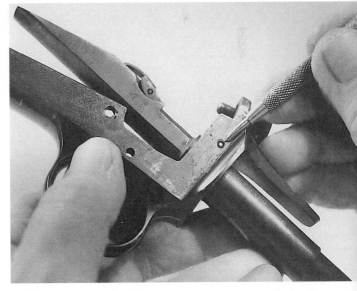

32. In normal takedown, the magazine housing is best left in place. However, if removal is necessary, this cross pin retains it in the lower receiver. After the pin is drifted out, the housing is moved forward out of the lower receiver. In removal of the magazine housing, there is always the possibility of damage.

Reassembly Tips:

1. When reinstalling the safety, remember that the flat recess goes toward the front and also that the shorter of its two ends goes toward the right side, as shown.

2. The trigger spring must be inserted through the trigger guard, and a tool is used to push it back into its tunnel. The proper orientation is shown. You will know it is properly in place when its rear bends are visible at the back of the lower receiver (see step 27).

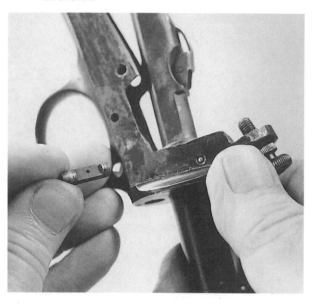

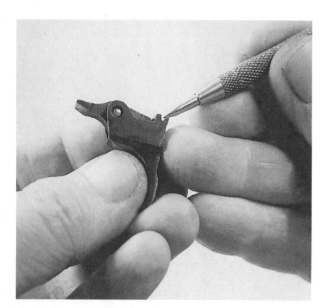

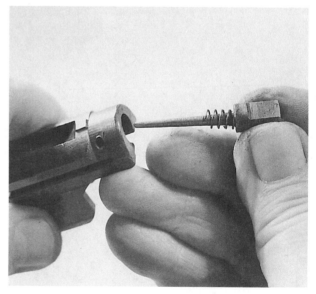

3. When installing the trigger and sear, and the sear spring, it is best to use a short slave pin to pre-assemble them, as shown. The slave pin is pushed out as the trigger pin is inserted. As the assembly is put in place, be sure the recess at the rear of the trigger engages the trigger spring.

4. Be sure the firing pin is installed in the orientation shown, with the long flat on top.

5. In rifles that have seen a lot of use, the firing pin retaining pin may be a loose fit. After it is reinstalled, it is best to stake the pin lightly on each side, as shown.

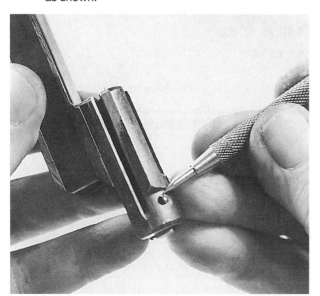

6. When replacing the recoil spring and its guide, start the spring onto the rod as the rod is pushed toward the rear, moving it in small increments. As the end is neared, use a tool to compress the spring forward while the threads are engaged.

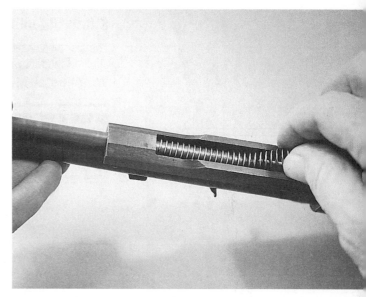

7. When installing the forend cap base, be sure it is perfectly centered to align with the opening in the forend. Also, be sure it is put back in the same orientation, as the screw holes are not always centered in the base.

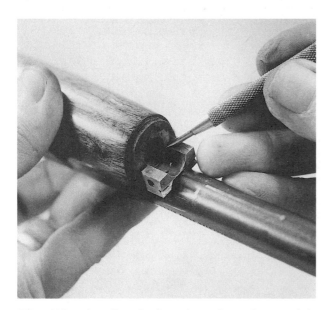

8. Use a tool to compress the cocking plunger spring, and insert a small tool in the hole provided to trap the spring. When the plunger has engaged the end of the recoil spring guide rod, and just before the forend cap is pushed into place, the tool is removed to release the spring.

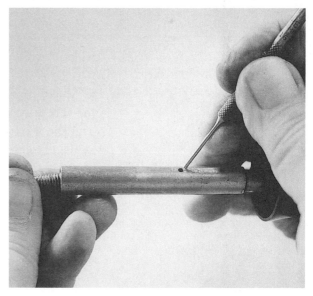

Winchester Model 67A

Similar/Identical Pattern Guns

The same basic assembly/disassembly steps for the Winchester Model 67A also apply to the following guns:

Winchester Model 67 Boy's Rifle   Winchester Model 677

Data:	Winchester Model 67A
Origin:	United States
Manufacturer:	Winchester Repeating Arms Co.
	New Haven, Connecticut
Cartridge:	22 Long Rifle
Overall length:	43 inches
Barrel length:	27 inches
Weight:	5 pounds

The Model 67 had a relatively long period of production, from 1934 to 1963. There was also a "boy's rifle," the Model 67BR, with a 20-inch barrel and a shorter stock. From 1937 to 1939, the Model 677 variation was made, with no sights, designed for use with a scope. All of the variations were the same, mechanically.

Disassembly:

1. Hold the trigger to the rear, open the bolt and remove the bolt toward the rear. Drift out the bolt cross pin.

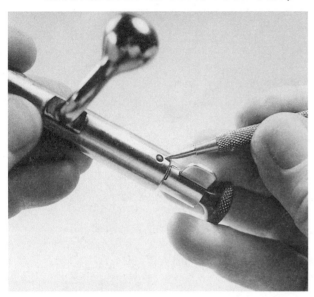

2. Remove the striker assembly toward the rear.

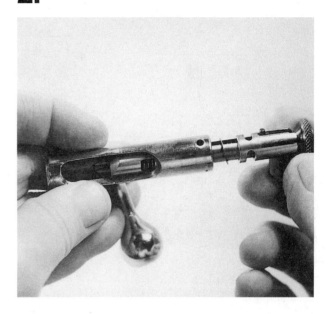

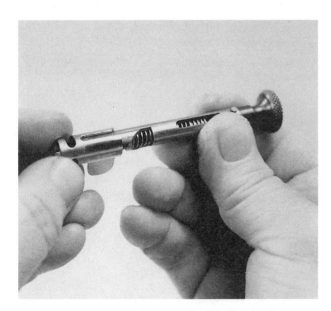

3. Remove the safety spring-washer toward the front. Remove the safety sleeve toward the front.

4. Drift out the striker knob pin. **Caution:** *Restrain the knob as the drift is removed, as the springs are under tension.* Ease the spring tension slowly, and remove the striker knob toward the rear. The rebound spring is easily removed from inside the striker knob shaft. Remove the striker spring and plunger from inside the striker.

5. Use a specially shaped screwdriver bit or a coin to back out the action mounting screw. This is a captive screw, and it will stay in its escutcheon in the stock. Remove the action from the stock.

6. The trigger guard is retained by two wood screws. An offset or angle-tip screwdriver will be necessary for the screw inside the guard.

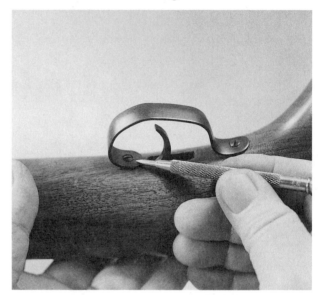

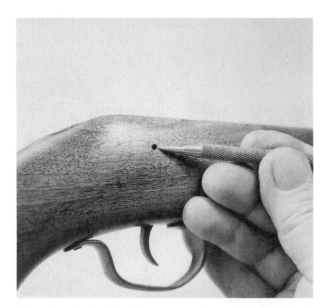

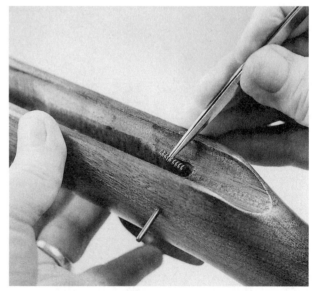

7. Push out the trigger cross pin. Use extreme care to avoid marring the stock. It is not necessary to remove the pinjust push it far enough to clear the trigger.

8. Remove the trigger upward. Remove the trigger spring from its well in the stock.

9. Slide the combination sear and ejector to the rear.

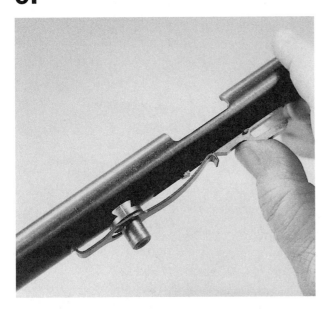

10. Pull the rear of the sear/ejector downward, just far enough to clear its rear upper projection, and remove it toward the rear.

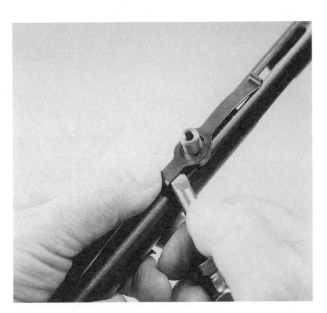

11. Lift the front of the sear spring just enough to clear its notch and push it rearward to align its exit hole with the post.

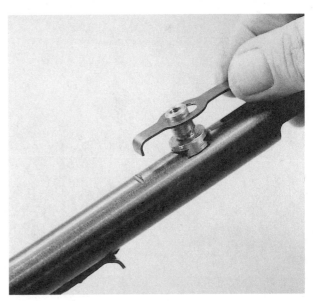

12. Remove the sear spring. If necessary, the post can be driven out of its dovetail toward the right. The front and rear sights are also dovetail-mounted, and are drifted out toward the right.

Reassembly Tips:

1. After the sear is reinstalled, push it back to the front, as shown.

2. When installing the trigger, drift the cross pin just far enough that the trigger can be put on it. Then, drift the pin into place. Again, take care not to mar the stock.

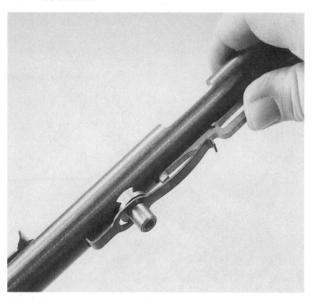

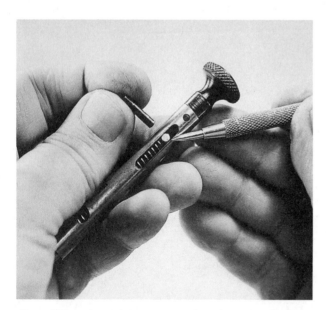

3. Use a slave pin to separate the rebound spring from the head of the striker spring plunger, as shown.

4. Viewed through the hole in the bolt body, use the slave pin as a guide to position the striker assembly for insertion of the bolt cross pin. The parts are shown here at the proper depth, but the slave pin head is a more precise guide.

Winchester Model 69

Similar/Identical Pattern Guns

The same basic assembly/disassembly steps for the Winchester Model 69 also apply to the following guns:

Winchester Model 69T **Winchester Model 697**
Winchester Model 69M **Winchester Model 69A**

Data:	Winchester Model 69
Origin:	United States
Manufacturer:	Winchester Repeating Arms
	New Haven, Connecticut
Cartridge:	22 Short, Long, or Long Rifle
Magazine capacity:	5 or 10 rounds
Overall length:	42 inches
Barrel length:	25 inches
Weight:	5 pounds

Made from 1935 to 1963, the Model 69 was also offered in target and match versions, the only difference in these being the addition of standard sling swivels and two different sights. Since they are mechanically the same, these instructions apply to all guns in the 69 series including the Model 697, except for removal of sights. The basic magazine was a 5-shot detachable box type, but a 10-shot version was available as an optional accessory.

Disassembly:

1. Remove the magazine and back out the main stock screw on the underside of the stock, forward of the magazine plate. Remove the action from the stock.

2. To remove the bolt, hold the trigger in the pulled position while opening the bolt and moving it out the rear of the receiver.

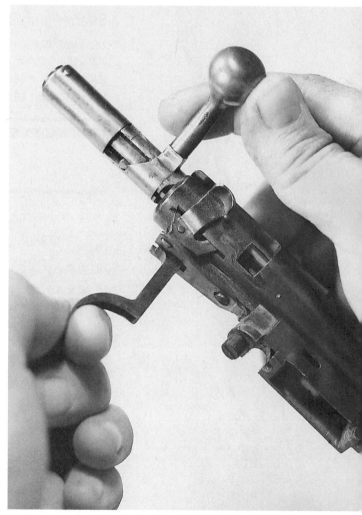

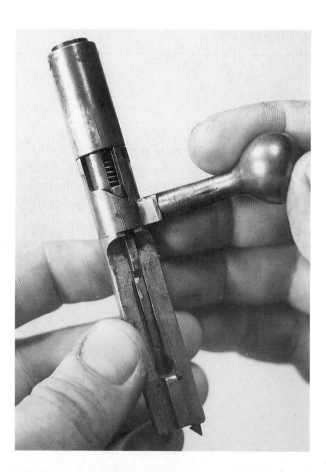

3. Grip the front portion of the bolt in a padded vise and turn the bolt handle to allow the striker to move forward to the fired position, partially easing the tension of its spring. The photo shows the bolt after the handle is turned, with the striker forward.

4. The screw-slotted end piece at the rear of the bolt is not a screw. The slot is there to aid reassembly. With the bolt still gripped in a padded vise, exert slight pressure on the end piece to control the tension of the striker spring, and push out the cross pin at the rear of the bolt. **Caution:** *The striker spring is under some tension, even when at rest, so control it and ease out the end piece.*

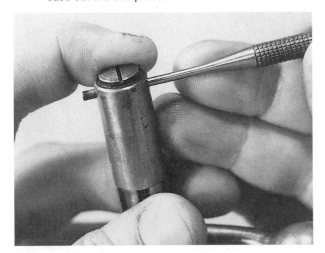

5. Remove the bolt end piece and the striker spring toward the rear.

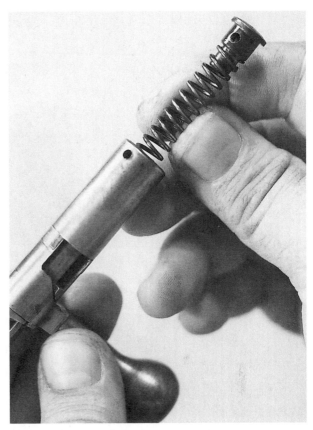

6. Remove the bolt sleeve toward the rear. The sleeve is often tightly fitted, and may require a few nudges with a nylon drift and hammer to start it off.

7. Move the bolt handle sleeve slightly toward the rear until the firing pin (striker) retaining cross pin is exposed and drift out the cross pin.

8. Move the bolt handle sleeve back forward, against its shoulder on the bolt, and turn it until the widest part of its internal opening is aligned with the firing pin on the underside of the bolt. Then, move the firing pin all the way to the rear, tip its rear end downward and remove it from the bolt. The clearances are very close here, so proceed with care.

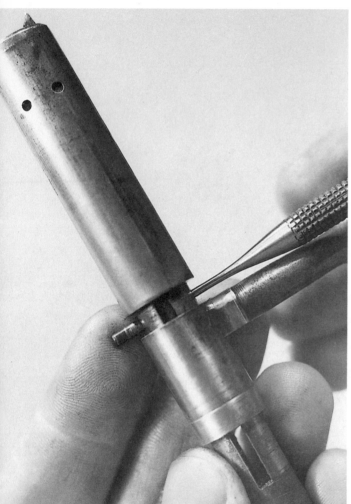

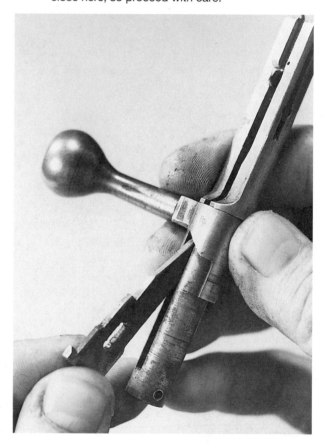

9. Remove the bolt handle sleeve toward the rear.

10. A drift punch of very small diameter is required to remove the vertical pins at the front of the bolt, which retain the two extractors. The punch shown was made in the shop for this purpose. The pins must be driven out upward, and the extractors and their small coil springs are taken off from each side.

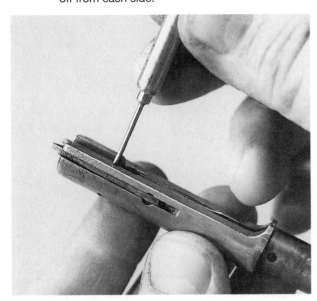

11. The formed steel that is the magazine catch is secured on the right side of the magazine housing by a single screw.

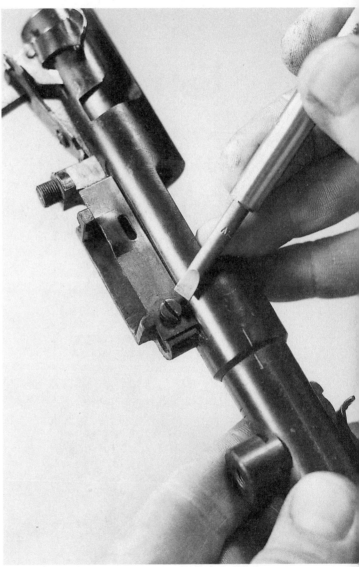

12. Remove the front magazine housing screw.

13. Remove the rear screw from the magazine housing and remove the magazine housing downward.

14. The magazine housing can be taken off without disturbing the trigger spring adjustment screw, but it is best to at least back it off to relieve the spring tension. If this is done, note its depth if the same weight of pull is desired on reassembly.

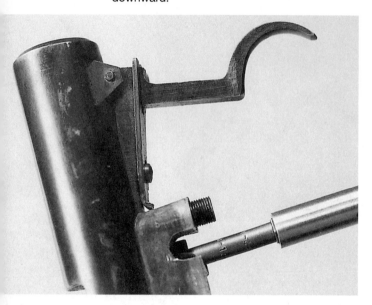

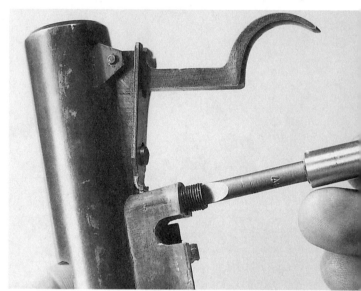

15. Drift out the cross pin that retains the trigger.

16. Remove the trigger and safety-lever downward.

17. Remove the screw on the underside of the front arm of the trigger, and slide the safety plate off toward the front. **Caution:** *Removal of the safety plate will release the safety positioning plunger and spring, so control them as the plate is taken off to prevent loss.*

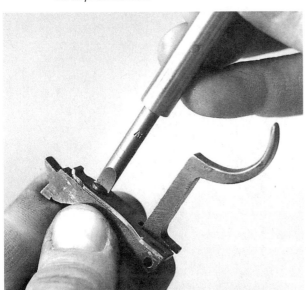

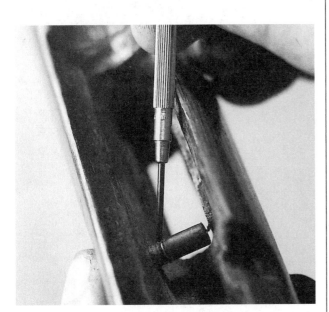

18. The magazine catch release button is retained in the left side of the stock by a circular spring clip which rests in a groove on the button shaft. Push the button in to give access to the clip, move it out of its groove and slide it off the shaft toward the right. The button and its coil spring can then be taken off toward the left.

Reassembly Tips:

1. When replacing the trigger and safety-lever, be sure the upper front arm of the lever goes into its slot in the receiver, and that the lower arm of the lever enters its slot in the safety plate on the trigger. Be sure the holes in the trigger and lever are aligned with the holes in the mount on the receiver before driving in the cross pin.

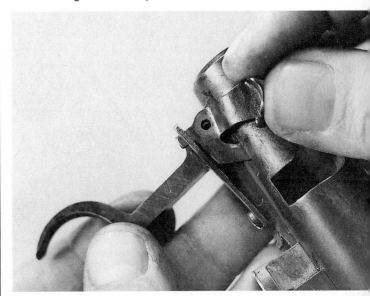

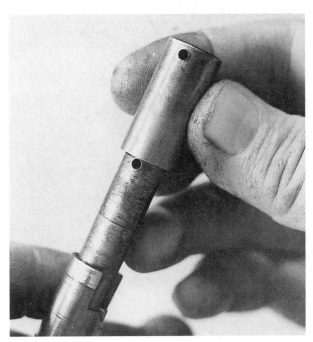

2. When replacing the bolt sleeve, be sure the cross pin holes at the rear are as closely aligned as possible with the holes in the bolt body before tapping the sleeve into place. When the sleeve is fully forward, insert a small drift punch through the holes to complete the alignment.

3. To reinstall the bolt end piece, grip the front portion of the bolt in a padded vise and push the end piece into place, holding it against the tension of the striker spring. Be sure the striker is in the fired position. Use a wide-bladed screwdriver to turn the end piece until the cross pin hole is in alignment with the holes in the bolt sleeve and body, and insert a drift punch to hold the end piece in place while driving in the cross pin.

4. Before the bolt is reinserted in the receiver, the striker must be in cocked position. With the bolt still gripped in the padded vise, turn the bolt handle to cock the striker. The photo shows the striker in the cocked position.

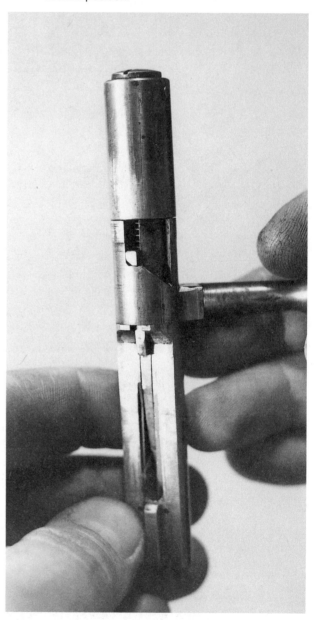

Winchester Model 74

Data:	Winchester Model 74
Origin:	United States
Manufacturer:	Winchester Repeating Arms Company
	New Haven, Connecticut
Cartridge:	22 Long Rifle, 22 Short (separate guns)
Magazine capacity:	14 in Long Rifle model, 20 in Short model
Overall length:	43¾ inches
Barrel length:	22 inches
Weight:	6¼ pounds

The Model 74 was originally intended to be an "economy" 22-caliber autoloader in the Winchester line, costing about one-third less than their Model 63. Made from just before World War II until 1955, the Model 74 had several unusual features. Among these were a top mounted cross-bolt safety and a bolt and firing mechanism that could easily be removed as a unit, without taking the rifle action out of the stock. The Model 74 was a simple and reliable gun, and many of them are still in use.

Disassembly:

1. Remove the magazine tube from the rear of the stock. Back out the large screw on the underside of the stock, and separate the action from the stock.

2. Press in the rear of the disconnector on the underside of the receiver to drop the striker to fired position (the safety must be on the "F" mark, of course). Then, push the takedown latch (at the left rear of the receiver) toward the right until its right end clears its recess in the receiver.

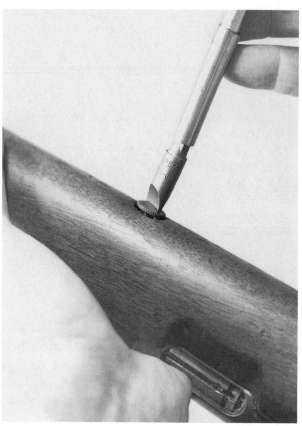

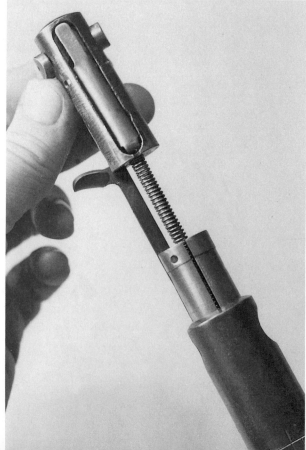

3. While holding the latch to the right, withdraw the bolt and firing mechanism assembly from the rear of the receiver.

4. Bring the bolt and sear housing (end piece) together until they meet to cock the striker. With a firm grip on the bolt and end piece, push out the cocking handle retaining pin, located at the right rear of the bolt. **Caution:** *Control the compressed bolt spring, and let the tension off slowly as you move the bolt and end piece apart.* Removal of the cocking handle will instantly release the two parts, so be prepared for it.

5. Remove the bolt spring and its guide from the bolt and end piece. At this point, the striker is still held in place by the sear. Grip the striker firmly, and release the sear by pressing its rear tab inward. **Caution:** *Keep the striker and end piece under control, and ease out the striker and its spring slowly.*

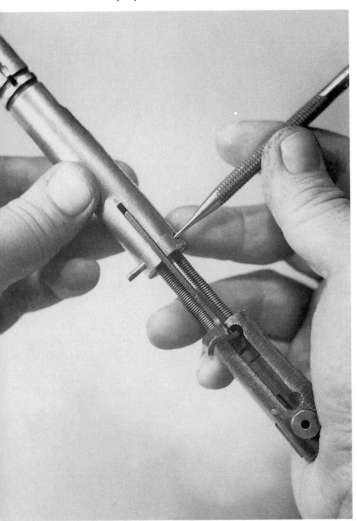

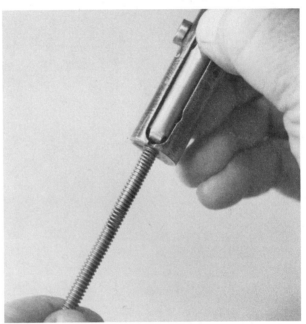

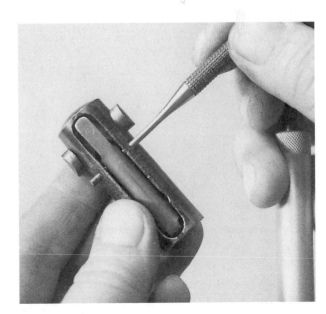

6. Drifting out the cross pin at the top of the end piece will release the sear for removal upward. Take the sear spring out of its well at the rear.

7. Partially depress the takedown latch until the hole in its upper surface aligns with a small hole inside the end piece, and use a very slim drift punch to drive out the retaining pin downward. **Caution:** *Be sure a punch of very small diameter is used, to avoid damaging the parts.* The punch shown was especially made in the shop for this purpose. When the pin is partially out, the small coil spring inside the latch will be released toward the right, so keep a fingertip over the hole in the right end of the latch to catch it. When the pin is out, the latch can be removed.

8. The extractor is retained by a vertical pin at the front of the bolt, accessible at the extreme rear of the open firing pin groove in the top of the bolt. The pin is driven out toward the bottom of the bolt. Here, again, use a very slim drift punch. When the pin is out, the extractor and its spring are removed toward the right.

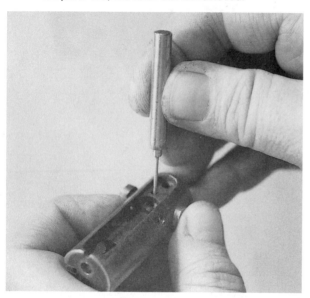

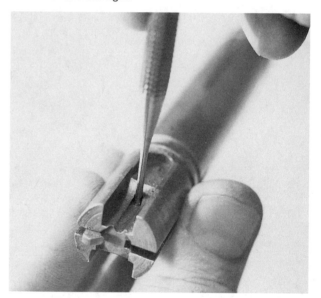

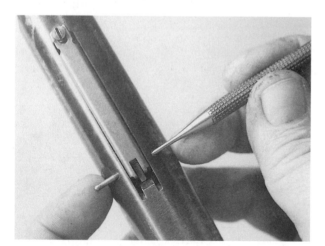

9. The disconnector is retained by a cross pin on the underside of the receiver.

10. When the cross pin is pushed out, the front end of the disconnector will be pulled into the receiver by its spring. Use a small tool to lift it slightly; then move it forward until its rear yoke clears the screw/post at the rear and remove the disconnector from the receiver. **Caution:** *Take care to lift the part only enough to ease it off. If you raise it too far, the spring may break.*

11. Backing out the screw/post at the rear of the disconnector slot will allow removal of the curved flat spring.

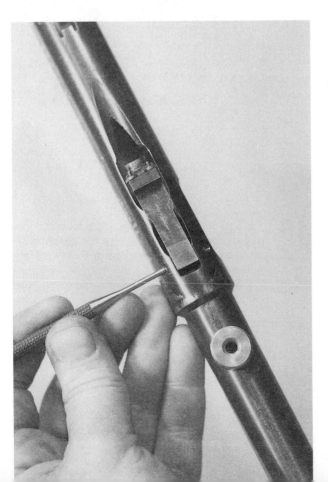

12. While observing the underside of the safety catch through the disconnector slot, insert a small tool from the rear of the receiver and carefully lift the tip of the safety spring just enough to allow the safety to be slid out of the top of the receiver. The spring is staked in place, and removal is not recommended except for replacement of a broken spring.

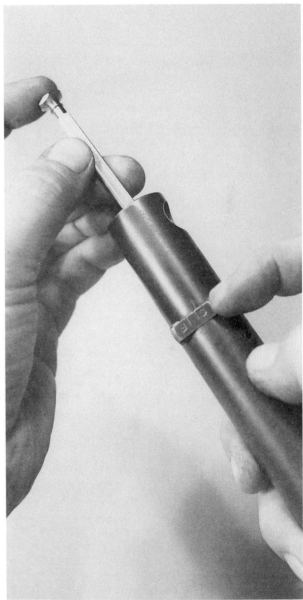

13. The cartridge feed guide is retained by a single cross pin on the underside of the receiver. After the feed guide is removed, the twin cartridge stops are easily detachable from it by swinging them outward on their fixed pins and removing them toward the rear.

14. The top cartridge guide is retained by a cross pin at the top front of the receiver, and is removed toward the rear and downward. The ejector is staked in place in the left wall of the receiver, and should not be disturbed in normal takedown.

15. Drift out the cross pin that passes through the stock above the trigger to free the trigger and its spring. The trigger is removed upward, but only after removal of the magazine tube.

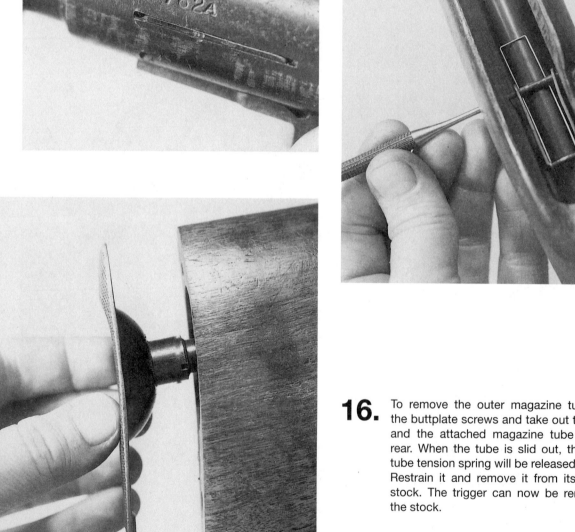

16. To remove the outer magazine tube, remove the buttplate screws and take out the buttplate and the attached magazine tube toward the rear. When the tube is slid out, the magazine tube tension spring will be released at the front. Restrain it and remove it from its well in the stock. The trigger can now be removed from the stock.

Reassembly Tips:

1. When replacing the magazine tube and buttplate assembly, use a tool to depress the magazine tube tension spring while sliding the magazine tube into place. Remember that the trigger must be put back in the stock before insertion of the magazine tube.

2. When replacing the takedown latch retaining pin, use a small screwdriver or drift to depress the internal spring beyond the pin location. Take care that the pin does not hit the spring and deform it.

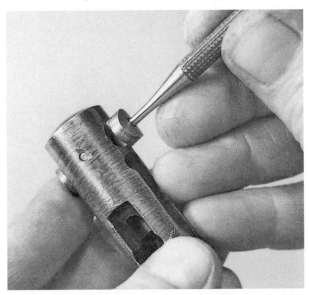

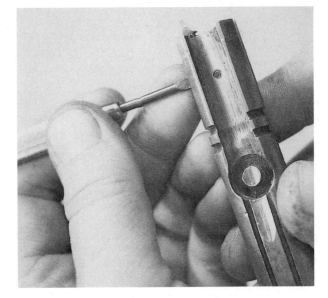

3. When replacing the extractor pivot pin, be sure the hole in the extractor lobe is exactly in alignment with the pin hole to avoid damage to the pin or the extractor. The pin must be driven in from the underside of the bolt, toward the top. Be sure the pin does not protrude into the firing pin groove.

4. When replacing the disconnector, lift the spring with a small tool and be sure the tip of the spring enters the opening at the front of the disconnector.

5. After hooking the front tip of the spring into the disconnector, insert a small screwdriver under the tip of the spring to hold it in place while sliding the disconnector forward, and then back to fit its rear yoke around the neck of the screw/post.

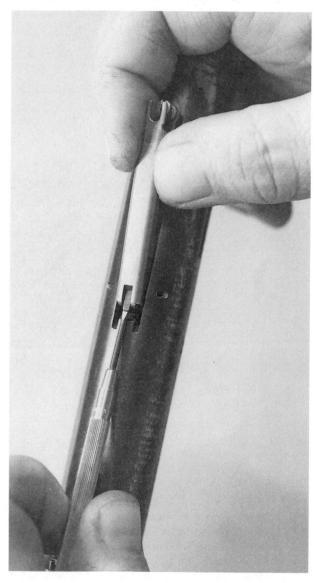

Winchester Model 77

Similar/Identical Pattern Guns

The same basic assembly/disassembly steps for the Winchester Model 77 also apply to the following gun:

Winchester Model 77 Box Magazine

Data:	Winchester Model 77
Origin:	United States
Manufacturer:	Winchester Repeating Arms
	New Haven, Connecticut
Cartridge:	22 Long Rifle
Magazine capacity:	15 rounds
Overall length:	40 inches
Barrel length:	22 inches
Weight:	5½ pounds

In comparison to other Winchester rifles, the Model 77 was made for a relatively brief period from 1955 to 1963. In a way, it was like a transition between the old and the new, with its beautiful solid steel receiver and a nylon/plastic trigger guard. The gun was made in two versions, box magazine and tube magazine, and the latter gun is covered here. Except for the difference in feed systems, the instructions can apply to either version. There are one or two very tricky points in the takedown/reassembly of the Model 77, and these are noted in the instructions.

Disassembly:

1. Remove the inner magazine tube and back out the screw on the underside of the stock, forward of the trigger guard. Back out the screw at the rear of the trigger guard and remove the action upward.

2. If the trigger guard is to be removed, take out the screw at the front of the guard. Note that this screw has a nut on the inside of the stock, which may have to be held while removing the screw.

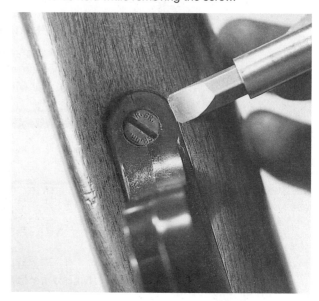

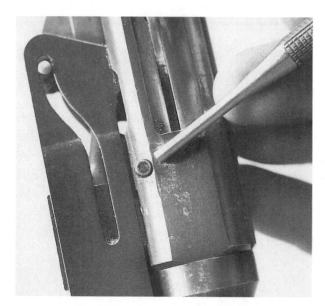

3. Pull the trigger to drop the striker to the fired position and push out the barrel retaining pin, which crosses the underside of the receiver below the chamber area.

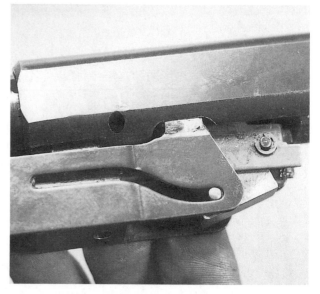

4. Move the barrel and bolt assembly forward until the upper rear arms of the operating slide are aligned with the exit cuts in the underside of the receiver. Spread the rear arms of the slide into the cuts to free the feed throat and carrier assembly.

5. Moving the rear arms of the slide into the exit cuts will free the side studs on the carrier assembly from the open tracks in the arms, and the carrier and feed throat can then be removed downward and toward the rear.

6. The carrier and feed throat assembly can be taken apart by careful removal of the C-clips from the ends of the cross pin on each side. When the carrier is removed from the feed throat, the feed platform and its spring will also be released from inside the carrier, so restrain these parts and ease them out. The cam pin across the front can also be removed.

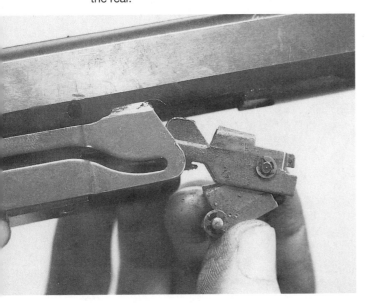

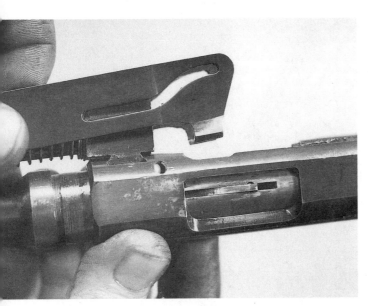

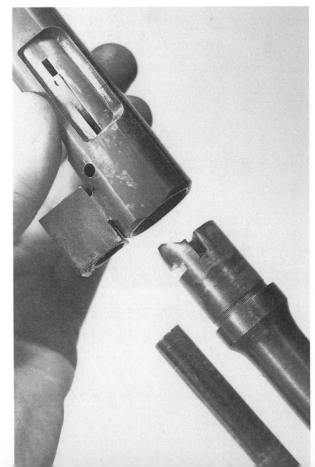

7. Restrain the action slide against the tension of the recoil spring, and disengage the rear upper arms of the action slide from their recesses in the underside of the bolt. Allow the action slide to move forward, relieving the tension of the spring.

8. Remove the barrel from the receiver.

9. Remove the action slide and recoil spring from the rear of the magazine tube.

10. The outer magazine tube may be removed by drifting out the small cross pin in the tube hanger loop. Move the tube out toward the front.

11. The hanger loop appears to be dovetail-mounted. Actually, it is keyed into a circular recess, and the loop is turned at a right angle to its normal position for removal.

13. Retract the timing rod spring and its collar from the rear tip of the rod, and remove the C-clip from the groove at the tip. Slowly release the tension of the spring, and remove the collar and spring toward the rear. Take out the timing rod toward the front.

12. Remove the bolt assembly toward the front.

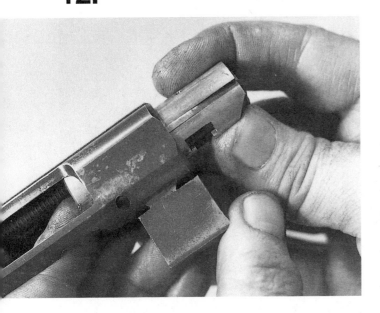

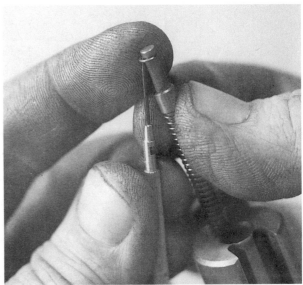

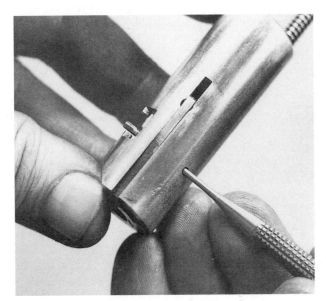

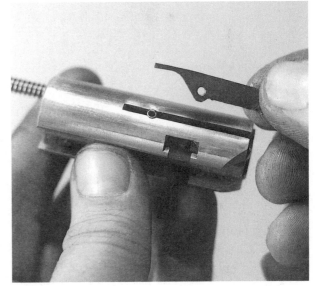

14. Drift out the vertical pin on the right side of the bolt, freeing the extractor, its spring and the firing pin inside the bolt.

15. Remove the extractor and its spring toward the right.

16. Removal of the extractor will release the firing pin assembly, and this can now be taken out toward the rear. If the return spring is not on the front of the firing pin, remove it from the firing pin tunnel and take care not to confuse it with the extractor spring, as they are not interchangeable.

17. The ejector is mounted inside the firing pin, along with its spring, and they are retained by a cross pin at the rear of the firing pin. Push out the pin, while restraining the spring, and remove the ejector and spring toward the rear.

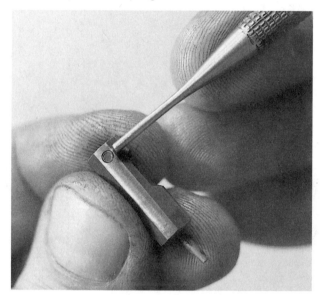

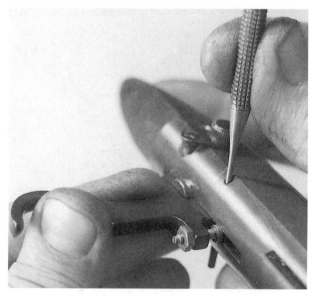

18. Remove the striker and its spring from inside the receiver. If they do not come out easily, pulling the trigger to relieve the sear tension should release them.

19. Restrain the trigger against the tension of the trigger and sear springs and push out the trigger cross pin.

20. Remove the trigger downward, slowly relieving the tension of its spring. It is not necessary to disturb the trigger adjustment screw.

21. Remove the sear and disconnector assembly downward.

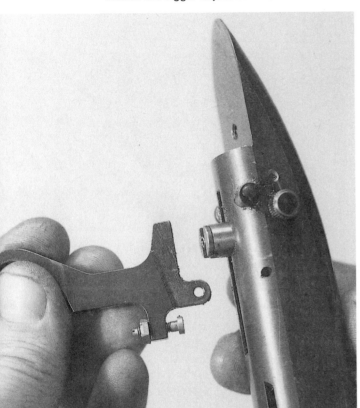

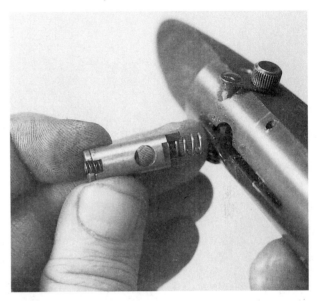

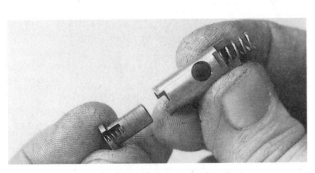

22. The sear, disconnector, and their attendant springs are easily separated.

23. The safety is retained by a C-clip on the end of its cross-shaft, on the left side of the receiver. Carefully remove the C-clip, restraining the safety spring and removing it from the end of the cross-shaft.

24. Remove the safety-lever toward the right.

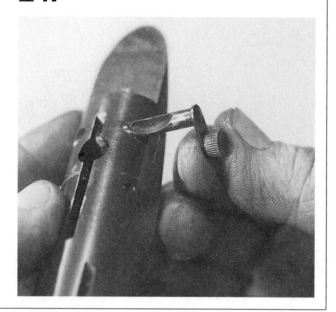

1. When replacing the firing pin in the bolt, insert a small screwdriver beside its cross pin at the rear to orient the firing pin within the bolt for mating with the pin lobe of the extractor.

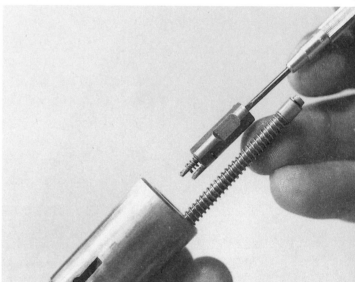

2. When replacing the sear/disconnector assembly in the receiver, note that the larger hole in the disconnector goes toward the rear, and that the shelf on the top of the sear goes toward the rear. This is an important point, as it is possible to reassemble them in reverse.

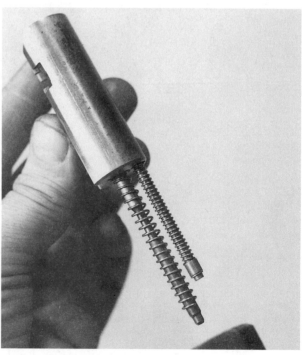

3. Replacement of the striker and its spring will be easier if they are placed in their hole in the rear of the bolt and inserted with the bolt.

Winchester Model 90

Similar/Identical Pattern Guns

The same basic assembly/disassembly steps for the Winchester Model 90 also apply to the following guns:

Winchester Model 1906

Rossi Model 62SA

Rossi Model 62A

Rossi Model 62SAC

Rossi Model 59

Data:	Winchester Model 90
Origin:	United States
Manufacturer:	Winchester Repeating Arms
	New Haven, Connecticut
Cartridge:	22 Short, Long, Long Rifle or WRF
	(separate guns)
Magazine capacity:	15 Short, 12 Long
	11 Long Rifle, 10 WRF
Overall length:	40 inches
Barrel length:	24 inches
Weight:	5½ pounds

Designed for Winchester by John M. Browning, the Model 1890 was made until 1932. Along the way, in 1906, a part was added to the carrier to allow the use of Short, Long, and Long Rifle rounds interchangeably, and that gun became the Model 1906. In 1932, the gun was slightly redesigned to become the Model 62, and this one was replaced very soon by the Model 62A, with production ending in 1959. The design returned in 1973, made by Rossi in Brazil, and the gun is still available. Except for the true Model 62, which has a different bolt/action slide system, the instructions will apply to any of the guns mentioned above.

Disassembly:

1. Back out the thumbscrew at the left rear of the receiver, and when its threads are clear, the screw will move slightly toward the left, out of its recess in the left side of the receiver, but will stay on the gun. If the screw is tight, a coin slot is provided to aid in starting it.

2. Set the hammer on the safety step, and move the rear portion of the gun off toward the rear.

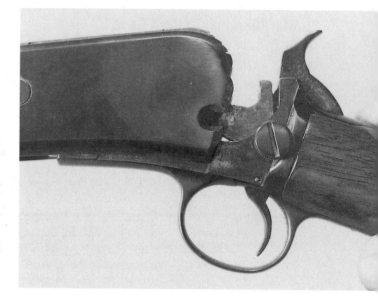

3. Remove the stock mounting screw, located at the rear tip of the upper tang, and take off the stock toward the rear. If the stock is very tight, it may be necessary to bump the front of the comb with the heel of your hand to start it.

4. To remove the takedown cross screw, use a very small diameter drift punch to drive out the transverse pin near its left tip. To make the pin accessible, the take down screw must be moved as far toward the right as it will go. After removal of the pin, the screw is removed toward the left.

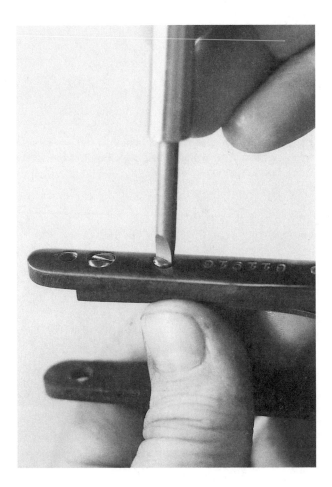

5. With the hammer lowered to the fired position, remove the hammer spring screw, the larger of the two screws at the rear of the lower tang. Removal will be made easier by first backing out the hammer spring tension screw, the smaller screw just forward of the other one.

6. Disengage the hammer spring hooks from the hammer stirrup, and remove the hammer spring toward the rear.

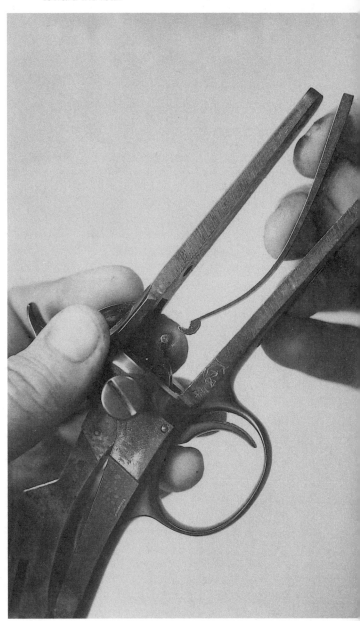

7. With a large diameter non-marring drift punch, push out the hollow hammer/carrier pivot toward the right.

8. Remove the carrier toward the front and upward.

9. The carrier lever spring is retained on the right side of the carrier by a vertical screw. Remove the screw and the spring upward.

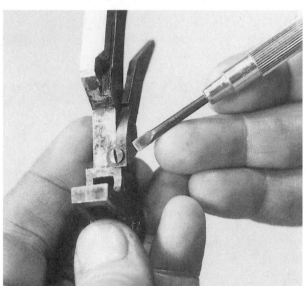

10. The carrier lever is retained on the carrier by a cross pin. When drifting out the pin, take care not to pinch the lever slot on the right side. After the pin is taken out, the lever is removed toward the front. The cross pin at the rear of the carrier is a limit pin that retains no part, and is not removed in normal takedown.

11. On the later models, after 1906-08, and including the Model 62A, there is a pivoting cartridge stop in the lower front projection of the carrier. Drifting out its cross pin will allow removal of the cartridge stop toward the front.

12. The previous removal of the hollow cross-piece has also released the hammer. Pull the trigger to clear its sear arm from the front, and remove the hammer upward.

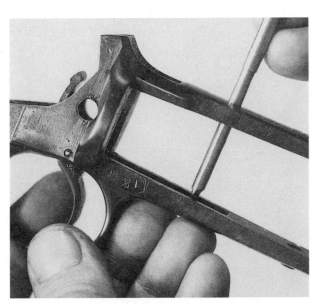

13. The trigger spring is retained by a vertical screw inside the lower tang. This screw can be removed by an offset or angled-tip screwdriver, or a small filler screw can be taken out of the upper tang, allowing a screwdriver with a very thin shaft to reach the screw from above, as shown. The screwdriver in the photo was specially made for this purpose.

14. Drifting out the trigger cross pin will allow the trigger to be removed upward. The sear is an integral part of the upper projection of the trigger.

15. Remove the slide coverplate screw, located on the left side of the receiver at the lower edge of the coverplate, and slide the coverplate off toward the front. Exerting slight inward pressure on the slide bar will make removal of the plate easier.

16. Use a non-marring tool to prop the slide bar out to the left, being sure its rear lug clears its track in the lower lobe of the breechblock. Depress the firing pin and hold it in while lifting the front of the breechblock upward, out of its locking recess in the receiver. Remove the breechblock toward the rear.

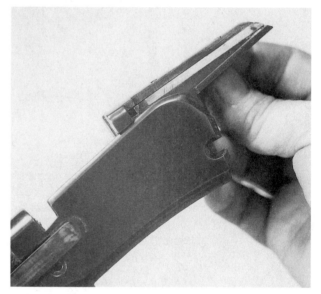

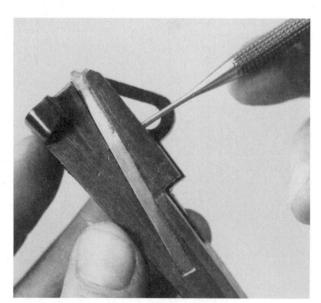

17. The extractor is retained on the right side of the breechblock by a vertical pin. Drift the pin out toward the top, and remove the extractor toward the right. The extractor is tempered to be its own spring. Note that the pin is installed at a right angle to the extractor, but not in relation to the other surfaces of the breechblock. In relation to these, it is slanted.

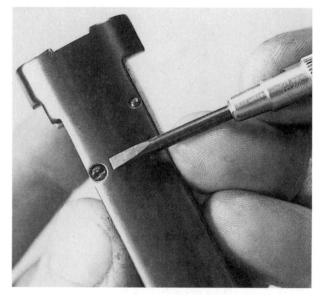

18. Removal of the two small vertical screws on top of the breechblock will release the firing pin retaining block, located on the left side.

19. After the screws are taken out, move the firing pin retaining block out toward the rear. **Caution:** *Do not try to remove the block toward the left, and especially avoid any leftward pressure on the rear tip of the block, as this will break the slim block at the rear screw hole.*

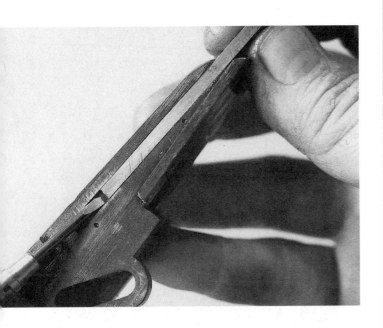

20. After the retaining block is removed, take out the firing pin and its coil return spring toward the rear.

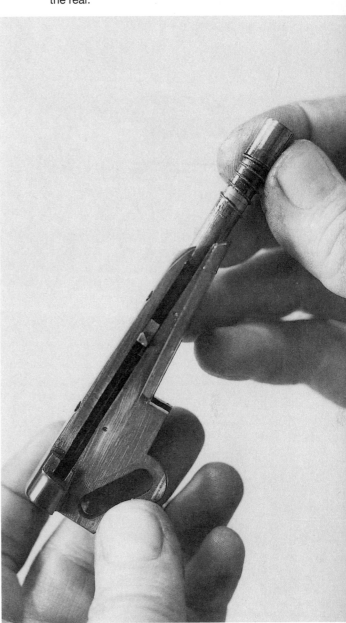

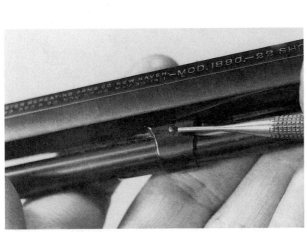

21. Remove the inner magazine tube, and drift out the cross pin in the rear magazine tube hanger loop. This will allow removal of the outer magazine tube toward the front, and the action slide and its handle can then be easily detached from the receiver. Removing the screws on each side of the handle will allow the action slide to be separated from the handle. On early guns, the magazine hangers are rotated to free them from the underside of the barrel. On later models, they are driven out of their dovetails toward the right.

22. The rear sight is secured at the front by a screw which enters a retainer in a dovetail cut. As the screw is turned, the sight base will climb off the top of the headless screw. Take care that the small screw and its base are not lost.

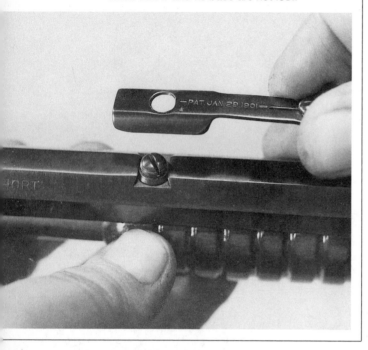

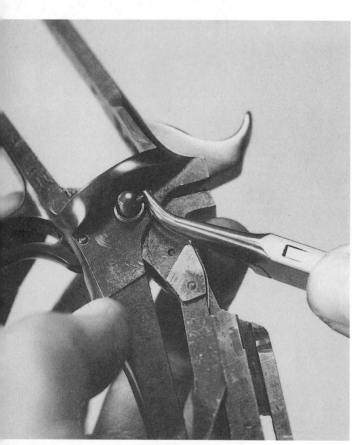

Reassembly Tips:

1. When replacing the screws that retain the firing pin block, insert a small diameter drift punch in one of the screw holes to hold the block in place while putting in the first screw.

2. When replacing the pin that retains the takedown screw, note that the pin is slightly smaller at one end, and be sure that this end is inserted in the hole. Grip the pin with sharp-nosed pliers to start it; then tap it into place with a small drift punch and hammer. Remember that the pin must have equal projection on each side of the takedown screw, to allow the screw to move toward the left during takedown and reassembly.

Winchester Model 190

Similar/Identical Pattern Guns

The same basic assembly/disassembly steps for the Winchester Model 190 also apply to the following guns:

Winchester Model 290　　　**Winchester Model 290 Deluxe**

Data:	Winchester Model 190
Origin:	United States
Manufacturer:	Winchester Repeating Arms Company New Haven, Connecticut
Cartridge:	22 Long Rifle
Magazine capacity:	15 rounds
Overall length:	39 inches
Barrel length:	20½ inches
Weight:	5 pounds

Introduced as the Model 290 in 1964, and in a "deluxe" version, this gun was offered in an economy style in 1974 as the Model 190. In this designation, it was made until 1980. Some very early guns will be found to have a plastic rear sight and a combination front sight and magazine tube hanger of the same material, and some elements of takedown involving those parts will be slightly different. However, the instructions will apply to either model.

Disassembly:

1. Cycle the bolt to cock the hammer and move the safety to the on-safe position. Remove the magazine tube and push out the large plastic cross pin located in the receiver just above the trigger. The pin can be pushed out toward either side.

2. Tip the trigger housing down at the rear and move it slightly toward the rear to disengage its forward stud from its recess inside the receiver. Remove the trigger group downward.

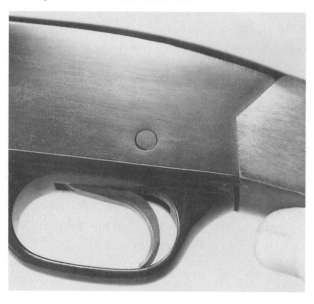

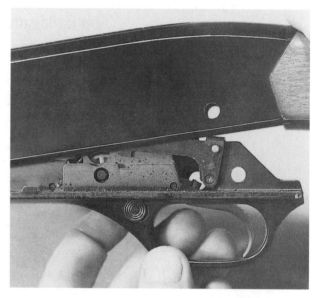

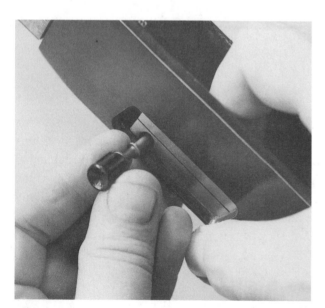

3. With the gun inverted, retract the bolt slightly and use a finger or tool to hold it inside the receiver. Lift the front of the bolt, and remove the bolt handle from its hole in the bolt.

4. Move the bolt toward the rear to clear its forward end from the barrel throat and tip the front of the bolt upward (the gun is still inverted) until it can be removed from the receiver. **Caution:** *The bolt spring is under tension. Ease it out.*

5. Remove the bolt spring and its nylon guide from the receiver.

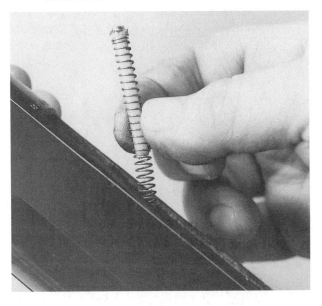

6. Removal of the buttstock requires a special socket wrench with a very deep end. It is possible to alter an ordinary socket for this, but in normal disassembly it is best to leave the stock in place. If the stock is removed, and the headless mounting bolt taken out, the recoil plate inside the receiver will be released for removal.

7. Drifting out the small, short cross pin in the magazine tube hanger near the muzzle will release the outer magazine tube for removal toward the front. This will allow the forend to be taken off downward. After removal of the forend, the nylon forend mount is easily slid out of its dovetail toward either side.

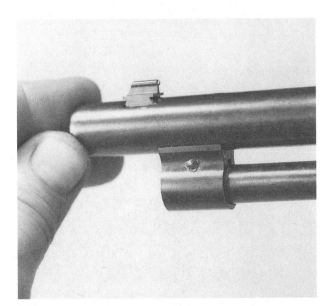

8. Flex the rear sight very slightly upward, and take out the sight elevator. Drifting out the rear sight toward the right will release the barrel collar cover for removal upward, giving access to the barrel collar.

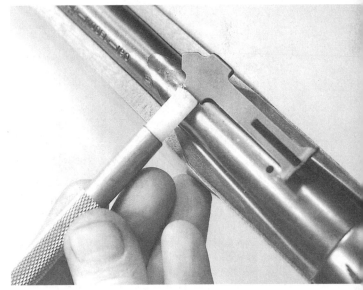

9. With the proper wrench (available from Brownells) turn the barrel collar counterclockwise (front view) until it is out of the receiver. Remove the barrel toward the front. **Note:** Because of the permanently attached magazine tube hanger, the barrel collar is not removable from the barrel.

10. If the barrel is very tight in the receiver, grip the barrel in a padded vise and tap the front of the receiver with a wood, leather or nylon hammer, moving the receiver off the rear of the barrel. **Caution:** *Take care not to deform the lower front of the receiver.*

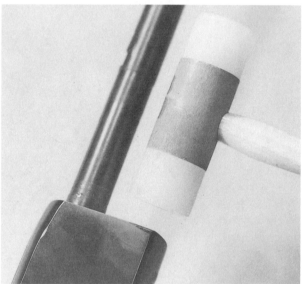

11. Drift out the vertical pin on the left side of the bolt to allow the firing pin to be moved toward the rear, easing the tension of the combination firing pin spring and extractor spring. **Note:** There is a steel ball bearing at each end of the spring. Take care that these are not lost. Remove the extractor pivot pin from its hole in the top front of the bolt. With the spring tension relieved, the pin should come out when the bolt is inverted and tapped with a light hammer. If the pin is tight, it can be nudged out by using a pointed tool in the stake mark on the underside of the bolt. Take care that this very small pin isn't lost.

12. Remove the extractor from the right side of the bolt, taking it out forward and toward the right.

13. Move the firing pin forward to nudge the spring out of its tunnel in the bolt and remove the spring and the two ball bearings from the extractor recess. Again, take care that the ball bearings aren't lost.

14. Move the firing pin toward the center of the bolt and remove the firing pin toward the rear.

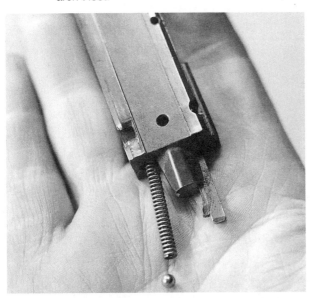

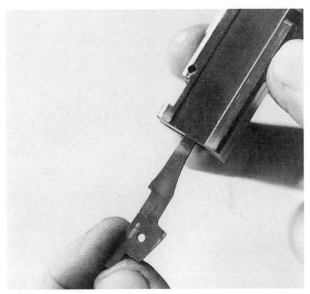

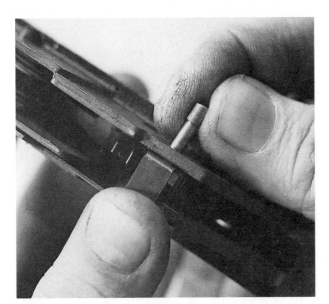

15. Move the safety to the off-safe position, restrain the hammer and pull the trigger, lowering the hammer to the fired position. Restrain the sear/disconnector assembly and remove its pivot pin toward the right.

16. Remove the sear/disconnector assembly upward. The sear and its spring are a permanent assembly inside the disconnector, the pivot pin being riveted in place at the factory. Routine removal is unwise in normal disassembly.

17. Push the hammer pivot out toward either side (left) and remove the hammer assembly upward (right). The hammer spring and its two nylon support pieces are easily removed from the hammer.

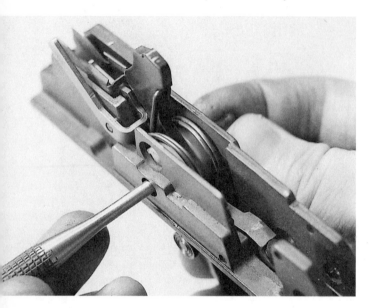

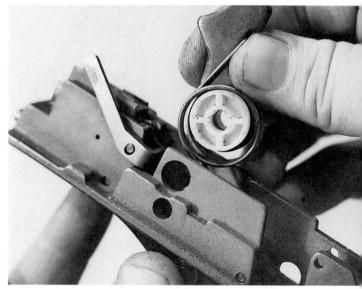

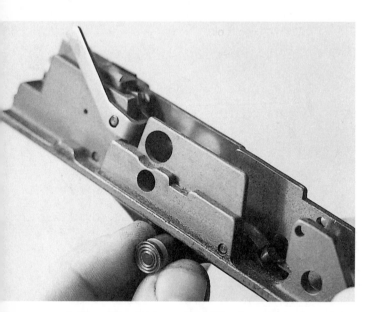

18. The right rear tail of the hammer spring retains the safety, and the safety can now be turned slightly and removed toward the left.

19. Push out the trigger pivot pin and remove the trigger from the top of the trigger housing. The sear contact stud on the trigger is factory-staked at the proper level, and it should not be disturbed.

20. The feed system is retained by three cross pins. The large pin at the rear (upper right in the photo) retains the carrier lever. When drifting it out, restrain the carrier, as its spring is under tension. Moving the carrier out to the rear will release the spring and its plunger, so proceed with caution. The cartridge feed guide is retained by a tiny roll pin near its center and by a larger pin near the lower edge of the housing. When these are removed, the guide can be taken out toward the top.

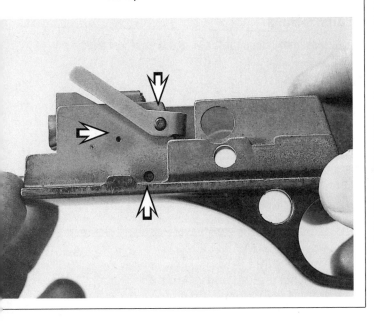

When replacing the safety in the trigger housing, remember that the end with the red ring goes toward the left, and be sure that the positioning recesses on the right side are at the top.

Note that the hammer pivot has one flat side, and be sure both of the nylon hammer spring supports are oriented so that their inside flats will align with the flat on the pin. If not, the support bushings may be damaged as the pin is pushed into place.

When driving in the firing pin stop pin on the left side of the bolt, insert the bolt handle temporarily to prevent the loss of the extractor pivot pin.

When replacing the bolt spring and guide, use a small screwdriver to push in the spring, a few coils at a time, while keeping pressure on the guide toward the rear. When the rear tip of the guide is in the spring hole, restrain the guide and spring with a tool or fingertip while inserting the bolt and bolt handle. Then, move the bolt back; being sure that the head of the guide engages its recess on the rear of the bolt.

When replacing the hammer assembly in the trigger housing, be sure the right lower tail of the hammer spring enters its recess inside the housing, so it will contact the positioning grooves in the safety. Be sure the left tail of the spring lies on its shelf in the housing, or it may bind the trigger.

Reassembly Tips:

1. When replacing the sear/disconnector assembly, be sure the lower end of the sear spring goes toward the rear, down the slope of the trigger.

2. When installing the outer magazine tube, be sure it is fully to the rear and the groove in its upper flange is aligned with the cross pin hole in the hanger before inserting the cross pin.

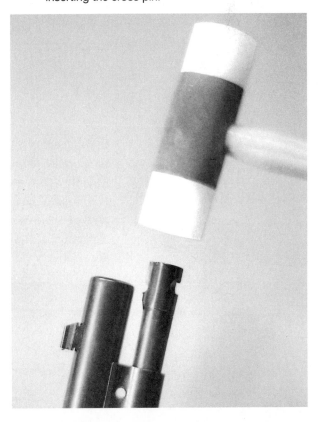

Winchester Model 9422

Similar/Identical Pattern Guns

The same basic assembly/disassembly steps for the Winchester Model 9422 also apply to the following guns:

Winchester Model 9422 XTR
Winchester Model 9422 XTR Classic
Winchester Model 9422M XTR
Winchester Model 9422M

Data:	Winchester Model 9422
Origin:	United States
Manufacturer:	Winchester Repeating Arms Co.
	New Haven, Connecticut
Cartridge:	22 Short, Long, Long Rifle
Magazine capacity:	21 Shorts, 17 Longs, 15 Long Rifles
Overall length:	37⅛ inches
Barrel length:	20½ inches
Weight:	6½ pounds

Introduced in 1972, the Model 9422 is the 22-caliber counterpart of the popular Model 94 centerfire gun. Externally it is very much like the Model 94, but the internal mechanism is quite different. The feed system is similar to the one used in the Model 61, making malfunctions extremely unlikely. The Model 9422 is fairly simple for a lever action, and with the exception of the cartridge stop and its spring, takedown and reassembly are relatively easy.

Disassembly:

1. Remove the magazine tube and take out the large coin-slotted cross screw at the rear of the receiver. A nickel fits the slot best. Separate the two sections of the gun, moving the rear portion down and toward the rear.

2. Remove the bolt assembly from the receiver toward the rear.

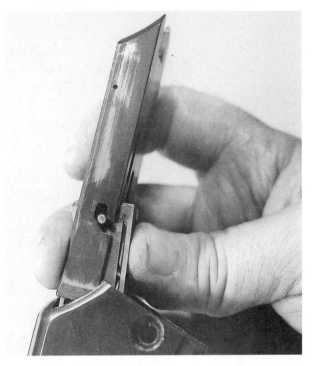

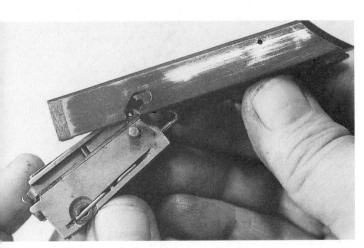

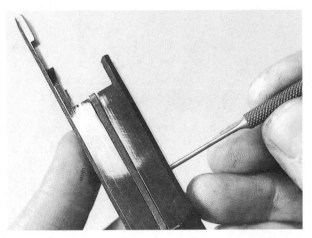

3. Separate the bolt from the bolt slide and take out the bolt cam pin which crosses the bolt at the rear. The cam pin does not fit tightly and can fall out, so take care that it isn't lost during disassembly.

4. Use a roll pin punch to drift out the cross pin in the bolt slide and remove the firing pin striker upward.

5. The firing pin is retained in the bolt by a roll pin across the upper rear, and the firing pin and its return spring are removed toward the rear.

6. A vertical pin on the left side of the bolt retains three parts the left extractor, the ejector, and the carrier pawl retainer. The extractor and pawl retainer are removed toward the left, and the ejector is moved out toward the rear. Take care that the small coil springs with the ejector and inside the carrier pawl are not lost.

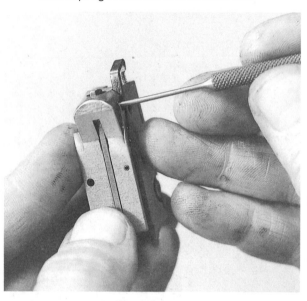

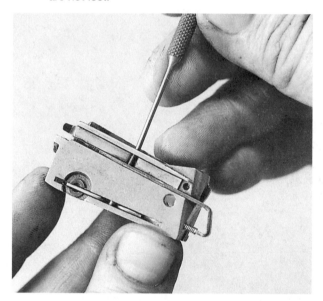

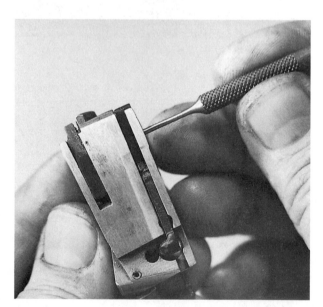

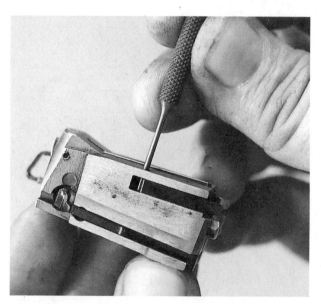

7. The right extractor is retained by a vertical roll pin on the right side of the bolt. The pin is accessible through a hole in the bottom right of the bolt, and is driven out upward. The extractor and its coil spring are taken off toward the right.

8. The lower extractor, part of the feed system, is retained by a vertical roll pin, accessible through a hole in the top of the bolt on the right side, and the pin is driven out downward. The lower extractor and its spring are then removed toward the right. Keep the spring with the lower extractor, and don't get it confused with the upper one, as they are not interchangeable.

9. Remove the buttplate, and use a B-Square stock bolt tool, or a long screwdriver, to take out the stock retaining bolt. When the bolt is out, take off the buttstock toward the rear.

10. Before removing the carrier and cartridge stop, carefully note the position and relationship of the combination spring which powers these parts, to aid in reassembly. Push out the cross pin which pivots and retains the cartridge stop, carrier, and the spring. All are removed upward, but the cartridge stop must be moved slightly forward before being lifted out. **Caution:** *The spring is under some tension, so keep the parts under control when pushing out the cross pin.*

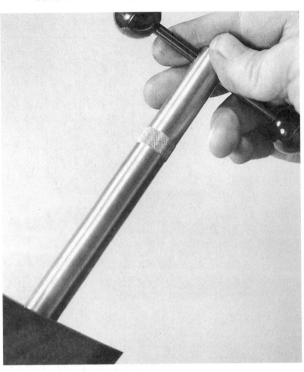

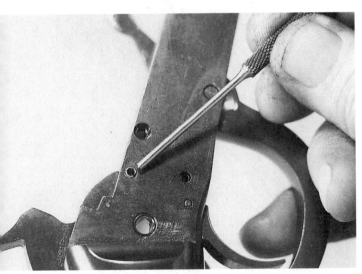

11. Use a roll pin punch to drift out the hammer stop pin, located just forward of the hammer. Set the hammer on its safety step while the stop pin is drifted out.

12. Restrain the hammer against its spring tension, pull the trigger to release it, and ease the hammer forward, past its normal down position. This will relieve the tension of the hammer spring, and the spring and its guide strut can then be removed from the rear, toward either side.

13. The hollow hammer pivot is now easily pushed out toward either side, and the hammer is removed upward. If the hammer pivot is tight, use a non-marring tool as large as its diameter, and take care not to deform its end edges.

14. With an Allen wrench of the proper size, take out the screw that retains the lever tension spring and its plate, and remove the plate and spring upward.

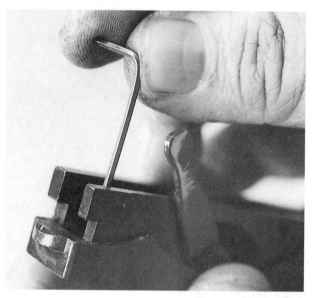

15. Push out the lever pivot pin toward the left, and remove the lever downward. Tip the upper lever arm toward the left as it is lifted out of its semi-circular opening and remove it.

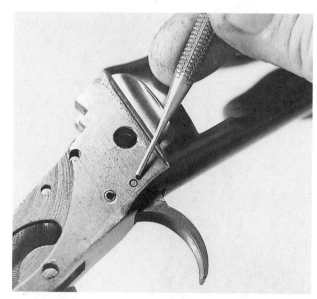

16. Drifting out the solid cross pin above the trigger will release the trigger downward. The trigger spring is retained by a roll pin, just forward of the trigger pin.

17. Remove the cross screw in the rear barrel band, and slide the band off toward the front. If the band is very tight, it will be necessary to nudge it with a nylon drift and hammer. Nudge it equally, on alternate sides, to avoid binding.

18. Remove the cross screw from the front barrel band, and slide the outer magazine tube out toward the front. Remove the forend forward and downward.

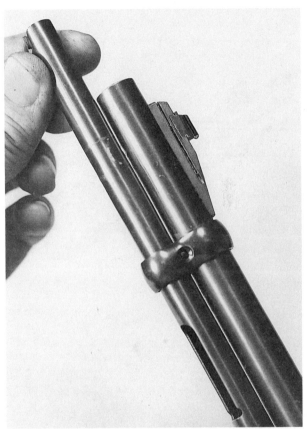

19. The barrel is retained in the receiver by a cross pin that is riveted on the right side. The pin must be driven out toward the left. The barrel can then be gripped in a padded vise and the receiver driven off with a wood or nylon mallet. In normal disassembly, however, the barrel is best left in place.

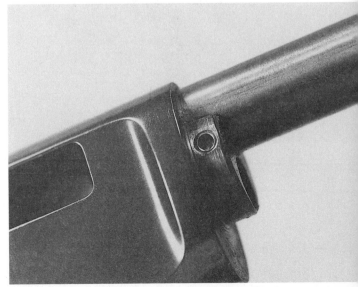

Reassembly Tips:

1. When replacing the outer magazine tube, be sure it is installed to its proper depth, and that the shallow groove in its top is aligned with the cross screw hole in the front barrel band.

2. To install the carrier, cartridge stop, and combination spring without great difficulty will require the use of a slave pin, a short length of rod stock to hold the parts together while they are positioned for insertion of the cross pin. The photo shows the proper arrangement of the parts and the spring, with the slave pin in place. The longer left arm of the spring goes below the hammer stop pin.

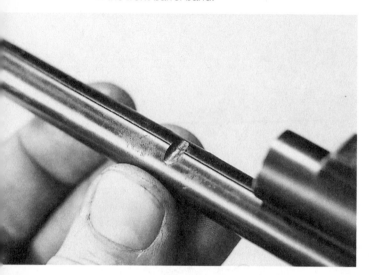

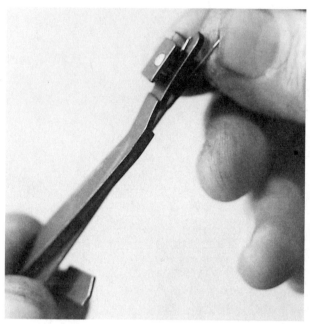

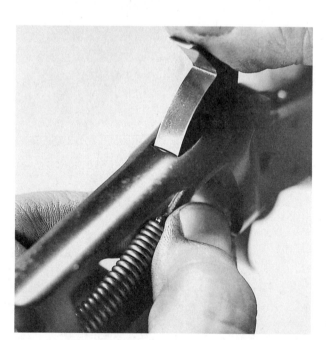

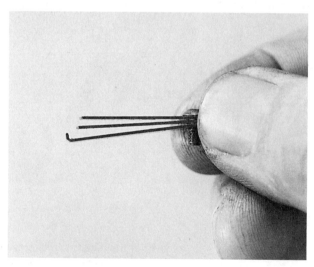

3. When replacing the hammer strut and spring, guide the spring at the rear to position the rear tip of the strut in alignment with its hole in the rear vertical bar of the trigger group. Be sure the front tip of the strut enters its recess on the rear of the hammer as the hammer is drawn back to the safety step.

4. When replacing the lever tension system in the front of the trigger group, note that the single or double spring leaves go on top, and the L-shaped plate on the bottom, with the short arm of the "L" upward.

5. When replacing the lever, note that the upper arm of the lever must be in position in the trigger group before the lever is moved into place.

6. When replacing the bolt assembly in the receiver, the bolt and bolt slide should be engaged as shown, with the bolt in the unlocked position, as the assembly is moved into the rear of the receiver.

Index/Cross Reference

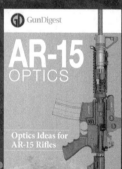
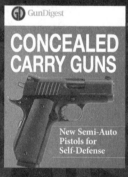